Financial Modelling in Power BI

Forecasting Business Intelligently

Dr. Liam Bastick with Jonathan Liau

Published in 2022 by SumProduct Pty Limited, Ground Floor, 470 St Kilda Road, Melbourne, VIC 3004, Australia. Simultaneously published in the USA by Holy Macro! Books, PO Box PO Box 541731, Merritt Island FL 32954.

Authors: Dr. Liam Bastick with Jonathan Liau

Editor: Kathryn Newitt

Indexer: Bill Jelen

Compositor: Joseph Kirubakaran

Cover Design: Shannon Travise

Distributed by Independent Publishers Group, Chicago, IL

ISBN 978-1-61547-072-3 Print, 978-1-61547-161-4 Digital

Library of Congress Control Number: 2022934126

Version 20220729a

About the Author

Dr. Liam Bastick FCA FCMA CGMA MVP

Starting off as a university lecturer, Liam has over 30 years' experience in financial model development / auditing, valuations, mergers and acquisitions, project finance, public private partnerships, strategy, training and consultancy. Indeed, he has been appointed as an independent expert for the courts of Victoria and New South Wales, in Australia.

He has considerable experience in many different sectors (*e.g.* banking, energy, media, mining, oil and gas, private equity, retail, transport and utilities) and has worked in many countries (including Australia, Belgium, Denmark, France, Germany, Hong Kong, Indonesia, Malaysia, Netherlands, New Zealand, Philippines, Singapore, Switzerland, United Kingdom, United States and Vietnam). He has worked with many internationally recognised clients, constructing and reviewing strategic, operational, planning and valuation models for many high profile International Public Offerings(IPOs), Leveraged Buy-Outs (LBOs) and strategic assignments.

With over 1,000 articles written for the accounting profession, he is a regular contributor to the American Institute of Certified Public Accountants (AICPA), Chartered Accountants Australia and New Zealand (CAANZ), Certified Practising Accountants Australia (CPAA), the Chartered Institute of Management Accountants (CIMA), the Institute of Chartered Accountants in England and Wales (ICAEW), Finance 3.0, Microsoft's Excel Blog and various LinkedIn specialist discussion groups.

Liam is a Fellow of the Institute of Chartered Accountants (FCA), a Fellow of the Institute of Chartered Management Accountants (FCMA), a Chartered Global Management Accountant (CGMA), and is also a professional mathematician, specialising in probability and number theory. In 2021, he was recipient of the inaugural Lifetime Achievement Award for financial modelling by the Financial Modeling Institute.

A frequent public speaker, Liam attends (virtually) Excel and Power BI conferences around the globe and has been a central organiser for the Excel Summit South and Excel Virtually Global. He has also authored and edited several books including *Introduction to Financial Modelling, Continuing Financial Modelling*, as well as the *Power BI MVP Book* and *Excel Insights*.

Since 2012, he has been recognised by Crimewatch and Microsoft, the latter as a Most Valuable Professional (MVP) in Excel, one of c.80 such awardees worldwide (as at the time of writing).

He still follows Derby County (if they survive bankruptcy) and the England cricket team (if they survive their current performances).

Jonathan Liau

Jonathan Liau was born in Singapore and lived in China as an ex-pat for most of his formative years. He served in the military in Singapore for two years before enrolling in the University of Sydney, studying Economics, Finance and IT. Until recently, Jonathan was a Senior Analyst at SumProduct Australia, specialising in Power BI projects.

Aside from work, Jonathan enjoys hiking and driving, the casual whiskey with friends, power lifting and tinkering with computers.

Preface

Thank **<expletive deleted>** that's over. Advertised forever, over a year late in its delivery, countless technical hurdles, software forever changing, something called COVID-19, a key member of the team leaving midstream, this was not the easiest book to write. On countless occasions, I was advised to scrap trying to do certain parts, but I steadfastly refused. It reminded me of a previous life as a post-graduate researcher…

I have (re)discovered I am still tenacious. They say if at first you don't succeed, then skydiving is not for you. For me, my reserve, reserve, reserve, reserve parachute failed to open, but fortunately, the ground broke my fall. But not my spirits. So I got inebriated and carried on regardless. I guess there are parts of this book where you will figure that is precisely what I did!

At the risk of sounding arrogant, I do think this is a ground-breaking book – and not just because of my (fictional) parachute accident. Detailed within these pages is a first stab to build a three-way integrated financial model *in Power BI*.

This book contains no discussion on visualisation. It doesn't really consider forecasting. It sidesteps opening balances. The model is very simple, but the concepts are deceptively awkward in places (*e.g.* inventory, depreciation, tax, and heck, even creating a line total!). Others have imported models or created one or two of the financial statements in Power BI, but this includes *all three*. This is one small step for a modeller but a giant leap for people who like to steal other people's quotations.

Please accept this book in the manner it's intended. This highlights the *start* of the financial modelling journey in Power BI. I invite fellow explorers to follow me in this expedition – maybe into oblivion – to gain greater insight into your financials, turning disorganised data into structured information, gleaned knowledge and segmented wisdom. It will take time, but it's a collaborative voyage and I am starting at Base Camp (once I have tidied up all my parachutes).

I have been lucky enough to have been appointed a Most Valuable Professional (MVP) by Microsoft for services to Excel – one of 80 or so – recognised "experts" as at the time of writing. Last year, I was fortunate enough to be awarded the inaugural Lifetime Achievement Award for Financial Modelling by the Financial Modeling Institute (yes, the spellings are deliberate!) too. In my acceptance speech, I promised I wasn't about to retire / go out to pasture. I insisted I was off to explore as noisily as possible the Brave New World of financial modelling in Power BI. Well, I've done it. See what you think!

I'd like to thank those that helped contribute to this book over the years (this one has been three years in the making). Thanks to Bill Jelen for sticking with me (this book has taken an eternity to put together), Kathryn Newitt for technically editing it and ignoring all the dad jokes, Jonathan Liau for the initial proofs of concept, Tim Heng and the SumProduct team for proofreading this thing to death (we've probably still missed things as you, dear reader, will be delighted to point out).

Finally, and most importantly, sincerest thanks to my immediate family, Nancy and no-longer-so-little Layla, who have always supported me – thinking that this book is going to earn them millions (good luck with that, gang). To that end, yet again, I let my 13-year old daughter, Layla Bastick, have the last (fore)word:

"So, he's written another book. Whether it's for the better or worse, I have no idea as I am yet to read it, but he has spent a lot of time on this so it's probably going to be, in the very least, interesting. I apologise in advance for the terrible jokes and puns in this book, but I have to admit they are funny. I am proud of my dad, especially with how long he has taken on writing this book and the effort he has put into it."

Liam Bastick, March 2022

www.sumproduct.com

Editor's notes

A few years ago, when we were undergraduates, I would studiously produce long and very boring assignments. I would be amazed to see the two sides of hand-written A4 that Liam would produce. Much to my frustration at the time, he always got better grades than me! That one piece of paper was always full of original and relevant ideas.

That is true of this book too, with the exception of the jokes. It is a brilliant idea, and it's taken a lot of hard work to complete. To get the most out of this book, you need to build the financial model. Start with our deliberately simple data set and work through the steps. Part of my role as editor has been to build the model repeatedly, and I can attest to the satisfaction of completing the Balance Sheet and admiring the result.

This is just the starting point. This is Power BI. The Financial Statements are more than just lines of data, they can be refreshed and drilled into, and they are fully integrated. All the visualisations you could wish for are at your disposal, along with insights and suggestions.

Since nothing like this has been successfully achieved before, your constructive comments and questions would be welcome. Less positive comments will be filtered before reading: I know how to clean up data.

So please, join us on a journey of discovery and find out how to build your Financial Statements in the intuitive and insightful world of Power BI. We hope you will get results as excellent as Liam's assignments.

Kathryn Newitt

www.sumproduct.com

(Unsolicited response from Liam: As always, Kathryn is far too modest. She was always the smarter of the two of us – and the more industrious. I spent my final year as an undergraduate trying to emulate her sheer dedication and diligence. If it wasn't for her, I would never have finished my academic studies in the first place. Ask any of my friends: I have always said that. Thank you Kathryn. You are far too generous with me.)

Downloadable Resources

Getting to grips with new ideas can be challenging. The easiest way to explore this book, is to use the same data file as us, and check your progress against the many images provided. We have set up a page on our website, where we will (for as long as our website and the internet as we know it still exist) provide the data file, example Power BI files and any other material that we think would be useful.

Head to our website at **https://www.sumproduct.com/book-3-resources** to download any files referred to in this book, as well as any additional information and examples.

Contents

CHAPTER 1: Introduction

They say third time's the charm.

You may or may not be familiar with the first two books in this series, *Introduction to Financial Modelling* and *Continuing Financial Modelling*. These weighty tomes covered how to model in Excel. But time moves on. And more and more of us are realising that whilst the humble spreadsheet is a powerful enabler, there's a young upstart in town, gaining traction every day.

Power BI – Microsoft's self-service business intelligence and data visualisation tool – is becoming both more versatile and more popular each month. Today's analysts need to use the best, most powerful and flexible analytical software for their work. More and more of us are realising Power BI fits the bill. We'd be foolish to stand still.

This book addresses the way forward for financial modelling. Many working in banking and finance are creating their financial models in Excel and then importing them into Power BI for graphical interpretation and further analysis. I am not going to do that. I'm going to build the model *in Power BI*.

I can't stress how far off the range we're taking the horses. If you are reading this, you are a true pioneer. I know of one or two IT programmers building the odd financial statement in Power BI, but all three? This is where you can gain a major advantage in the workplace.

Why?

If I build the calculations for financial statements in Power BI, I can produce statements by product, by customer, by geography, by … Get the picture? The limitation will be restricted to the granularity of the underlying data. If you build the statements elsewhere and import them in, how do you propose drilling down to that level of detail?

Newsflash: you can't.

Don't get me wrong; there is nothing wrong with building financial models in Excel or else downloading them from some third party management information system. This is just the next step. It's evolution. You can carry on building interactive spreadsheets if you wish. The dinosaurs were useful but did not inherit the Earth. Instead, they power our economies and pollute our skies. Or you can start the revolution of evolution. In just a few short years, Power BI has come from nowhere to become the business intelligence software of choice. Want to push it to its limits?

I thought so.

So, what's this book about? I am planning to take you on a journey of discovery. You will realise my jokes are very bad (having a co-author has had little effect) and that Power BI can do more than you might think. I will have to cover some old ground for those that have read this book's predecessors, as I will have new readers. If you are a returning reader, don't let that put you off: approaches may be similar, but precise techniques will differ.

This is NOT a "basic" book on Power BI. If you know nothing about Power BI, you might be able to follow the gist here, but I would strongly advise reading an introductory text first. All functions used here will be explained, but not in copious detail, as and when they are needed (almost as "asides"). Knowing your way around Power BI is "assumed knowledge". Having said that, *most* of the formulae used do not require a PhD in Mathematics either. As always with these books, the devil is in the concept, not the detail.

The plan for this book is as follows:

- **Power BI introduction:** Just in case you have been living under a rock for the past millennium, I provide a brief overview of Power BI
- **Discussion on "Best Practice" methodology:** To be honest, just getting the model to work in Power BI may seem a sufficient challenge, but here I remind what constitutes "Best Practice" financial modelling at a high-level. This will help keep these principles front and centre when developing our model
- **Financial statements theory:** I tell this joke every time, but it's no secret that it was the phrases "double entry" and "working with models" that attracted me to this profession. How disappointed was I? On a serious note though, I want to revisit the key outputs of a financial model to fully understand what "three-way integrated" means and the ramifications for the modeller. Further, I actually go back to understand what is an Income Statement, a Balance Sheet and a Cash Flow Statement. Yes, you may know what they are – but I want to do it from the perspective of understanding the purpose of each statement so that it guides you in determining the order of building a financial model. No matter what you build, the derived order may be applied to all future model developments
- **Control accounts:** Just like the Excel version of this topic, it all revolves around control accounts, *i.e.* analysing what causes movements in Balance Sheet items. Using this very simple approach – adopted throughout this book – you will find Balance Sheet errors will become a thing of the past
- **Getting started in Power BI:** This section doesn't deal with installation points (that was earlier, see above); this section is more about tips on setting up the data, so that loading and calculation times are not unnecessarily long, as well as considering parameterisation for scenario and sensitivity analyses at the outset. These are key considerations if working with voluminous data
- **Example of a model build:** Oh yes, it might be an idea to actually build up a case study, and this constitutes the main body of this text. The approach will be methodical and discuss the order of calculations and alternative methods available at times. Formulae will chiefly be built in **DAX**, rather than **M**, for reasons that will become clear later in the book.

As always, let me stress one last thing: this book is a *practical* book. There are lots of supporting examples to play with and use, to visualise the important concepts discussed here. The aim is to understand the concepts, not the specifics, because you will never build this case study again in your life – but you will want to apply the lessons learned to your own scenarios.

So, no excuses, make sure you are sitting comfortably and open up Power BI. It's a great visualisation tool, but now you and I, dear reader, we are going to pummel it into submission and make it a modelling tool too.

Let's get going!

CHAPTER 2: Introduction to Power BI

Power BI is a business intelligence (BI) tool developed by Microsoft for the purposes of data preparation, analysis and visualisation. Unlike many other business intelligence and data visualisation tools on the market, it offers the analyst a user-friendly environment to connect to and transform their datasets, without needing to rely upon IT departments to obtain the results for them.

When people look at Power BI, they see it as being valuable for several different reasons:

- **Data transformation and cleansing** The first step of the business intelligence process is to collect data and ensure that it is in a format that is ready for analysis. This is also known as data cleansing. This process involves taking a raw set of data and removing any errors, inconsistencies and inserting any calculation steps or transforming the data in order to prepare it for presentation and analysis.

  Often, this process is conducted wherever the data is being stored. If it is being stored in a database, there are usually queries or views that will present the final, cleaned dataset for BI tools to use. If data is stored in an Excel file, a process will usually require a user to open the file and modify the contents prior to loading it into the BI process.

  Power BI gives users the ability to quickly and simply adapt and transform data using the Power Query editor. This is the same technology that you find in Excel (also sometimes known as Get and Transform), but slightly newer and improved. Typically, Power Query in Power BI tends to be six to 12 months ahead of the equivalent tool in Excel, with new functions and features rolled out first.
- **Data visualisation** Once data is cleaned, it can be presented in the form of reports and dashboards. Power BI distinguishes reports as being a series of visualisations that are connected back to a single dataset, whereas dashboards are considered to be summaries of multiple reports. Power BI allows you to generate reports using a combination of visualisations.

  While most software tools will give you a wide range of visualisations to use, including charts, tables, maps and so on, Power BI has a unique capability allowing you to download custom visuals that have been created by the community. These custom visuals let you adapt your reports and customise them beyond the built-in charts and tables.
- **Sharing insights across a team** The primary thing people consider Power BI for is to share reports and dashboards that have been created across their wider team. This may be shared to individuals, team workspaces or even embedded into a corporate intranet or external website. Sharing in Power BI has the additional benefit in that roles can be set up to restrict the ability of shared users to access information.
- **Self-service business intelligence** Finally, many people are switching to Power BI to allow users to create their own reports. Traditionally, BI tools are managed by IT teams, with reports and dashboards that are pre-defined, and require IT change requests to adjust or to create new ones. Power BI is designed for users to be able to swiftly create their own reports and adjust existing ones, provided that they have access to the dataset.

With all the things that people expect Power BI to do, it needs to be extremely capable. As such, there are several key elements to Power BI that enable it to perform all of these tasks in different ways.

- **Power BI Desktop** This is the tool where a Power BI user will perform the heavy lifting of data transformation and cleansing. Using the Power Query editor to work with data and using Power Pivot technology to relate tables and perform complex aggregations and time-series calculations, Power BI Desktop is where most of the changes and insights are generated. While the visualisation engine is relatively seamless and can display historical records without fuss, any calculations that might be required to report on KPIs or metrics that do not exist in the dataset will need to be created using Power BI Desktop.

  Power BI Desktop also has the greatest range of database services that it can connect to. Online or on-premises, you can connect to a range of files, databases, online services or anything that has an ODBC connection.

  Power BI Desktop is used for data transformation and cleansing, followed by data visualisation. Once reports have been prepared, the data needs to be published to the Power BI Service in order to share these with colleagues.

- **Power BI Service** This is the formal name for the website version of Power BI that you can log into. It lacks the data transformation and calculation capabilities of Power BI Desktop, but it is a simpler process to connect to certain data sources, even if it doesn't have the flexibility and range of data services.

  The primary role of the Power BI Service is to distribute reports and dashboards and any other insights that might be generated. Once a report has been uploaded to the Service, it can be shared with individuals or with entire teams.

  The Power BI Service is also where you can run insights and analytics tools over your datasets. Two key features – Get Quick Insights, and Q&A – are useful at generating quick visualisations to inspire further research or answering spur-of-the-moment questions.

- **Power BI Mobile** Power BI Mobile is the phone and tablet version of the Power BI Service. It loses further functionality (you can no longer create new datasets and reports) but it allows users to move away from their desktop environment and quickly pull open their reports and dashboards in a portable interface.

- **Power BI Gateway** Once data is published to the Power BI Service, it sits there until it is subsequently refreshed. Although you can refresh it manually by republishing the data, you can also set it up to be automatically refreshed on a schedule. For online data sources, this is straightforward. However, for on-premises data sources such as SQL servers and Excel files, this requires a gateway to be installed on an on-premises computer that effectively connects the Power BI Service with the local data sources.

- **Power BI Report Server** Designed for those companies that don't want their data being stored in the cloud, the Power BI Report Server is a local version of the Power BI Service that can be installed on a computer. It provides data privacy and control, at the expense of more limited functionality.

Getting Power BI

If you are completely new to all this, obviously, the first thing you need is Power BI. From above, you can see there are two parts:

1. **Power BI Desktop:** where the main modelling work will be undertaken, all done from the familiarity and comfort of your own computer
2. **Power BI Service:** the website version has three main variants, colloquially known as Power BI Free, Power BI Pro and Power BI Premium.

Here's how you get what you want…

POWER BI DESKTOP

There are two main ways to get Power BI Desktop. The first way is to head to powerbi.com, follow the links to the Power BI Desktop page, and download it. This requires you to regularly go back to the page to download the latest updates, in order to access the latest and greatest features.

The other option is to download it from the Microsoft Store in Windows. This will keep the software automatically updated through the Windows Update process. However, this version is generally a slightly older version, which trades off access to the latest features for a more stable working environment.

Most importantly, it needs to be noted that Power BI Desktop is absolutely free. No matter how you use it or where you get it from, it will cost nothing at all.

POWER BI FREE

The Power BI Service is free to use as an individual. Go to the powerbi.com website, sign up for an account using a corporate email address (*i.e.* no Gmail, Hotmail, *etc.*), and you're good to get started.

There are a few restrictions with using the free license. The key difference between free and paid versions is that the free version will not allow you to share your dashboards, reports and datasets with other individuals, whether they are a part of your team or not. This essentially means that your free Power BI Service is a tool for self-reporting only, though there is nothing stopping you from emailing the Power BI Desktop file to a colleague, and letting them upload the dataset to their own personal Power BI Service.

POWER BI PRO

Power BI Pro is the paid version of your Power BI Service access. As implied earlier, this gives you the ability to share your dashboards, reports and datasets with your colleagues (and others). This also gives you the ability to create template reports and datasets for your colleagues to use. This is best for smaller businesses (*i.e.* where there are less than *c.*300 staff who would use Power BI) who may use the Service only occasionally.

POWER BI PREMIUM

Power BI Premium is an enterprise solution that enables users to cost-effectively have hundreds or thousands of users without paying for a full Power BI Pro license for each of them (you cheapskates: it's a wonder Microsoft can make ends meet). Given that the vast majority of users in an organisation are likely to be report consumers, and only a handful, usually finance and IT, are likely to be power users, the Power BI Premium service provides dedicated capacity for an organisation at a fixed fee, with Pro licenses only required for those power users.

The Power BI Premium license also gives you access to Power BI Report Server, which enables you to host your dashboards and reports onsite instead of the cloud, meaning that you can work around any privacy and data policy restrictions that might stand in the way of using Power BI. This is only really cost effective if you have several hundred users in an organisation, however.

And finally...

I will mainly be focused on Power BI Desktop in this book as this is where analysts will spend the majority of their time. While the other tools are important for their respective purposes, I will refer to them as and when I need to.

CHAPTER 3: Best Practice Methodology

I am not working in Excel this time, but the principles of "Best Practice" modelling in Excel do still transfer over to Power BI and remain pertinent, so a quick summary is probably worthwhile. The whole intention of this book is to provide a text that can be handed to someone who is looking to build financial models as part of their role. Jokes aside, I am assuming for those of you with no more than a passing acquaintance with Power BI and accounting, this book will get you – as the (would-be?) modeller – up to speed with the requirements and concepts associated with financial model development.

Modellers should strive to build "Best Practice" models. Here, I want to avoid the semantics of what constitutes "best" in "Best Practice". "B" and "P" are in capitals deliberately as I see this as a proper noun insofar no method is truly "best" for all eventualities. There's plenty of texts out there that include copious amounts on what thou shalt and shalt not do regarding building a spreadsheet. They all have one thing in common: they are not right for all occasions.

I would rather consider the term as a proper noun to reflect the idea that a good model has four key attributes:

- **C**onsistency;
- **R**obustness;
- **F**lexibility; *and*
- **T**ransparency.

Our company calls this **CRaFT**. We try to keep it simple. Looking at these four attributes in turn can help model developers decide how best to design financial models.

Consistency

Models constructed consistently are easier to understand as users become familiar with both their purpose and content. This will in turn give users more comfort about model integrity and make it easier to add / remove business units, categories, numbers of periods, scenarios *etc*.

Consistent formatting and use of styles cannot be over-emphasised. Humans take in much information on a non-verbal basis. Power BI is a fantastic visualisation tool. Use it! Those of you familiar with the models supplied with this book may now realise I exploit this mindset: the variables and parameters used to vary outputs and perform what-if? analysis all use slicers, option buttons, timelines and other such obvious visual tools. Nobody *ever* reads instructions – so make everything so simple a child could use it. And probably delete it.

There are other key elements of a workbook that should be consistent. These include:

- Formulae should be copied uniformly across ranges, to make it easy to add / remove periods or categories as necessary (this is pretty much forced in Power BI's table and matrix visualisations)
- Sheet titles and hyperlinks should be consistently positioned to aid navigation and provide details about the content and purpose of the particular sheet

- For forecast spreadsheets incorporating dates, the dates should be positioned uniformly, the number of periods should be consistent where possible and the periodicity should be constant (the model should endeavour to show all sheets monthly or quarterly, *etc.*). If periodicities must change, formulae must still work. That's a key issue here, which differentiates Power BI from Excel. I must model at the lowest level of granularity and aggregate, otherwise calculations will not work. But more on that later.

This should reduce referencing errors, increase model integrity and enhance workbook structure. Talking of which...

Robustness

Models should be materially free from error, mathematically accurate and readily auditable. Key output sheets should ensure that error messages such as *#DIV/0!*, *#VALUE!*, *#REF!*, *#Brown*, *#Pipe etc*. cannot occur (ideally, these error messages should not occur anywhere).

Removing these *prima facie* errors is straightforward and often highlights that the modeller has not undertaken a basic review of their work after completing the task. When building, it is often worth keeping in mind hidden assumptions in formulae. For example, a simple gross margin calculation may calculate profit divided by sales. However, if sales are non-existent or missing, this calculation would give *#DIV/0!* This is where Power BI is great: the Data Analysis eXpressions (**DAX**) function takes all of that into account – so use it!

Flexibility

One benefit of modelling in a software package such as Power BI is to be able to change various assumptions and see how these adjustments affect various outputs.

Therefore, when building a model, the user should consider what inputs should be variable and *how* they should be able to vary. This may force the model builder to consider how assumptions should be entered. Most of the time this will be by using slicers, for example.

I strongly recommend that all inputs are entered as positive numbers, wherever possible, just change the descriptions accordingly. If I were to tell you that last year, costs were $10,000 but they have increased by 10% this year. You would understand me. But what would you make of me telling you costs were minus $10,000 and had increased by -10%!?

The aim is to have a model provide sufficient flexibility without going overboard.

Transparency

As stated above, many modellers often forget that key decision makers base their choices on printed materials: consequently, models must be clear, concise, and fit for the purpose intended. I always say if you can follow it on a piece of paper (*i.e.* no Formula Bar), it's transparent.

Most Excel users are familiar with keeping inputs / assumptions away from calculations away from outputs. However, this concept can be extended: it can make sense to keep different areas of a model separate, *e.g.* revenue assumptions on a different worksheet from cost(s) of goods sold assumptions, and capital expenditure assumptions on a third sheet, and so on. I have many control accounts to construct as part of the case study; it will be best to keep them separate from the rest of the model, in order to avoid confusion.

In summary

It's all about design and scoping. The problem is, we just like to get on with it. Consequently, we dust off old templates, fit square pegs into round holes and produce mistake-laden spreadsheets time and time again resulting in costly management decisions. But we can't do that this time. Modelling in Power BI is *new*. NO ONE is doing this. They might say they are, but all they are doing is importing models into Power BI and then rendering cool visualisations. But let me be clear: that's not what we are doing. Therefore, since we have no old habits to perpetuate, we can try and set a good example from the outset!

Chapter 4: Financial Statements Theory

Before jumping straight into Power BI, warts and all, I need to talk through the financial statements. Yes, I realise many of you will work in finance, be accountants or experienced analysts, but I need to ensure we are all on the same page. And I apologise if you have purchased / stolen the first two books, because I do need to include this topic again.

The reason is simple. I wish to propose a method of building up a financial model. I want to put it all together to explain why you should build the model in a particular order, but I appreciate no one likes to learn by rote. I need to explain *why*. That is why I need to summarise the layout and purpose of each financial statement. And my editor will be delighted that this section is lifted straight from those chapters – so feel free to skip this if you have heard it all before. Because you just might have.

To emphasise, this book is not an accounting book. It is simply intended to provide a "jump start" into the world of financial modelling. I am not going to talk about Accounting Standards (such as the International Financial Reporting Standards, IFRS, or the US Generally Accepted Accounting Principles, US GAAP), but rather just explain generic principles. I appreciate things work differently in different parts of the world so I intend to be as general as I can be.

Nevertheless, most accounting regimens recognise the same three primary financial statements, so let's start with reviewing all of them.

Income Statement

Also known as the profit and loss account, revenue statement, statement of financial performance, earnings statement, operating statement or the statement of operations, this is the financial statement that shows the net operating profit of an entity for a given period of time. It works on an accruals basis, which whether you are an accountant or no, is probably how you think. Allow me to explain.

Most of you will be employees, presumably paid monthly. Do you find you have too much month at the end of the money? Most try not to get into that situation; we **accrue**. The Income Statement is essentially the Net Operating Profit (accrued income less accrued expenditure) for a period of time after tax.

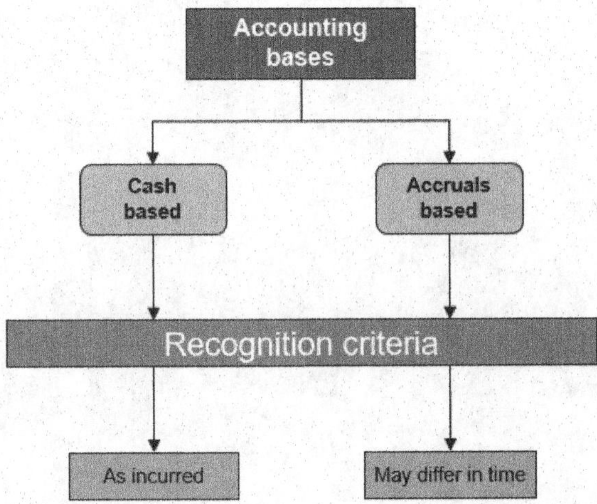

Income is recognised when products are delivered or services are provided, not when payment is received. Similarly, costs are attributed to the period they are incurred, not when they are necessarily paid. If our company sells one million widgets within the financial year at $1 each and incurs direct costs of 75c per widget, I would expect a Gross Profit of $250,000, *viz.*

Number of Widgets:		1,000,000
Unit Price:	$	1.00
Unit Cost:	$	0.75

	$
Sales	1,000,000
Cost of Goods Sold	(750,000)
Gross Profit	**250,000**

The cash position could be radically different. The company may have had to pay all of the costs and not yet received any monies. However, this is not how we think. We all attribute on an accruals basis, *i.e.* what pertains to the period in question.

And there's more. If I asked, what would you model first, then second, then third, who here was thinking, revenue, costs of goods sold and then operating expenditure? Like it or not, we are all walking talking Income Statements:

Revenue	X
COGS	(X)
Gross Profit	**X**
Operating Expenditure	(X)
EBITDA	**X**
Depreciation	(X)
EBIT	**X**
Interest Expense	(X)
Net Profit Before Tax (NPBT)	**X**
Tax Expense	(X)
Net Profit After Tax (NPAT)	**XX**

Now most of us are familiar with this Income Statement, but do you fully appreciate the reason for its order? The order shouldn't just be learned by rote; it should be understood. For example, Revenue being first makes perfect sense for any company endeavouring to turn a profit. But why is Costs of Goods Sold (COGS) above Operating Expenditure?

Who here was thinking COGS is a variable cost whilst Operating Expenditure is a (stepped) fixed cost? That may be true up to a point, but that explains little. The point is that Costs of Goods Sold is defined as costs **directly** attributable to the sale. Direct costs may include raw materials and some labour costs. Indirect costs, on the other hand, are legitimate costs of the business too, just not directly attributable to the sale. Typical examples include rent and utilities. Some could be argued either way (*e.g.* freight); the aim is to be consistent. Therefore, it makes sense that the direct costs are attributed first so that the Gross Profit (often referred to as **contribution**) can be assessed before the allocation of other costs, which in some instances may be rather arbitrary.

Clearly, Tax Expense is the final expense as it encapsulates all of the other incomes and expenses, but why does Depreciation Expense come before Interest Expense? This is perhaps not so clear cut and I offer two reasons, both of which can be argued with:

1. **Funding:** If you consider the Income Statement to contain the period's "fair share" of income and expenditure, one significant cost is Capital Expenditure. I am going to talk about this large cost in detail later, but essentially this is ascribed to the purchase of significant business assets to generate future profits for more than one year, that are held for continuing use in the business. It would be wrong to apportion all of this expenditure to one period if the benefit will extend over several / many years and depreciation is the allocation of that cost to the period in question. If financing, you often want to compare the funding – and its associated costs – against this allocated amount. Therefore, Depreciation Expense should be stated ahead of Interest Expense in the Profit and Loss account.
2. **Valuation:** It is hard to believe that Discounted Cash Flow (DCF) valuations and Net Present Value (NPV) analysis are still fairly recent valuation tools. Prior to the popularity of these approaches, the main method of choice was based on earnings multiples. For example, if companies A and B were similar in operation and profit margins, but B were twice the size of A, shouldn't B have a valuation approximately double A? It's difficult to argue with this logic. Capital structures (*i.e.* the mix of debt to equity) are irrelevant as if a company is purchased, the chances are the capital structure will be revised by the purchaser. Since depreciation is a relevant expense in the earnings multiple calculation, it should appear ahead of the debt expense (*i.e.* interest) so that the earnings figure to be used is readily visible.

Why have I made such a big deal of the order? Go and ask a non-accountant the order they would build a model in: the vast majority would build the income calculations first, the direct costs second and so on. The reason the Income Statement is always so popular is this is how people think. I am a great believer in "if it ain't broke, don't fix it" and this ideology very much applies here.

We should seriously consider building a model in the P&L order as this is most intuitive to modellers and users alike.

Balance Sheet

How would you explain the Balance Sheet to the good old Clapham ombudsman (*i.e.* the ordinary person on the London bus)? For those going, "it's the comparison for a moment in time of an entity's assets, liabilities and equity", please explain "assets", "liabilities" and "equity".

The Balance Sheet used to be known as the Net Worth statement; the Income Statement reports on financial performance, the Balance Sheet summarises the corresponding financial position. For a particular moment in time (the date stated) it displayed what a business was worth. It is a cumulative statement aggregating all of the factors that contribute to the value:

Non-Current Assets	
Property, plant and equipment	X
Other non-current assets	X
Total Non-Current Assets	***X***
Current Assets	
Cash	X
Account receivable	X
Other current assets	X
Total Current Assets	***X***
Total Assets	**X**
Current Liabilities	
Accounts payable	X
Other current liabilities	X
Total Current Liabilities	***X***
Non-Current Liabilities	
Debt	X
Other Non-Current Liabilities	X
Total Non-Current Liabilities	***X***
Total Liabilities	**X**
Net Assets	**X**
Equity	
Ordinary Equity	X
Net Profit After Tax (NPAT)	X
Retained Earnings	X
Total Equity	**X**

There are various ways of presenting the Balance Sheet. I am quite fond of this approach as it places Current Assets (items worth something to the business that will be held for less than or equal to one year) next to Current Liabilities (amounts owed that need to be paid within the next year). The ratio Current Assets divided by Current Liabilities assesses a business's ability to pay its bills and Current Assets less Current Liabilities shows the working capital of a business on the face of a primary financial statement.

The line items down to Net Assets are often colloquially known as the "top half" of the Balance Sheet (even if it is nearer 90% of all line items!) and the Total Equity section is known as the "bottom half". What is good about this presentation is the top half summarises what is controlled by a business whereas the bottom half communicates ownership.

This is why debt is not in the bottom half of the Balance Sheet. In the past, the Equity section was often headed "Financed by" and that always confused me as I did not understand why debt was not there. The reason it is not, is because the shareholders of the business (the Equity stakeholders) control the debt repayments and servicing. Yes, banks and other financial institutions may put contracts in place, but that is so they may go to court to force companies to pay if payment is not made voluntarily. Consequently, debt is "controlled", it usually is for a period of greater than one year and hence it is not in the bottom half but rather in the Long Term Liabilities section instead.

It may be clearer with another example. Ever bought a house? Did you buy it outright for cash? Chances are if you are lucky enough to be climbing the real estate ladder, in your first purchase you were not the principal stakeholder. So what about the risks and rewards? If the house goes up significantly in price, will you be splitting the profits in proportion to the amount financed? Of course you won't.

Similarly, imagine the house were to be damaged in a storm. Would you be on the phone the next day to get them to arrange someone to fix it? Good luck with that. "Do we know you?" may be the polite response, although more common replies may end in "off" instead.

The house would be a non-current (fixed) asset. The mortgage would be the linked non-current liability and – assuming the debt is less than the value of the house – the difference between these items would be your equity stake. You control the house and the debt (top half), the equity goes in the bottom half. Easy.

Modellers tend to create Balance Sheets as a bit of an afterthought, but they are more important than that. Values may not be stated in the dollars of the day when purchased (this is known as **historical cost accounting**), which makes any summary meaningless as you are comparing apples with pears, but it is still better than nothing.

In fact, modellers *hate* Balance Sheets. They never seem to balance, reconcile or be understood. But this can all be circumvented with **control accounts** which I shall discuss in the next chapter. Balance Sheets are essential.

There is one other issue. Balance Sheets by their very nature are cumulative. They are stated at a point in time. They must *balance*. So what if the Balance Sheet did not balance at the model start date? As a modeller, there is nothing you can do about this: this is an opening assumption (the Opening Balance Sheet). If this were to happen to you, reject the Opening Balance Sheet and wait until someone who knows what they are doing gives you a proper one.

Furthermore, here, in our case study, I will simplify and use a "blank" or "zero" Opening Balance Sheet. There are two key reasons for this:

1. The main purpose of this book is to discuss key concepts and explain the continuing, rather than the opening process. A non-zero Opening Balance Sheet detracts from this key objective adding noise.
2. Not for a second am I suggesting the issues surrounding an Opening Balance Sheet are either trivial or that the statement is irrelevant. However, every Opening Balance Sheet will be calculated differently and I cannot mitigate for all possibilities. Therefore, I have excluded it from the scope of this book.

You should note that opening balances may have a dramatic effect and cause complications (*e.g.* depreciation for opening Non-Current Assets). The point is, each scenario may represent a different circumstance and thus needs to be modelled differently. Therefore, I exclude these issues, at least, from *this* book. "Get Out of Jail Free" card well and truly played.

But do remember:

All a modeller may ever be held accountable for is that the change in Net Assets equals the change in Total Equity.

Cash Flow Statement

The Cash Flow Statement never used to be one of the so-called primary financial statements. Originally, it was the reconciliatory note that demonstrated how the cash stated on the Balance Sheet had been derived. Changes in Balance Sheet and Income Statement numbers are often known as a "revision of accounting policies" and as long as the auditors and shareholders agree the changes everyone nods sagely and does not even bat an eyelid. If you start messing around with the Cash Flow Statement that's called fraud and you can go to jail. Recent high-profile collapses and embezzlements have given greater prominence to this financial statement – even though it should have had equal standing from the beginning.

There are three sections to the Cash Flow Statement:

- Operating
- Investing
- Financing.

Can you think of an example of an Operating Cash Flow? Who said Revenue? That *isn't* one. Cash Receipts is the cash flow equivalent of Revenue. Be careful: it's making mistakes like this in modelling that cause Balance Sheets not to balance. Similarly, an example of Investing Activities might be Purchases of Non-Current Assets rather than "Capital Expenditure". Debt drawdowns and repayments would be two examples of Financing Activities, and so on.

Now, what about the other way around? Where does Interest Paid go? (You didn't realise you were taking a multiple-choice exam?) The "proper" answer is Operating Activities, although I imagine you might be thinking Financing Activities. Three points:

1. As a company expands, sometimes its working capital (essentially cash and cash equivalents readily available after setting aside current bills) is insufficient to facilitate the growth required. Business owners may put more cash into their business (equity) or alternatively take out financing (debt). Should they choose the latter option, the mandatory servicing of that debt is an operational cost of the business – so Interest Paid should go in Operating Activities
2. If all you read above was "blah blah blah... Operating Activities", I think you might not be alone. A simpler – although not quite correct – explanation is as follows. As detailed above, the Income Statement is essentially the Net Operating Profit after tax. Interest Expense is clearly an expense in the Profit and Loss Account. Therefore, it makes sense that the cash equivalent of Interest Expense – Interest Paid – is in the cash proxy for the P&L, namely the Cash Flows from Operating Activities section
3. Some companies do indeed place Interest Paid in the Financing section of the Cash Flow Statement. This has been due to past practices (consistency) and case law precedent. So it can reside here, although it probably makes more sense to be in Operating Activities as explained above.

Hopefully, that makes sense. So what about Interest Received? Where should that be placed? Operating? Investing? Financing? Well, as Meat Loaf once said, two out of three ain't bad:

- Banks and other financial institutions may place Interest Received in Operating Activities. This is because Interest Received may be their main source of income, *e.g.* from mortgages and unsecured loans
- Other companies may place Interest Received in Investing Income. In this instance, interest has been earned and received from surplus cash on deposit.

Do you see in either scenario it would be incorrect to net off this amount with Interest Paid? The only time the two line items are in the same section (Operating Activities) is when Interest Received is essentially Cash Receipts and why would you want to combine this with debt servicing? This clearly highlights the accounting point of **no net off**. It is better if line items are shown gross so that end users may better understand their financials / forecasts.

One last thing: let's consider Dividends Paid. This line item goes in Financing Activities. Some people do not understand why Interest Paid and Dividends Paid are (usually) placed in different sections of the Cash Flow Statement. Interest Paid is the *mandatory* servicing of debt; Dividends Paid is the *voluntary* servicing of equity. Hence it is a financing decision and therefore placed in the Financing Activities section.

I have concentrated on these elements as this is where many modellers make mistakes. Hopefully, this discussion makes things clearer and will prevent you from falling for some of the same traps your peers have repeated time and time again.

This all leads us nicely into the example Cash Flow Statement:

Operating Cash Flows	
Cash Receipts	X
Cash Payments	X
Interest Paid	X
Tax Paid	X
Net Operating Cash Flows	**X**
Investing Cash Flows	
Interest Received	X
Dividends Received	X
Purchase of Non-Current Assets	X
Net Investing Cash Flows	**X**
Financing Cash Flows	
Debt Drawdowns	X
Debt Repayments	X
Ordinary Equity Issuance	X
Ordinary Equity Buybacks	X
Dividends Paid	X
Net Financing Cash Flows	**X**
Net Inc / (Dec) in Cash Held	**X**

The above is an example of what is known as a **direct** Cash Flow Statement. Pardon? What is one of those?

There are two forms to the Cash Flow Statements: direct and indirect. In many accounting jurisdictions it is stipulated that one variant must be displayed in the financial statements and the other should be the reconciliatory note to said accounts. It usually does not matter which way round this is done, as long as it is consistent from one period to the next.

Both variants affect the Net Operating Cash Flow section only of the Cash Flow Statement. They are defined as follows:

- **Direct:** This can reconcile Operating Cash Flows back to a large proportion of the bank statements. It is a summary of Cash Receipts, Cash Paid, Interest Paid and Tax Paid
- **Indirect:** This starts with an element of the Income Statement and adds back non-cash items (deducting their cash equivalents) and adjusts for working capital movements.

A typical indirect Cash Flow Statement may compare to the direct version as in the below illustration:

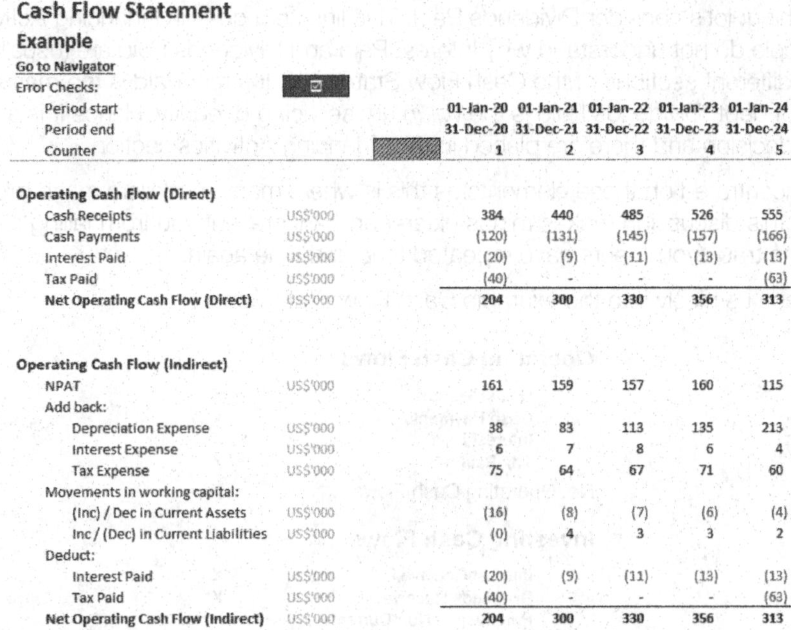

Cash Flow Statement Example

Go to Navigator

Error Checks:						
Period start		01-Jan-20	01-Jan-21	01-Jan-22	01-Jan-23	01-Jan-24
Period end		31-Dec-20	31-Dec-21	31-Dec-22	31-Dec-23	31-Dec-24
Counter		1	2	3	4	5
Operating Cash Flow (Direct)						
Cash Receipts	US$'000	384	440	485	526	555
Cash Payments	US$'000	(120)	(131)	(145)	(157)	(166)
Interest Paid	US$'000	(20)	(9)	(11)	(13)	(13)
Tax Paid	US$'000	(40)	-	-	-	(63)
Net Operating Cash Flow (Direct)	US$'000	**204**	**300**	**330**	**356**	**313**
Operating Cash Flow (Indirect)						
NPAT	US$'000	161	159	157	160	115
Add back:						
Depreciation Expense	US$'000	38	83	113	135	213
Interest Expense	US$'000	6	7	8	6	4
Tax Expense	US$'000	75	64	67	71	60
Movements in working capital:						
(Inc) / Dec in Current Assets	US$'000	(16)	(8)	(7)	(6)	(4)
Inc / (Dec) in Current Liabilities	US$'000	(0)	4	3	3	2
Deduct:						
Interest Paid	US$'000	(20)	(9)	(11)	(13)	(13)
Tax Paid	US$'000	(40)	-	-	-	(63)
Net Operating Cash Flow (Indirect)	US$'000	**204**	**300**	**330**	**356**	**313**

As explained above, the indirect version is calculated as follows:

- Start with a line item from the Income Statement (here, Net Profit After Tax)
- Add back non-cash items (Depreciation Expense, Interest Expense and Tax Expense)
- Adjust for working capital movements (increases and decreases in Current Assets and Current Liabilities) not included above
- Deduct the cash equivalents of the non-cash items added back:
  - Instead of Interest **Expense** deduct Interest **Paid**
  - Instead of Tax **Expense** deduct Tax **Paid**
  - Instead of Depreciation Expense *don't do anything*.

Que? Why is Depreciation Expense excluded altogether? Hands up those that said, "It's not a cash item". Well, Interest Expense and Tax Expense are not cash items either. That is an insufficient reason. What is the cash equivalent of Depreciation Expense? It's the Purchase of Non-Current Assets – and that is found in Investing Activities. The reason

Depreciation Expense is excluded is for two reasons: (1) yes, it is a non-cash item, but (2) it is a double count.

So which one should you model? The vast majority of modellers prefer the indirect version as it is easier to model: most will have modelled an Income Statement and (at least extracts from) the Balance Sheet, so it is easy.

This is dangerous. This is often what causes problems in Balance Sheet reconciliations. If you implement the direct method, this facilitates the incorporation of **control accounts** and control accounts are a financial modeller's best friends. I will explain further in the next chapter. Use the direct method and calculate the indirect variant later, if required.

There is another important consideration for the Cash Flow Statement as well. Here is a sanitised version of a chart produced from a real-life model:

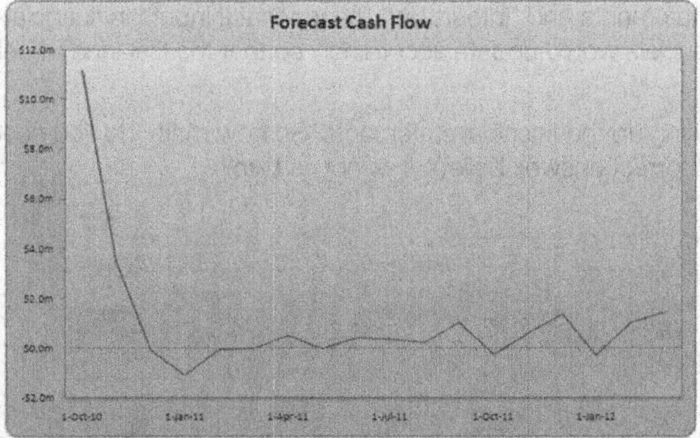

Picture yourself as the Board were back in 2010. Cash is tight and you are trying to determine precisely how much of a bank overdraft facility you require. What might you decide? About $1m? Look again.

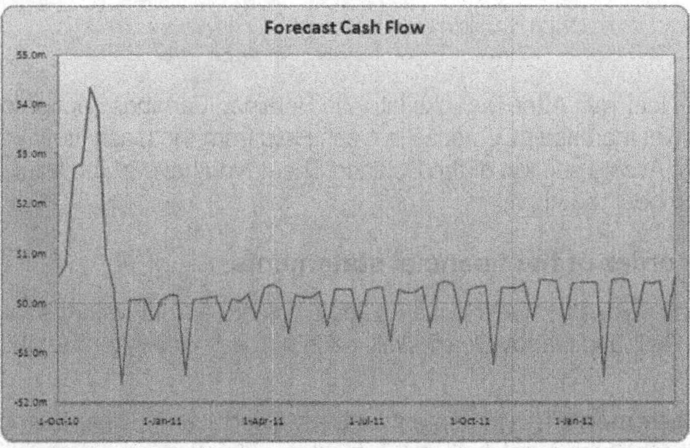

The first chart forecast cash flows on a monthly basis; the second displayed the same data weekly and looks more like my dental x-ray. Clearly, there is cyclicality in the cash flows and the troughs are deeper than the monthly output suggests. $1m would be insufficient according to the second chart. It may be even worse if modelling were undertaken on a daily basis.

The reason we prefer Income Statements to Cash Flow Statements is because the P&L frequently smooths out the inherent volatility in the latter. That is fine for understanding the trends in profitability and the overall financial performance of the business, but it may be inadequate to manage a business on a day-to-day basis. Determining the correct periodicity in a financial model is paramount in order to optimise the information available in financial forecasts.

Model Cash Flow Statements on a direct basis and use the periodicity required by the business to make effective business decisions.

Linking financial statements

You may have heard of the phrase "three-way integrated". It's not quite as kinky as it sounds. With regard to financial statements, "three-way" simply means incorporating all three financial statements and "integrated" means that if inputs in financial data were to change, the financials would update accordingly so that the Balance Sheet would still balance.

This requires linking up the financial statements. So how many do you need? One? Eight? 50? The correct answer, believe it or not, is **two**:

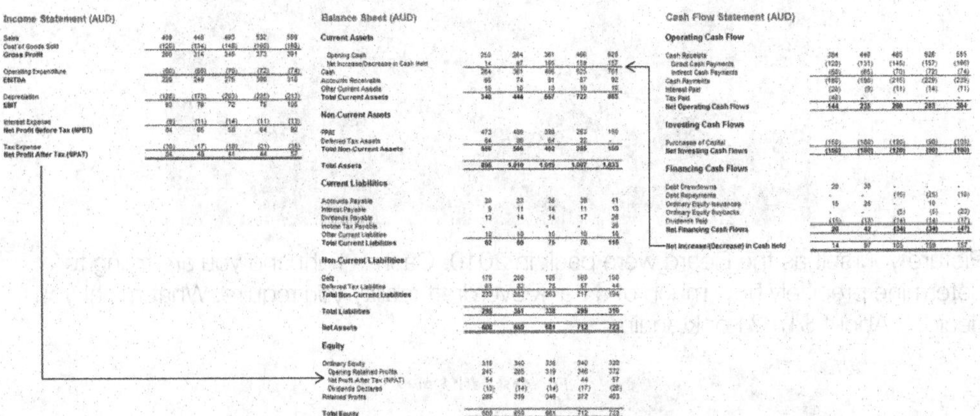

Income Statement (AUD)

Sales	409	448	493	532	559
Cost of Goods Sold	(120)	(134)	(148)	(159)	(168)
Gross Profit	289	314	346	373	391
Operating Expenditure	(60)	(65)	(70)	(72)	(74)
EBITDA	229	249	276	300	316
Depreciation	(136)	(173)	(203)	(226)	(212)
EBIT	93	76	72	75	105
Interest Expense	(9)	(11)	(14)	(11)	(13)
Net Profit Before Tax (NPBT)	84	65	58	64	92
Tax Expense	(30)	(17)	(18)	(21)	(35)
Net Profit After Tax (NPAT)	54	48	41	44	57

Balance Sheet (AUD)

Current Assets					
Opening Cash	250	264	361	466	625
Net Increase/Decrease in Cash Held	14	97	105	159	157
Cash	264	361	466	625	781
Accounts Receivable	65	74	81	87	92
Other Current Assets	10	10	10	10	15
Total Current Assets	340	444	557	722	885
Non-Current Assets					
PP&E	473	408	338	263	150
Deferred Tax Assets	84	38	64	22	-
Total Non-Current Assets	556	566	402	285	150
Total Assets	896	1,010	1,059	1,007	1,033
Current Liabilities					
Accounts Payable	28	33	36	38	41
Interest Payable	9	11	14	11	13
Dividends Payable	13	14	14	17	28
Income Tax Payable	-	-	-	-	35
Other Current Liabilities	12	10	10	10	15
Total Current Liabilities	62	68	75	78	116
Non-Current Liabilities					
Debt	170	200	185	160	150
Deferred Tax Liabilities	63	82	78	57	44
Total Non-Current Liabilities	233	282	263	217	194
Total Liabilities	295	351	338	295	310
Net Assets	600	659	681	712	723
Equity					
Ordinary Equity	315	340	335	340	320
Opening Retained Profits	245	285	319	346	372
Net Profit After Tax (NPAT)	54	48	41	44	57
Dividends Declared	(13)	(14)	(14)	(17)	(28)
Retained Profits	285	319	346	372	403
Total Equity	600	659	681	712	723

Cash Flow Statement (AUD)

Operating Cash Flow					
Cash Receipts	384	442	485	526	551
Direct Cash Payments	(120)	(131)	(145)	(157)	(166)
Indirect Cash Payments	(60)	(65)	(70)	(72)	(74)
Cash Payments	(180)	(196)	(215)	(229)	(239)
Interest Paid	(20)	(9)	(11)	(14)	(11)
Tax Paid	(40)	-	-	-	-
Net Operating Cash Flows	144	238	260	283	304
Investing Cash Flows					
Purchases of Capital	(150)	(180)	(120)	(90)	(100)
Net Investing Cash Flows	(150)	(180)	(120)	(90)	(100)
Financing Cash Flows					
Debt Drawdowns	20	30	-	-	-
Debt Repayments	-	-	(15)	(25)	(10)
Ordinary Equity Issuances	15	25	-	10	-
Ordinary Equity Buybacks	-	-	(5)	(5)	(20)
Dividends Paid	(15)	(13)	(14)	(14)	(17)
Net Financing Cash Flows	20	42	(34)	(34)	(47)
Net Increase/(Decrease) in Cash Held	14	97	105	159	157

As long as the Net Profit After Tax links into the Retained Earnings section of the Balance Sheet and the Net Increase / Decrease in Cash Held from the Cash Flow Statement links into the Current Assets section of the Balance Sheet, you have all the links you require to put a financial model together.

Appropriate order of the financial statements

Right, it's time to invoke the Goldilocks Analogy. You are familiar with the tale of Baby Bear, Mummy Bear and Daddy Bear? Well, each of these is akin to one of our financial statements.

- **Income Statement:** This statement is "Baby Bear". I am neither talking about the magnitude of the numbers nor the number of line items within the financial statements. I am considering how small or large the Income Statement is conceptually compared with the other statements.

  The Income Statement considers the Net *[Operating]* Profit After Tax (NPAT). The Cash Flow Statement considers Operating Cash Flows, but it also considers

Investing and Financial ones too. The Balance Sheet incorporates the summary (NPAT) of the Income Statements so must also be at least as large. Therefore, the Income Statement is the baby of the bunch.

- **Cash Flow Statement:** At the risk of sounding sexist (before you all send me hate mail, I am talking about typical size only, not importance), this one is "Mummy Bear". As discussed above, it considers more factors than the Income Statement (albeit from a different perspective), but since it is also summarised in the Balance Sheet (Cash), it is the 'middle' statement.
- **Balance Sheet:** So by a process of elimination, the Balance Sheet is "Daddy Bear". Not only does it summarise the other two financial statements, but it also details financials not captured elsewhere, *e.g.* movements between Non-Current and Current, and transfers in Reserves.

Now while you are all wondering what my drug of choice is, I had better explain why this is important. Earlier, I stated that when commencing model development, in general, we start to work our way down the Income Statement. That made sense and is commensurate with the magnitude of the concept of the financial statement. It also suggests that the Cash Flow Statement should be built second, which again makes sense, given the Balance Sheet includes a summary of the other two statements. This gives us our conceptual order of constructing three-way integrated financial statement in a model:

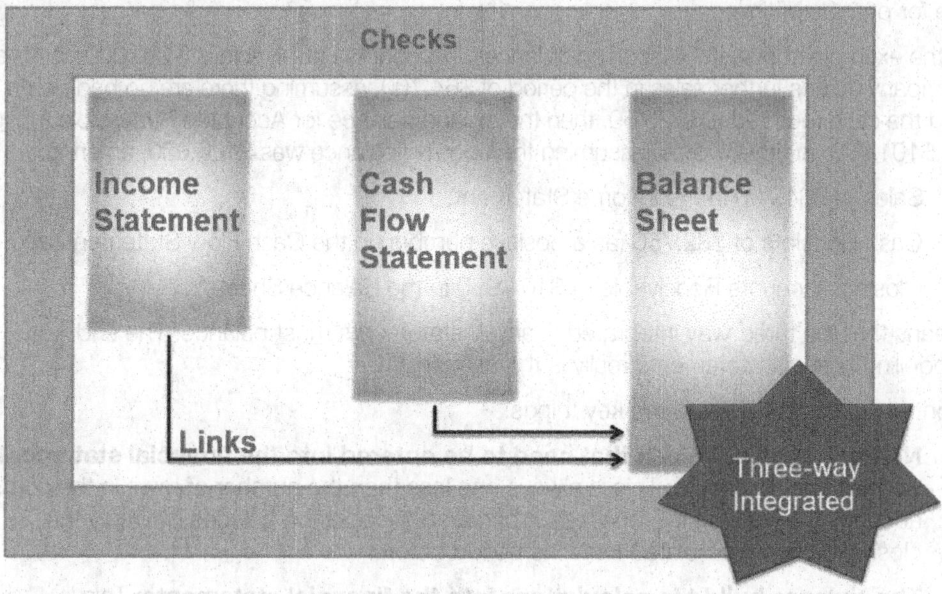

To summarise, we should:

- Develop the three financial statements, building up by line item and total
- Link the Income Statement and Cash Flow Statement into the Balance Sheet
- Add error checks to ensure no errors, that the Balance Sheet balances and is solvent (for example).

We have a plan...

CHAPTER 5: Control Accounts

It's time to bring out the big guns and use my secret weapon – the one that always makes my Balance Sheet balance, and my financial statements integrate (they can't do calculus though, but my teeth can).

They are easy to construct and even simpler to understand. Consider the reconciliation of the line item Accounts Receivable (or Debtors):

	$
Accounts Receivable b/f	**120,000**
Sales	**64,700**
Cash Receipts	**(82,750)**
Accounts Receivable c/f	**101,950**

Chances are you have probably seen something similar to this before, maybe from accounting / finance studies. This reconciliation is known as a **control account**: it is a reconciliation of a Balance Sheet item from one period to the next ("b/f" means brought forward or last period and "c/f" means carried forward or current period).

Typically (although not always), the line items between the opening and closing balances come from the Income Statement and Cash Flow Statement. This is consistent with the idea that the Balance Sheet is stated at a point in time whereas the other two statements are for periods of time.

In the example above, if the opening balance of Accounts Receivable is $120,000 and the company makes further sales in the period of $64,700, assuming there are no bad debts and the cash received is $82,750, then the closing balance for Accounts Receivable must be $101,950. In other words, assuming the opening balance was $120,000, entering:

- Sales of $64,700 in the Income Statement;
- Cash Receipts of $82,750 (as a positive number) in the Cash Flow Statement; *and*
- Closing Accounts Receivable of $101,950 in the Balance Sheet

means that the three-way integrated financial statements must balance. The end. Modelling financial statements really is that simple.

Control accounts tell you three key things:

1. **Number of calculations that need to be entered into the financial statements so that they balance:** This is always one less than the number of rows in the control account. The reason it is one less is because the opening balance is simply the closing balance calculated from the period before
2. **The order to build the calculations into the financial statements:** This is always row 2 first, then row 3, then row 4 and so on. Think of it this way: assuming no opening balance (which there would not be in the beginning), if there were no sales, there could be no payments received. If there are no sales and no receipts, the difference between them (the amount owed, the Accounts Receivable) would also be zero. It is a logical order
3. **It identifies the key driver:** Often you want to undertake sensitivity and scenario analysis in your models, but sometimes you may be unsure which variables should

be included in the analysis. Line 2 of the control account is always the key driver. As above, if there were no sales, there could be no payments received. If there are no sales and no receipts, the difference between them (the amount owed, the Accounts Receivable) would also be zero. To make a point, I have repeated myself deliberately. To make a point, I have repeated myself deliberately. To make a point, I have repeated myself deliberately...

Therefore, in the example, the conclusions are:

- In order to make the Balance Sheet balance I need to construct three calculations which need to be incorporated into the financial statements: Sales, Cash Receipts and closing Accounts Receivable
- The order to calculate them should be Sales, Cash Receipts and finally closing Accounts Receivable.
- The key driver of Accounts Receivable is Sales.

The last two points do not appear to be too controversial, but have you reflected on the first point? If you have had any sort of accounting training whatsoever, you will have had double entry rammed down your throat *(I argued long and hard to keep this one in with my editor...)*.

The whole concept of double entry is you do one thing, then do another and *voila!* everything balances. Everything is performed in pairs. But I am telling you that you need to create **three** calculations. Does that go against everything you believe? Have I discussed debits and credits anywhere? (The answer is yes, in that last sentence.) Often in accounting, we talk about "reversing journals": this is code for "given we are forced into a double entry system, this is incorporated as a fiddle factor to make it work". In fact, in the example case study coming up shortly, very few control accounts contain an even number of calculation entries. So much for double entry.

From the last two chapters, I can now formulate an action plan regarding the order to construct a financial model:

Building a Financial Model in Power BI

This approach remains moot on the order of calculation construction. This is how to build a hassle-free, three-way integrated financial model:

1. Begin with the Income Statement, take the first line item in this account (*e.g.* Revenue)
2. Create calculations if not already computed
3. Construct control account
4. Add checks if necessary
5. Move to the next line item in the financial statement not yet calculated
6. Return to Point 2
7. Once the Income Statement is completed, consider the first line item on the Cash Flow Statement not yet linked
8. Once the Cash Flow Statement is also completed, consider the first line item on the Balance Sheet not yet linked
9. Once the Balance Sheet has been completed, add in the Opening Balance Sheet
10. Correct any opening balance errors if necessary.

It seems a lot, but it really isn't as bad as it sounds. The main simplification I have in this case study is I assume the opening Balance Sheet is zero, because with Power BI you can take your data back as far as you want (well, to 31 December 1899 anyway!), so you just calculate *all* your data. This may be impractical in the real world, but remember, the main thing here is I am trying to get the key concepts across and making adjustments for the opening Balance Sheet may cause confusion and will be specific to your situation, which I can't give adequate discussion to in this book. Hopefully, you shall forgive me!

CHAPTER 6: Getting Started

This chapter is intended to give you the background information you will need to understand the construction of the model from a technical perspective. Just as I am not assuming you are an expert in accounting, I am also not assuming that you are a database administrator or software developer either. If the chapter seems a little disjointed, that's because it is. There are other books available which will help you to become a programming guru or a wizard on data warehousing. I will introduce the data I am using and the techniques I will use to mould the data into the model. In many ways, the order of the sections is irrelevant, but since you will start by opening Power BI Desktop, I begin with a warning.

Power BI keeps updating!

Just one word of caution as you progress through this book. It takes *time* to put this together, but Microsoft's updates are *relentless*. Indeed, as I have written this, my colleagues and I have had to rewrite several times and keep taking revised screenshots because things keep updating and changing. Tricks documented in here may no longer be necessary by the time you read them. The layout of Power BI might change. But the concepts will still be relevant.

Please don't get annoyed if the book seems out of date here and there. Be pleased instead that Microsoft has been listening and modifying things accordingly. Buy lots of copies of this book and I will issue you with new editions hourly (for the litigious amongst you, this is written tongue firmly placed in cheek and constitutes no legally binding obligation!!).

Unable to open document (old PBI version)

In Chapter 2, I described how to install Power BI Desktop. Depending on how I have chosen to install Power BI Desktop, there is an error that may be encountered the first time I try to open the **pbix** file from File Explorer (or from an email attachment).

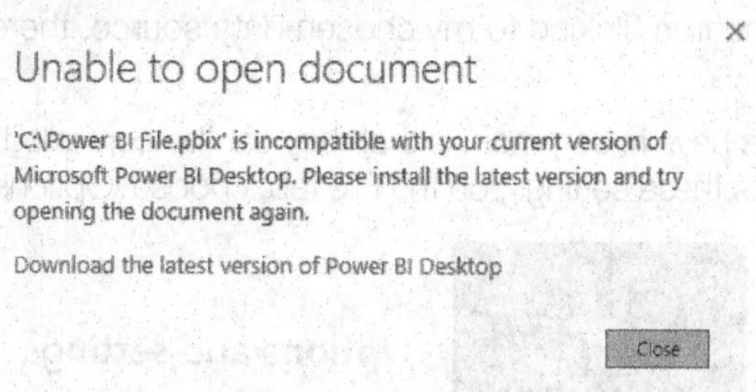

This means that the file was created with a different (typically, later) version of Power BI Desktop than the one that File Explorer thinks it should be using. If you encounter this, your first corrective action should be to open Power BI Desktop, and then open the file from there. If you still encounter problems, then you must check that Power BI Desktop is up to date. As previously explained, if you have downloaded Power BI Desktop from the Microsoft website, you may need to check back for updates on a regular basis (it is easy to miss the messages in Power BI Desktop itself). This problem is less likely to be encountered if you have installed Power BI Desktop from the app store. If Power BI Desktop appears to be up to date and you still have problems, you should remove and reinstall Power BI Desktop. If that doesn't work, check out the SumProduct website where we will soon start selling laptop-destroying axes for as little as $19.99, excluding delivery and taxes.

Privacy warning

Power BI Desktop is a fantastic visualisation tool taking raw data and transforming it into informative and insightful dashboards. Data is a valuable resource, and some companies will set up firewalls and access restrictions to protect data. Whilst I can't possibly know the situation at your company, there are a couple of scenarios that are sometimes encountered when linking source data to Power BI. This section is not intended to replace the excellent Microsoft help pages, which contain very detailed descriptions to explain exactly why these messages can occur. Just before we begin, I wish to highlight two errors that might be triggered when linking to the source data in the Power Query Editor (more on how to access this later):

Formula.Firewall: *Query 'Source Data' (step 'Source') references other queries or steps, so it may not directly access a data source. Please rebuild this data combination.*

The reasons why this error can occur are complex, and are to do with the way that queries can potentially be made more efficient for relational databases by applying filters directly to the source. In the model for this book, I am using a 'flat' data file which can't be filtered at source, but the restrictions may still be encountered. Another message that could be invoked is:

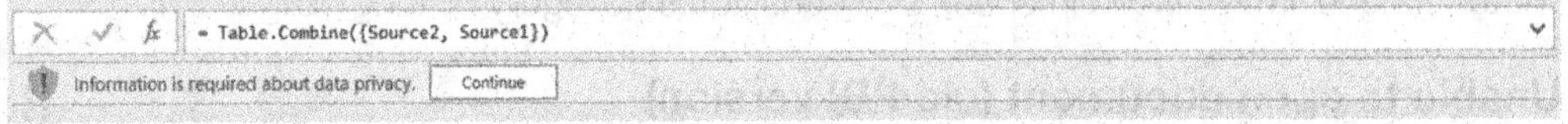

Information is required about data privacy.

This example could happen if I decided to get the data from a couple of sources where I needed to enter logon details. These are two [2] examples of privacy related messages that would prevent me from linking to my chosen data source, there are others on a similar theme.

What these messages have in common, is that they can be controlled by the privacy settings in Power BI. To access these settings, on the File tab, choose 'Options and settings':

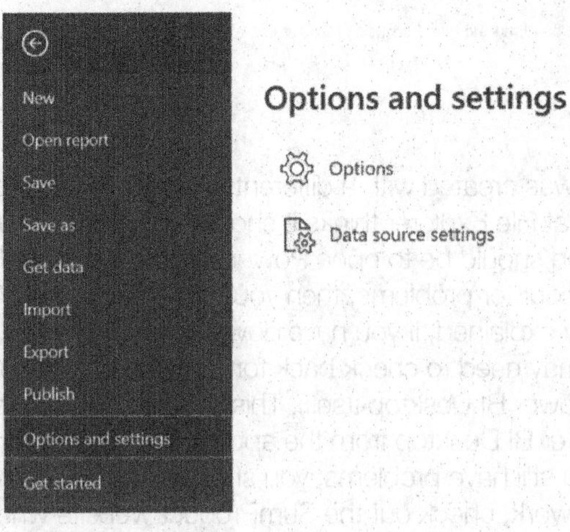

In the Options dialog, select the Privacy tab under the 'Current file' section, where the default option is to 'Combine data according to your Privacy Level settings for each source'. Changing this to 'Ignore the Privacy Levels and potentially improve performance' should remove the messages I gave examples of. However, the information icon warns about making this choice:

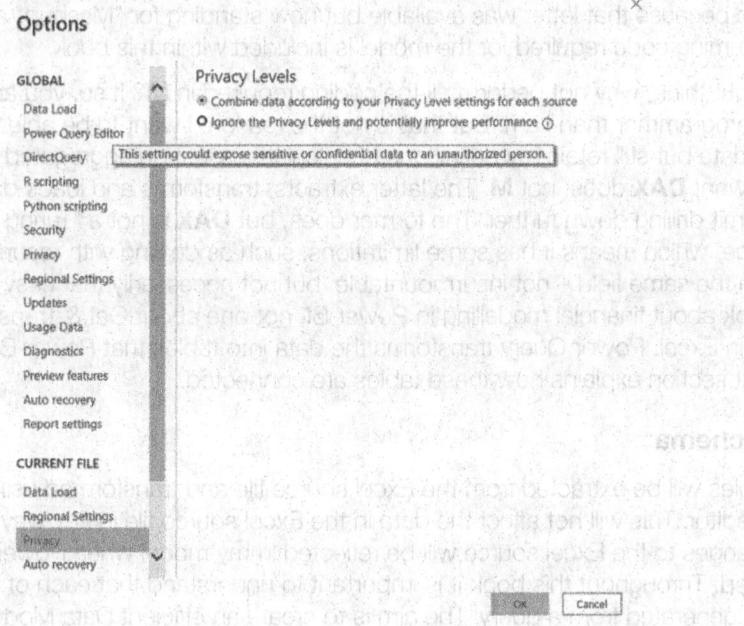

To explore this topic, click on 'Learn more about Privacy Levels' to access the Microsoft help pages.

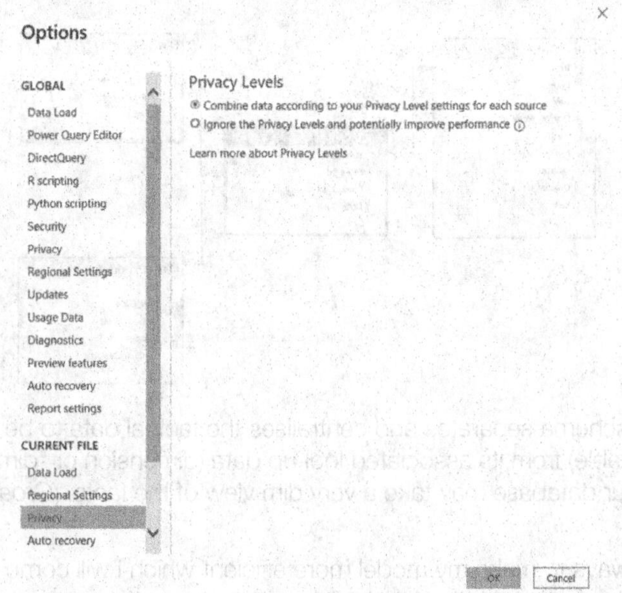

Moving on, let's look at the engines driving Power BI: the programming languages…

Programming languages

Power BI Desktop uses two programming languages, and I will be using both to create the financial model. The language used to create measures and calculated columns is **DAX** (Data Analysis eXpressions, **DAX**). When I create tables for the model, I will be transforming data using the Power Query engine – this uses a language called **M** (chosen because that letter was available but now standing for "Mashup" allegedly). All programming code required for the model is included within this book.

You might think, why not perform all the coding required in **M**? If so, you are a much better programmer than I am. But that is not the reason. I want to be able to drill down on my data but still retain my definitions of calculations just on aggregated or filtered data. This is what **DAX** does; not **M**. The latter extracts, transforms and loads data but does not permit drilling down further. The former does, but **DAX** is not a "Turing complete" language, which means it has some limitations, such as dealing with recursion and other items in the same field – not insurmountable, but not necessarily that easy either. This is a book about financial modelling in Power BI, not one about Get & Transform (Power Query) in Excel. Power Query transforms the data into tables that Power BI can use, and the next section explains how these tables are connected.

Star schema

The tables will be extracted from the Excel source file and transformed using the Power Query editor. This will not affect the data in the Excel source file in any way; however, any changes to the Excel source will be reflected in my model when Power Query is refreshed. Throughout this book it is important to understand that each of the tables used is generated from a query. The aim is to create an efficient Data Model to power the visuals. An efficient Power BI table only includes the columns (fields) that will be used. Tables should ideally be connected via a star schema, and there should ideally be one designated Date Table. A star schema looks like this:

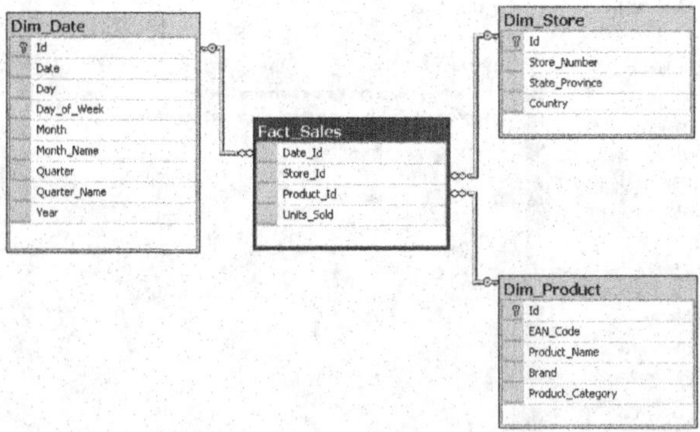

Basically, a star schema separates and centralises the factual data to be analysed (a factual or "fact" table) from its associated lookup data (dimension or "dim" tables). If you don't do this, your database may take a very dim view of the facts. *(Groan! I need a pay rise – Ed.)*

There are more ways to make my model more efficient which I will come to later in the chapter. First, I should look at the data I will be using in more detail.

Introducing the data

The data I will be using all comes from one file:

Source data.xlsx.

This, and Power BI files for various points in the model, may be found at:

www.sumproduct.com/book-3-resources

In real life, the data may originate from a multitude of sources, such as Excel, Access, SAP, bespoke databases, websites and old tissue boxes crammed full of receipts (yes, I had a state-of-the-art filing system when I was self-employed too). It does not matter; just employ the appropriate Power BI data connector to extract, transform and load your data. The fact that all my data comes from one source should not detract from your enjoyment of the book, as I have written it in such a way there should be no enjoyment whatsoever in any case…

In this source Excel workbook, there are various tables. In summary, the following screenshot provides an *aide memoire* of what is situated where, in terms of "dummy" financial code:

Code	Description
1000	Sales
2000	Costs of goods sold (COGS)
2100	Inventory
3000	Operating expenditure
4000	Capital expenditure
5100	Debt
5200	Debt repayments
6100	Equity issued
6200	Equity buyback
7000	Dividends

For example, the depreciation table contains a list of 'Capital expenditure' amounts throughout the two years. Like all our data tables, I am going to assume our data is in $'000, although I will only use $ as the currency indicator here, for simplicity. Forgive me if this upsets you, but I wanted the numbers to be sizeable enough to mean something, but not so large that all screenshots in the book would only show three columns as the fields had to be wide enough to accommodate large numbers! I am sure you will agree this is an acceptable compromise and we are working with data directly imported from *La La Land* in any case. Any complaints may be sent through to the usual channels, *i.e.* anyone but me.

	A	B	C
1	Account	Date	Amount
2	4000	1-Jan-21	1,000
3	4000	1-Feb-21	75
4	4000	1-Mar-21	75
5	4000	1-Apr-21	75
6	4000	1-May-21	75
7	4000	1-Jun-21	800
8	4000	1-Jul-21	75
9	4000	1-Aug-21	75
10	4000	1-Sep-21	75
11	4000	1-Oct-21	75
12	4000	1-Nov-21	75
13	4000	1-Dec-21	1,200
14	4000	1-Jan-22	75
15	4000	1-Feb-22	75
16	4000	1-Mar-22	75
17	4000	1-Apr-22	75
18	4000	1-May-22	75
19	4000	1-Jun-22	2,000
20	4000	1-Jul-22	75
21	4000	1-Aug-22	75
22	4000	1-Sep-22	75
23	4000	1-Oct-22	75
24	4000	1-Nov-22	75
25	4000	1-Dec-22	2,000

The depreciation table is shown in the Excel source file. I have configured the date in a format which makes it clear what the month is, whether you write dates properly (*e.g.* "17/9/67") or you're an American. Before I open Power Query, there is a setting I must change to enable me to display dates with the month name. This is not necessary to build the model, it is included to explain how I managed to display the dates in this way because this is a question I get asked all the time.

Using Windows Settings to control Power Query date display

Since Power Query is generally used to transform and edit data to be displayed in applications such as Excel or Power BI, the options to change the way the data is displayed in Power Query are limited. This means that the date format is determined by the locale, for example UK or US. For example, 12th Jan 2021 would be represented as 12/01/21 in UK format, or 01/12/21 in US format. Since I want all my readers to interpret the dates correctly, I would like to show the month name by default for all dates. There is currently no setting in Power Query to do this. There is however a setting in Windows 10 that I can use.

In the Windows 'Settings' app, there is an option called 'Time & Language':

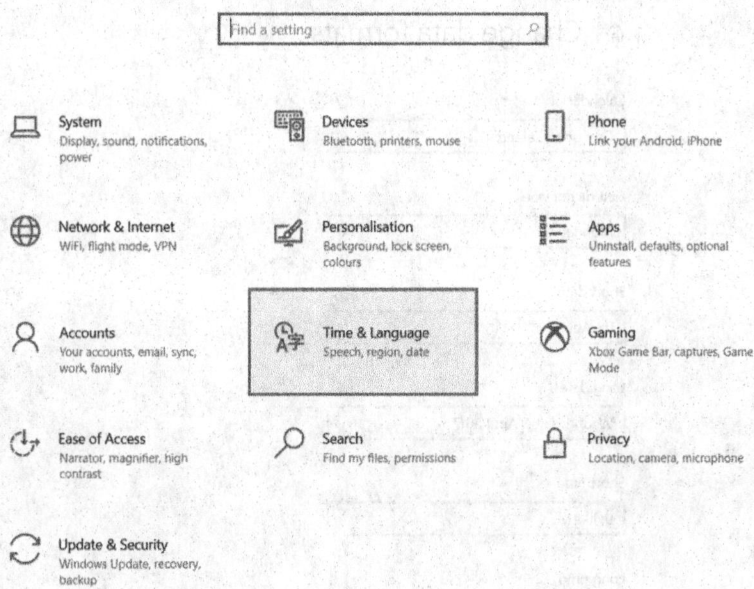

If I choose the 'Region' tab on the 'Time & language' dialog, in my case, I can set my 'Regional format' to **English (Australia)**. Note the 'Short Date' setting in 'Regional format data': this is the key to displaying dates in Power Query as I have them presented in this book. It should be noted that this option is *not* available for all territories. But don't blame me!

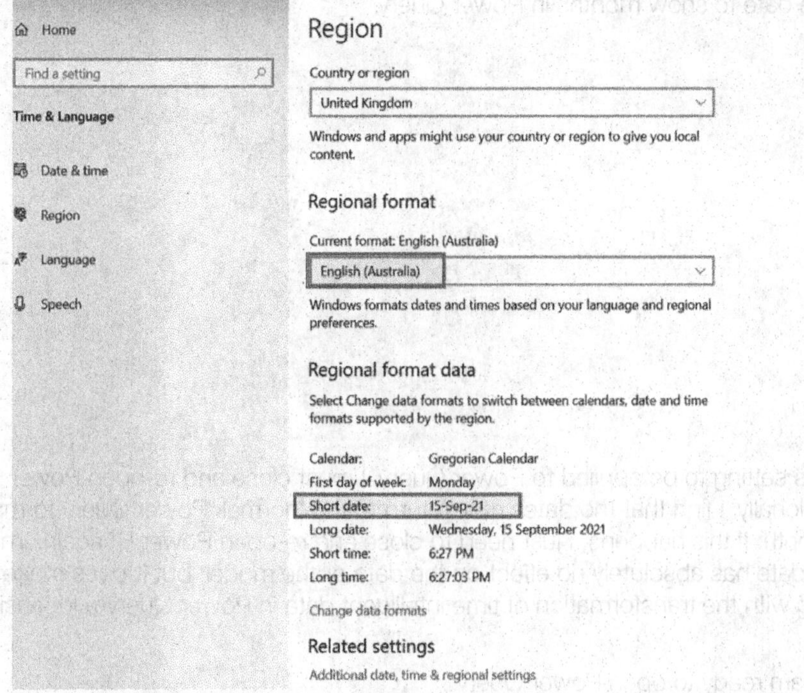

I can use the blue 'Change date formats' area to access the 'Change date formats' dialog.

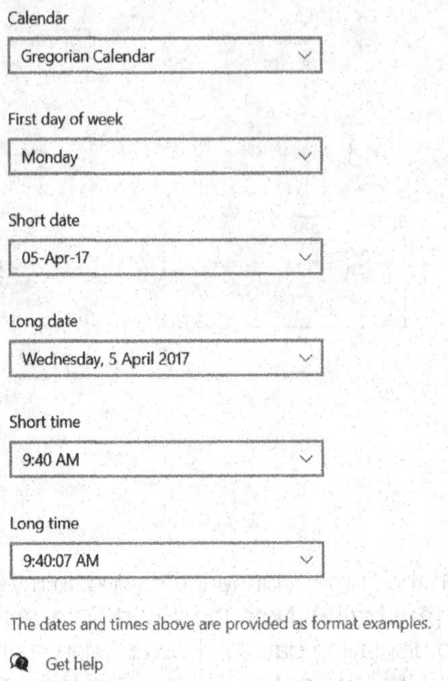

The dropdown for 'Short Date' gives me lots of options, but I must pick '05-Apr-17' to get the date to show months in Power Query.

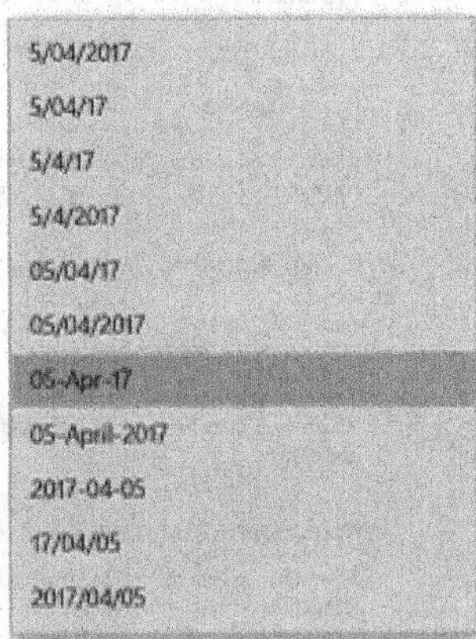

For this setting to be applied to Power Query, I must close and re-open Power BI. Occasionally, I find that the dates may return to the 'normal' Power Query format without the month: if this happens, I just need to close and re-open Power BI again. The format of the date has absolutely no effect on the data or the model, but it does make a book dealing with the transformation of time intelligent data in Power Query a lot easier to follow!

Now I am ready to open Power Query.

Opening the Power Query editor

Having successfully opened Power BI Desktop, I want to extract my data. I could do this from the Home tab using the 'Get Data' dropdown in the Data section, but because I am going to be clever about the way I link to the source data, I am going to use 'Transform data' in the Queries section.

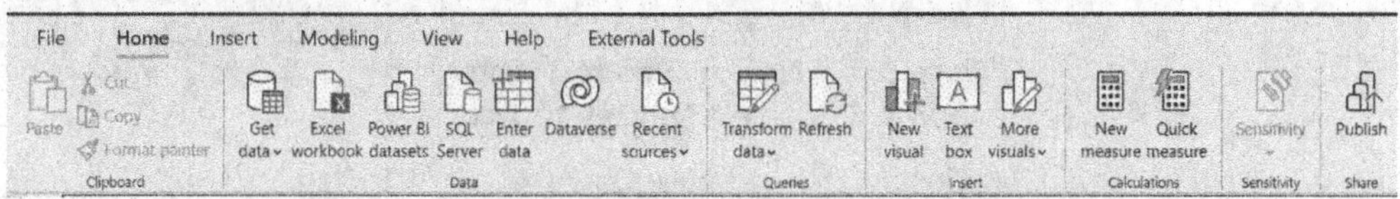

From here, I can access the Power Query editor from the 'Transform data' option.

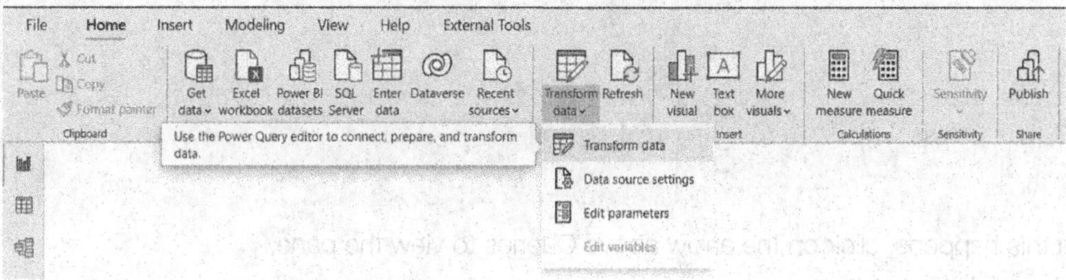

This will display the Power Query editor.

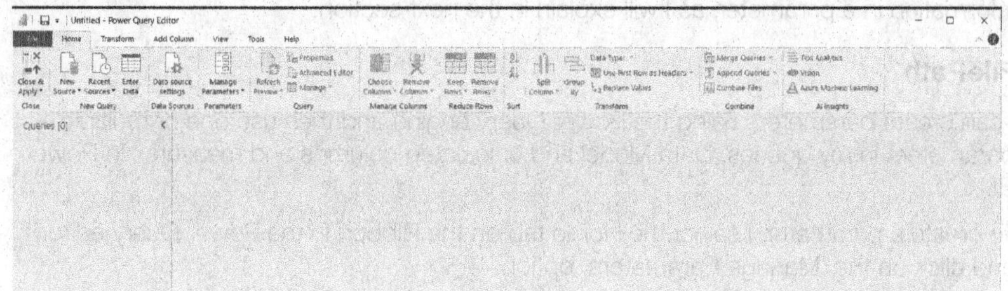

On the previous screen, I have a Queries pane to the left, which may appear closed.

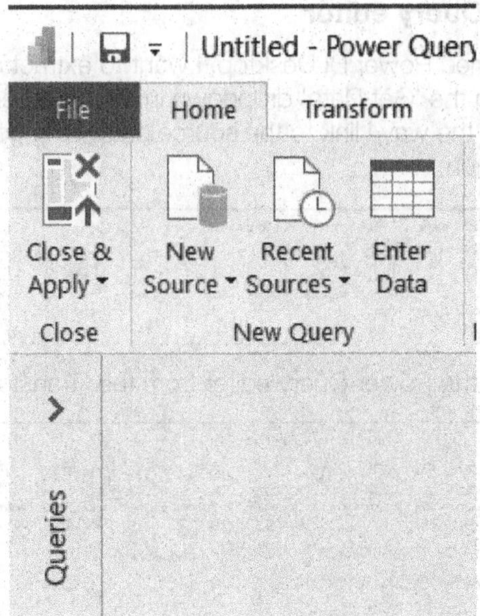

If this happens, click on the arrow above Queries to view the pane.

I am ready to access the data, but as I said, I am going to be clever about this. To make it very clear where the Excel Workbook is, and what it is called, I am going to store this information in a parameter, as I will explain in the next section.

FilePath

I can create parameters using the Power Query engine and then use one or multiple parameters in my queries, Data Model and calculated columns and measures in Power BI.

To create a parameter, I select the Home tab on the Ribbon in the Power Query editor, and click on the 'Manage Parameters' option:

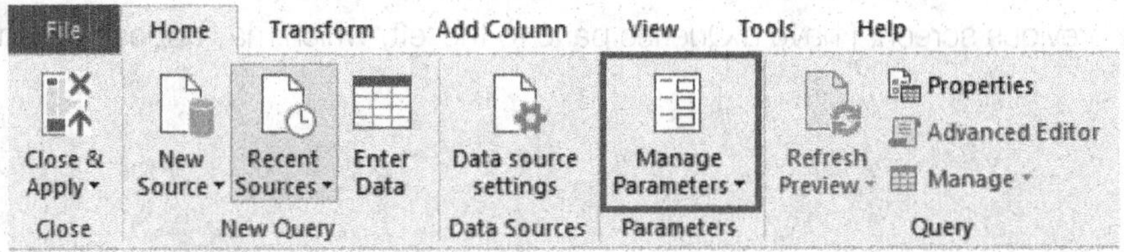

The 'Manage Parameters' dialog will appear. Here, I click on the 'New' option at the top of the dialog:

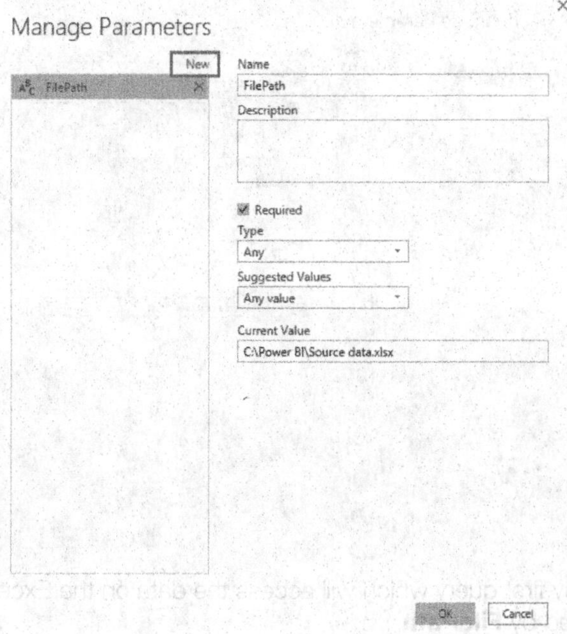

The **FilePath** parameter should point to the file location of the source file **Source data.xlsx**. Whilst in principle the **pbix** file and the source file do not have to be in the same location, keeping them close together limits network latency, ensuring that queries execute efficiently. Whilst I was imprisoned writing this book, an old lag taught me that.

I can also select whether the parameter is required (the check box in the image). This will mean that Power BI will require a value to be assigned to this parameter.

I can also assign a data type. In this case, I have used the default data type 'Any', which means there is no restriction on the type of data that can be entered as a value:

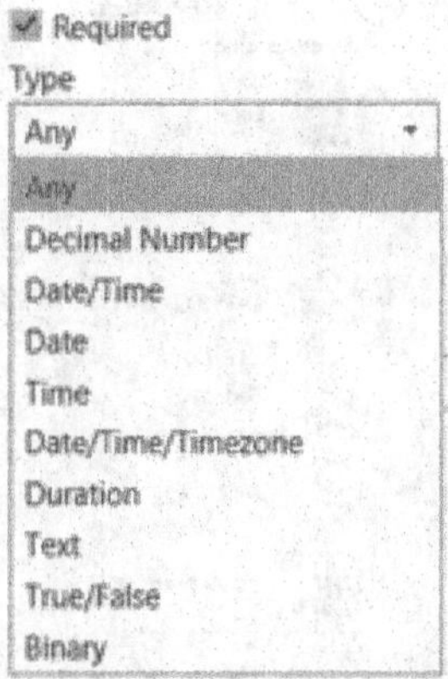

This parameter should allow 'Any Value' in the suggested values. I type the location and file name into the 'Current Value' field.

Manage Parameters

New

FilePath

Name: FilePath

Description

Required

Type: Any

Suggested Values: Any value

Current Value: C:\Power BI\Source data.xlsx

OK Cancel

I can now create my first query which will access the data on the Excel Workbook using the location provided by **FilePath**.

Source data

I am ready to create my first query. Rather than allow the Power Query engine to automatically bring in all the data I need, I am going to create a new Blank Query and create a simple query that will only access the Excel Workbook identified by **FilePath**.

I can create a Blank Query from the dropdown from 'New Source' on the Home tab.

This is a good point to check that I have access to the Formula Bar and the Query Settings.

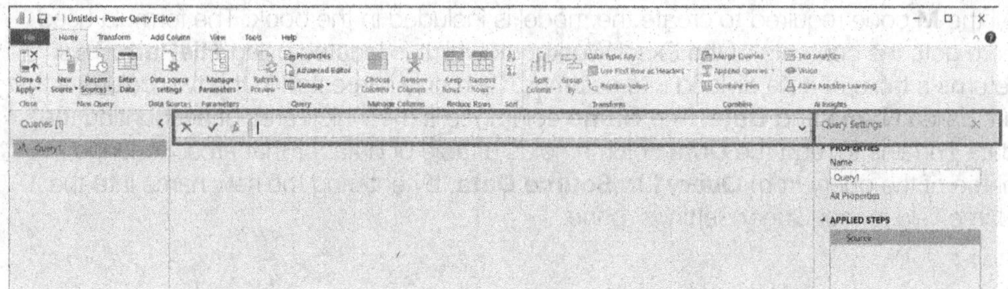

If I don't have access to either of these areas, I can change the settings on the View tab.

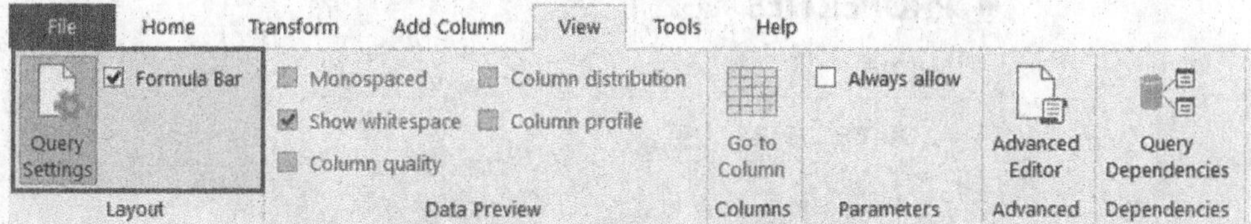

The 'Query Settings' button allows me to view or hide the Query Settings pane and the checkbox next to Formula Bar should be ticked as this is where the **M** code for a Query Step appears.

I can now type the **M** code I need for my first step into the Formula Bar:

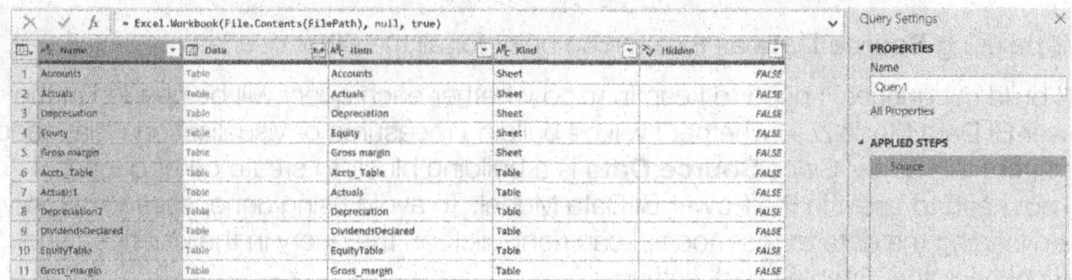

The **M** code I have used is:

```
= Excel.Workbook(File.Contents(FilePath), null, true)
```

Like Excel, each formula begins with an equals sign (=). Microsoft Intellisense helps me with the syntax. You have probably discovered that **M** is case sensitive, and must be typed exactly as shown in the previous image.

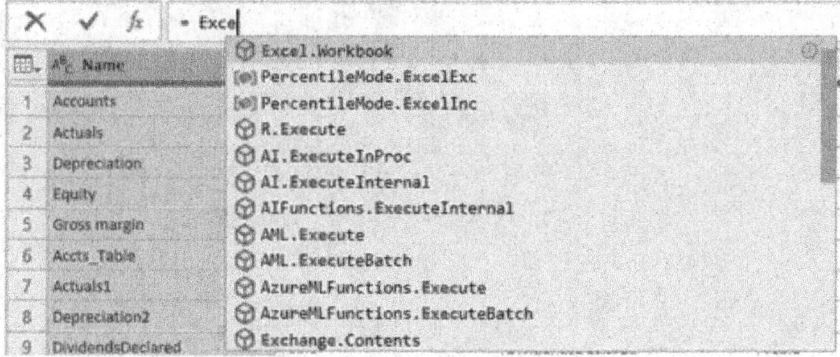

All the **M** code required to create the model is included in the book. The formula used here gets the contents of the Excel Workbook which is located using **FilePath.** This returns a table of data divided into columns. I am only interested in the two columns that are called **Name** and **Data**. The **Name** column tells me which area of accounting the data pertains to, and the **Data** column holds a table of data for that area. I change the name of the query from **Query1** to **Source Data**, by entering the new name into the Name field in the 'Query Settings' pane.

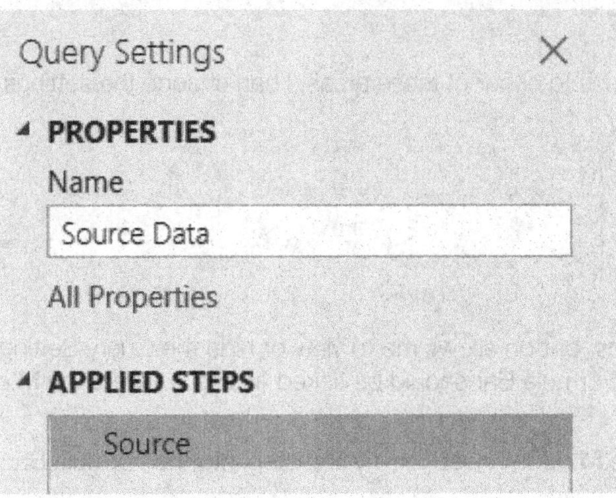

I will be using **Source Data** as the starting point for all the other queries.

As I build my queries, I need to keep in mind whether each query will be needed in the Power BI Data Model, *i.e.* whether I will be building measures or visualisations that need data from this query. Since **Source Data** is a building block to create other queries, I will not need to use it in the Power BI Data Model. To avoid using unnecessary memory when loading the data to the model, I can right-click on the query in the Queries panel and uncheck the 'Enable Load' setting.

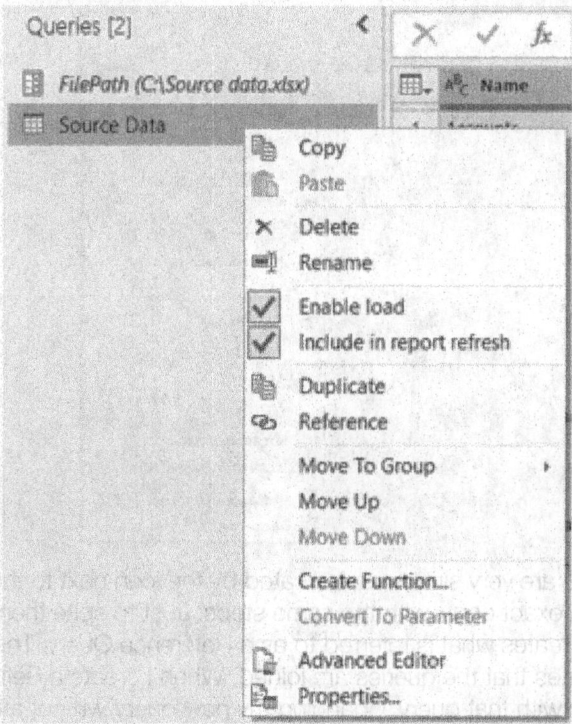

The query will then be displayed in *italics* to make it easier to see which queries will and *will not* be loaded into the model.

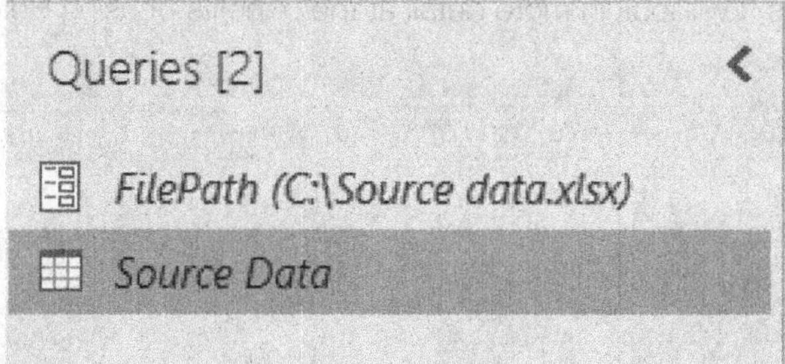

Referencing a query

I can now create a new query by using Source Data as a starting point. There are several ways I can do this, which I can see if I right-click on Source Data as I did when I unchecked 'Enable Load'.

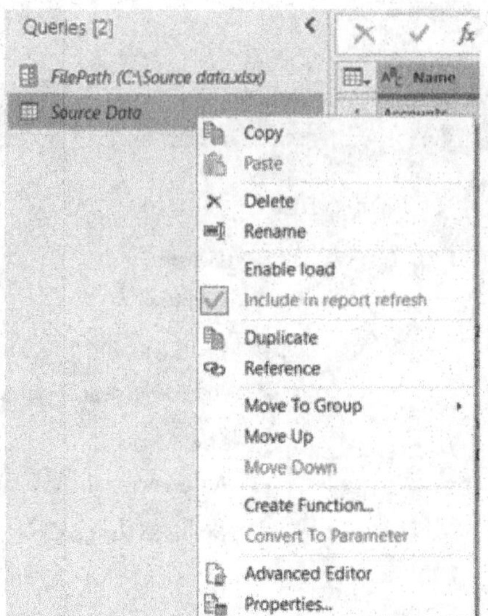

Copy and Duplicate are very similar, as indicated by the icon next to them. Using either will create an exact copy, with the same steps. Just to spite them, I will be using Reference, which creates what is referred to as a Reference Query. The chain icon next to Reference indicates that the queries are joined. When I create a Reference Query, I start my new query with that query. Changing my new query will not affect the original query, **Source Data**, but any changes to **Source Data** will automatically be picked up by my new query. This is exactly what I want: if the Excel data accessed by **Source Data** changes for any reason, I don't want to have to go and change all my queries. Before I create more queries, I will look in more detail at the benefits of using Reference Queries.

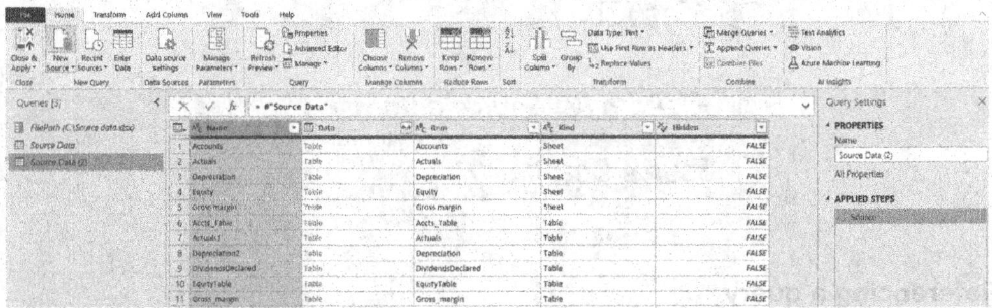

Reliable references

You may skip this section if you wish, it is included to provide more detail on what Reference Queries are and how they interact with other queries. Reference Queries are used extensively when creating the tables for the accounting model, because they are extremely useful when creating multiple tables from the same source.

Sometimes, you create two similar tables in Power BI. They are identical for the first few 'APPLIED STEPS', but then a proverbial fork in the road appears and the two tables part ways. For example, consider the following base table:

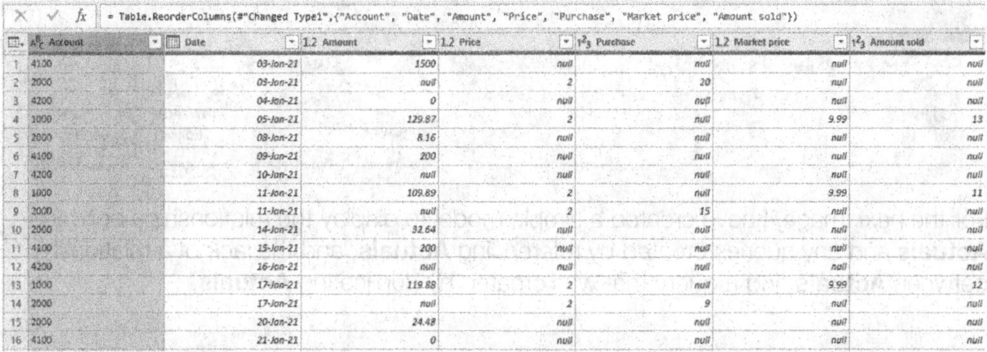

= Table.ReorderColumns(#"Changed Type1",{"Account", "Date", "Amount", "Price", "Purchase", "Market price", "Amount sold"})

	Account	Date	Amount	Price	Purchase	Market price	Amount sold
1	4100	03-Jan-21	1500	null	null	null	null
2	2000	03-Jan-21	null	2	20	null	null
3	4200	04-Jan-21	0	null	null	null	null
4	1000	05-Jan-21	129.87	2	null	9.99	13
5	2000	08-Jan-21	8.16	null	null	null	null
6	4100	09-Jan-21	200	null	null	null	null
7	4200	10-Jan-21	null	null	null	null	null
8	1000	11-Jan-21	109.89	2	null	9.99	11
9	2000	11-Jan-21	null	2	15	null	null
10	2000	14-Jan-21	32.64	null	null	null	null
11	4100	15-Jan-21	200	null	null	null	null
12	4200	16-Jan-21	null	null	null	null	null
13	1000	17-Jan-21	119.88	2	null	9.99	12
14	2000	17-Jan-21	null	2	9	null	null
15	2000	20-Jan-21	24.48	null	null	null	null
16	4100	21-Jan-21	0	null	null	null	null

This is the **Actuals** table which I will be creating shortly. When I come to calculate the inventory control account, I will have to create a similar table, where I will need to perform further grouping, which is unique to the rows relating to inventory only. However, I still need the **Actuals** table. If I group the **Actuals** table on the rows required for inventory, I will lose data on other accounts. The answer here is to create two copies.

In this case, I want my copy to start with this query, and I only want to make changes to the original query.

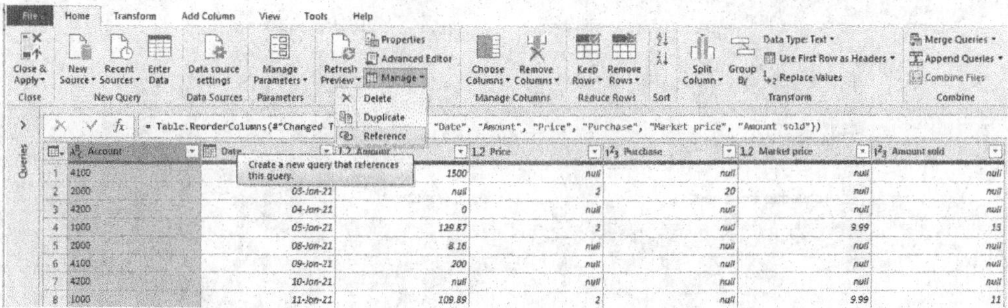

I will show another method to create a Reference Query with the query to be referenced open. From the Manage option in the Query section of the Home tab, I can choose to create a Reference Query.

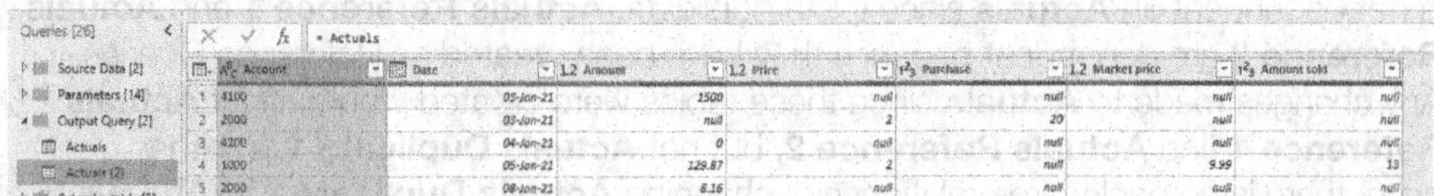

My new query has only one step: Source. In the Formula Bar, I can see that the Source step is pointing at my original query.

```
= Actuals
```

Anything I add to this query will have no impact upon my source query. This is the reason for the attachment icon next to the 'Reference' option: I am attaching my original query to my new query.

On the View tab there is a 'Query Dependencies' window.

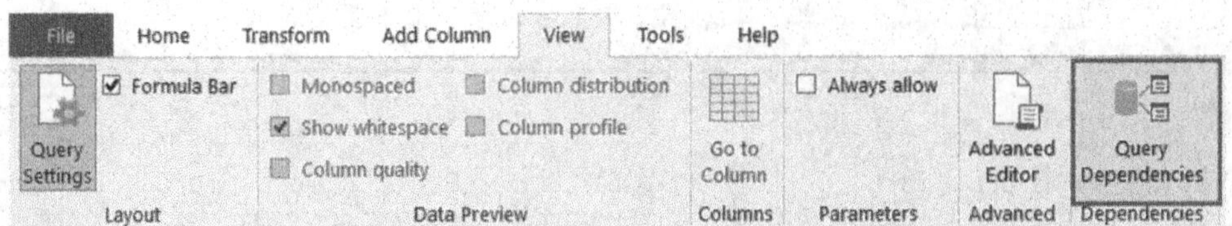

For the next image, I have created a simple model to display the relationships between **Actuals** and any queries created by referencing **Actuals**, and the lack of a relationship between **Actuals** and a query that was created by duplicating **Actuals**:

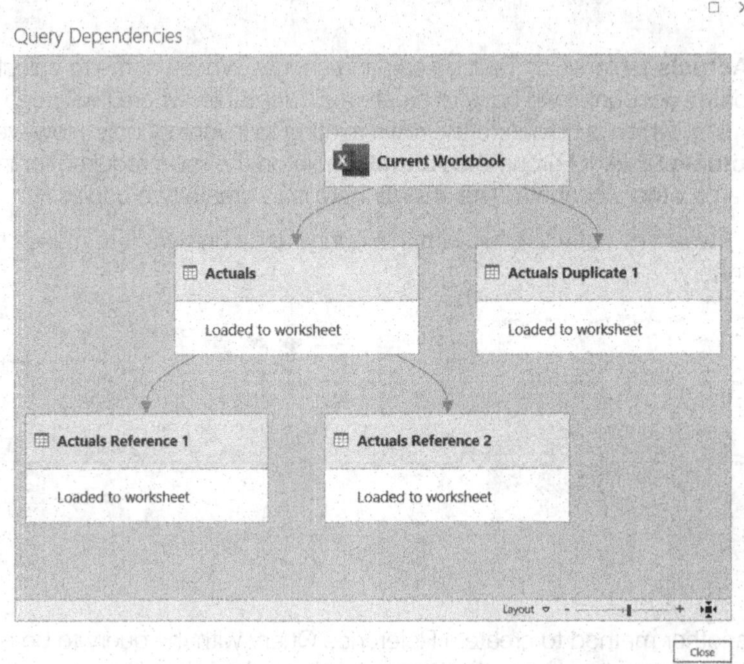

In this example, the 'Query Dependencies' window shows that whilst **Actuals Duplicate** is not dependent on **Actuals** since it is a duplicate, **Actuals Reference 1** and **Actuals Reference 2** are dependent because they have been created as Reference Queries. Any changes made to **Actuals** since these tables were created would affect **Actuals Reference 1** and **Actuals Reference 2**, but not **Actuals Duplicate 1**. In either case, there is no backwards relationship: changing **Actuals Duplicate 1** or **Actuals Reference 1** will *not* affect **Actuals**.

When I **merge** queries later in the book, this process creates a Reference Query, which stops me from changing the original tables when I create new steps. **Appending** queries as new would also create a Reference Query for similar reasons. Reference Queries are useful whenever I want to preserve my original query, but I also need to make sure that my new query is kept in line with the original query.

So now you know! Now, I will return to creating the tables that will be the starting point for the accounting model.

Source tables

I will set up the tables listed in the next visual. For many of the queries, the starting point is **Source Data,** but as I progress, I will be building on existing queries as I shall explain. To follow along with the steps taken in Power Query to create these tables, please refer to the first Power BI file in the additional resources:

Table Name	Description
Source Data	Reference source data query
Actuals	Table that houses all the data
Depreciation	Table that has all the Capex values
Dividends	Table that displays the planned dividend amounts
Equity	Table that shows equity issuances and buybacks
Calendar	Date table with contiguous dates
Control account measures	Housing table for control accounts measures
Financial account measures	Housing table for financial statements measures

You may disagree with the architecture here. However, in reality, source data comes from a myriad of sources, often with little rhyme or reason. I wanted to generate that sort of scenario here. It is for the case study illustration only and in no way is meant to reflect Best Practice.

Depreciation

I will come to **Actuals** later, as it builds on the other tables. First of all though, I shall start with **Depreciation**. I have made a Reference Query from the **Source Data**:

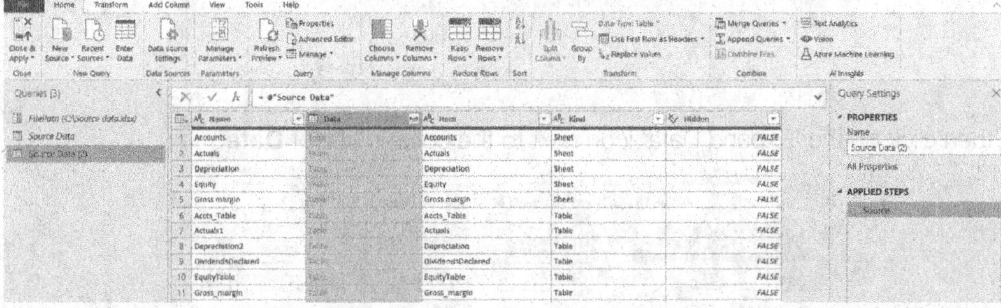

I rename my query **Depreciation** and filter the **Name** column for 'Depreciation' using the dropdown icon next to the column title. There are other ways I can extract the data as I will show later, but for this first table I will go through the individual steps.

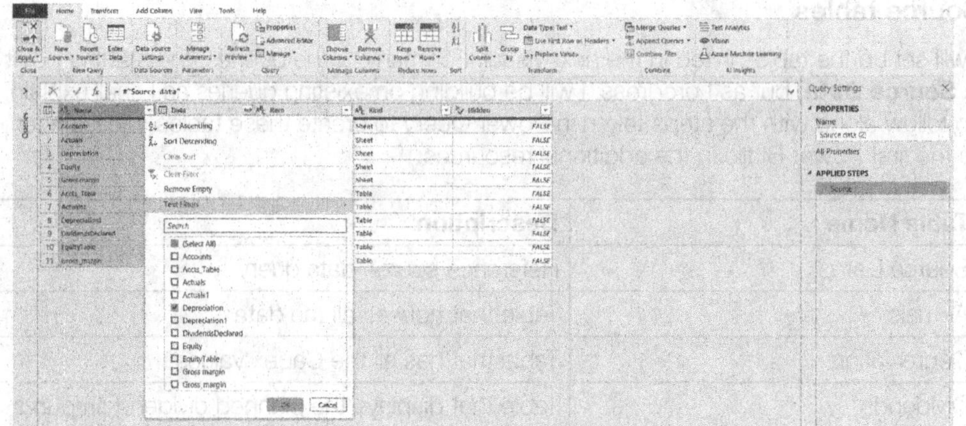

I select the **Data** column and right-click to select the 'Remove Other Columns' option.

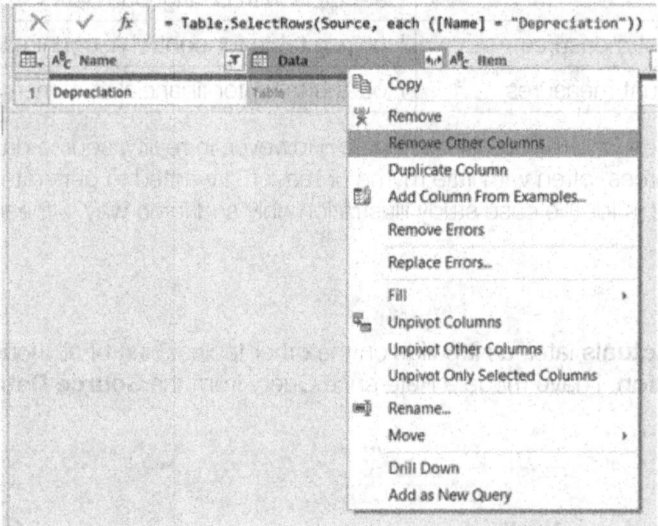

I then click on the 'Expand Data' icon next to the column title of **Data**:

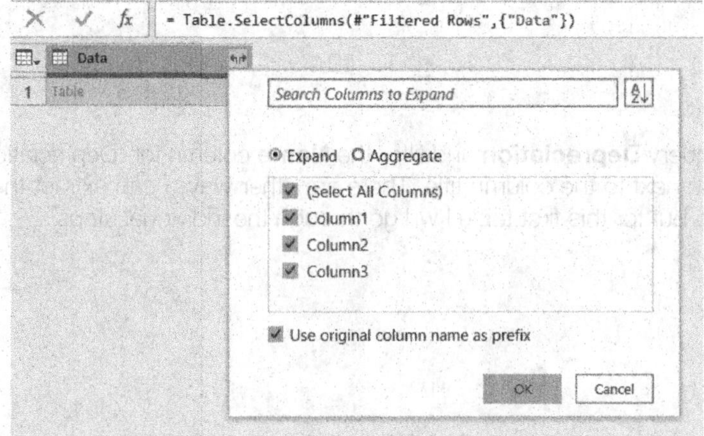

I untick the 'Use original column name as prefix' option (this is typically only useful when you have existing columns with similar names so you may distinguish between sources and because you can't have the same field name twice). When I click 'OK' the row is extended:

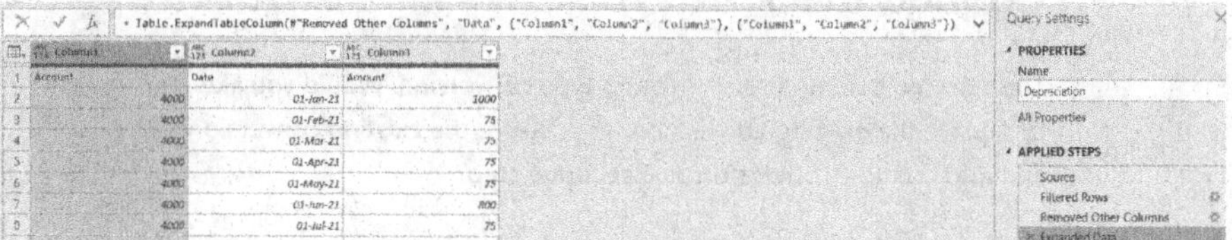

The next step is to 'Use First Row as Headers'; this option can be found in the Transform group on the Home tab of the Ribbon:

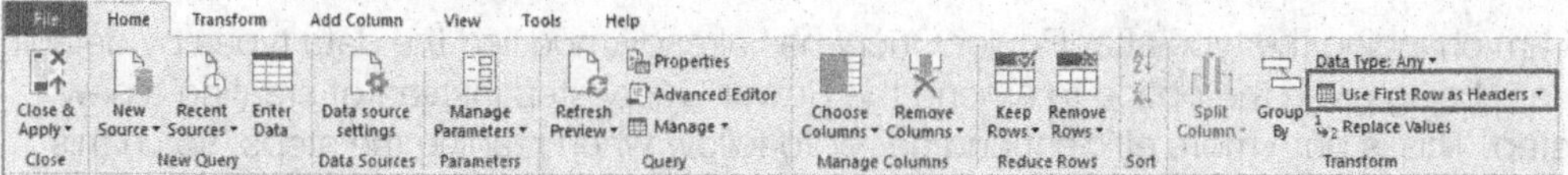

Power BI then automatically changes the data types for me, based upon a sample of the data:

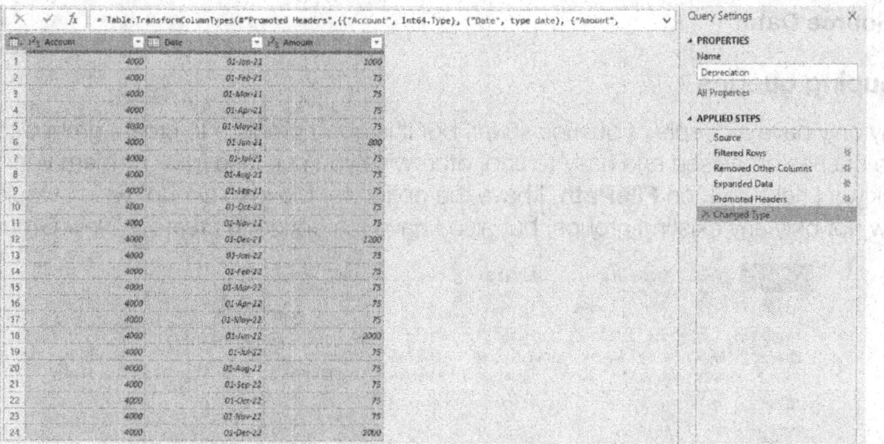

Although Power Query will use algorithms to select the default data types, I can change them as I know my data. There is a minor tweak to be made here. I know that although **Account** is identified by numbers, the number must be in text form, so I can filter the values in Account in my **DAX** measures later (this is specific to this example and isn't something you would necessarily do). Therefore, I must change the data type for the **Account** column to text.

I can see on the Home tab that the data type is currently 'Whole Number':

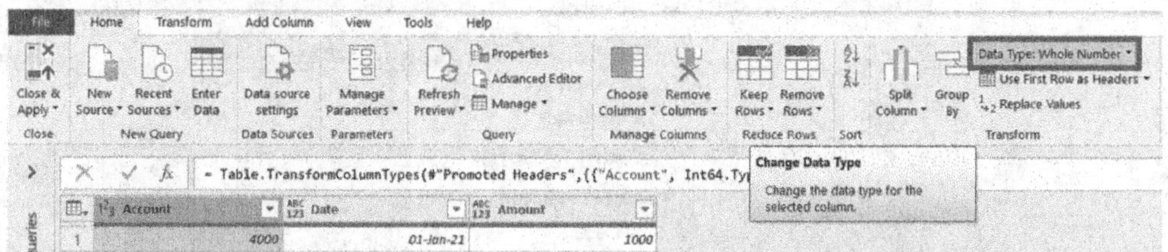

I can change this using the dropdown to 'Text'. When I do this, Power Query prompts me with a question:

Change Column Type
The selected column has an existing type conversion. Would you like to replace the existing conversion, or preserve the existing conversion and add the new conversion as a separate step?
Replace current
Add new step
Cancel

I am changing the type after Power Query has already modified the data types by default. I am being given the option to amend the Power Query step instead of creating a new step. This is both more efficient and easier to follow when reading the steps, so, in this instance, I will choose to 'Replace current'.

Depreciation will be used to create queries needed by the model, but it should not be loaded to the model. Therefore, the 'Enable Load' setting should be unchecked as it was for **Source Data**.

Grouping queries

I may only have a couple of queries so far, but it is good practice to create groups to keep queries organised and easy to find, otherwise you can lose track of them *very* quickly. If I right-click on **FilePath**, I have the option to 'Move to Group' which would show not only any existing groups, but also I have the option to create a 'New Group'.

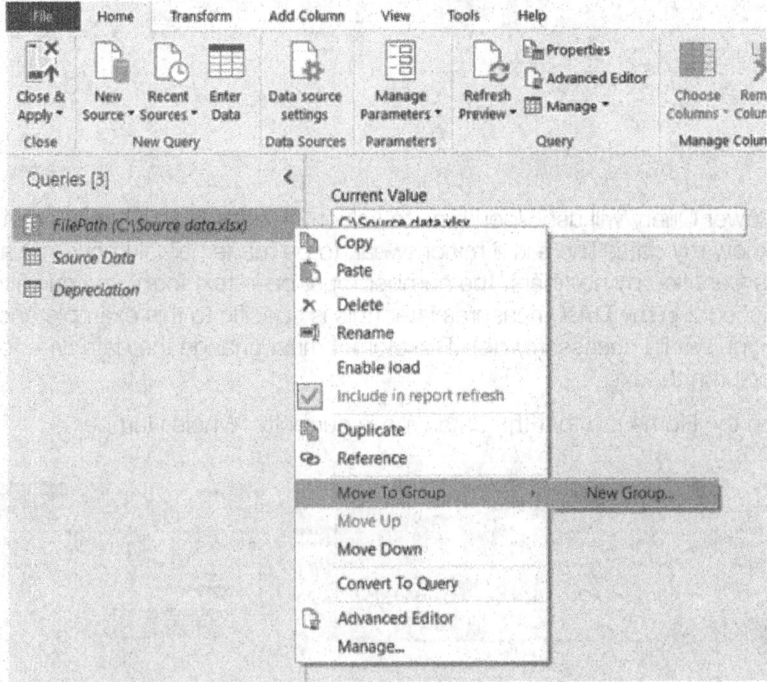

I choose to create a group called 'Parameters'.

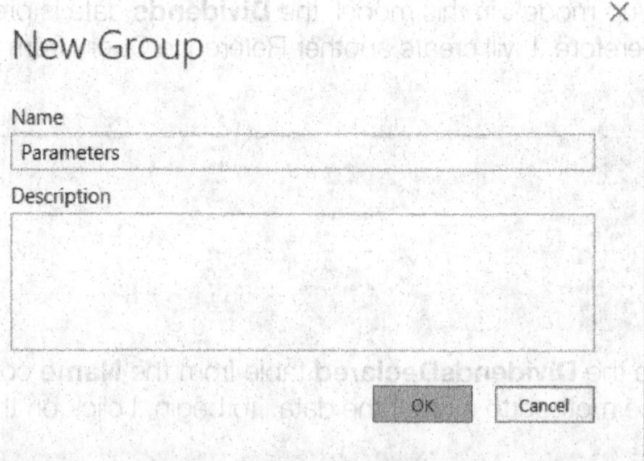

Since I have created a group, Power Query automatically creates a group for the other queries called (you guessed it) 'Other Queries'. It's not very imaginative, you know.

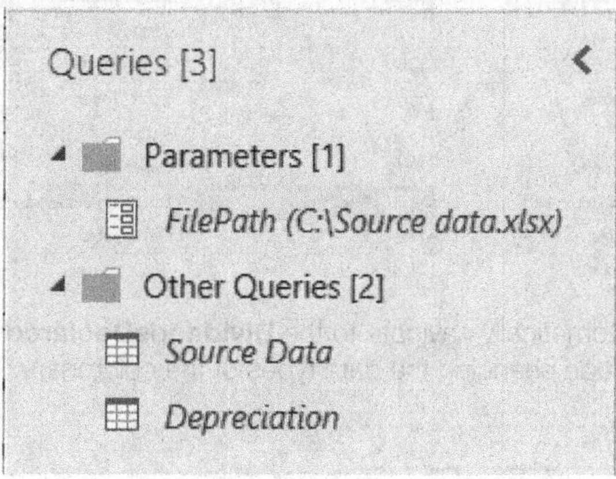

I create more meaningful groups for the other queries. I will be adding more queries to the 'Parameters' and the 'Output Query' groups as I create them.

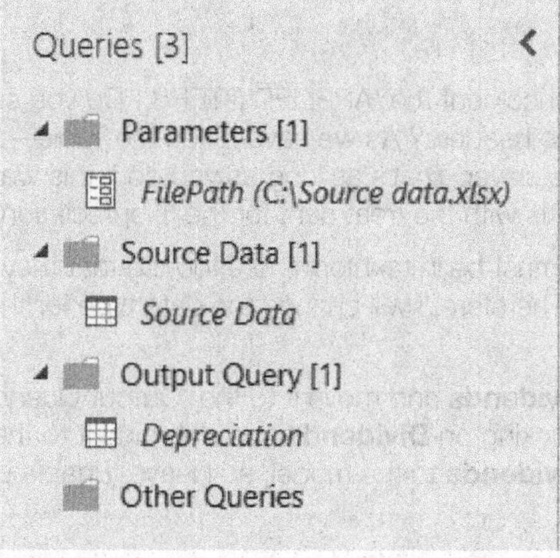

Dividends

Whilst I am in "set up mode", in this model, the **Dividends** data is presented in a separate table. Therefore, I will create another Reference Query from **Source Data**.

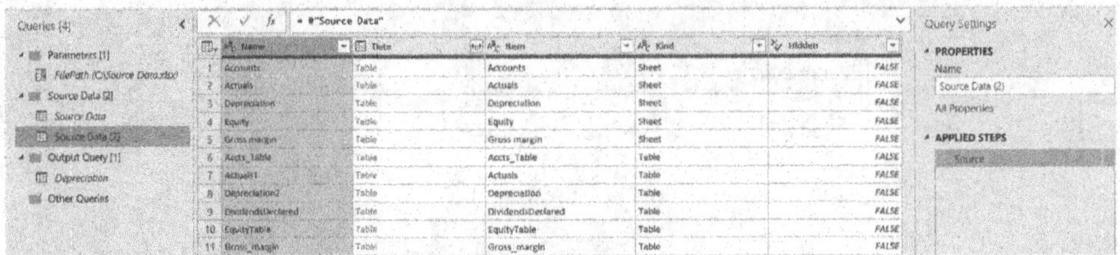

From here, I locate the **DividendsDeclared** table from the **Name** column. This time, I will use a difference method to extract the data. To begin, I click on the yellow **Table** text.

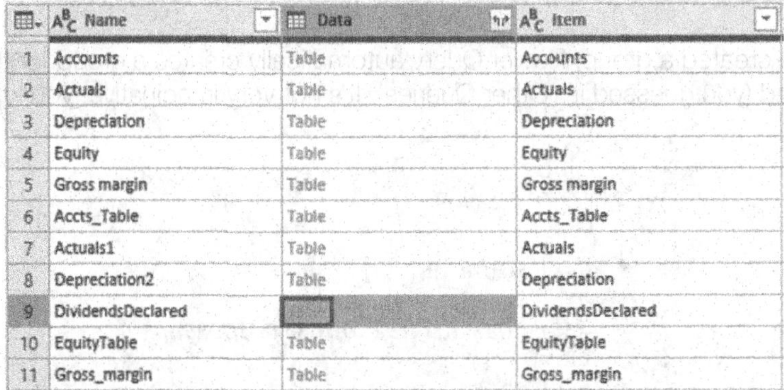

	Name	Data	Item
1	Accounts	Table	Accounts
2	Actuals	Table	Actuals
3	Depreciation	Table	Depreciation
4	Equity	Table	Equity
5	Gross margin	Table	Gross margin
6	Accts_Table	Table	Accts_Table
7	Actuals1	Table	Actuals
8	Depreciation2	Table	Depreciation
9	DividendsDeclared		DividendsDeclared
10	EquityTable	Table	EquityTable
11	Gross_margin	Table	Gross_margin

Power BI will then automatically navigate to the **DividendsDeclared** table and extract the data. This will include changing the data types of the columns:

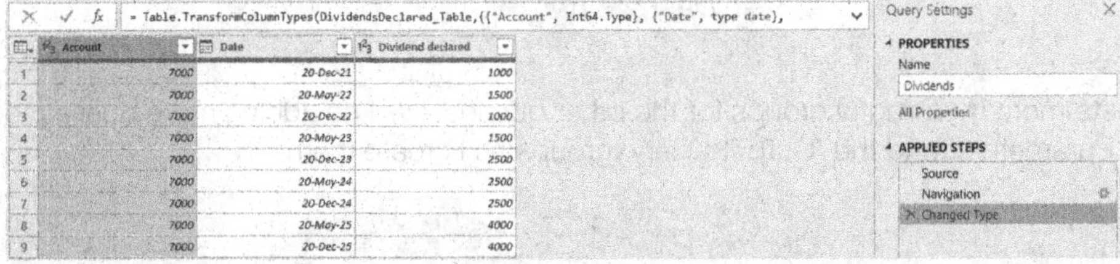

Just before I continue, check out the 'APPLIED STEPS'. Do you see how there is no mention of promoting the headers? As we have taken the Table – and not the sheet, the Power Query Editor gets clever. That's as long as you do it this way; you might want to compare and contrast this with the treatment for the 'Depreciation' table *(above)*.

The **Account** numbers must be in text form here too, so that they can be properly filtered by my **DAX** measures. Therefore, I will change the data type for the **Account** column to text.

I rename the table to **Dividends** and move it to the 'Output Query' group. Now the group exists I can do this by clicking on **Dividends** and dragging it to the position I want in the group. I want to load **Dividends** to the model, so I leave 'Enable Load' ticked.

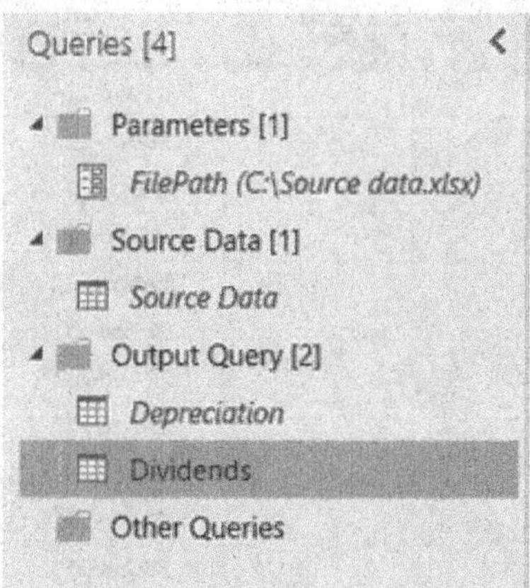

Equity

In this model, the equity issuances data is in a separate table. I create another Reference Query from **Source Data**, and click on the yellow **Table** text next to **EquityTable**.

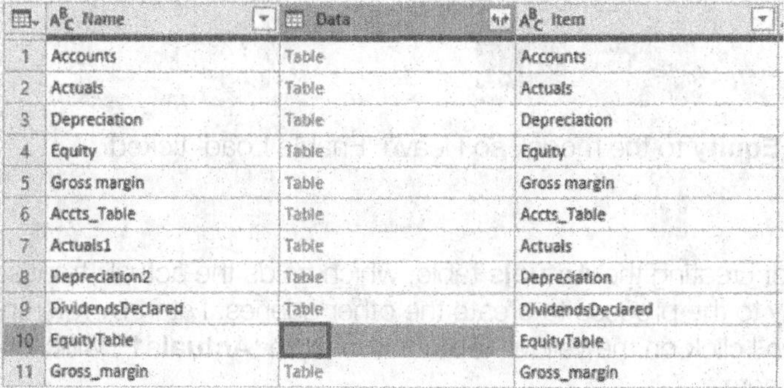

	Name	Data	Item
1	Accounts	Table	Accounts
2	Actuals	Table	Actuals
3	Depreciation	Table	Depreciation
4	Equity	Table	Equity
5	Gross margin	Table	Gross margin
6	Accts_Table	Table	Accts_Table
7	Actuals1	Table	Actuals
8	Depreciation2	Table	Depreciation
9	DividendsDeclared	Table	DividendsDeclared
10	EquityTable		EquityTable
11	Gross_margin	Table	Gross_margin

Power BI will then automatically navigate to the **EquityTable** table and extract the data. This will include changing the data types of the columns:

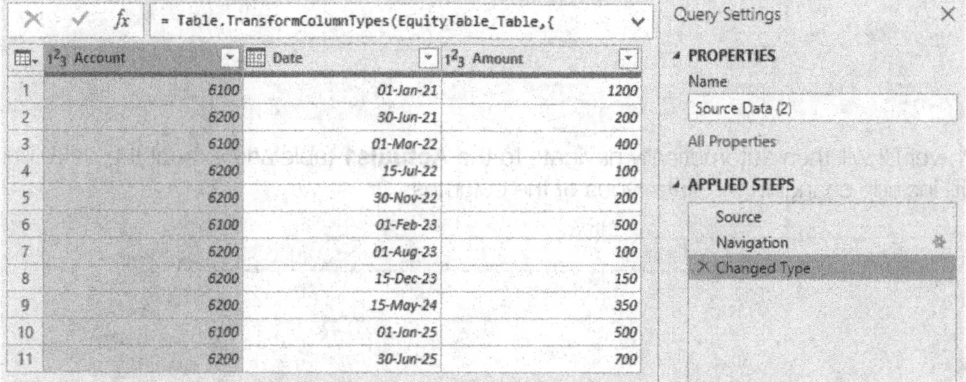

	Account	Date	Amount
1	6100	01-Jan-21	1200
2	6200	30-Jun-21	200
3	6100	01-Mar-22	400
4	6200	15-Jul-22	100
5	6200	30-Nov-22	200
6	6100	01-Feb-23	500
7	6200	01-Aug-23	100
8	6200	15-Dec-23	150
9	6200	15-May-24	350
10	6100	01-Jan-25	500
11	6200	30-Jun-25	700

As I did for **Dividends**, I change the data type for the **Account** column to text.

	Account	Date	Amount
1	6100	01-Jan-21	1200
2	6200	30-Jun-21	200
3	6100	01-Mar-22	400
4	6200	15-Jul-22	100
5	6200	30-Nov-22	200
6	6100	01-Feb-23	500
7	6200	01-Aug-23	100
8	6200	15-Dec-23	150
9	6200	15-May-24	350
10	6100	01-Jan-25	500
11	6200	30-Jun-25	700

All that is left now is to rename the table to **Equity** and move it to the Output Query group. In this case I have chosen to rename my query from the Queries pane by right-clicking on the **Equity** query:

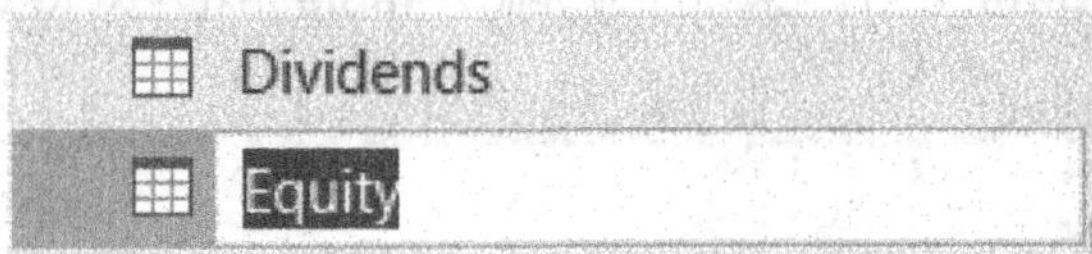

I want to load **Equity** to the model, so I leave 'Enable Load' ticked.

Actuals

The process for creating the **Actuals** table, which holds the actuals transactions, begins in a similar way to the process to create the other queries. I start by referencing **Source Data**, and then I click on the yellow **Table** text next to '**Actuals1**', which is the Table I wish to select here.

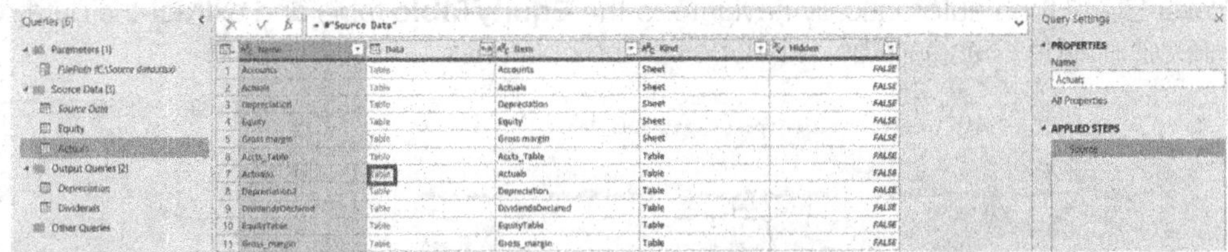

Power BI will then automatically navigate to the **Actuals1** table and extract the data. This will include changing the data types of the columns:

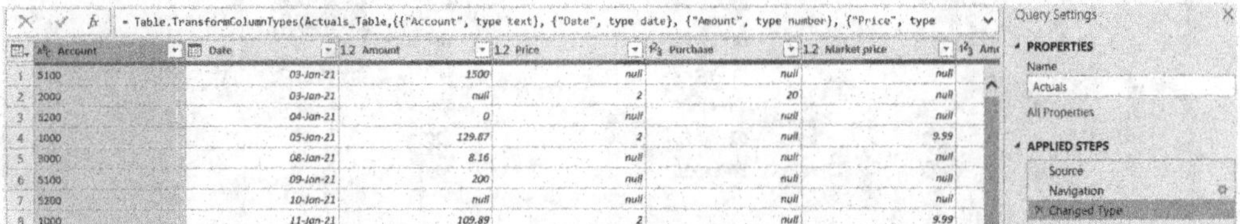

I need to check the data type of the columns. As for the other tables, I need to set the data type on **Account** to text. I also need to make sure that the other columns are correct for my data. For example, I know that some of my **Price** data includes decimal places, but since Power Query currently bases the data type defaults on only the first 100 rows, it has defaulted **Price** to a whole number.

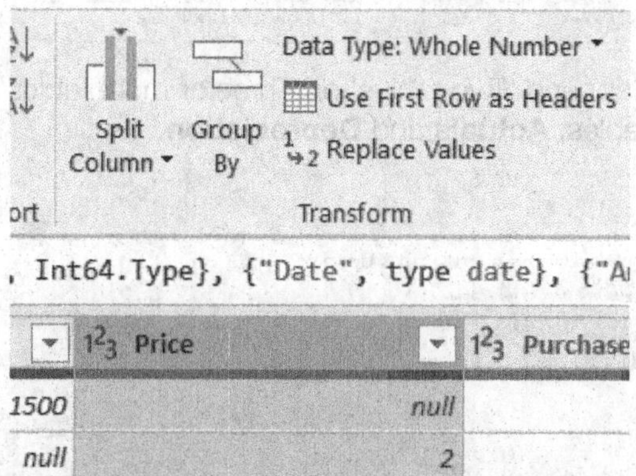

Whilst I should make any changes I can now, I can come back and do this later if I find one of the data types is wrong. It is important to remember that Power Query transforms my data without changing the original data in any way, so I can never lose any detail. Since I know that some values in **Price** contain decimal places, I click on the icon next to the column heading and change the data type of **Price** to a 'Decimal Number':

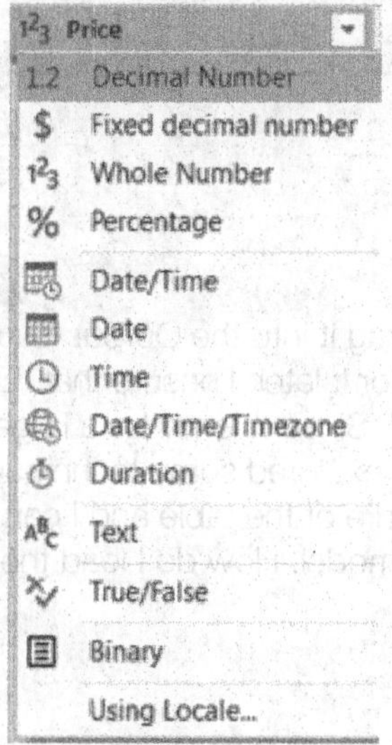

To create the complete table, I need to append my **Depreciation** query to this query, so that I have all the transaction dates in one table ready to create my **Date Table**.

Appending queries

In the Home tab, there is an option to 'Append Queries', *i.e.* position one or more queries beneath another. I can either 'Append Queries' or 'Append Queries as New'. 'Append Queries as New' will create a new query, referencing the queries being appended, whereas 'Append Queries' will append queries to my current query. I choose to 'Append Queries'. If you do accidentally create a new query (which would be given the name **Append1**), simply delete it and go back and use 'Append Queries' from **Actuals** instead.

I can either choose to append 'Two tables' or 'Three or more tables'. In this case, I just need to append two tables, **Actuals** and **Depreciation**.

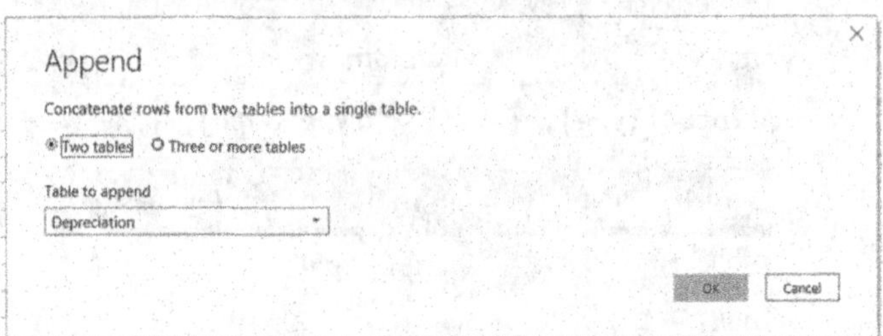

This will append the **Depreciation** data to the **Actuals** query. Not all columns from the **Actuals** table are present on the **Depreciation** table. This is not an issue as **Depreciation** does contain the columns we will need for calculations. Any columns that do not have values on **Depreciation** will be populated with *null* values. When viewed in the Power Query Editor, **Actuals** still looks the same, but has more rows.

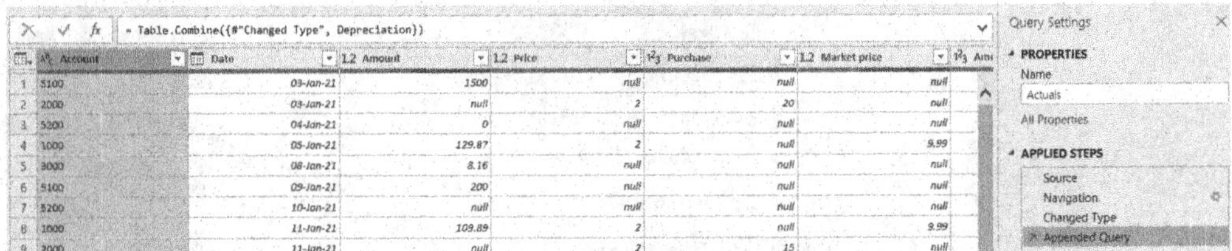

I name this table **Actuals** and drag it into the Output Query group. This query is not complete yet; I have more data for it later. I ensure that 'Enable Load' is allowed as this table will be loaded to my model. Since this will be a large table, this is one of the reasons I will revisit **Actuals** when I have explored some techniques to improve load efficiency. However, I have the basic structure of the table and I can load the data to Power BI Desktop and start to create my model. How do I load the data? Well, I'm glad you asked…

Close & Apply

Whenever I want to view my transformed data in Power BI, I can use the 'Close & Apply' dropdown from the Home tab.

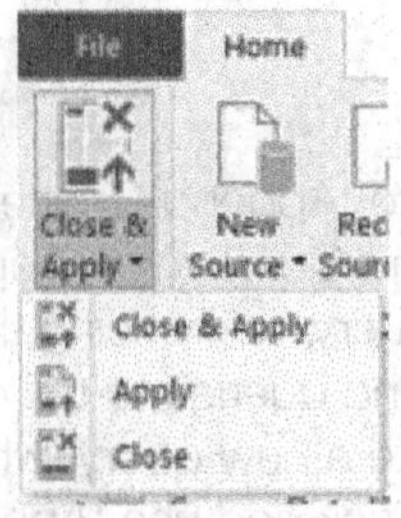

I can either choose to 'Apply' my changes without returning to the Power BI Desktop screen, 'Close' to go back to the Power BI screen without applying changes yet, or 'Close & Apply' to make my changes and go back to the Power BI screen. If I do not choose to apply changes, I have the option of discarding them. Once in the Power BI Desktop, I can choose whether to apply the changes or discard them from there.

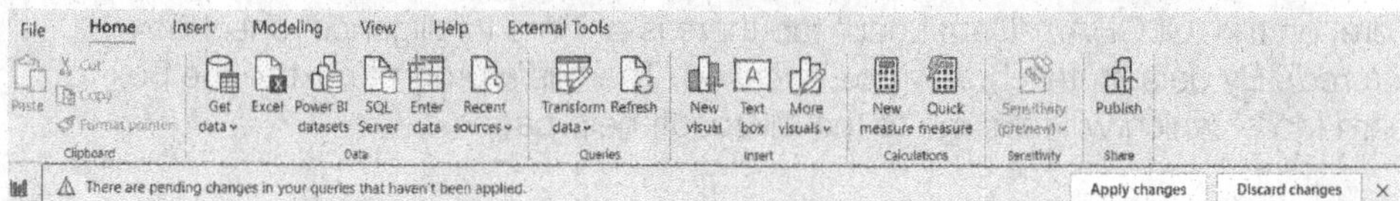

Having applied the changes, any queries with 'Enable Load' set will appear in the Fields pane.

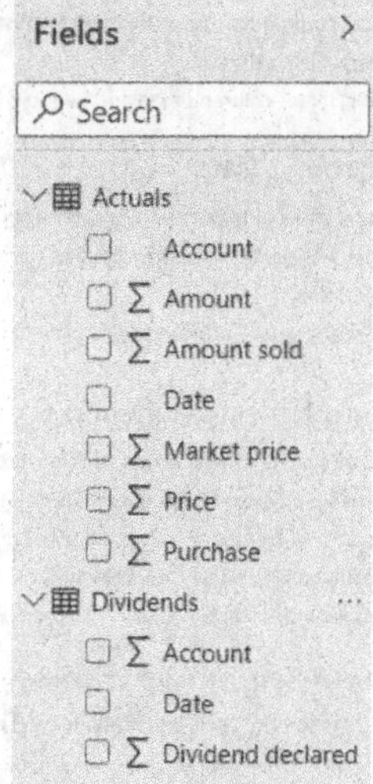

Now I have some data loaded, it is time to think about how I will need to construct my model. Talking of time…

Auto Date / Time

In order to construct the accounting model, I need time intelligence data. I need some way of linking the data so that I can perform calculations at a day level, and then summarise to months, quarters or years. To do this, I need a **Date Table**, often referred to as a *Calendar* table. Before I go on to describe how I will do this in Power Query, let me explain why I am creating the table in this way.

A **Date Table** or Calendar has exactly one row (record) per day for the time period that covers the dataset in the Power BI model. To be clear, the very earliest date and the latest date recorded in any table must be captured (and it can be necessary to go back at least one calendar year earlier and one later than this too, if undertaking comparative analyses such as year-on-year).

The table must contain a date column (noted as such), and may contain other columns according to the needs of the Data Model. This could include the year, month name, period *etc*. The **Date Table** allows a date hierarchy to be applied to any table in the model which includes a date.

Be careful here. There is some inbuilt functionality in Power BI Desktop which will create the date hierarchy for any table that includes a date. This means that I do not have to create my own **Date Table**. It is worth digressing and exploring what this functionality does, before turning it off, because it can cause issues.

From the File tab, I can access an 'Options' menu (through 'Options and settings'), where, on the 'GLOBAL' 'Data Load' tab there is a 'Time intelligence' checkbox *(pictured)*. By default, this box will be checked. There is a prompt next to the box to 'Learn More' which will take me to the Microsoft help pages.

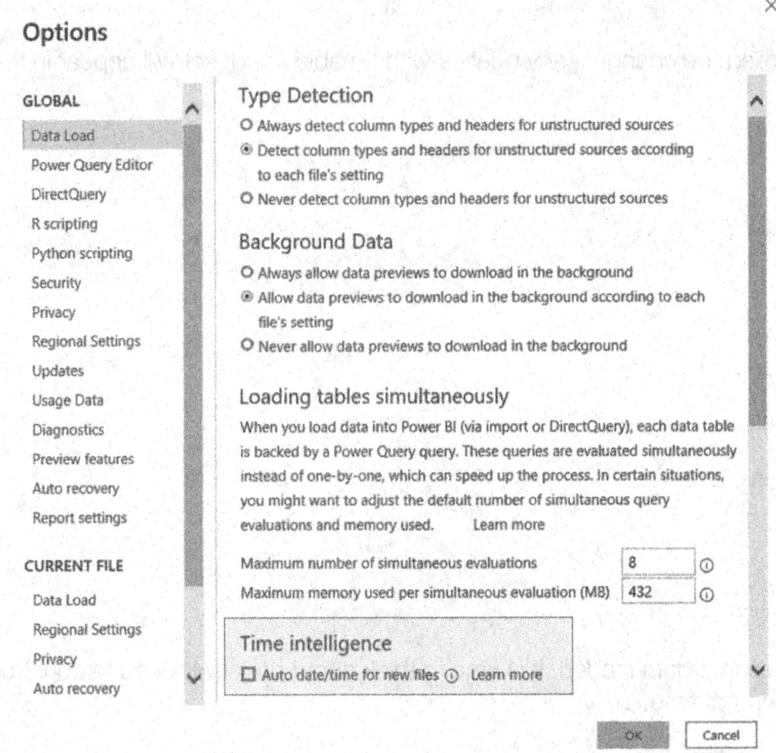

The important part to note from the help pages is this:

```
The Auto date/time is a data load option in Power BI Desktop. The purpose
of this option is to support convenient time intelligence reporting based
on date columns loaded into a model. Specifically, it allows report authors
using your Data Model to filter, group, and drill down by using calendar time
periods (years, quarters, months, and days). What's important is that you
don't need to explicitly develop these time intelligence capabilities.

When the option is enabled, Power BI Desktop creates a hidden auto date/time
table for each date column, providing all of the following conditions are
true:

•   The table storage mode is Import
•   The column data type is date or date/time
•   The column isn't the "many" side of a model relationship
```

For the model I am creating, every data table has at least one date associated with it. Therefore, using the automated feature would produce lots of hidden auto date / time tables. There is no way to selectively enable the creation of hidden date / time tables; it is an all or nothing scenario.

This is not the only reason for choosing to create my own **Date Table**. The hidden tables come with their own hierarchy for year, quarter, month and day. This is useful, but it is fixed (*i.e.* limited). If I am creating slicers based upon this hierarchy, I can choose a day, but not a weekday or even a week. Further, the year and quarters assume that the year begins on January 1st and finishes on December 31st. This cannot be customised. To have full control over the way the date hierarchy works, I need my own **Date Table** – which means I do not want to use the automated functionality.

I could just ignore the hidden data and use my own **Date Table**, but the automated process will continue to create multiple tables and hierarchies, which is a drain on memory usage. This is a key factor in determining how responsive my final Power BI model will be. There is another issue with memory use too, but I have forgotten what that was…

I need to turn 'Time intelligence' off on the 'Data Load' tab for my 'CURRENT FILE'. I also turn it off for the 'GLOBAL' settings, which will affect any new reports. When changing 'Time intelligence' for the 'CURRENT FILE' for other existing reports, I should take care in case I have created any visuals which rely on hidden date / time tables. These would need to be fixed using a manually created **Date Table**. I will discuss the best way to create a **Date Table** next.

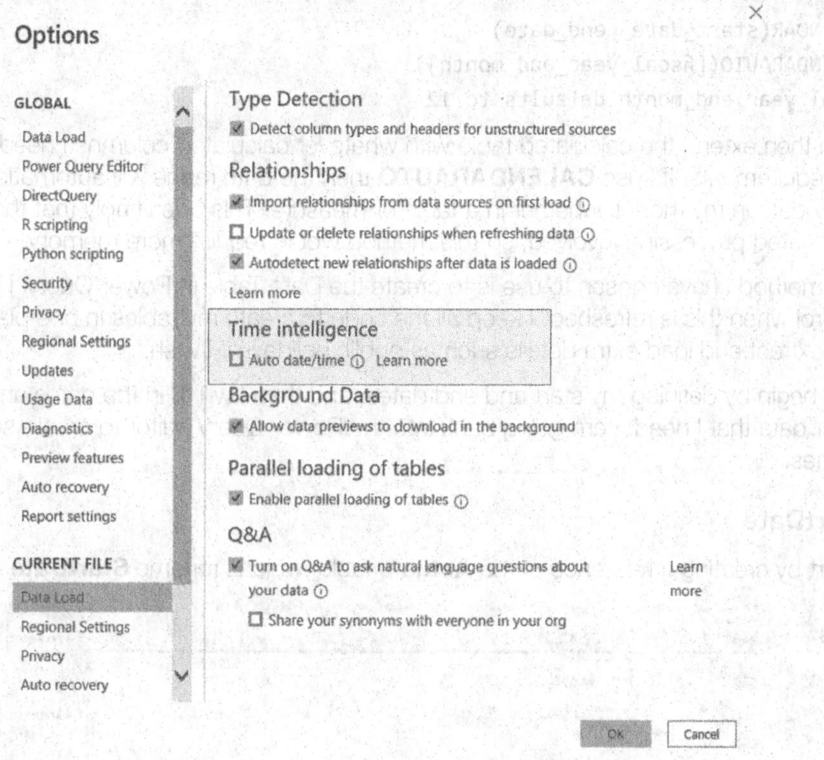

Date Table

I have explained that to enable time intelligence functions in Power BI Desktop, I need a Date Table. There are some qualities that are essential in a Date Table:

- the earliest date in the table must be before or equal to the earliest date in any other table in the associated model
- the final date in the table must be on or after the latest date in any other table in the associated model (and in this case a year after, to ensure the calculations work correctly)
- dates must be in ascending order, increasing in increments of one day, with no duplication
- there must be no gaps (omissions) in the dates (*e.g.* public holidays and / or weekends must all be included). This is also known as congruous or contiguous data.

There are several ways I can create a Date Table. I can import a whole Date Table from an external source using the Power Query engine to extract the data. If I am working with a source which already includes a Date Table (alternatively known as a **Calendar**), then the best method is to extract that table using Power Query. That way I know that my Date Table is up to date and suitable for linking to the rest of the model.

If I do not have a Date Table in my source, I could use **DAX**. I can generate a Date Table using either the **CALENDAR** or the **CALENDARAUTO** functions. Each function returns a single-column table of dates.

```
CALENDAR(start_date, end_date)
CALENDARAUTO([fiscal_year_end_month])
fiscal_year_end_month defaults to 12
```

I can then extend the calculated table with whatever calculated columns I need to suit my requirements. If I use **CALENDARAUTO** then the date range will automatically cover every date in my model, whether in a table or measure. This does imply that there is automated processing involved, so this method would require more memory.

The method I have chosen to use is to create the Date Table in Power Query. I can control when this is refreshed, I keep all the code to create my tables in one place and I can extract and load extra details such as public holidays if I wish.

I will begin by defining my start and end dates, and then I will fill in the dates and add any other data that I need. I am going back into the Power Query editor to create some more queries.

StartDate

I start by creating a reference of the **Actuals** table, which I rename **StartDate.**

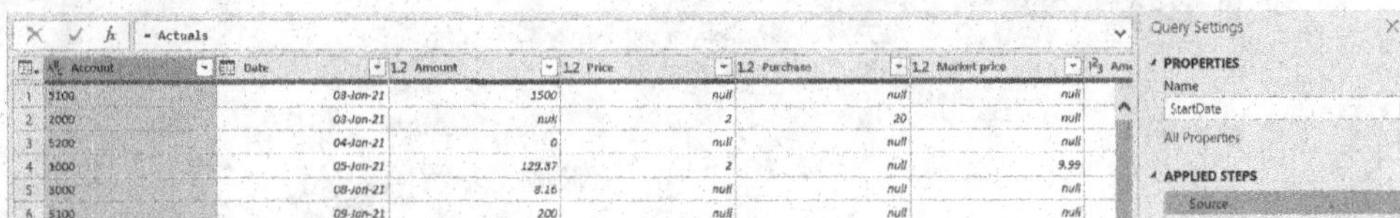

I only need to keep the **Date** column, so I select this and choose to 'Remove Other Columns'.

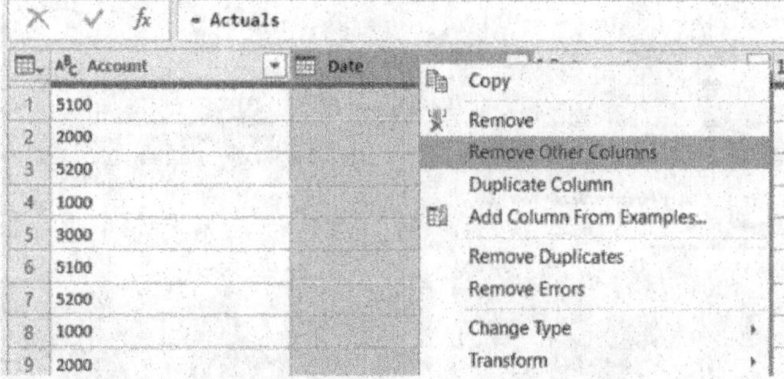

I sort the **Date** column using 'Sort Ascending'.

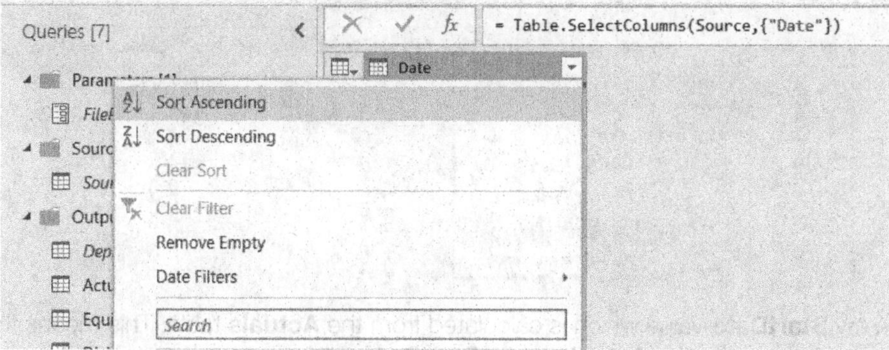

As this is the **StartDate** that I am setting up, I only want the first entry, so I keep the first row. I can access this functionality on the Home tab under the 'Keep Rows' icon.

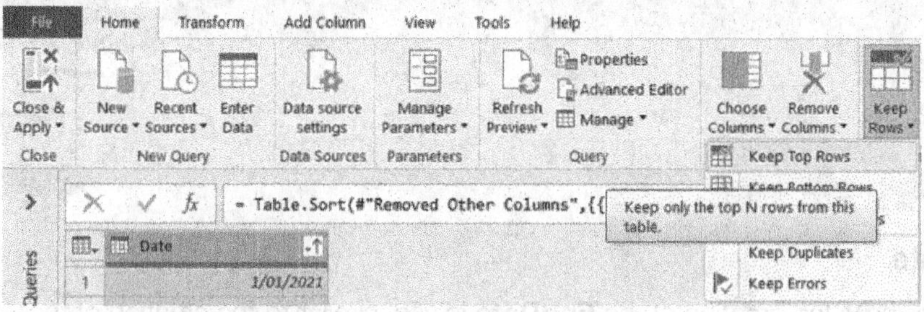

In the dialog, I choose to keep the top row.

Keep Top Rows

Specify how many rows to keep.

Number of rows

1.2 | 1

OK | Cancel

I change the data type from a date to a whole number: when I come to create the **Calendar** table later, I will be using list functionality which works with numbers, but not dates.

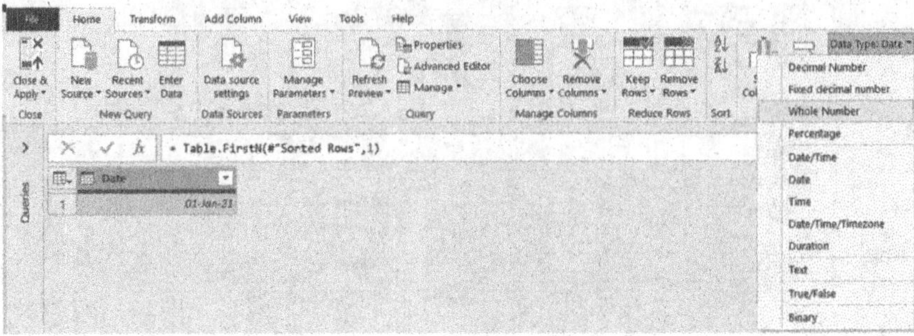

Finally, I need to drill down into my value, so that this query will return a single value.

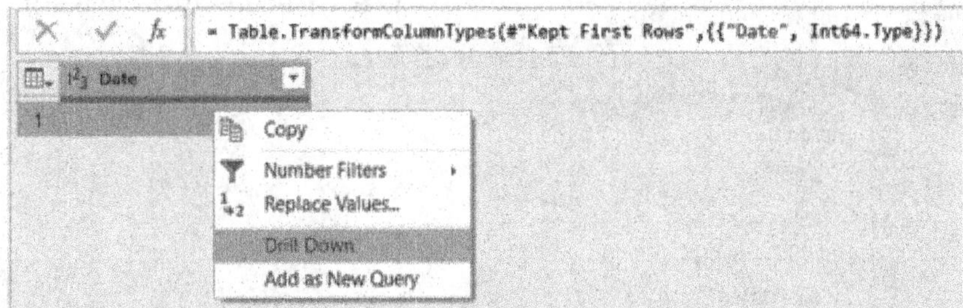

I have my **StartDate** value which is calculated from the **Actuals** table. This means that if older data is added to the **Actuals** table, **StartDate** will be updated accordingly.

EndDate

Unsurprisingly, the creation of the **EndDate** is very similar to the creation of the **StartDate**. As previously, I create a Reference Query from **Actuals,** remove all the columns apart from **Date**, and then I sort the rows, but this time I 'Sort Descending'. I rename this query EndDate.

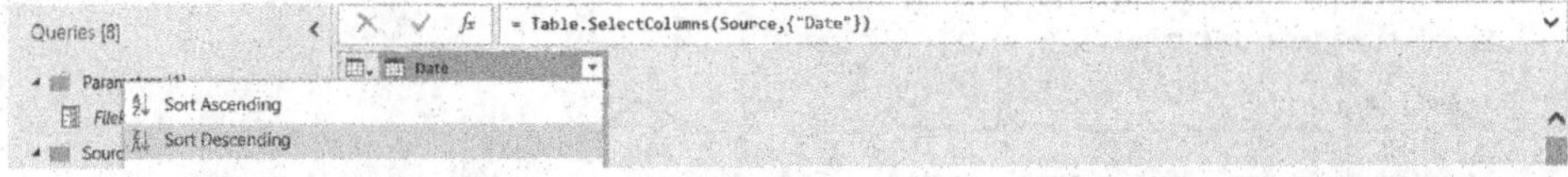

As before, I keep the first row. This time, however, I want to allow for a Power BI Desktop feature. Power BI does not calculate numbers properly if the Date Table ends on the last date of the dataset, so I add a year to the date using a 'Custom Column' from the 'Add Column' tab.

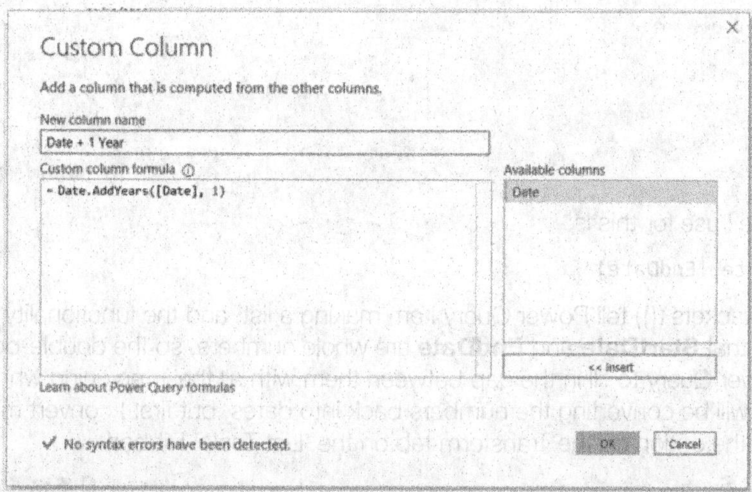

I create a new column **Date + 1 Year** which is a year on from **Date**. The **M** code used is:

```
= Date.AddYears([Date], 1)
```

I can then remove my original **Date** column.

I then change the data type to whole number and drill down as I did for **StartDate**, until I am left with a single value **EndDate** which will change if newer data is added to the **Actuals** table.

Calendar

To create our Date Table (which I am going to call '**Calendar**' in due course), I start with a Blank Query as I did for the **Source Data** query, by using the dropdown from 'New Source' on the Home tab. Then, I create my table by creating a list of all numbers between **StartDate** and **EndDate** entered in the Formula Bar.

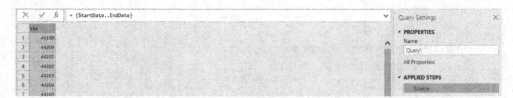

The **M** code I use for this is:

```
= {StartDate..EndDate}
```

The curly brackets ({}) tell Power Query I am making a list, and the functionality recognises that **StartDate** and **EndDate** are whole numbers, so the double-dot ellipsis (..) tells Power Query to fill in the gap between them with all the intervening whole numbers. I will be converting the numbers back into dates, but first I convert my list into a table using the option on the Transform tab on the 'List Tools' Ribbon.

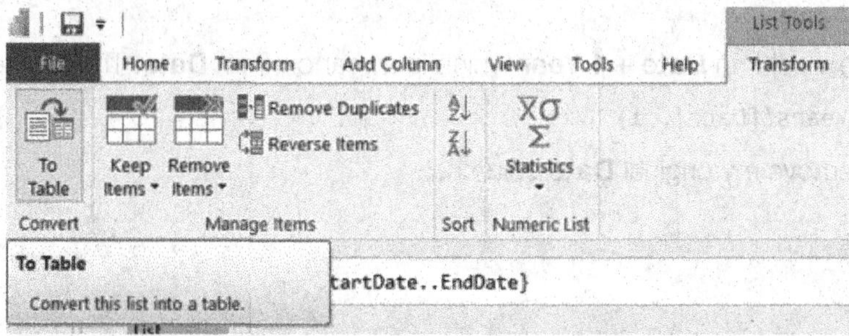

The dialog that appears includes options that are useful for more complicated lists: I can accept the defaults and click OK:

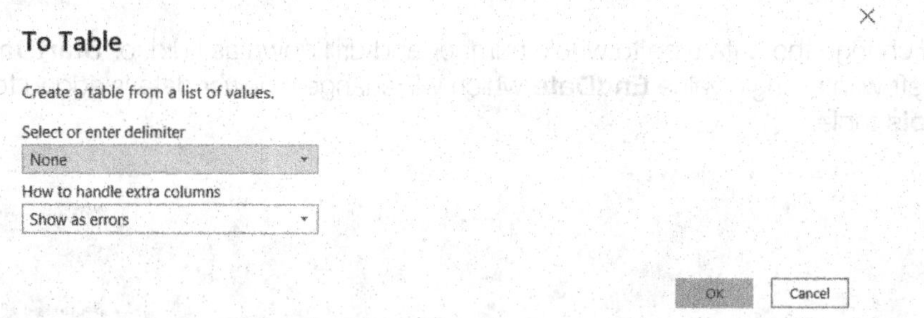

I set the data type of my column to 'Date' and rename it **Date**. I rename the query to Calendar.

I am now ready to add more columns to **Calendar.** To do this, I can use the date functions available on the 'Add Column' tab. I will start by adding the 'Year' to get a **Year** column.

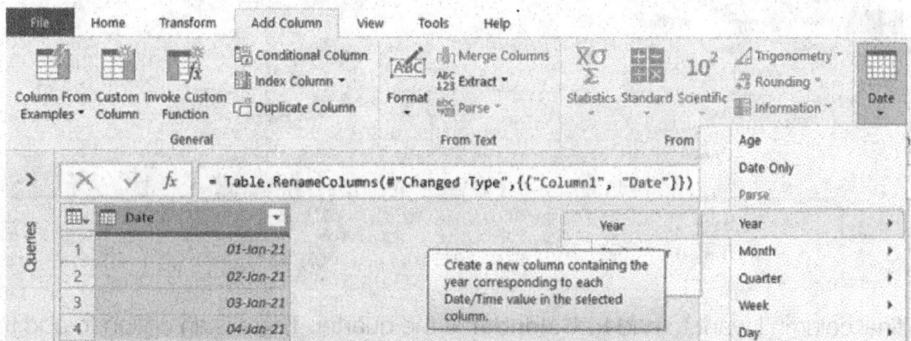

I repeat this process, selecting **Date** each time, to add **Month, Month Name** and **Day**.

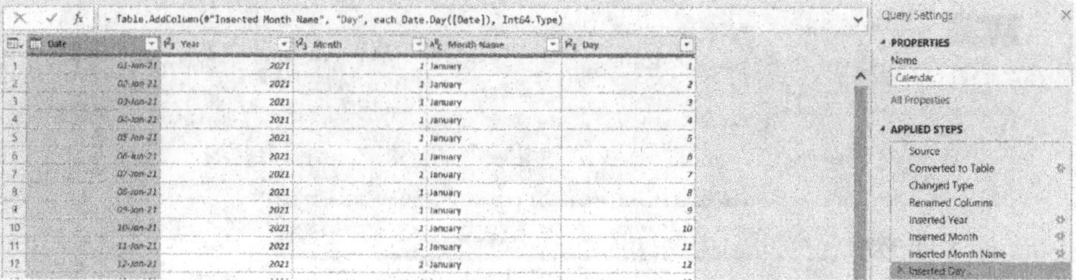

The **Month Name** is the full name of the month. I would like to just use the first three letters of each month instead. There are several ways I can do this. I choose to extract the part of the **Month Name** that I need. To do this, I select **Month Name** and choose to Extract 'First Characters' from the 'Text Column' section of the Transform tab.

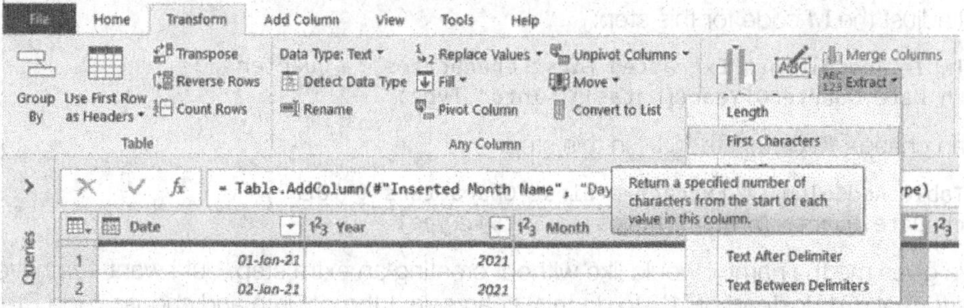

I choose the first three characters.

Extract First Characters

Enter how many starting characters to keep.

Count

3

OK Cancel

This reduces **Month Name** to three [3] characters:

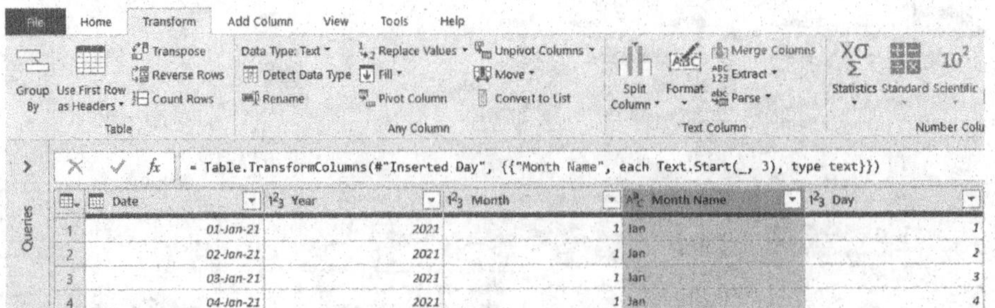

The final column I want to add to **Calendar** is the quarter. There is an option to add the quarter from the 'Date' functions on the 'Add Column' tab, but I want to modify it. I select **Date** and add a **Quarter** column from the 'Add Column' tab.

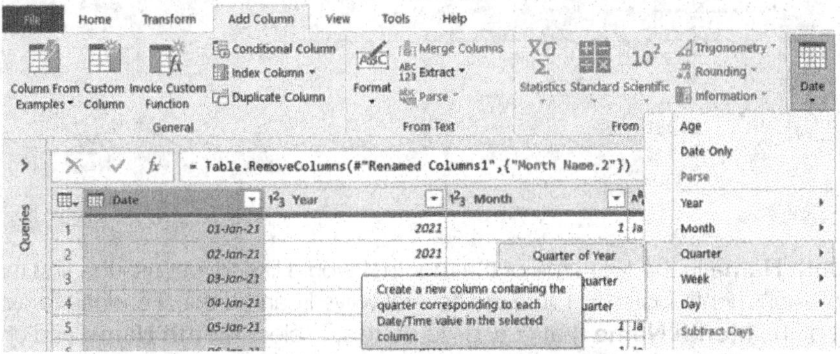

I want to change the name of this column to 'Qtr'. To show another way of doing this, I will adjust the **M** code for this step:

```
= Table.AddColumn(#"Extracted First Characters", "Quarter",
each Date.QuarterOfYear([Dates]), Int64.Type)
```

I can change "Quarter" to "Qtr" in this step:

```
= Table.AddColumn(#"Extracted First Characters", "Qtr",
each Date.QuarterOfYear([Dates]), Int64.Type)
```

This gives me the name I would like without creating an extra step, but I want it to have the format 'Q1' instead of '1'. To do this, I can select the column and choose 'Add Prefix' from the Format dropdown in the 'Text Column' section of the Transform tab.

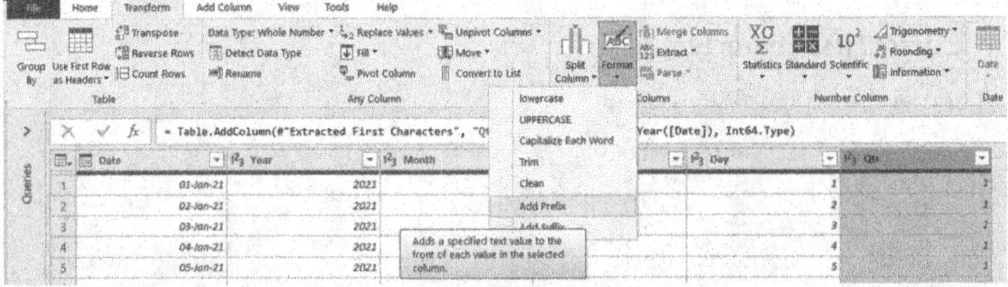

Note that even though the column is currently a whole number, Power Query will still allow me to use an option from the 'Text Column' section and will automatically change the data type of the column. I enter the prefix in the dialog.

Prefix

Enter a text value to add to the front of each value in the column.

Value

Q

OK Cancel

This creates a single step 'Added Prefix' which changes Quarter into a text column with the prefix I have specified.

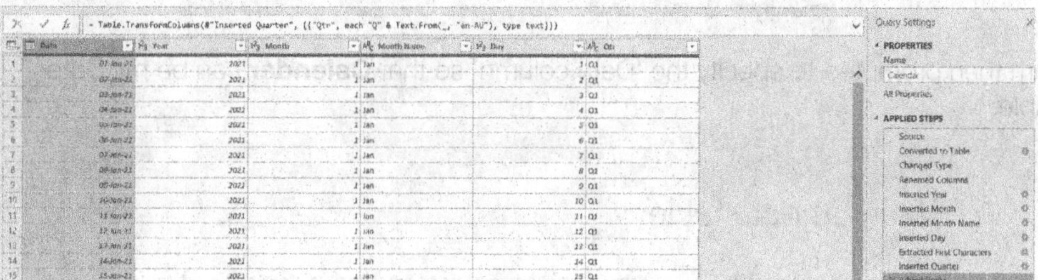

Now I have completed the **Calendar** table, I leave the 'Enable Load' checked, as I will be needing it in my model. I uncheck 'Enable Load' on **StartDate** and **EndDate**, as I do not need them in the model. I drag all three queries to the Output Query folder to keep everything neat.

I must set **Calendar** as my Date Table in Power BI Desktop, so that it knows it is a special type of table (*i.e.* a date table). I 'Close & Apply' my query changes so far and go to the 'Data' tab on the Power BI Desktop.

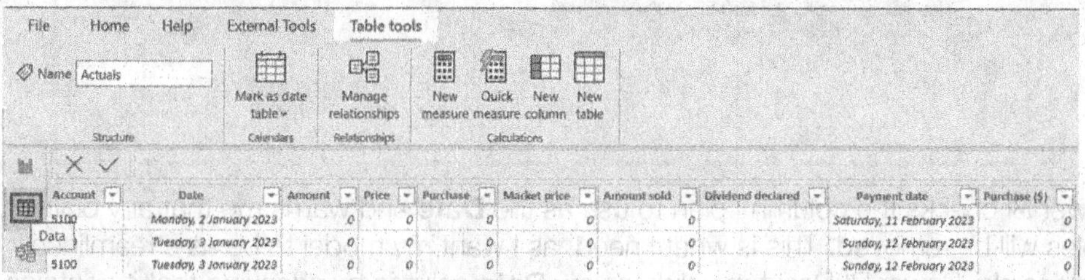

I select the **Calendar** table in the Fields pane. You may need to sort **Calendar** in ascending order of date using the arrow next to the column heading.

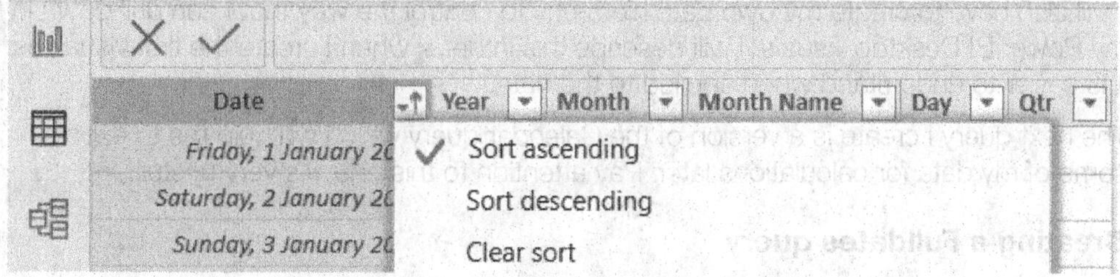

The option to 'Mark as date table' is in the 'Table Tools' tab.

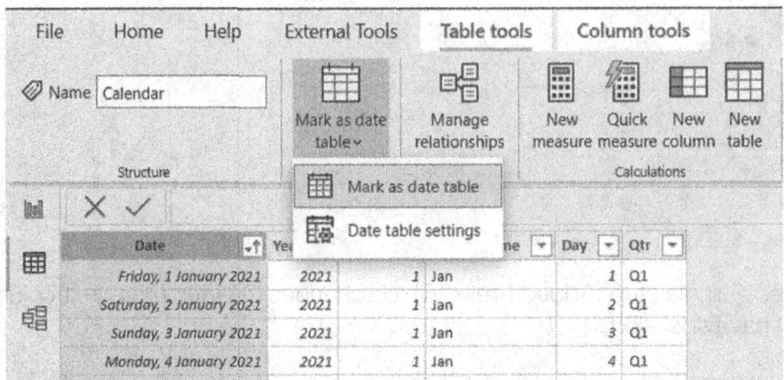

I am then prompted to specify the 'Date column' so that **Calendar** can be my Date Table.

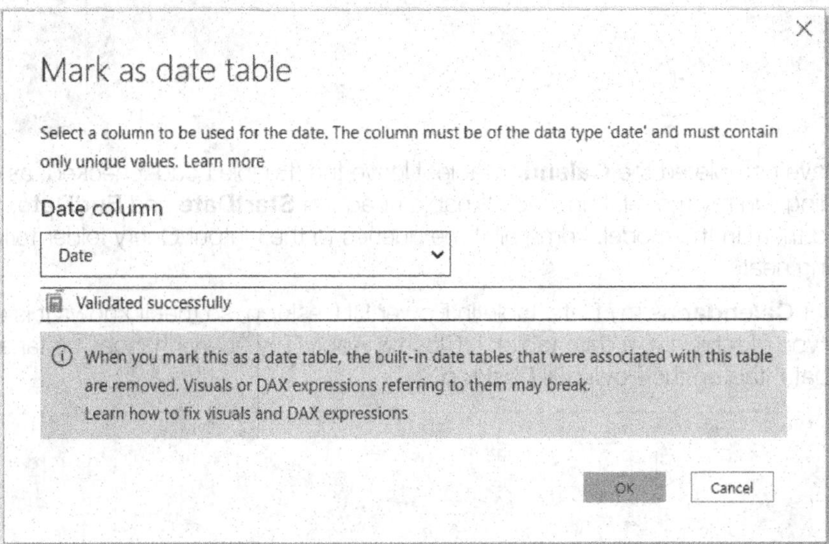

Power BI checks the column I plan to use as the **Date** and warns me that any built-in tables will be removed. This is what I need, as I want my model to be as streamlined as possible. Power BI Desktop validates my **Date** column by checking that it contains unique, contiguous (no gaps) date values, with no *null* values and the correct Date / Time data type.

I will also have to create my own date hierarchy to control the way that I can drill down in my Power BI Desktop visuals. I will describe this in detail when I create the first visual, as it is easier to understand when applied to the data.

The next query I create is a version of the Calendar query which will help me to expand some of my data for calculations later. Pay attention to this one; it's very useful!

Creating a Fulldates query

To create this query, I return to the Power Query editor where I will first create a second calendar table, but this calendar table will just contain the dates and no other columns. I can duplicate the calendar table.

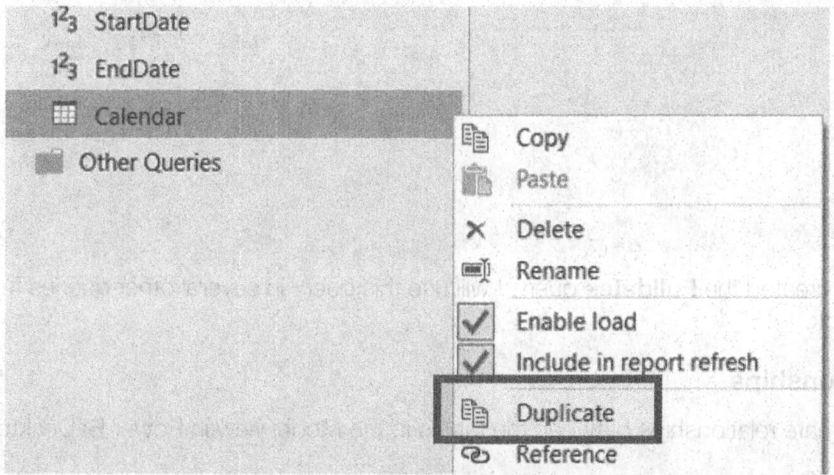

From here, I can navigate to the step right before I create columns in the **Calendar** table. In this example, this would be the 'Renamed Columns' step. I select the step below it, 'Inserted Year', right-click that step and select the 'Delete Until End' option:

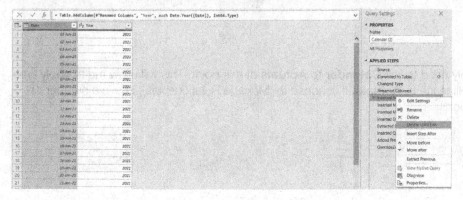

I can ignore the warning that appears and continue with the 'Delete' action:

Delete Step

Are you sure you want to delete until the end? This will delete the current step and subsequent steps from your query.

I am left with a query that contains the dates from the beginning to the end of the model. I shall rename this query to **Fulldates**. I have also disabled load since it does not need to be loaded to the report.

Having created the **Fulldates** query, I will use this query in several other queries further in this book.

Relationships

I can create relationships between the tables in the Model view in Power BI Desktop.

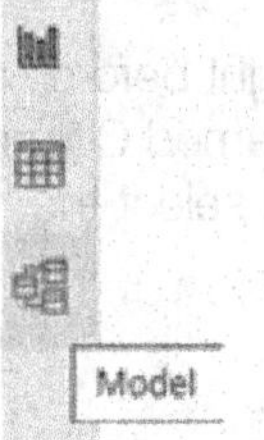

I only need to link **Calendar** to **Actuals** at this point. This will allow me to apply time intelligence to **Actuals.** If I choose to 'Manage Relationships', I have a number of options:

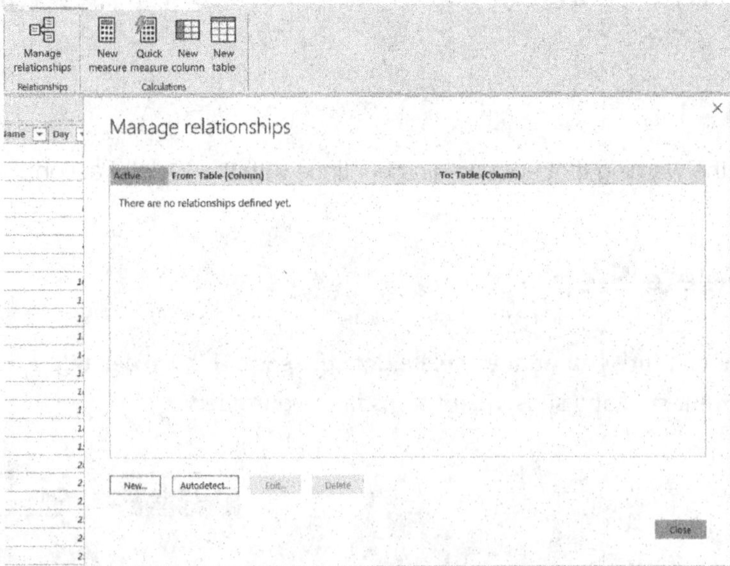

I can create a 'New' relationship, or 'Autodetect' relationships, where Power BI will look for suitable connections. I choose to create a 'New' relationship.

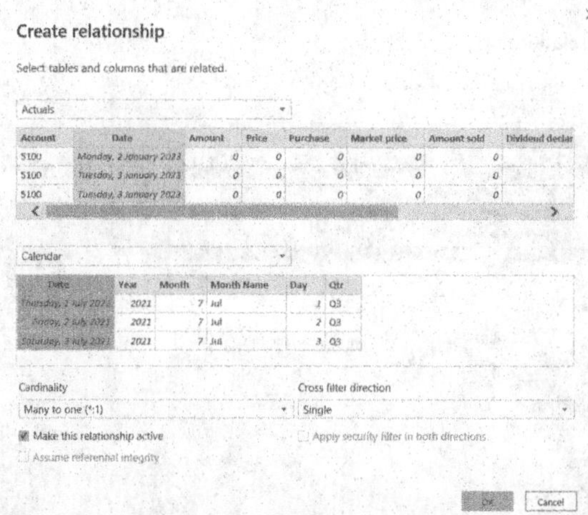

I choose to create a relationship between **Actuals** and **Calendar**, based upon **Date**. Power BI Desktop defaults the 'Cardinality' and 'Cross filter direction' and sets the 'Make this relationship active' to checked. I can create more than one relationship for two tables, but only one may be active.

Cross filter direction

There are only two values for 'Cross filter direction':

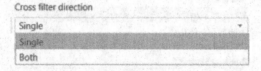

This value controls whether filtering data on one table will apply the filter to the other table. I would never want to filter the **Calendar** table based upon a filter on **Actuals**, so for me 'Single' is the right choice.

Once I have created my relationship, I can view it on the diagram, *viz*.

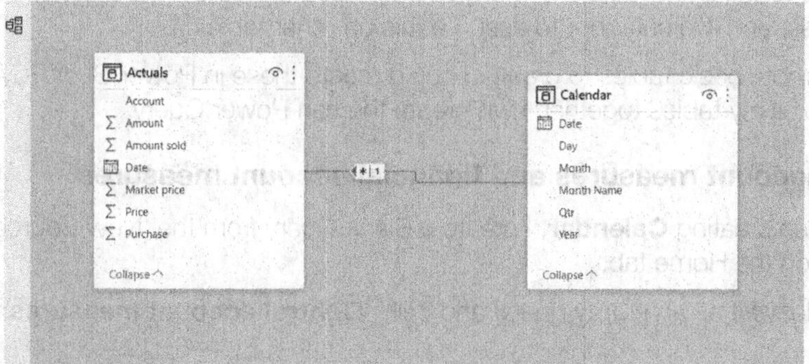

I can either double-click on the relationship icon, or right-click and choose 'Details' to view and change the details using the 'Edit Relationship' pane.

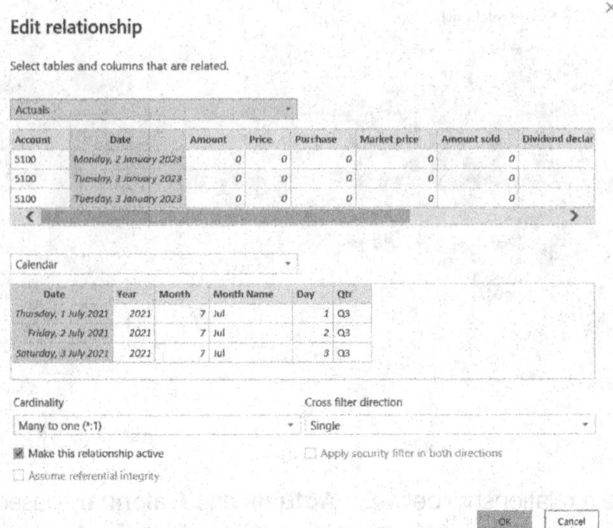

Cardinality

There is a dropdown list under 'Cardinality'.

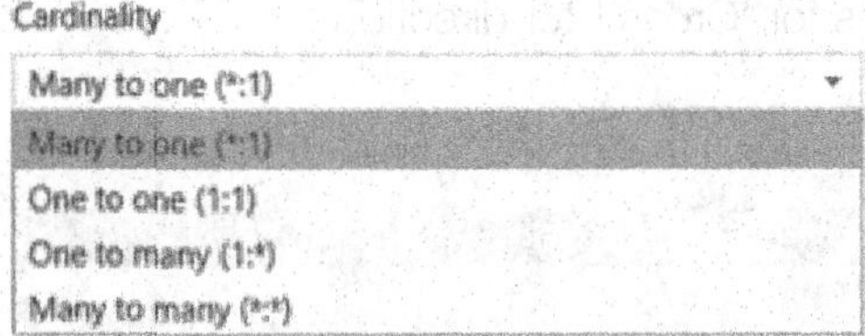

The default for **Actuals** to **Calendar** is 'Many to one'. This means that there could be more than one row with the same date in **Actuals**, but a unique value in **Calendar**.

'One to one' would mean both tables had unique values, and 'One to many' would imply that **Actuals** had unique values and **Calendar** had duplicate values. Links from other tables to the Date Table are 'Many to one' because I know the Date Table contains unique dates, and it is safer not to assume this on other tables.

I have two more basic tables to create. I could create these in Power BI or Power Query, but to keep all my tables together, I will create them in Power Query.

Control account measures and financial account measures

As I did when creating **Calendar**, I create a Blank Query from the 'New Source' dropdown on the Home tab.

This time I leave it as an empty query, and call it **Control account measures**.

I create a duplicate or copy of **Control account measures** and create another Blank Query called **Financial account measures.** Both queries will be left as 'Enable Load' as I will be using these queries to organise the **DAX** measures that I create. I will keep them in the Output Query folder.

ABC Control account measures

ABC Financial account measures

The icon next to them indicates that they contain a single text value rather than a table. This means that they will have very little impact upon the time and resources used to load the data to the model. However, now that the model is expanding, it is time to consider how to ensure that loading data to it is as efficient as it can be.

Memory usage

The greatest enemy of an efficient Data Model is the inefficient use of memory. Throughout this model I will be making use of two concepts in Power Query:

1. **Buffering:** storing data in memory where it is isolated from changes
2. **Table.View:** this emulates a feature used in something known as "query folding", which is the ability for a routine to generate a single query statement to retrieve and transform source data. This technique is used to reduce the number of times a query is read when loading to the Power BI Desktop Data Model.

Remember how I left **Actuals** waiting for the rest of the data it needed? I will be using both methods to streamline the way **Actuals** is loaded, which means I can use it as an example for both functions.

It is difficult to predict how much memory usage will be saved using these techniques. The effects of buffering will vary according to the amount of memory available, which in turn depends upon the environment that Power BI Desktop is running in. Buffering steps and **Table.View** steps do not affect calculations. Buffering is added before running a step that would otherwise re-read data already in memory. **Table.View** must be the last step in the query, so I will cover this when I have completed the **Actuals** query.

First, I will explore the function I am going to use for buffering, **Table.Buffer**…

Table.Buffer

```
Table.Buffer(table as table) as table
```

This function buffers a **table** into memory (*i.e.* it "pre-loads" it), isolating it from external changes during evaluation. In essence, this basically pulls a copy of the table into memory (random access memory, RAM) so that it can be referenced instead of the actual table.

Buffering can be useful, but it is important to check that it is actually helping. There are some known disadvantages to it: if I am working with a relational database, I can't use query folding and table buffering at the same time. In this model, I am dealing with flat files (*i.e.* they have no internal hierarchy), so this is not a problem.

Table.Buffer() should be used with caution with very large datasets. The buffering uses RAM, and the amount of RAM that is held by Power Query is limited, which means that if the limits are exceeded, the RAM must come from the hard drive. This would *seriously* slow things down. This does not apply to my model, so I can go ahead and use **Table.Buffer**. If you think that the buffering steps are not helping, then they can be omitted without losing any model functionality.

Table.Buffer() is a function which is applied to a step in my query: in this case **Actuals**. Whilst I can add steps from the Formula Bar (as I did for **Source Data** and **Calendar**), because **Table.Buffer()** is linked to other steps, the easiest place to apply it, is in the Advanced Editor. The Advanced Editor can be accessed from the Home tab:

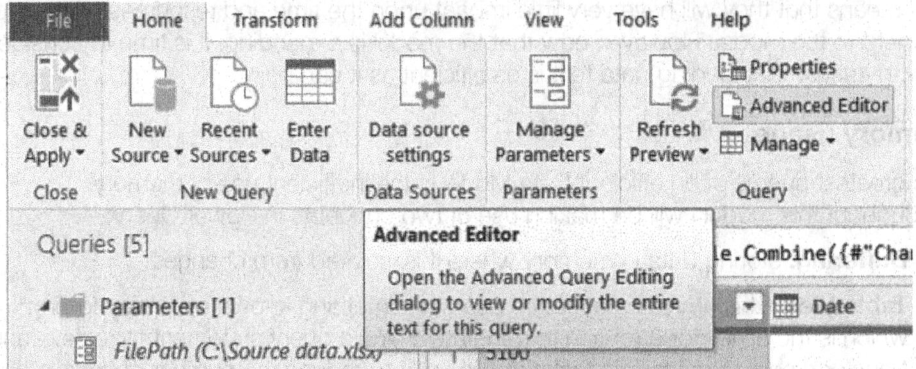

By allowing me to view the entire text for this query, the Advanced Editor shows me how the **M** code for my query is constructed.

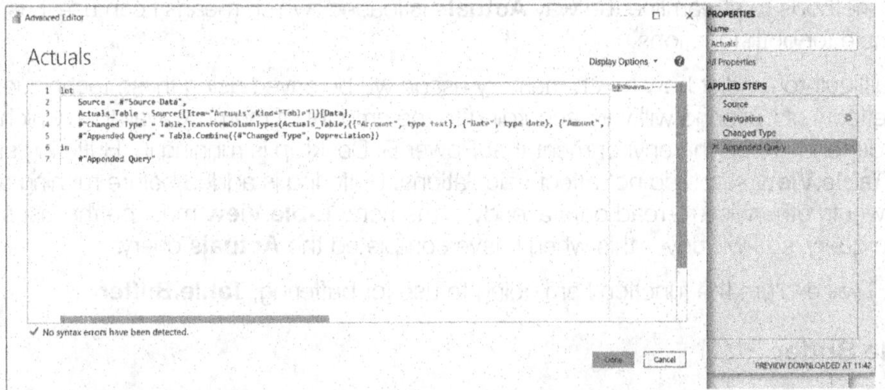

In the previous visual, I have lined up the Advanced Editor to show that all the steps in the 'APPLIED STEPS' section appear between a 'let' and an 'in' statement. The hash (**#**) sign before a name in speech marks (**""**) tells Power Query to ignore the space in the name. This is why I have '**Source =**' on the first step and '**#"Appended Query" =**' on the last step. The code finishes with the name of the last step. Technically, each step is a table: it represents the format of the table or query at that point in the transformation. The **M** code from the Advanced Editor is reproduced below:

```
let
 Source = #"Source Data",
 Actuals_Table = Source{[Item="Actuals",Kind="Table"]}[Data],
```

```
 #"Changed Type" = Table.TransformColumnTypes(Actuals_Table,{{"Account", type text}, {"Date", type date}, {"Amount", type number}, {"Price", type number}, {"Purchase", Int64.Type}, {"Market price", type number}, {"Amount sold", Int64.Type}}),
 #"Appended Query" = Table.Combine({#"Changed Type", Depreciation})
in
 #"Appended Query"
```

I am going to add a new line before the 'Appended Query' step:

```
BufferedTable = Table.Buffer(Depreciation),
```

Note the comma at the end (it means another line of code will follow). 'BufferedTable' is the name I am giving to the step. The rest is telling Power Query to buffer the **Depreciation** table.

I also need to change the 'Appended Query' step:

```
 #"Appended Query" = Table.Combine({#"Removed Other Columns1", BufferedTable}),
```

When I append the queries, I want to use the buffered table read in isolation, instead of reading **Depreciation** while combining the tables.

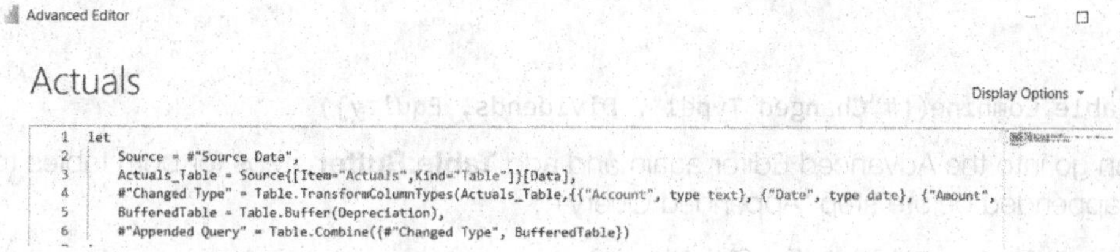

Advanced Editor

Actuals

Display Options

```
let
    Source = #"Source Data",
    Actuals_Table = Source{[Item="Actuals",Kind="Table"]}[Data],
    #"Changed Type" = Table.TransformColumnTypes(Actuals_Table,{{"Account", type text}, {"Date", type date}, {"Amount",
    BufferedTable = Table.Buffer(Depreciation),
    #"Appended Query" = Table.Combine({#"Changed Type", BufferedTable})
```

```
let
 Source = #"Source Data",
 Actuals_Table = Source{[Item="Actuals",Kind="Table"]}[Data],
 #"Changed Type" = Table.TransformColumnTypes(Actuals_Table,{{"Account", type text}, {"Date", type date}, {"Amount", type number}, {"Price", type number}, {"Purchase", Int64.Type}, {"Market price", type number}, {"Amount sold", Int64.Type}}),
 BufferedTable = Table.Buffer(Depreciation),
 #"Appended Query" = Table.Combine({#"Changed Type", BufferedTable})
```

The merge should now be much quicker. Now I can add the rest of the data to the **Actuals** query, and again I will be adding a **Table.Buffer** step to help.

I need to append the data from **Dividends** and **Equity.** Before I append the data, I need to check the data type on my existing table, to avoid encountering problems with the data types on the appended data. I need to make sure all my data types are correct – **Account** should be set to text, **Purchase, Price** and **Market price** should be decimal numbers. If I need to change the data type on any of these columns, then a step 'Changed Type1' will be generated.

I am using 'Append Queries' from the Home tab again (not 'Append Queries as New'), and this time I can choose to append more than two queries.

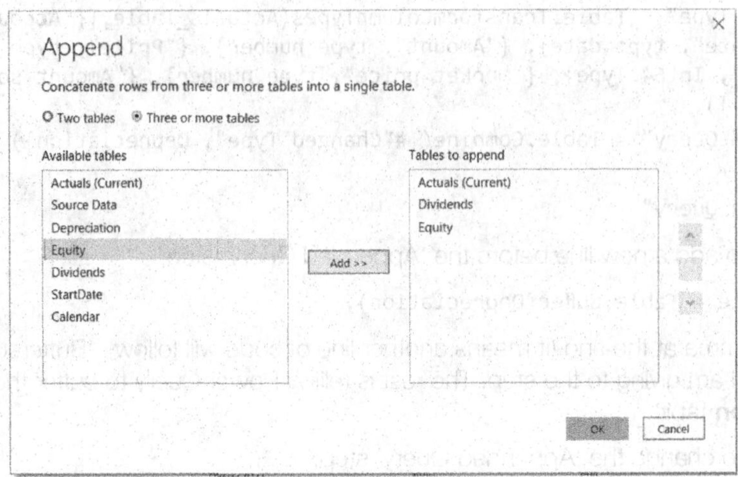

Now I have the **M** code for this append query:

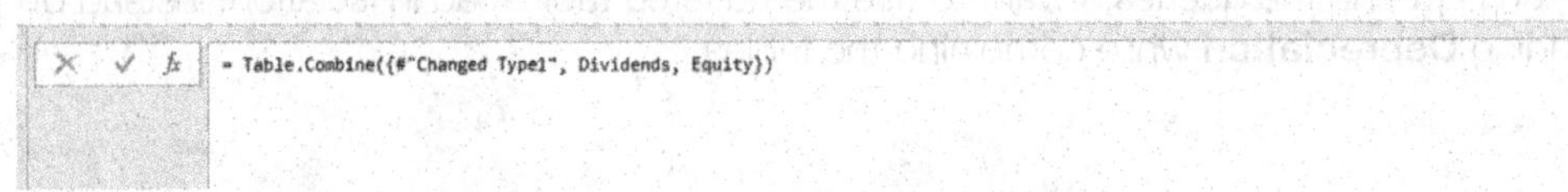


```
= Table.Combine({#"Changed Type1", Dividends, Equity})
```

I can go into the Advanced Editor again and add **Table.Buffer** steps for both tables to be appended before step 'Appended Query1':

```
Table.Buffer1 = Table.Buffer(Dividends),
Table.Buffer2 = Table.Buffer(Equity),
```

I can then change the 'Appended Query1' step to:

```
= Table.Combine({#"Changed Type1", Table.Buffer1, Table.Buffer2})
```

My **M** code for the query now looks like this (including the 'Changed Type1' step referred to previously):

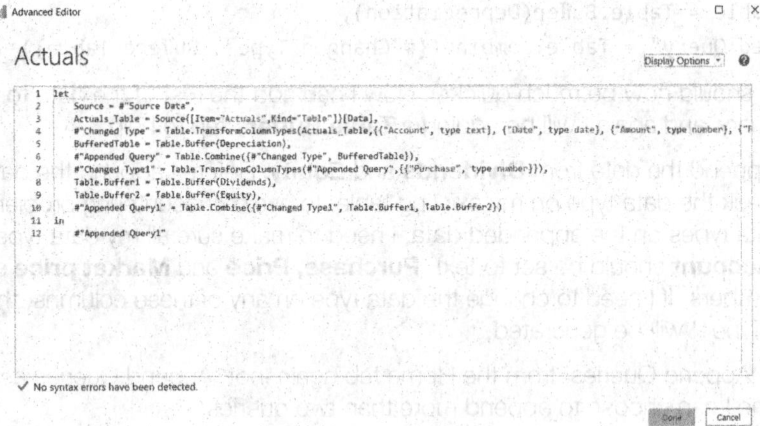

```
let
 Source = #"Source Data",
 Actuals_Table = Source{[Item="Actuals",Kind="Table"]}[Data],
 #"Changed Type" = Table.TransformColumnTypes(Actuals_Table,{{"Account", type
text}, {"Date", type date}, {"Amount", type number}, {"Price", type number},
{"Purchase", Int64.Type}, {"Market price", type number}, {"Amount sold",
Int64.Type}}),
 BufferedTable = Table.Buffer(Depreciation),
 #"Appended Query" = Table.Combine({#"Changed Type", BufferedTable}),
 #"Changed Type1" = Table.TransformColumnTypes(#"Appended Query",{{"Pur-
chase", type number}}),
 Table.Buffer1 = Table.Buffer(Dividends),
 Table.Buffer2 = Table.Buffer(Equity),
 #"Appended Query1" = Table.Combine({#"Changed Type1", Table.Buffer1, Table.
Buffer2})
in
 #"Appended Query1"
```

Now I need to use the second technique to make the load to the Data Model more efficient: **Table.View()**.

Table.View() optimisations

Before I explain **Table.View()**, please be aware that this is an advanced concept in Power Query. The only reason I am using it, is because my model uses flat files as a source. For the purposes of understanding why I am using **Table.View()**, a flat file is simply a file which is not part of a relational database. I want the data from the Excel Workbook to be loaded to the Power BI model as efficiently as possible, and **Table.View()** is going to help me to do that.

In Power Query, queries that use data from relational databases are subject to a process called **query folding**. To be folded and loaded as efficiently as possible, the query should be able to be expressed as a single **SQL** (Server Query Language) statement. Folded queries are only accessed once when loaded into Power BI Desktop. This helps with load times and query evaluation efficiencies. However, queries that use flat files such as Excel, are not folded and are accessed twice.

Since my model is only using a flat file, I am only interested in why it is being accessed twice, and how I can avoid it. The load process reads the query once with filters that return with zero rows in order to determine just the column information. The process will then read the query again but this time with no filter, allowing the rows to be read so that the data can be loaded into a table in Power BI Desktop.

The trick here is to use the **Table.View()** function to make the Power Query engine run the zero-row filter queries instantly. This will ALWAYS be the last step in the query because it must have the final list of all columns and their data type.

The **Table.View()** function uses the following syntax:

```
Table.View(table, handlers) as table
```

This function returns a view of the table as specified by the **handlers**. In this case, the table parameter is set to *null*, since I am loading the table for the first time, not extending it.

```
Table.View(null, handlers)
```

In the **handlers** section, I provide the column names and column type information, which would have been automatically accessed in the zero-row filter query. This means that this step is only run when creating the query and not when refreshing it. There are three **handlers**, which work together to pass the required information to Power Query. These are:

1. **GetType**: this is called when the Power Query engine needs to know about the data types of the columns of the table returned by this expression. This is where I need to know all the columns and their types, in order to fully describe the structure of my table. The types used in my model are:

   Date = Date.Type
   Decimal = Number.Type
   Text = Text.Type
   Whole number = Int64.Type
   Any = Any.Type
   Percentage = Percentage.Type

2. **GetRows**: this is called when the Power Query engine wants all the rows from the table (for example, when it's loading data into the dataset). In this case, I use the previous step name (#"Appended Query1")
3. **OnTake**: this is called when the Power Query engine only wants the top **n** rows from the table. A count of zero [0] means just provide the structure, otherwise the rows from my previous step would be counted.

I shall add the **Table.View()** function to the end of the **Actuals** query here to optimise load times. I find the easiest way to do this is to open the Advanced Editor in Windowed mode, and position it just below the column titles so I can see what the column names are, and also what data type they are. You should note that if you have given any columns a slightly different name, put them in a different order or they have a different data type, then the list of columns and associated data types MUST match the final step in YOUR query. I'll show later what you will see if the step is not quite right. I replace the final step and the 'in' statement with the following code:

```
#"Appended Query1" = Table.Combine({#"Changed Type1", Table.Buffer1, Table.
Buffer2}),
OverrideZeroRowFilter = Table.View(
null,
[
GetType = () =>
type table[
Account = Text.Type,
Date = Date.Type,
Amount = Number.Type,
Price = Number.Type,
Purchase = Number.Type,
Market price = Number.Type,
Amount sold = Int64.Type,
Dividend declared = Int64.Type
],
GetRows = () =>
#"Appended Query1",
OnTake = (count as number) =>
if count = 0 then
#table(
type table[
Account = Text.Type,
Date = Date.Type,
Amount = Number.Type,
Price = Number.Type,
Purchase = Number.Type,
Market price = Number.Type,
Amount sold = Int64.Type,
Dividend declared = Int64.Type
```

```
],
{}
)
else
Table.FirstN(#"Appended Query1", count)]
)
in
 OverrideZeroRowFilter
```

The previous step **#"Appended Query1"** is included to show that the last step is referenced. The previous step must be referenced in the **GetRows()** and **Table.FirstN()** parameters, so that the **Table.View()** step is being applied to the last step of the query. There are some errors that are easy to make when creating **Table.View()** steps. If the columns do not match the exact names, or the correct type, errors will occur. If a comma is not added to the end of the previous step (in this case **#"Appended Query1"**), then errors will occur. I will give examples of what these errors look like and how they can be corrected later in this section. If this step is hard to get right, it can be omitted without causing calculation problems, but the load to the Power BI Desktop model will be slower. The next visual shows the final step correctly applied:

There are three main errors you can make with **Table.View()** and Power Query's powers of detection diminish as we go!

The first error is impossible to miss:

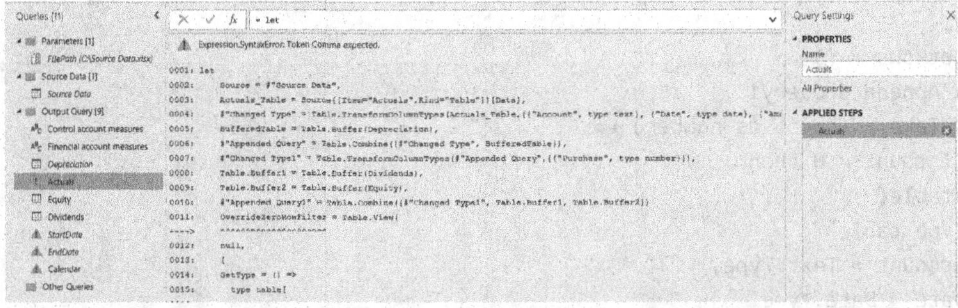

In fairness, Power Query does issue an error for this in the Advanced Editor, but if I click 'Done' without checking, I could assume that I'd lost all my steps! In this case, it is a common error: I missed a comma at the end of the 'Appended Query1' step.

Advanced Editor

Actuals

Display Options

```
let
    Source = #"Source Data",
    Actuals_Table = Source{[Item="Actuals",Kind="Table"]}[Data],
    #"Changed Type" = Table.TransformColumnTypes(Actuals_Table,{{"Account", type text}, {"Date", type date}, {"Amount", type number}, {"Price", type number}, {"Purchase", Int64.Type}, {"Market price", type number}, {
    BufferedTable = Table.Buffer(Depreciation),
    #"Appended Query" = Table.Combine({#"Changed Type", BufferedTable}),
    #"Changed Type1" = Table.TransformColumnTypes(#"Appended Query",{{"Purchase", type number}}),
    Table.Buffer1 = Table.Buffer(Dividends),
    Table.Buffer2 = Table.Buffer(Equity),
    #"Appended Query1" = Table.Combine({#"Changed Type1", Table.Buffer1, Table.Buffer2})
    OverrideZeroRowFilter = Table.View(
    null,
    [
    GetType = () =>
      type table[
      Account = Text.Type,
      Date = Date.Type,
      Amount = Number.Type,
      Price = Number.Type,
      Purchase = Number.Type,
      Market price = Number.Type,
      Amount sold = Int64.Type,
      Dividend declared = Int64.Type
    ],
    GetRows = () =>
      #"Appended Query1",
    OnTake = (count as number) =>
      if count = 0 then
      #table(
      type table[
      Account = Text.Type,
      Date = Date.Type,
      Amount = Number.Type,
      Price = Number.Type,
      Purchase = Number.Type,
      Market price = Number.Type,
      Amount sold = Int64.Type,
      Dividend declared = Int64.Type
    ],
      {}
    )
    else
```

Token Comma expected Show error

Done Cancel

Clicking on 'Show error' highlights the next step after the comma was expected, so I correct it by adding a comma. This tells Power Query another step is coming; only the last step has no comma at the end.

Advanced Editor

Actuals

Display Options

```
let
    Source = #"Source Data",
    Actuals_Table = Source{[Item="Actuals",Kind="Table"]}[Data],
    #"Changed Type" = Table.TransformColumnTypes(Actuals_Table,{{"Account", type text}, {"Date", type date}, {"Amount", type number}, {"Price", type number}, {"Purchase", Int64.Type}, {"Market price", type number}, {
    BufferedTable = Table.Buffer(Depreciation),
    #"Appended Query" = Table.Combine({#"Changed Type", BufferedTable}),
    #"Changed Type1" = Table.TransformColumnTypes(#"Appended Query",{{"Purchase", type number}}),
    Table.Buffer1 = Table.Buffer(Dividends),
    Table.Buffer2 = Table.Buffer(Equity),
    #"Appended Query1" = Table.Combine({#"Changed Type1", Table.Buffer1, Table.Buffer2}),
    OverrideZeroRowFilter = Table.View(
    null,
    [
    GetType = () =>
      type table[
      Account = Text.Type,
      Date = Date.Type,
      Amount = Number.Type,
      Price = Number.Type,
      Purchase = Number.Type,
      Market price = Number.Type,
      Amount sold = Int64.Type,
      Dividend declared = Int64.Type
    ],
    GetRows = () =>
      #"Appended Query1",
    OnTake = (count as number) =>
      if count = 0 then
      #table(
      type table[
      Account = Text.Type,
      Date = Date.Type,
      Amount = Number.Type,
      Price = Number.Type,
      Purchase = Number.Type,
      Market price = Number.Type,
      Amount sold = Int64.Type,
      Dividend declared = Int64.Type
    ],
      {}
    )
    else
```

✓ No syntax errors have been detected.

Done Cancel

Once I add the comma, I have the green tick, and I can click Done to see that my steps are still there.

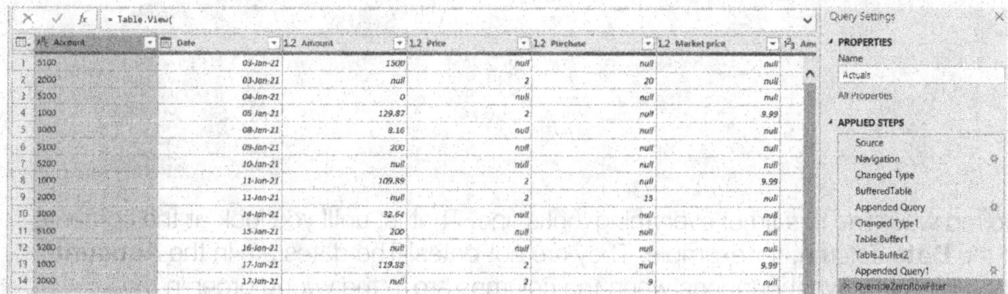

= Table.View(

	Account	Date	Amount	Price	Purchase	Market price
1	5100	03-Jan-21	1500	null	null	null
2	2000	03-Jan-21	null	2	20	null
3	5200	04-Jan-21	0	null	null	null
4	1000	05-Jan-21	129.87	2	null	9.99
5	3000	08-Jan-21	8.16	null	null	null
6	5100	09-Jan-21	200	null	null	null
7	5200	10-Jan-21	null	null	null	null
8	1000	11-Jan-21	109.89	2	null	9.99
9	2000	11-Jan-21	null	2	15	null
10	3000	14-Jan-21	32.64	null	null	null
11	5100	15-Jan-21	200	null	null	null
12	5200	16-Jan-21	null	null	null	null
13	1000	17-Jan-21	119.88	2	null	9.99
14	2000	17-Jan-21	null	2	9	null

The next error is more subtle.

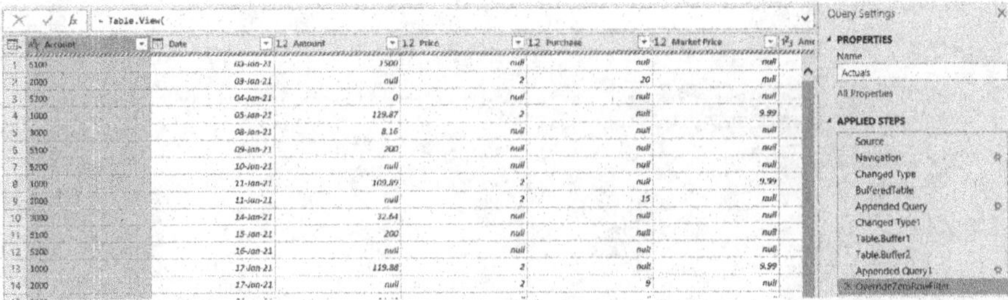

Ah yes, the red wavy line. This means that there is something wrong with the last step. I have made a deliberate mistake, which is the most common one I have seen when applying a **Table.View()** step.

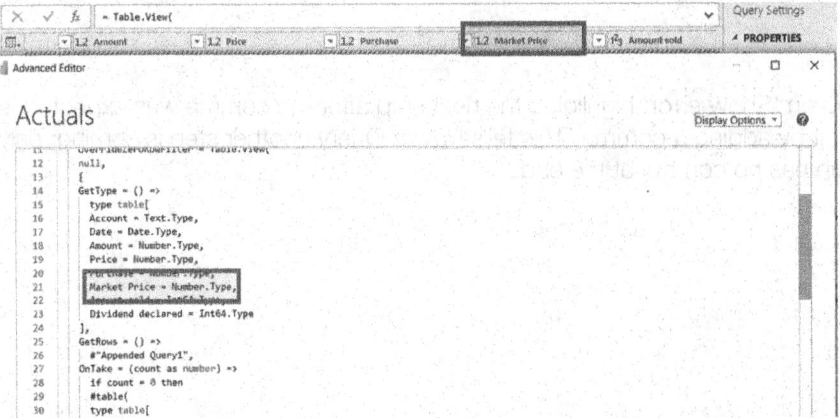

In this case, the name of the column on the previous step was **Market price** (note the lowercase "p"), but in the **Table.View()** step I have called it **Market Price**. The Advanced Editor will not detect this as an error, and the column will appear with the name **Market Price** on the final step. If the final step has a red wavy line, check the column names (even extra spaces can cause this) and data types in the **Table.View()** step against the PREVIOUS step.

The final error is not picked up by Power Query at all, but you will soon notice when you try to use the data!

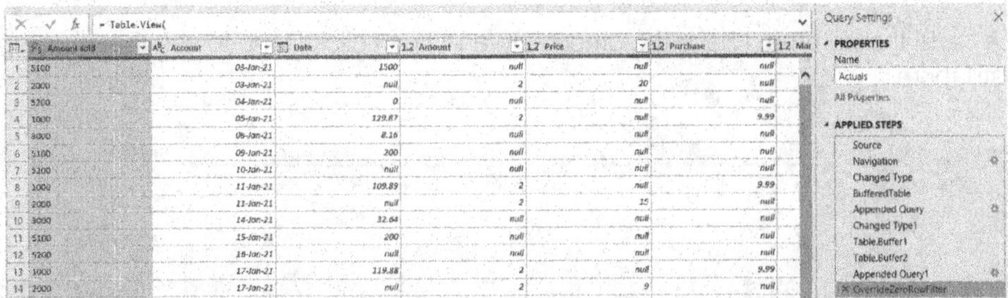

No red wavy line this time: everything looks fine. That is, until you look at the contents of the **Date** column, for example. They are not dates! The dates are in the **Account** column. This is what happens when the columns are in the wrong order in the **Table.View()** statement, compared with the previous step. The **Amount sold** field should not appear before **Account**.

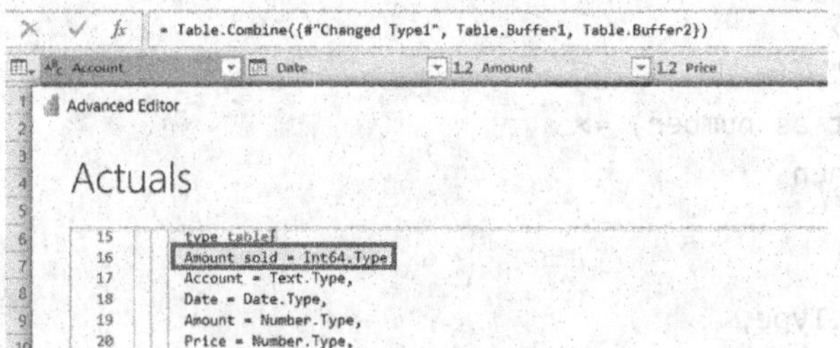

This is something to look out for when copying and pasting from the book: the order of the columns MUST be the same as the previous step. This applies to the **GetType()** and **OnTake()** parameters. You will get no warning for this error: you simply must check!

Incidentally, if the line under the column heading is partially grey, it is an indication of how many *null* values are in that column and this is not a problem.

Now I've covered how to make the **Table.View()** step error-free, I can apply it to any query that I will be uploading to the Power BI model. I can check this by looking for queries that are NOT displayed in italics (*i.e.* they are set to 'Enable Load'). This includes the **Dividends, Equity** and **Calendar** tables which I have already created, so I will add their final steps now.

Dividends Table.View step

```
let
 Source = #"Source Data",
 DividendsDeclared_Table = Source{[Item="DividendsDeclared",Kind="Table"]}
[Data],
 #"Changed Type" = Table.TransformColumnTypes(DividendsDeclared_Table,{{"Ac-
count", type text}, {"Date", type date}, {"Dividend declared", Int64.Type}}),
 OverrideZeroRowFilter = Table.View(
 null,
 [
 GetType = () =>
 type table[
 Account = Text.Type,
 Date = Date.Type,
 Dividend declared = Int64.Type
 ],
```

```
GetRows = () =>
#"Changed Type",
OnTake = (count as number) =>
if count = 0 then
#table(
type table[
Account = Text.Type,
Date = Date.Type,
Dividend declared = Int64.Type
],
{}
)
else
Table.FirstN(#"Changed Type", count)]
)
in
OverrideZeroRowFilter
```

Equity Table.View step

Advanced Editor

Equity

Display Options

```
let
    Source = #"Source Data",
    EquityTable_Table = Source{[Item="EquityTable",Kind="Table"]}[Data],
    #"Changed Type" = Table.TransformColumnTypes(EquityTable_Table,{{"Account", type text}, {"Date", type date}, {"Amount", Int64.Type}}),
    OverrideZeroRowFilter = Table.View(
    null,
    [
    GetType = () =>
      type table[
      Account = Text.Type,
      Date = Date.Type,
      Amount = Int64.Type
    ],
    GetRows = () =>
      #"Changed Type",
    OnTake = (count as number) =>
      if count = 0 then
      #table(
      type table[
      Account = Text.Type,
      Date = Date.Type,
      Amount = Int64.Type
   ],
      {}
    )
    else
     Table.FirstN(#"Changed Type", count)]
  )
in
    OverrideZeroRowFilter
```

```
let
Source = #"Source Data",
EquityTable_Table = Source{[Item="EquityTable",Kind="Table"]}[Data],
```

```
 #"Changed Type" = Table.TransformColumnTypes(EquityTable_Table,{{"Account",
type text}, {"Date", type date}, {"Amount", Int64.Type}}),
 OverrideZeroRowFilter = Table.View(
 null,
 [
 GetType = () =>
 type table[
 Account = Text.Type,
 Date = Date.Type,
 Amount = Int64.Type
 ],
 GetRows = () =>
 #"Changed Type",
 OnTake = (count as number) =>
 if count = 0 then
 #table(
 type table[
 Account = Text.Type,
 Date = Date.Type,
 Amount = Int64.Type
 ],
 {}
 )
 else
 Table.FirstN(#"Changed Type", count)]
 )
in
 OverrideZeroRowFilter
```

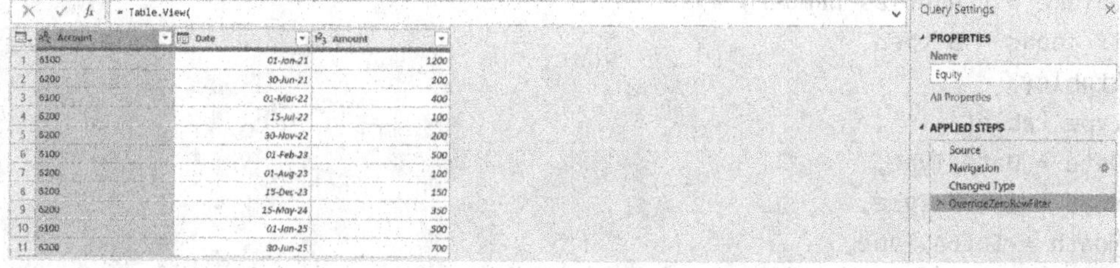

Calendar Table.View step

```
 #"Added Prefix" = Table.TransformColumns(#"Inserted Quarter", {{"Qtr", each
"Q" & Text.From(_, "en-GB"), type text}}),
 OverrideZeroRowFilter = Table.View(
 null,
 [
 GetType = () =>
 type table[
 Date = Date.Type,
 Year = Int64.Type,
 Month = Int64.Type,
 Month Name = Text.Type,
 Day = Int64.Type,
 Qtr = Text.Type
 ],
 GetRows = () =>
 #"Inserted Prefix",
 OnTake = (count as number) =>
 if count = 0 then
 #table(
 type table[
 Date = Date.Type,
 Year = Int64.Type,
 Month = Int64.Type,
 Month Name = Text.Type,
 Day = Int64.Type,
 Qtr = Text.Type
 ],
 {}
 )
 else
 Table.FirstN(#"Inserted Prefix", count)]
 )
in
```

`OverrideZeroRowFilter`

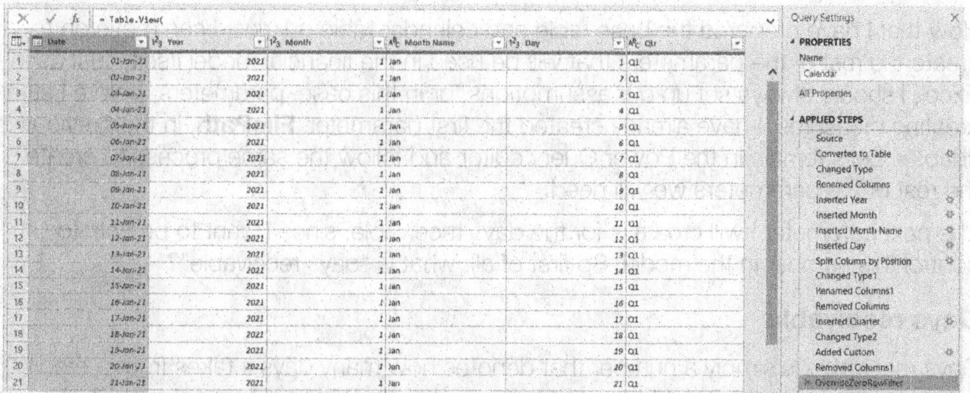

This is the last of the queries I need to change for now: I will add view steps when I create queries that I set to 'Enable Load'. Before I create any more queries, I need to create the rest of my parameters.

CHAPTER 7: Creating Parameters

Now that I have prepared the base table and calendar table queries, I can move on to create the rest of the parameters that will be used in the financial model itself. Just as in Excel, I should always set up our assumptions, or in this case, parameters, before I start creating measures. I have already created the first parameter, **FilePath**, in the previous chapter. Let's remain in the Power Query editor and follow the same process to create the rest of the parameters we will need.

The next parameter I will create is for the days receivable, since I want to be able to control this number in the model. So first of all: what is "days receivable"?

Days receivable

Days receivable is simply a number that denotes how many days it takes from a credit sale being made to the actual payment being received. This should only be applied to credit sales. If some sales are made on a cash basis (*i.e.* monies are paid when the item or service is procured), these sales should be excluded from calculating this number, otherwise incorrect management decisions may be made.

For example, if I have $100,000 of sales and days receivable were seven [7] days, I would expect $100,000, net of any sales costs, in my bank account, a week later. However, if 50% of sales were paid for at the time of purchase, and these sales were included in calculating the average time, I would be wrong. For the average to be seven days, the credit sales must be on 14 days' terms, since (0 + 14) / 2 = 7. Therefore, a week after all sales are made, our company would still only have $50,000, as the credit sales monies will not yet have been received. If the company was to rely on $100,000 being in the bank account at this time, it could have serious cash flow repercussions. This is why days receivable (and days payable for that matter) should only be calculated for the relevant credit items. Watch out!

For simplification purposes in this book, I will assume all sales are made on credit terms. (Where some sales are made on a cash basis, you would simply exclude these items from the modelling and treat them as sales made on zero [0] days receivable.)

Back to creating parameters

After my little intermission, let's return to creating my first parameter of the chapter:

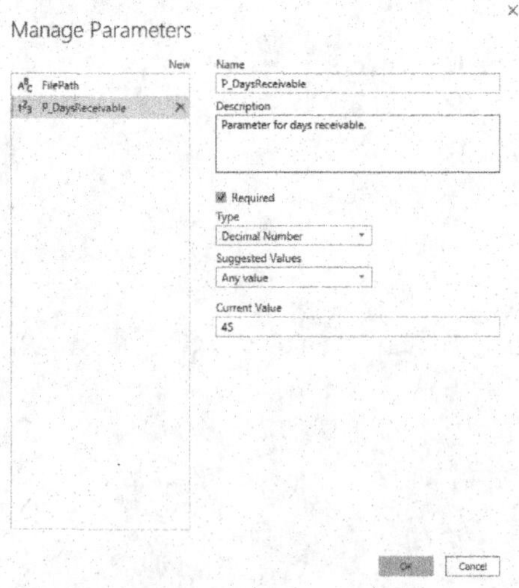

The '**P_**' at the front of the parameter name stands for 'parameter'. This is so if I have an ordered list of items, I will be able to locate all my parameters easily. Honestly! I'm not taking the "P"! I have also given the parameter a short description. This description is optional.

I can select whether the parameter is required (the check box in the image). This will mean that Power BI will require a value to be assigned to this parameter.

There are other options to consider:

- when creating parameters (at time of writing), Power BI Desktop only allows certain data types as parameters. In this case, I have selected the 'Decimal Number' type:

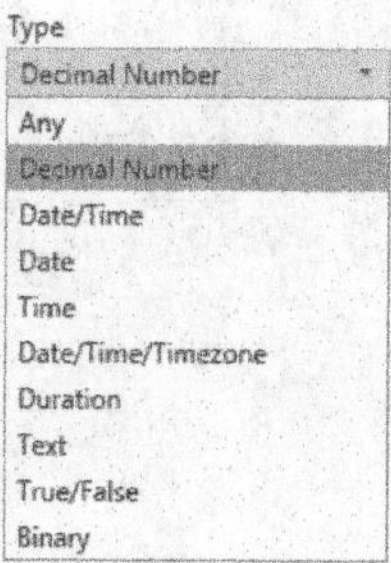

  - parameters that are percentages, or whole numbers must be classified as a 'Decimal Number' for the moment, as there are no other data types available. This does not affect the outcome of the calculation

- There are currently three [3] options I could choose in the 'Suggested Values' dropdown:

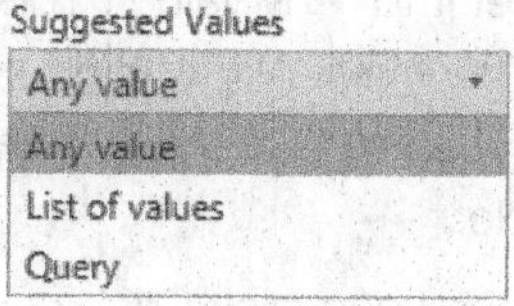

  - I will be using 'Any value' for this parameter, but if I were to select the 'List of values' option, this would allow me to create a list of set values that the end user could choose from:

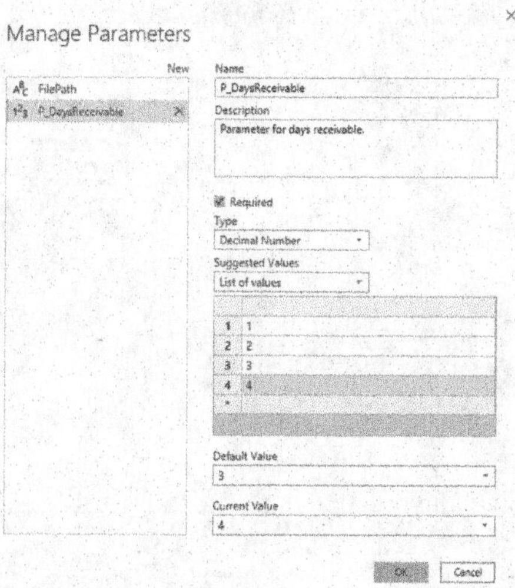

- the Query option would allow the parameter's values to be determined by a query:

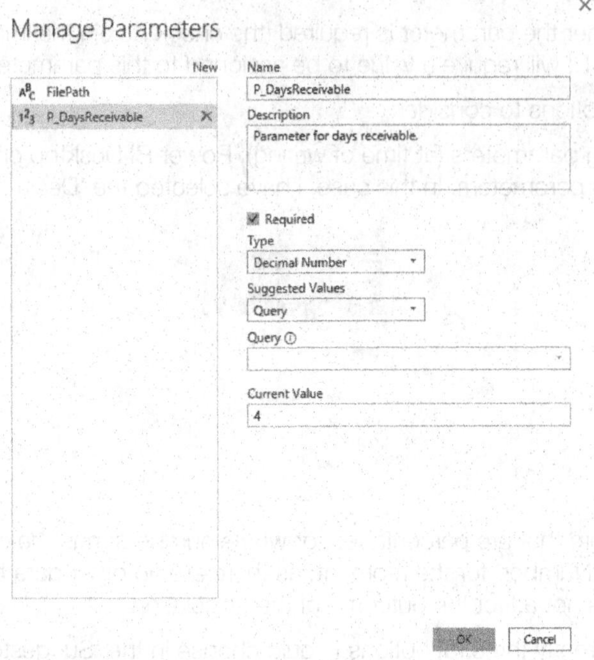

- for this example, I have set it to 'Any value'. This will allow the end user to assign any number to the days receivable parameter

- I have also populated the 'Current Value' option with 45. This will be the default value which I will use for my example.

When I am done with my parameter, I can click OK.

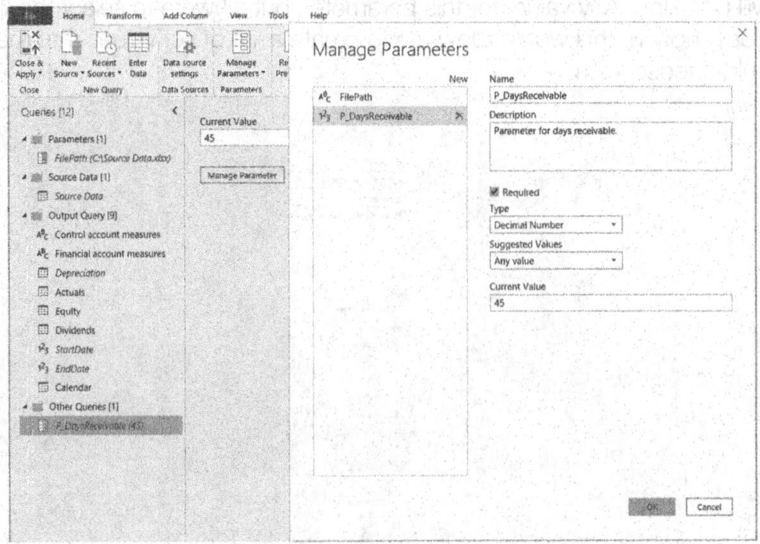

I will create the rest of the parameters that I will need in this model. Rather than explain them all here, I will describe each parameter as I use it to create the model. For now, I have provided a table which contains all the information needed to create each parameter. The **Name** column denotes the name of the parameter: to follow along with the book, please use the same name. The **Required** column indicates whether to tick the Required box to determine if the parameter is required. The **Type** indicates the data type for the parameter. The **Suggested Values** option determines if I am restricting the values used, as described previously. Note that the **Gross margin** parameter is actually a table created from a query, which I will cover later. You will also recall **FilePath** was created earlier and must be set to the file path of wherever you save your source data. And if you don't recall, then hey, stop reading this book out of order!

Name	Required	Type	Suggested Values	Current Value
FilePath	Yes	String	Any Value	C:\Power BI\ Source data.xlsx
Gross margin	Yes	Table	Gross margin %	Multiple
P_DaysReceivable	Yes	Decimal Number	Any Value	45
P_DaysPayable	Yes	Decimal Number	Any Value	40
P_DebtCode	Yes	Text	Any Value	5100
P_DepreciationYears	Yes	Decimal Number	Any Value	5
P_DebtRepaymentCode	Yes	Text	Any Value	5200
P_EquityBuyBackCode	Yes	Text	Any Value	6200
P_EquityIssueCode	Yes	Text	Any Value	6100
P_InterestRate	Yes	Decimal Number	Any Value	0.07
P_InventoryCode	Yes	Text	Any Value	2000
P_OpexCode	Yes	Text	Any Value	3000
P_SalesCode	Yes	Text	Any Value	1000
P_TaxAssetAnnualRate	Yes	Decimal Number	Any Value	0.5
P_TaxAssetLife	Yes	Decimal Number	Any Value	4
P_TaxRate	Yes	Decimal Number	Any Value	0.3

The list of parameters, (not including **Gross margin**) sorted into alphabetical order, should display as follows:

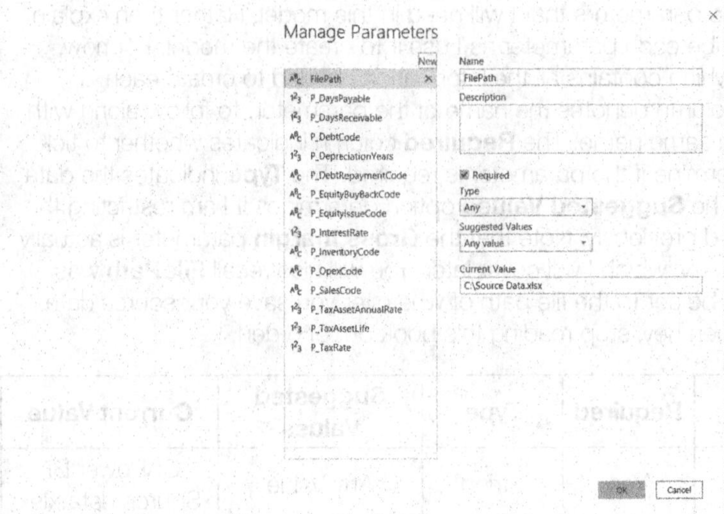

I move all the parameters to the Parameters Query group.

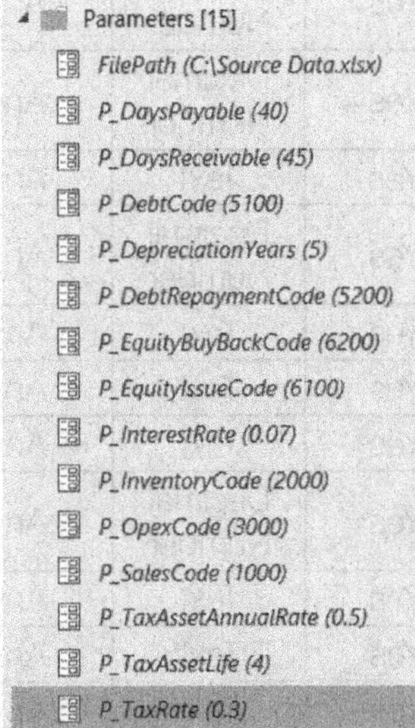

The final parameter is **Gross margin**. To create this, I need to create a query.

The first step here is to reference my base query **Source Data**, and rename the new query **Gross margin**:

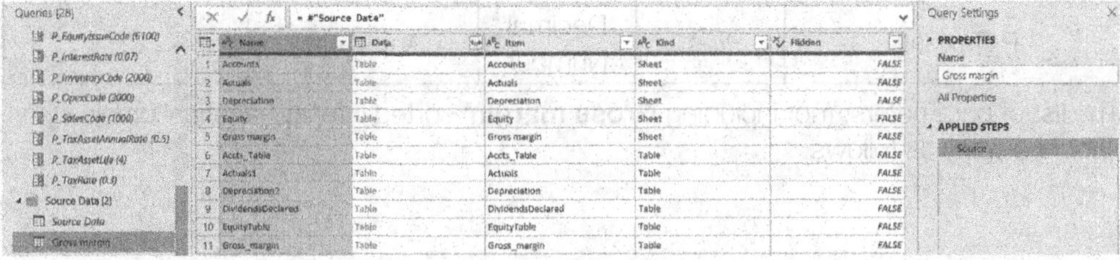

I look for 'Gross margin' in the **Name** column and click on the yellow Table option in the **Data** column.

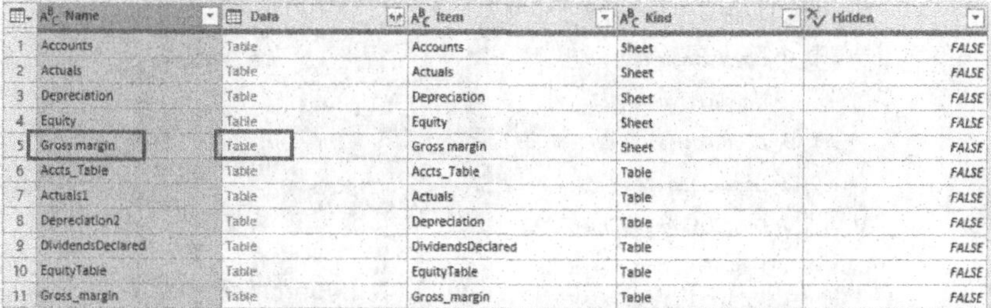

	Name	Data	Item	Kind	Hidden
1	Accounts	Table	Accounts	Sheet	FALSE
2	Actuals	Table	Actuals	Sheet	FALSE
3	Depreciation	Table	Depreciation	Sheet	FALSE
4	Equity	Table	Equity	Sheet	FALSE
5	Gross margin	Table	Gross margin	Sheet	FALSE
6	Accts_Table	Table	Accts_Table	Table	FALSE
7	Actuals1	Table	Actuals	Table	FALSE
8	Depreciation2	Table	Depreciation	Table	FALSE
9	DividendsDeclared	Table	DividendsDeclared	Table	FALSE
10	EquityTable	Table	EquityTable	Table	FALSE
11	Gross_margin	Table	Gross_margin	Table	FALSE

After clicking on the yellow table text, Power BI should automatically perform the necessary transformations to produce the table.

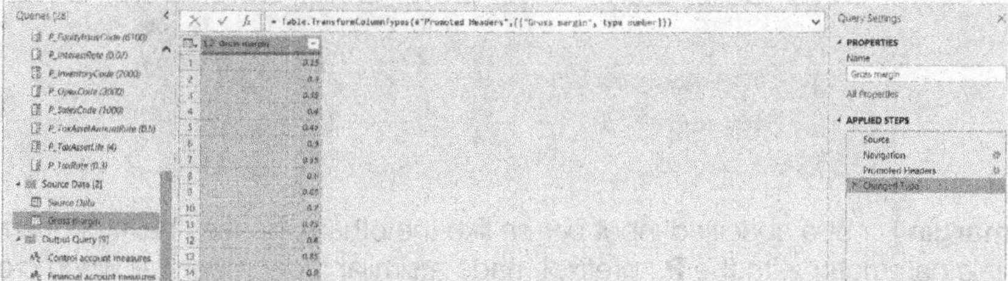

I change the data type to a percentage. As for the other queries, I accept the prompt to replace the existing conversion in the 'Changed Type' step.

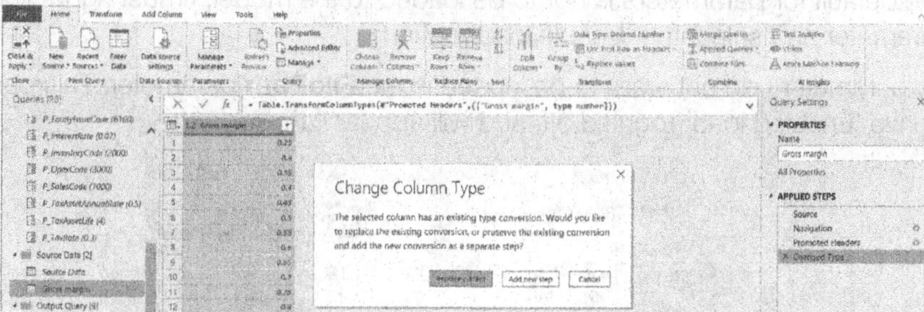

The **Gross margin** table should now look like this:

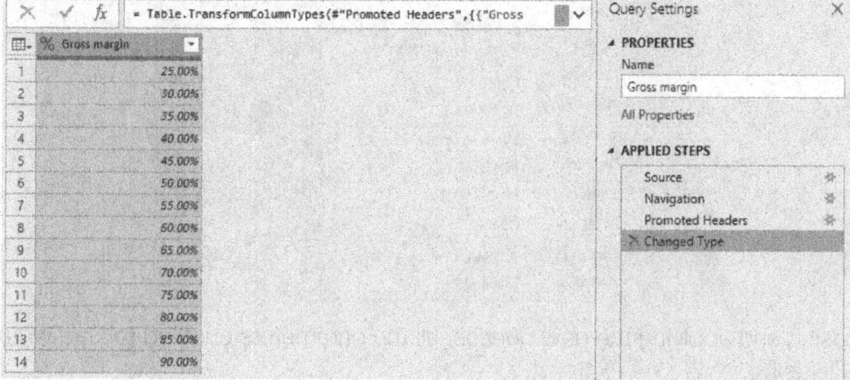

	Gross margin
1	25.00%
2	30.00%
3	35.00%
4	40.00%
5	45.00%
6	50.00%
7	55.00%
8	60.00%
9	65.00%
10	70.00%
11	75.00%
12	80.00%
13	85.00%
14	90.00%

I move this query into the Parameters Query group with the rest of the parameters:

Gross margin is not a specified input *per se* like the others, hence I have chosen not to start this parameter with the **P_** prefix. I made a similar judgement call when creating the **FilePath** parameter. If you disagree, that's your preference. However, if you are constructing the model from the book, I'd recommend using the same name.

Since the default for parameters is not to be loaded to the model, I must right-click on each parameter and select the 'Enable load' option:

The only parameter I do not want to be loaded is the **FilePath** parameter. This parameter should have 'Enabled load' toggled off, and will appear *italicised*.

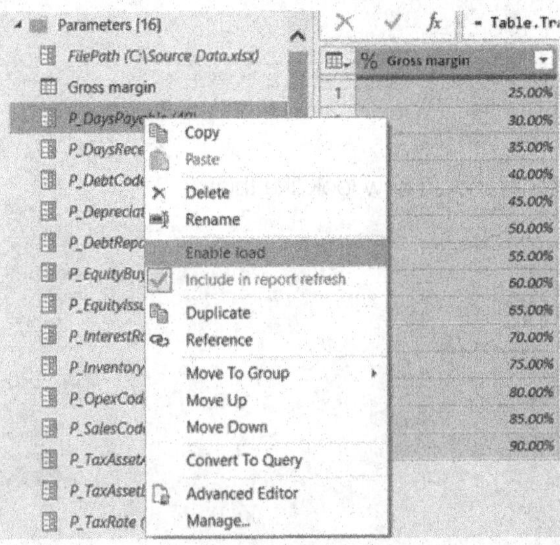

After closing and applying the new queries, all the parameters enabled to load will appear on my Fields list.

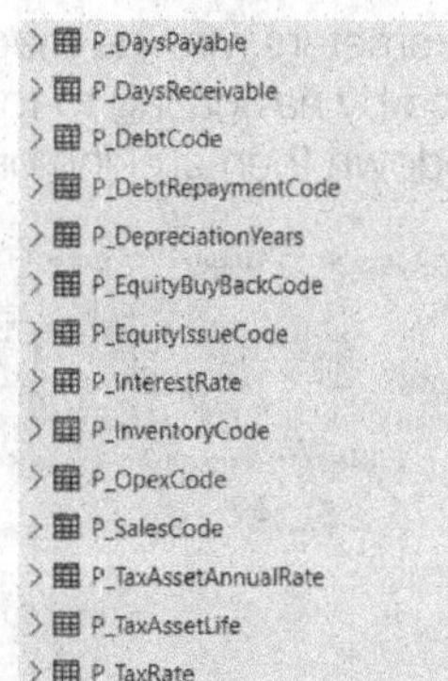

When building the model, I will not need to refer to these parameters on the Fields list (except for the **Gross margin** table). Therefore, to keep things cleaner, I choose to hide them. To hide a parameter or field, right-click on it and select the Hide option. The Hide feature will also be used to display the **Control account measures and Financial account measures** at the top of the list of tables later, but I cannot use this until I have added measures to those tables.

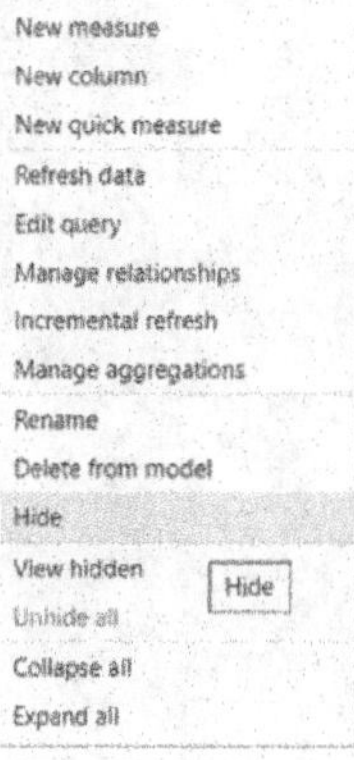

My Fields pane now looks neater:

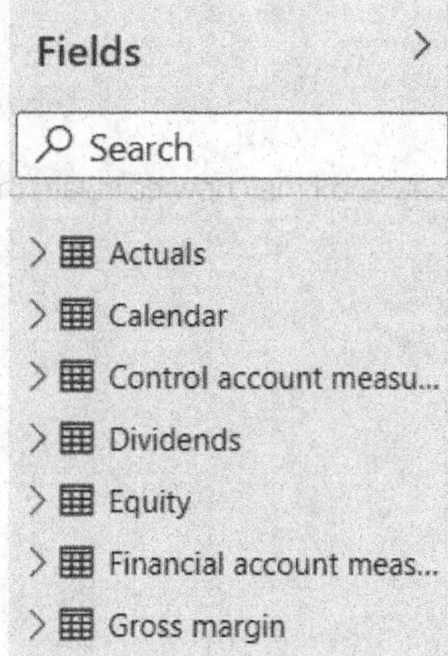

From now on, value changes to parameters may be made via the 'Edit Parameters' dialog box. This dialog may be called by navigating to the Home tab on the Ribbon, selecting the 'Transform data' dropdown then clicking on 'Edit parameters', *viz.*

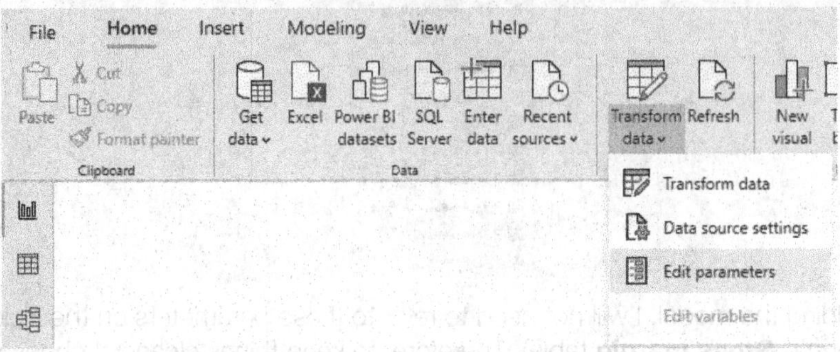

Parameter changes can be performed in this dialog. When finished, click OK. Power BI will then prompt me to commit the changes as the parameters are held in the Power Query section of the model.

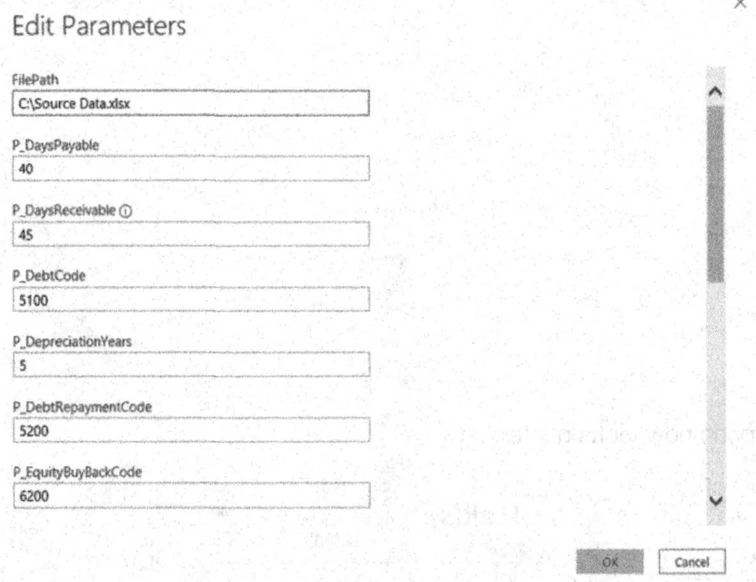

I now have all my parameters set, and I may now calculate the sales control account. Bring it on!

CHAPTER 8: Calculating Sales

Three million pages in and we may finally make a start! Earlier, I suggested we would be best working down our financial statements, starting with the Income Statement – and use the principle of control accounts to assist. Therefore, in this chapter, I will outline the method I used to calculate the four line items that comprise the sales control account:

1. Sales opening receivables
2. Sales
3. Sales cash receipts
4. Sales closing receivables.

Before creating the calculations here, I want to explain the working capital assumption and how it works. As explained earlier, if money is owed, the people who owe it are **Debtors** and, assuming no write-offs of sales made, the amounts owed are known as **Accounts Receivable** or simply **Receivables**. This amount owed is viewed as an asset of the business. It isn't cash but it should convert to cash *soon*. Cynical businesses may quite rightly think if only it were that simple, but it is for the purposes of this case study.

Consider the following example (using the alternative "Debtor" nomenclature):

Control Account

Opening Debtors	-	*BS*
Sales in Period	**1,000**	*IS*
Cash Receipts	**(753)**	*CFS*
Closing Debtors	**247**	*BS*

Imagine a company has just started off in business (*i.e.* has no amounts due) and generates sales of $1,000 in the period. At the end of the period, assuming no bad debts, $753 has been paid, leaving a closing debtor balance of $247. This difference is what I refer to as the **working capital adjustment**. If I had modelled the sales of $1,000 in the period, how might I generate the cash receipts forecast such that if the assumptions changed, the receipts would calculate appropriately?

Clearly, if I am given the closing debtor balances, the problem becomes trivial, so I will assume that this is not so. Therefore, I am going to consider an alternative approach and some of the associated underlying issues that need to be considered when modelling. Let me first derive an alternative method.

I will assume that the sales accrue evenly over the period of time and for the sake of this example, that period is one year (365 days). Presuming (i) all sales are made on credit terms, (ii) all customers pay their invoices on the day the amounts fall due and (iii) no bad debts are incurred, this can be reflected graphically as follows:

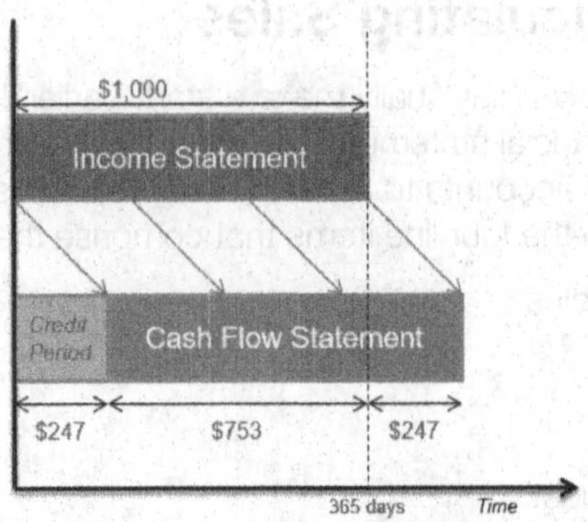

Clearly, the credit period is the "gap" at the beginning of the time period, *i.e.* 247/1000 x 365 days = 90 days. This can be represented formulaically as:

Days Receivable = (Closing Debtors x Days in Period) / Sales in Period

Rearranging, this becomes:

Closing Debtors = (Sales in Period x Days Receivable) / Days in Period,

e.g. in our example: 247 = (1000 x 90) / 365.

Therefore, when modelling in Excel, I often set the number of days receivable (and days payable) as key assumptions for cash flow forecasting. However, it is not always as simple as that here. Let me explain. Consider I am planning to build a monthly model (assuming 30 days in a month) and sales for the month are again $1,000. Debtor days remain at 90 days.

Based on these calculations, I would generate the following control account:

Control Account

Opening Debtors	-	BS
Sales in Period	1,000	IS
Cash Receipts	2,000	CFS
Closing Debtors	3,000	BS

Erm, that's right: make sales of $1,000 and have $3,000 (= 90/30 x 365) owing to you by the end of the month. Also, the company pays $2,000 to customers a reclaimable $2 for each $1 spent. That's nonsense, unless your company happens to be called Loan Sharks R Us – and yet, as an experienced model auditor I have seen this erroneous calculation crop up on a regular basis. The problem is, in this current economic climate most businesses want to prepare monthly – sometimes weekly and even daily – cash flow projections.

Power BI allows you to drill down to this level. Clearly, if the days receivable or days payable assumption exceeds the number of days in each forecast period this approach is inappropriate and will lead to calculation errors. Indeed, opening and closing balances may not reconcile on this basis either too.

Since I need to be able to drill down to the lowest level of granularity (here, daily), this approach will not work. This is a prime example of where a simple calculation in Excel simply falls over in Power BI.

The only way this will work – and reconcile – in Power BI is to calculate the day payment will be received for each record. I use this payment date to aggregate the cash for different periods. This means I will have two dates for each of our records, the sales date and the payment date. This in turn will mean I will need two links between our fact table and our **Calendar** table (and need to switch between them using **USERELATIONSHIP**) – the date of the sale (main link) and the date cash is received (secondary link). But I will consider that scenario later. Here, I will simply parameterise the difference between the date of the sale and the date the cash is received. That's the thinking behind the development of the calculation in this section.

Let's make a start.

Sales opening and closing receivables are simply functions of the Sales and Sales cash receipts. Therefore, I will come back to these two items later.

The first measure I will create is the **Sales** measure:

```
1 Sales =
2 CALCULATE(
3     SUM(Actuals[Amount]),
4     Actuals[Account] = "1000"
5 )
```

```
Sales =
CALCULATE(
 SUM(Actuals[Amount]),
 Actuals[Account] = "1000"
)
```

Yes, I know I have hard coded "1000" in the expression above, having just extolled the virtues of variables and parameterisation. Keep reading; I am building up to the parameters I have created recently. But let's keep it simple to begin with. To create a measure, use the 'New measure' button on the Home tab.

Just before I dive into the **SUM** function, I should explain a couple of presentation points: how to make separate lines in **DAX** code in Power BI, and how to control where measures are stored.

If the cursor is at the beginning of the **CALCULATE** function, and I want to type code in the next line (3).

```
1 Sales =
2 CALCULATE(
```

I press **SHIFT + ENTER** on the keyboard. This will take me to the next line of code (3) in the **DAX** editor:

```
Sales =
CALCULATE(

```

When I create a measure, Power BI needs to associate it with a table, which is called the 'Home table' for that measure (see the next image). The 'Home table' defaults to the table I have open when I create the measure. To move a measure to another table, I can change the Home table to any table in the Fields pane. At the time of writing, I cannot move a measure by clicking and dragging in the Fields pane; there is a balance to be struck between moving measures easily and moving them accidentally. This balance has already affected the way date hierarchies are created, as I will show shortly.

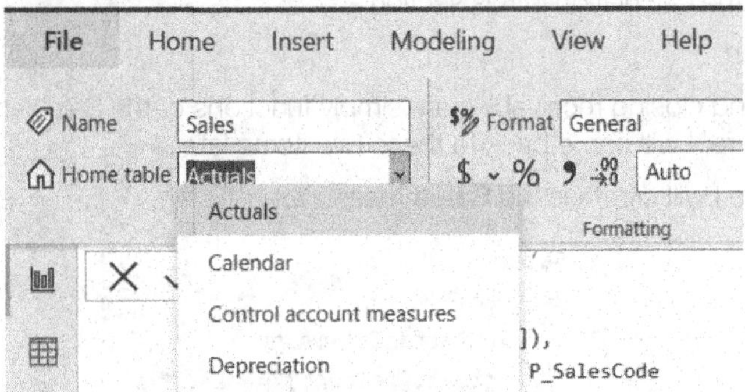

I can change 'Home table' to **Control account measures** to keep my measures together.

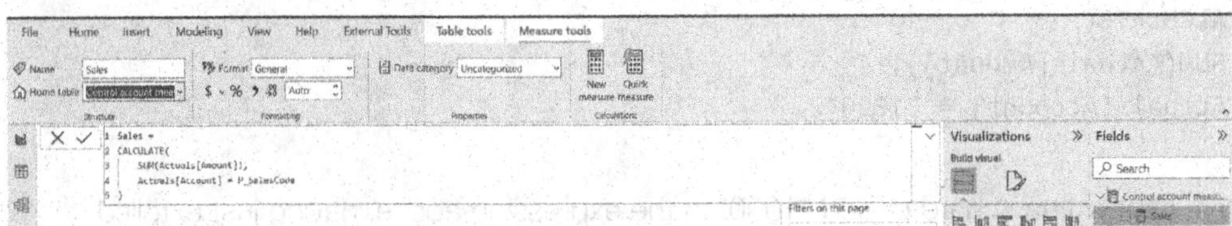

This is a good point to check the Format setting and the decimal places setting below it.

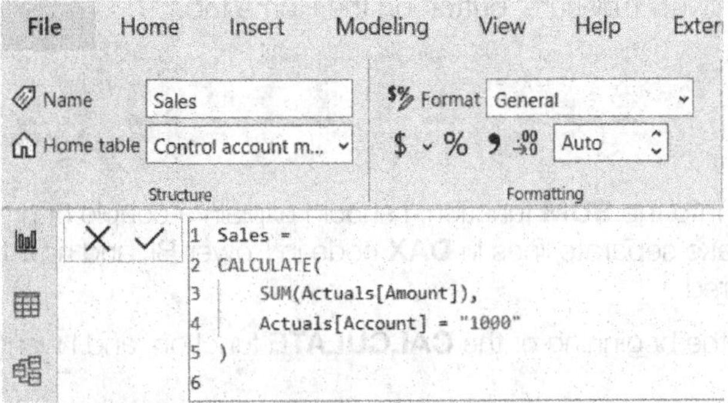

These should be set to General and Auto respectively. If you find that yours is 'Whole Number', then I probably know why.

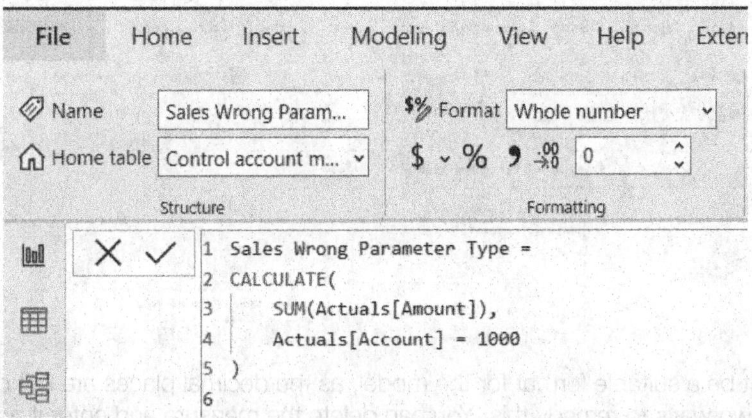

I have created another measure where I have deliberately omitted the speech marks around the 1000 I am using in my filter. Power BI just assumes that I only want the numeric values from the **Account** field and sets the format accordingly. It is not until it comes to display the measure, that Power BI announces the error.

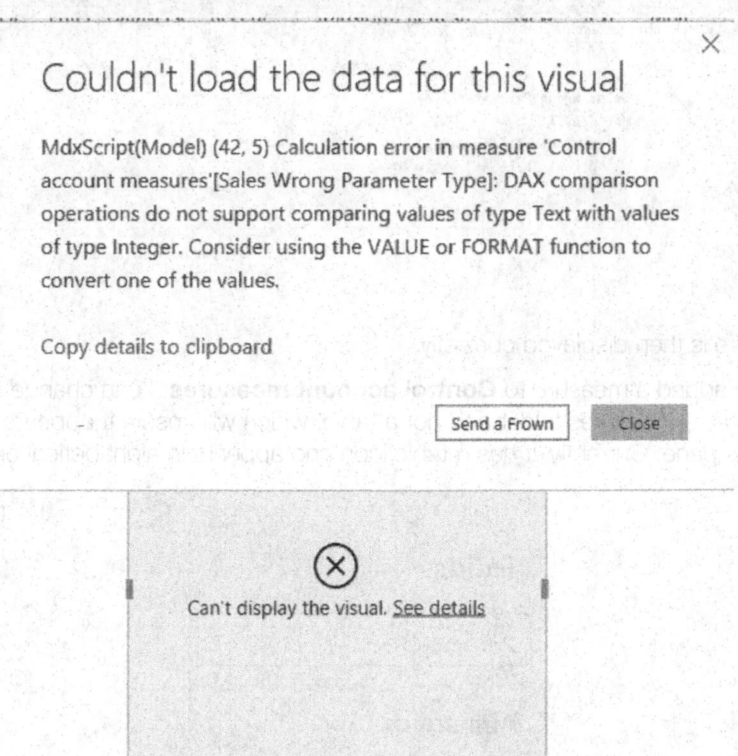

Couldn't load the data for this visual
MdxScript(Model) (42, 5) Calculation error in measure 'Control account measures'[Sales Wrong Parameter Type]: DAX comparison operations do not support comparing values of type Text with values of type Integer. Consider using the VALUE or FORMAT function to convert one of the values.
Copy details to clipboard
Send a Frown
Close
Can't display the visual. See details

(This part of the error may also occur if the filter is on a parameter of the wrong data type.)

You can go back and correct the measure, but the format is already set:

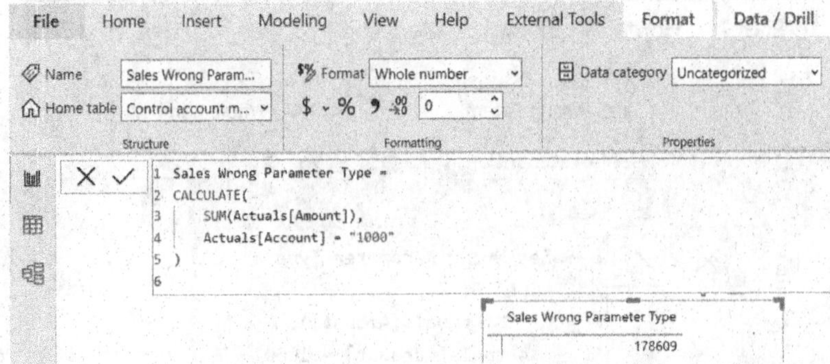

This will not be a suitable format for the model, as the decimal places are not displayed. There are two ways to remedy this. You can delete the measure and enter it again or else you can adjust the Format.

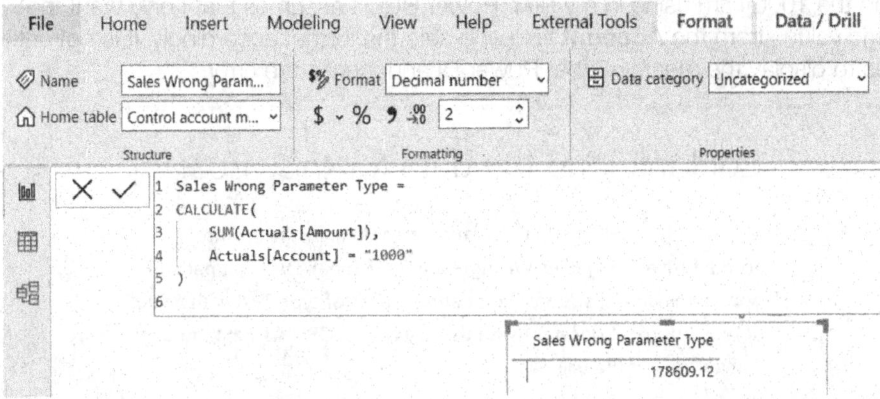

The measure is then displayed correctly.

Now I have added a measure to **Control account measures**, I can change this to be recognised as a measures folder and not a table, which will ensure it appears at the top of the Fields pane. Currently, it has a table icon and appears in alphabetical order with the other tables.

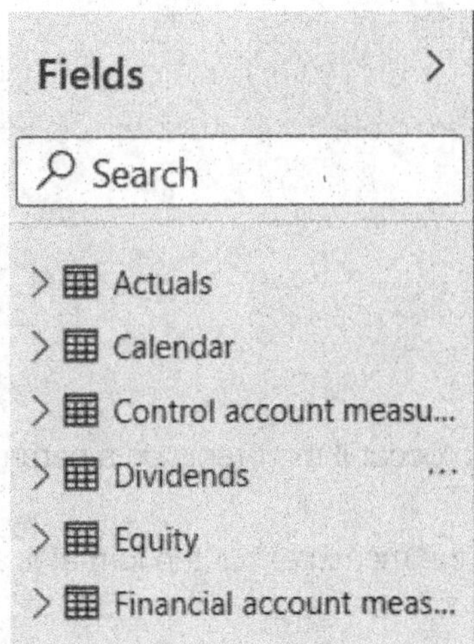

To change this, I hide the only column on the table. Earlier, I showed how to hide items whilst in the Report view. This time I am in the Model view, where I can click on the eye to hide or unhide items from the Report view. I could also have done this by hiding **Control account measures** before I used it as a 'Home table', but that would mean it would not have been displayed in the Report view. The Model view shows all the hidden items loaded to the Data Model with the crossed-out eye icon, so if you accidentally hide something you want to see on the Report view, it can be undone here.

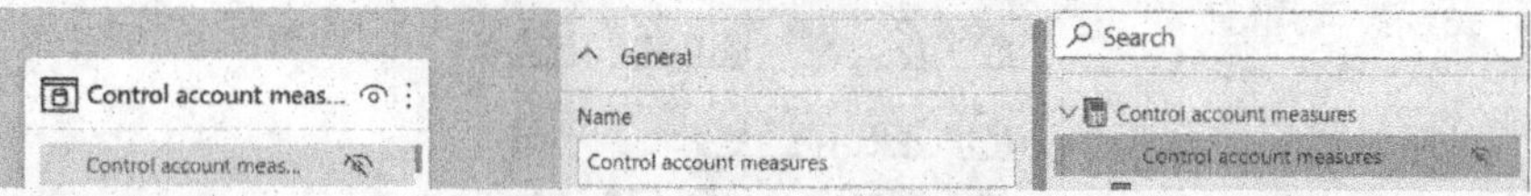

Back in the Report view, my measure folder is no longer treated as a table, and will appear at the top of the list:

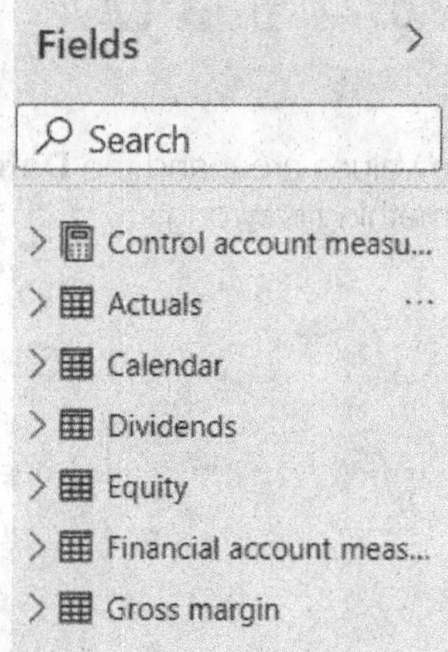

I will do the same for **Financial account measures** when I add a measure to this table.

Now that I have the **Sales** measure, I will use the **Matrix** visualisation to display my sales values ordered by time period. Keanu Reeves watch out. Looking at the Visualizations pane, I select the **Matrix** visualisation:

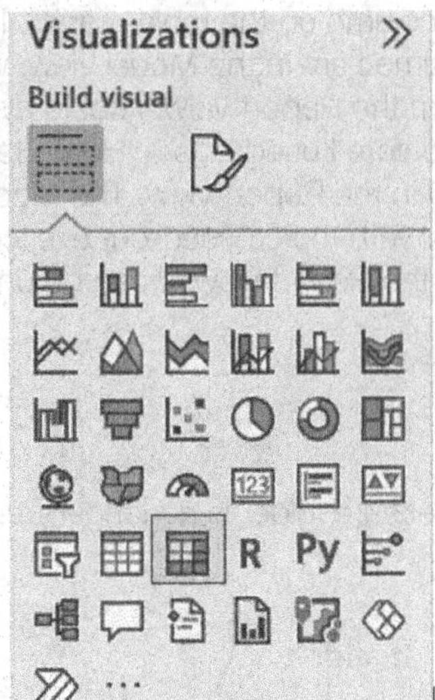

I plot the **Sales** measure into the Values area, and the **Date** field, from the **Calendar** table into the Columns area. Something is wrong.

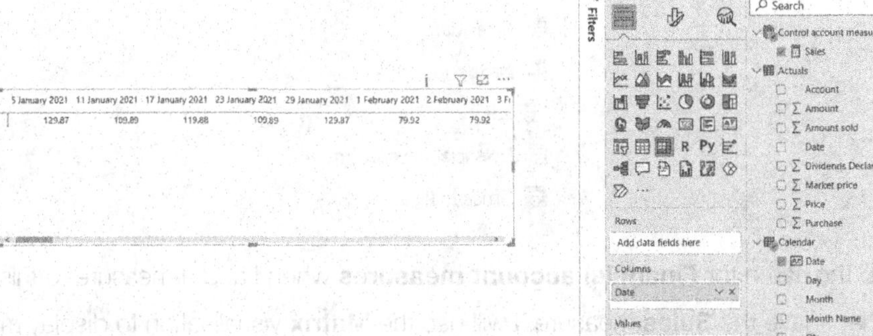

Although all the fields I need to drill up and down by day, month, quarter and year are on the **Calendar** table, I have not created a hierarchy. Having turned off the automatic Date Table creation, I need to create a hierarchy for **Calendar**. In previous versions of Power BI, I could have done this by dragging **Qtr**, **Month** and **Day** into **Year**. However, this is where the balance of making things easy versus not doing things accidentally comes in again. Users were accidentally creating hierarchies all over the place and Microsoft decided to jettison this functionality. Now, I must create the hierarchy by selecting **Year** and right-clicking.

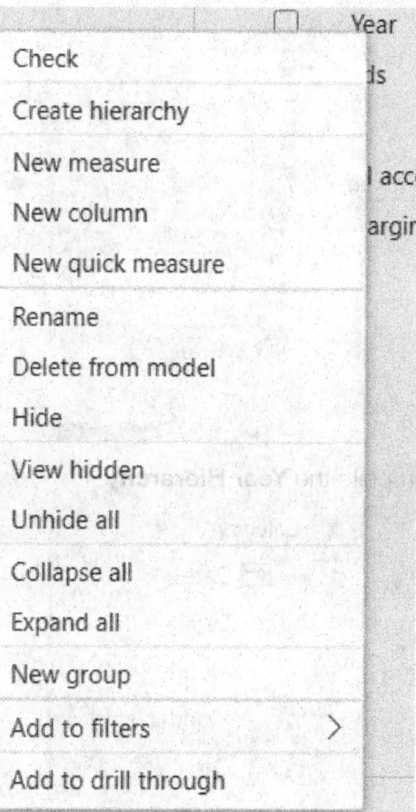

If I choose to 'Create hierarchy', a hierarchy under **Year** called **Year Hierarchy** is provided.

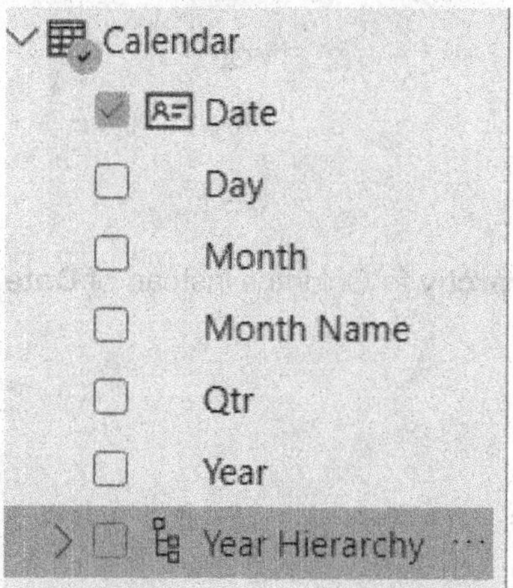

I can add **Qtr**, **Month Name** and **Day** to this hierarchy by right-clicking on each of them and choosing to add them.

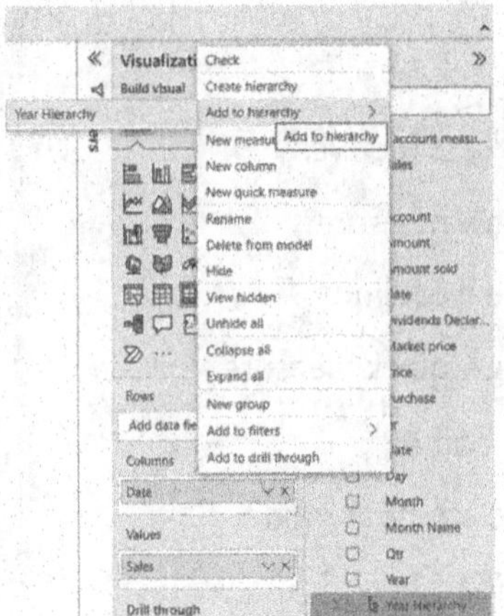

I repeat this process to complete the **Year Hierarchy**.

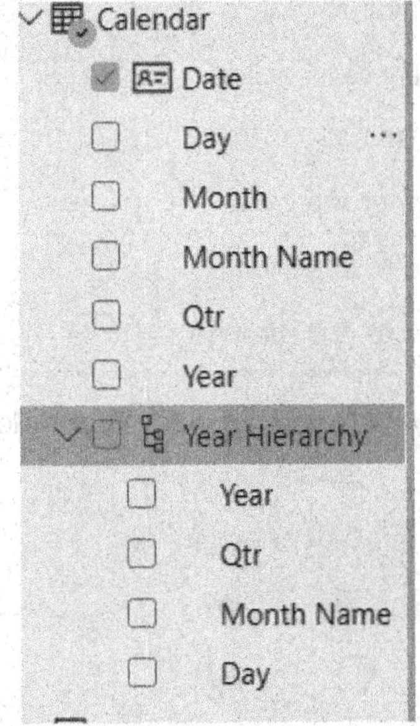

Now if I drag the **Year Hierarchy** to Columns instead of **Date**, I have drill down options:

Finally, I can right-click on **Year Hierarchy** and rename it to **Date hierarchy**:

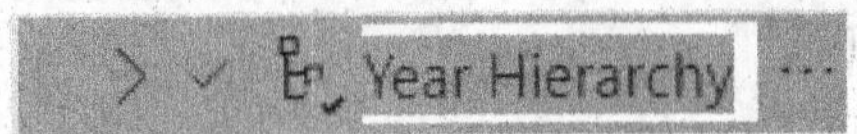

From here, there are still some changes to be made to make it look more like a traditional financial reporting line in Excel. With the visualisation selected, I click twice on the fork option 'Expand all down one level in the hierarchy':

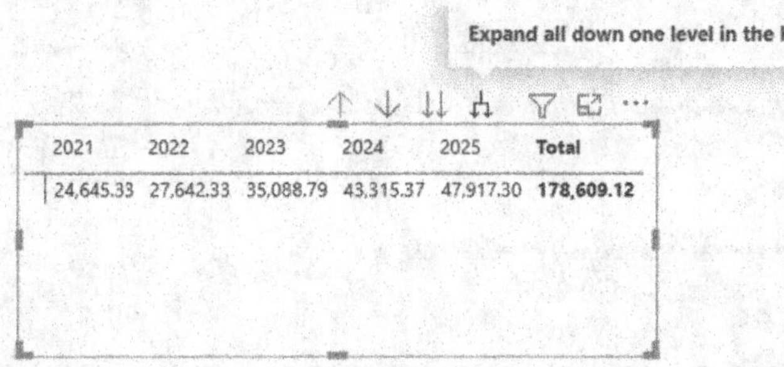

The resulting visualisation will now look like this:

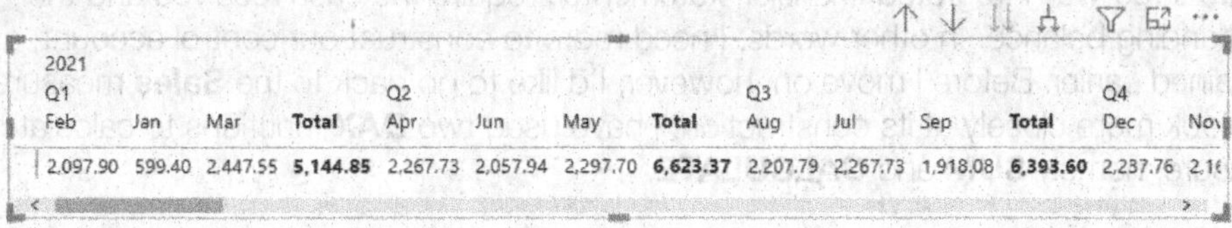

I have months, but they are not in the right order. I can solve this by going to the Data view and selecting **Calendar.** I select the **Month Name** column and then choose the 'Sort By' dropdown and choose to sort by **Month**, which is the month number.

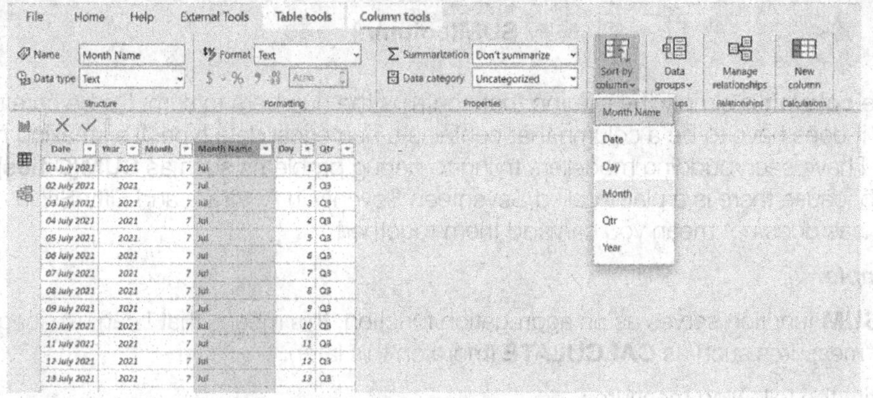

Now when I go back to my visualisation:

2021													
Q1				Q2				Q3				Q4	
Jan	Feb	Mar	**Total**	Apr	May	Jun	**Total**	Jul	Aug	Sep	**Total**	Oct	Nov
599.40	2,097.90	2,447.55	**5,144.85**	2,267.73	2,297.70	2,057.94	**6,623.37**	2,267.73	2,207.79	1,918.08	**6,393.60**	2,077.92	2,167

The months are in the right order.

The next step is to remove the total columns appearing at the end of each quarter. With the visualisation selected, I select the Format tab and toggle 'Column subtotals' to Off.

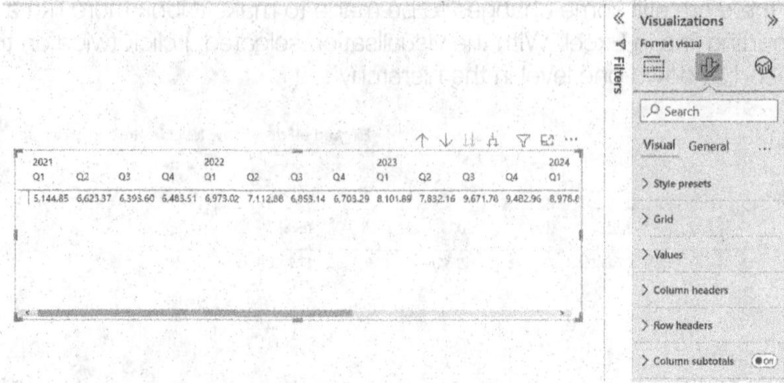

There we have it: **Sales**. This identifies the purchases made by our company's customers and will be the head figure in our Income Statement. However, let's not forget that to create three-way integrated financial statements I require the cash received and the outstanding balance. In other words, I need more to construct our control account, as explained earlier. Before I move on, however, I'd like to go back to the **Sales** measure and look more closely at its construction. I have used two **DAX** functions to calculate this measure, namely **SUM** and **CALCULATE**.

The SUM function

In short, the **SUM** function adds all the numbers referenced. The syntax is very straightforward:

SUM(column)

where **column** is simply the column that contains the numbers to sum. Do be careful here: it does have to be a column that contains a numerical data type. It's amazing how often I have seen budding modellers trying to debug problems such as **SUM(Cities)**. Just because there is a place called Seventeen Seventy in Australia and Fifty-Six in Arkansas does not mean you can add them together!

Example

The **SUM** function serves as an aggregation function, this means that I can use it again in other measures such as **CALCULATE** (more on this later).

If I write the following measure :

```
SUM example =
    SUM(Actuals[Amount])
```

```
SUM example =
 SUM(Actuals[Amount])
```

It will sum every value in the **Amount** column in the **Actuals** table. I can demonstrate this by plotting this measure onto a Table visualisation:

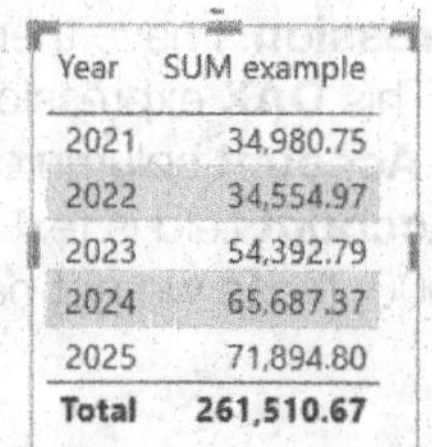

Year	SUM example
2021	34,980.75
2022	34,554.97
2023	54,392.79
2024	65,687.37
2025	71,894.80
Total	**261,510.67**

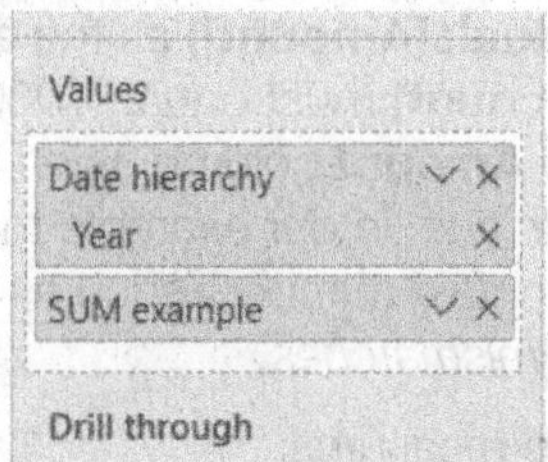

To properly calculate the sales amounts for each year, I must filter out other account numbers and just sum accounts that are "1000". The **SUM** function has no built-in method of filtering out values in the column. Therefore, I must use the **SUM** function in conjunction with another function: **CALCULATE**.

The CALCULATE function

Any avid Excel user will know the usefulness of the **SUMIF** function. Unfortunately, **SUMIF** does not work in Power BI. However, there is a viable alternative – and it is much more powerful.

The **CALCULATE** function evaluates an expression in a context that is modified by prescribed filters. Does this sound like Excel's **SUMIF** function?

The syntax for **CALCULATE** is:

CALCULATE(expression, filter1, [filter2, ...])

The **expression** may be a field or a formula, with each **filter** located in any table imported to Power BI, assuming the tables have had proper relationships established (it sounds like old fashioned courting!). You should note that **CALCULATE** is not "context specific" (*i.e.* the data used does not need to pertain to the row or column headers of any PivotTable the expression may be in), and the filters used do not need to be included in the PivotTable either.

See where I am going with this?

Example

Recalling the original measure that I created earlier in this Section:

```
Sales =
CALCULATE(
    SUM(Actuals[Amount]),
    Actuals[Account] = "1000"
)
```


```
Sales =
CALCULATE(
 SUM(Actuals[Amount]),
 Actuals[Account] = "1000"
)
```

I have used **SUM(Actuals[Amount])** as the **expression**. I have then added a filter whereby **Actuals[Account]** must equal "1000". This **DAX** expression now reads, 'Sum all of the values in the **Amount** column when the **Account** column equals "1000"'. As noted earlier, "1000" is text. In our example the **Account** field is text, but if it was set to any, and allowed to contain numbers such as 1,000, these will <u>not</u> be included. You must avoid what I call *type mismatches*.

Let's compare the two measures:

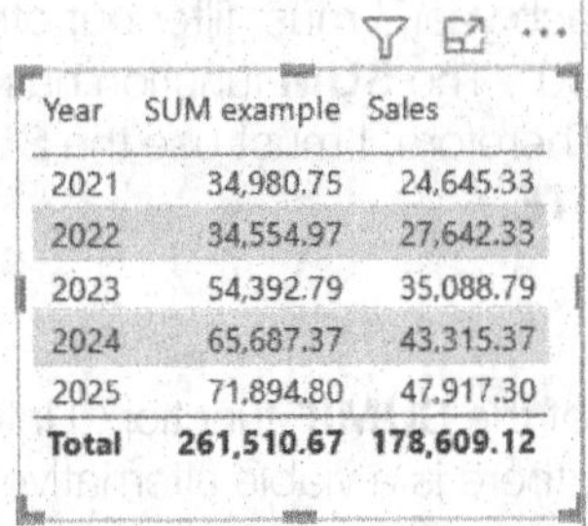

Year	SUM example	Sales
2021	34,980.75	24,645.33
2022	34,554.97	27,642.33
2023	54,392.79	35,088.79
2024	65,687.37	43,315.37
2025	71,894.80	47,917.30
Total	**261,510.67**	**178,609.12**

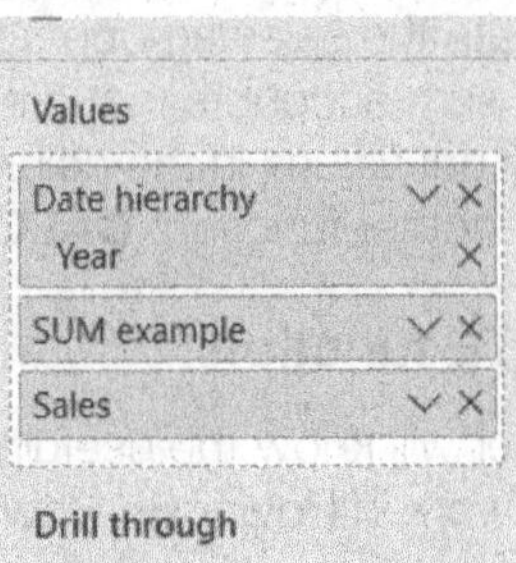

The **CALCULATE** function correctly calculates the **Sales** amounts in my dataset.

Returning to my model, I will now adjust the measure to use the **P_SalesCode** parameter that I created earlier:

```
Sales =
CALCULATE(
    SUM(Actuals[Amount]),
    Actuals[Account] = P_SalesCode
)
```

```
Sales =
CALCULATE(
 SUM(Actuals[Amount]),
 Actuals[Account] = P_SalesCode
)
```

This way, if the account code for sales changes, I will just need to change it once in the parameters, and it will be reflected throughout the model. That's the whole point of modelling: I may sensitise and / or adjust, and all calculations will simply update accordingly.

Returning to the Data Model, the next measure to create is the **Sales cash receipts** measure. This requires an understanding of the movements in working capital.

To demonstrate my Power BI approach, consider the following. A sale of $100 is made on the 1st of January 2021. Let's assume days receivable for credit sales are 45 days. That means that the payment is transferred to my bank account on the 15th February 2021, *i.e.* 45 days later. Again, I will keep this simple and ignore the effects of working days, weekends, public holidays, coronaviruses and alien invasions.

I can adjust for this by using the **DATEADD** function.

The DATEADD function

The **DATEADD** function is a time intelligence function. This means that it requires a calendar table with strict ascending and contiguous dates, meaning dates with no gaps.

The syntax of this function is:

DATEADD(dates, number_of_intervals, interval)

The **DATEADD** function returns the table of column of dates that is shifted either forward or backwards in time specified by the **number_of_intervals**.

Example: Take Care with DATEADD

You must be careful with **DATEADD**. I shall introduce a very simple dataset that is separate to the main dataset I have worked with so far:

	A	B
1	Month	Sales
2	31-Jan-20	0
3	29-Feb-20	50
4	31-Mar-20	60
5	30-Apr-20	73
6	31-May-20	87
7	30-Jun-20	94
8	31-Jul-20	115
9	31-Aug-20	122
10	30-Sep-20	116
11	31-Oct-20	144
12	30-Nov-20	138

In this example, I shall call this table the **Sales** table. This Table is separate to the main model I am creating.

Given this is all my data is, I see no reason to create a calendar table. However, I will create a measure for my sales, which I will call **Total Sales**:

```
Total sales =
SUM(Sales[Sales])
```

```
Total sales =
SUM(Sales[Sales])
```

All I want to do is compare these sales with the sales from the previous month.

```
Total sales 1 month ago =
CALCULATE([Total sales],
    DATEADD(Sales[Month],
    -1,
    MONTH
    )
)
```

```
Total sales 1 month ago =
CALCULATE([Total sales],
 DATEADD(Sales[Month],
```

```
  -1,
  MONTH
  )
)
```

There is a problem though:

Month	Total sales	Total sales 1 month ago
Sunday, 31 January 2021	0	
Monday, 1 February 2021	50	
Wednesday, 31 March 2021	60	
Friday, 30 April 2021	73	
Monday, 31 May 2021	87	73
Wednesday, 30 June 2021	94	
Saturday, 31 July 2021	115	94
Tuesday, 31 August 2021	122	115
Thursday, 30 September 2021	116	
Sunday, 31 October 2021	144	116
Tuesday, 30 November 2021	138	
Total	**999**	**861**

What!? Why aren't some months showing? This was not the intention at all. For those of you who think this would all be fixed by using a calendar table, it might, depending upon how the data was stored – but the issue is essentially a little simpler than that.

Imagine our data was all collected on the **28**th of each month instead, *i.e.*

	A	B
1	Month	Sales
2	28-Jan-21	0
3	28-Feb-21	50
4	28-Mar-21	60
5	28-Apr-21	73
6	28-May-21	87
7	28-Jun-21	94
8	28-Jul-21	115
9	28-Aug-21	122
10	28-Sep-21	116
11	28-Oct-21	144
12	28-Nov-21	138

In this instance, our **Total sales 1 month ago** would work as envisaged:

Month	Total sales	Total sales 1 month ago
Thursday, 28 January 2021	0	
Sunday, 28 February 2021	50	0
Sunday, 28 March 2021	60	50
Wednesday, 28 April 2021	73	60
Friday, 28 May 2021	87	73
Monday, 28 June 2021	94	87
Wednesday, 28 July 2021	115	94
Saturday, 28 August 2021	122	115
Tuesday, 28 September 2021	116	122
Thursday, 28 October 2021	144	116
Sunday, 28 November 2021	138	144
Total	**999**	**861**

The problem is **DATEADD(Sales[Month], -1, MONTH)** means take the date PRECISELY one month ago. Given I do not have contiguous data, my original calculations were drawing a blank when there were no sales for the corresponding day of the month for the previous month. This is a classic *gotcha* and one you must look out for.

Incidentally, there is a way around this using the original data. Instead of using **DATEADD**, I may use the **PREVIOUSMONTH** function instead, *viz*.

```
Total sales 1 month ago =
CALCULATE([Total sales],
    PREVIOUSMONTH(
        Sales[Month]
    )
)
```

```
Total sales 1 month ago =
CALCULATE([Total sales],
 PREVIOUSMONTH(
 Sales[Month]
 )
)
```

This provides the desired result:

Month	Total sales	Total sales 1 month ago
Sunday, 31 January 2021	0	
Sunday, 28 February 2021	50	0
Wednesday, 31 March 2021	60	50
Friday, 30 April 2021	73	60
Monday, 31 May 2021	87	73
Wednesday, 30 June 2021	94	87
Saturday, 31 July 2021	115	94
Tuesday, 31 August 2021	122	115
Thursday, 30 September 2021	116	122
Sunday, 31 October 2021	144	116
Tuesday, 30 November 2021	138	144
Total	**999**	

DATEADD(Date, -1, MONTH) and **PREVIOUSMONTH** are *not* quite the same thing. The problem is, **PREVIOUSMONTH** does not help me here; I may need to drill down to fortnightly, weekly or even daily analyses, so I must remember to take care with our logic and watch out for these sorts of issues. And what's with the summation too? Yes, not *quite* the right function, thank you.

Another workaround would involve using days instead of months in the **DATEADD** function. This way, instead of shifting one month I shift by a specified number of days:

```
Total sales 1 month ago =
CALCULATE([Total sales],
    DATEADD('Calendar'[Date],
    -30,
    DAY
    )
)
```

```
Total sales 1 month ago =
CALCULATE([Total sales],
 DATEADD(‘Calendar’[Date],
 -30,
 DAY
 )
)
```

This would provide me with the following result:

Year	Quarter	Month	Day	Total sales	Total sales 1 month ago
2021	Qtr 1	January	31	0	
2021	Qtr 1	February	28	50	
2021	Qtr 1	March	2		0
2021	Qtr 1	March	30		50
2021	Qtr 1	March	31	60	
2021	Qtr 2	April	30	73	60
2021	Qtr 2	May	30		73
2021	Qtr 2	May	31	87	
2021	Qtr 2	June	30	94	87
2021	Qtr 3	July	30		94
2021	Qtr 3	July	31	115	
2021	Qtr 3	August	30		115
2021	Qtr 3	August	31	122	
2021	Qtr 3	September	30	116	122
2021	Qtr 4	October	30		116
2021	Qtr 4	October	31	144	
2021	Qtr 4	November	30	138	144
2021	Qtr 4	December	30		138
Total				**999**	**999**

This is acceptable, as I am going to sum up from a daily basis. If there aren't sales received on a particular day, it's not a problem; it means there were no sales on the date referred to. This is different from my previous month example where the dates were omitted instead. In this instance, they will be aggregated on the day that they are actually received. Hence, if I want a weekly, monthly, quarterly or annual summary, I just aggregate our daily analyses. This will ensure consistency too.

This is how I must model in Power BI. In Excel, I may assume a proportion of the sales for the period will be outstanding on a given date, because I am approximating and not varying the periodicity (usually!). However, in Power BI, I may drill down from year to quarter to month to day – I must have consistency throughout. There is no other way of achieving this.

Sales cash receipts measure

Going back to my model I can write my **Sales cash receipts** measure:

```
Sales cash receipts =
    CALCULATE(-[Sales],
        DATEADD('Calendar'[Date], -P_DaysReceivable, DAY)
    )
```

```
Sales cash receipts =
 CALCULATE(-[Sales],
 DATEADD('Calendar'[Date], -P_DaysReceivable, DAY)
 )
```

Note I include a negative sign (-) right before the **[Sales]** measure: this is so that I can properly calculate the amount of cash still outstanding in my control account.

Plotting this measure onto my visualisation I get the following result:

2021									
Q1						Q2			
Jan		Feb		Mar		Apr		May	
Sales	Sales cash receipts	Sales	Sales cash receipts	Sales	Sales cash receipts	Sales	Sales cash receipts	Sales	Sales c
599.40		2,097.90	-239.76	2,447.55	-1,358.64	2,267.73	-2,297.70	2,297.70	

Something does not seem quite right; I want the measures to display on the rows of the measure not the columns of the measure. To change this, I go to the 'Format visual' pane, click on the Values section, find the Options subsection and then toggle the 'Switch values to rows' option to On.

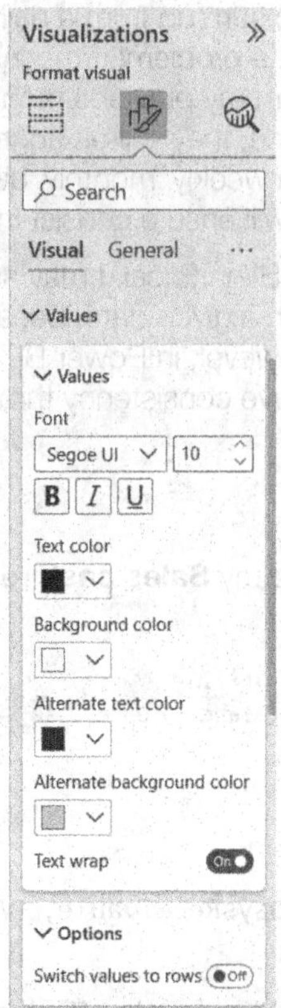

Each field will now be displayed on the rows, rather than the columns of the visualisation:

Year	2021										
Qtr	Q1			Q2			Q3			Q4	
	Jan	Feb	Mar	Apr	May	Jun	Jul	Aug	Sep	Oct	Nov
Sales	599.40	2,097.90	2,447.55	2,267.73	2,297.70	2,057.94	2,267.73	2,207.79	1,918.08	2,077.92	2,167.83
Sales cash receipts		-239.76	-1,358.64	-2,297.70	-2,397.60	-2,317.68	-2,207.79	-2,217.78	-2,167.83	-2,177.82	-1,818.18

I'd like to add some conditional formatting to the measure, so that negative numbers will be displayed with brackets around them and be coloured red.

I head to the 'Format visual' pane and click on the 'Cell elements' option. Here, Power BI will allow me to pick which measure I wish to apply the formatting to. In this case I want to apply the formatting to the **Sales cash receipts** measure.

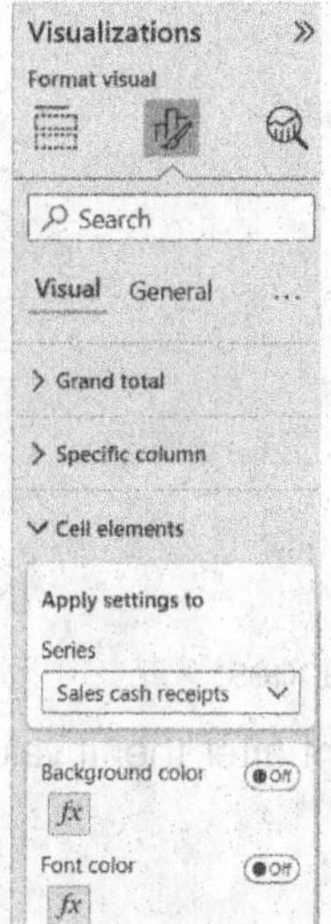

I toggle the 'Font color' option to On. This enables the 'fx' icon, allowing me to apply rules for conditional formatting:

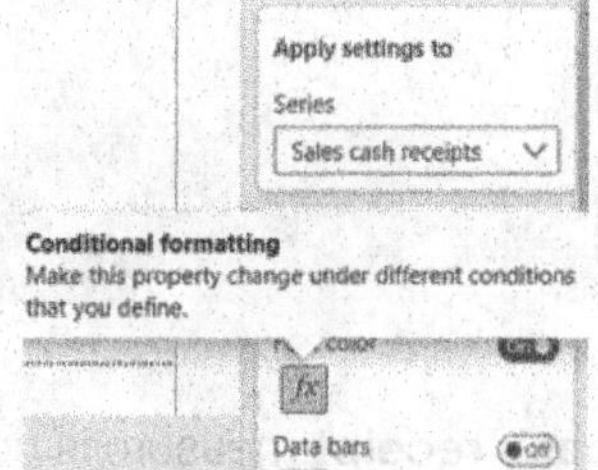

This reveals the 'Advanced controls' option.

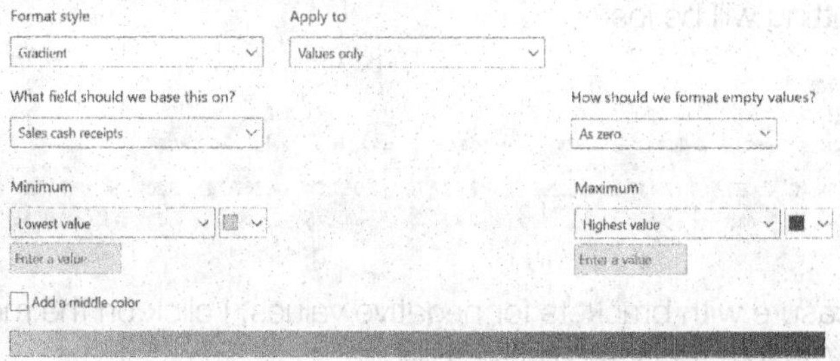

The quickest way to apply red to this measure is by changing the 'Format style' option to Rules:

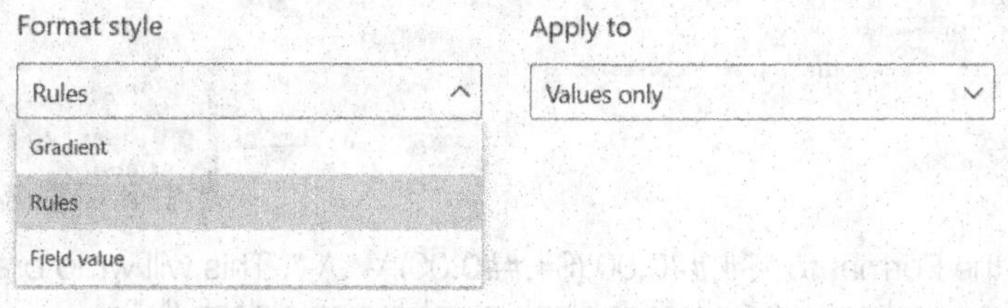

This will reveal the rules interface:

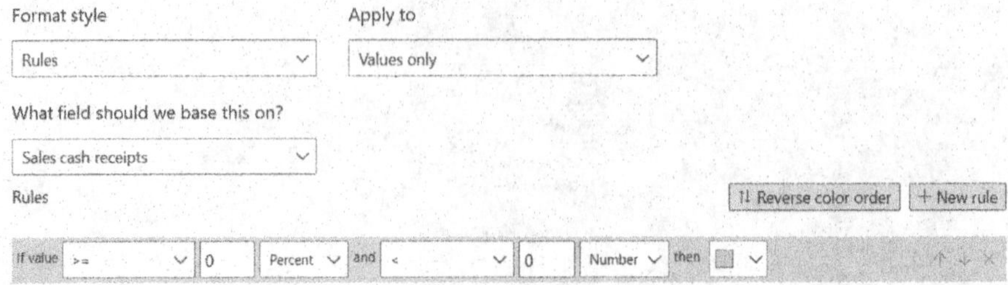

From this point, I will make three changes:

1. I will delete the zero [0] value right after the 'If value >=', changing it to Minimum
2. change the value to Number
3. change the colour to red.

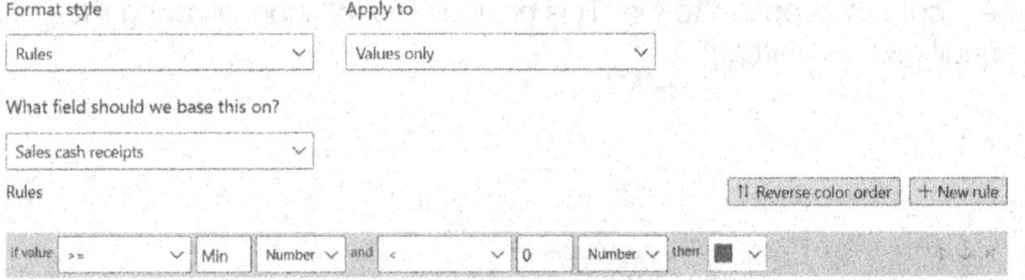

I then click OK, and my **Sales cash receipt** measure is now styled red. It is important to note that conditional formatting will only be applied to this measure within the visualisation. If I remove the measure and place it back into the same visualisation, the conditional formatting will be lost.

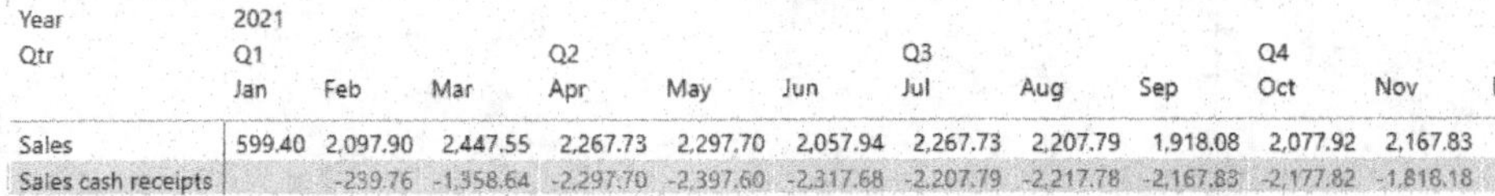

Year	2021										
Qtr	Q1			Q2			Q3			Q4	
	Jan	Feb	Mar	Apr	May	Jun	Jul	Aug	Sep	Oct	Nov
Sales	599.40	2,097.90	2,447.55	2,267.73	2,297.70	2,057.94	2,267.73	2,207.79	1,918.08	2,077.92	2,167.83
Sales cash receipts		-239.76	-1,358.64	-2,297.70	-2,397.60	-2,317.68	-2,207.79	-2,217.78	-2,167.83	-2,177.82	-1,818.18

To format the measure with brackets for negative values, I click on the measure, and navigate to the 'Measure tools' tab on the Ribbon:

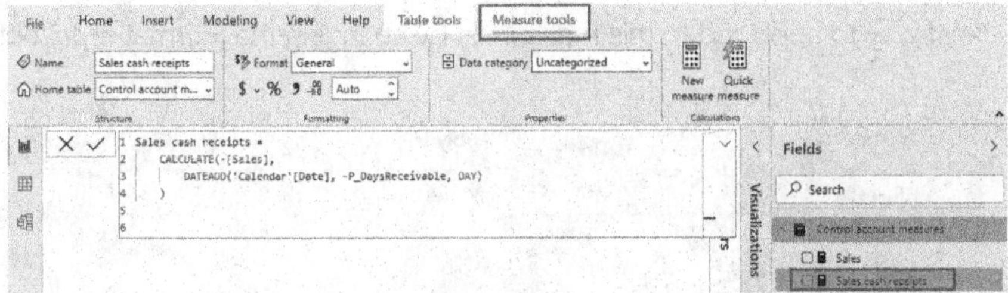

I then change the Format to "$#,##0.00;($#,##0.00);\- ; \-". This will wrap brackets around negative numbers, and present blank numbers as a dash ("-"):

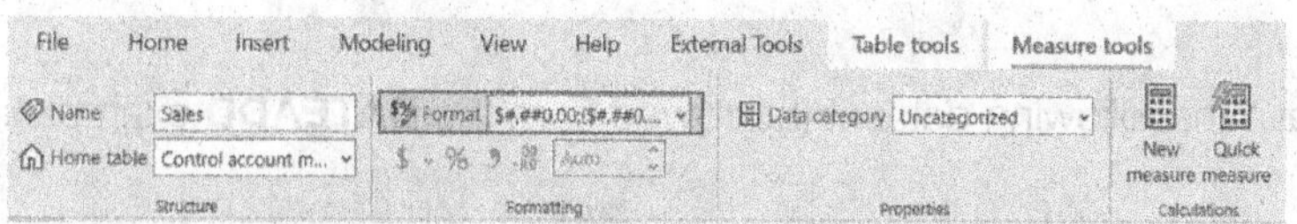

For consistency, I should also apply the same Formatting settings to the **Sales** measure.

The measures should now look like this:

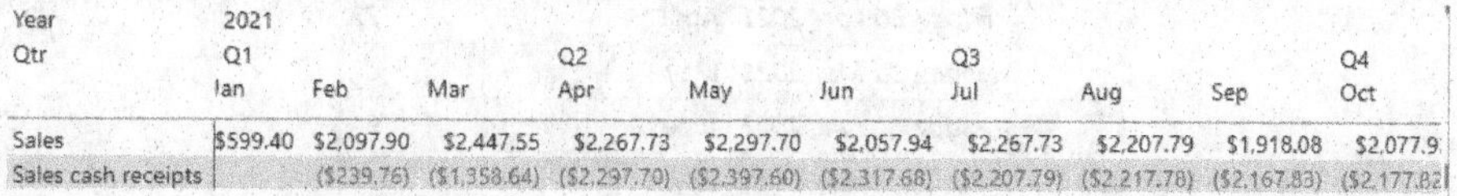

Year	2021									
Qtr	Q1			Q2			Q3			Q4
	Jan	Feb	Mar	Apr	May	Jun	Jul	Aug	Sep	Oct
Sales	$599.40	$2,097.90	$2,447.55	$2,267.73	$2,297.70	$2,057.94	$2,267.73	$2,207.79	$1,918.08	$2,077.9
Sales cash receipts		($239.76)	($1,358.64)	($2,297.70)	($2,397.60)	($2,317.68)	($2,207.79)	($2,217.78)	($2,167.83)	($2,177.82

For those of a nervous disposition, who pay meticulous attention to *detali,* you may not be comfortable with the non-alignment of the digits in Sales, due to the brackets for negative numbers. If this is of major concern to you:

1. Note that the Excel custom number format "$#,0.00_);($#,0.00);\- ; \-", in which the underscore "makes space" for the following character, here a close bracket, does not work presently for Power BI. Maybe one day!
2. Seek therapy.

At this point, I need two more measures to complete my sales control account: **Sales opening receivables** and **Sales closing receivables**. To calculate the **Sales opening receivables** measure, I need to create two helper measures. These two measures should calculate the cumulative amounts of **Sales** and **Sales cash receipts**.

Calculating the cumulative amounts can be tricky. However, there is a way to do it, using the **FILTER, ALL** and **MAX** functions. If we are going to play sweet music here, I should at least introduce the band.

The FILTER function

The **FILTER** function returns a table that represents a subset of another table or expression. It has the following syntax:

FILTER(table, filter)

where:

- **table** is the **table** to be filtered, which can also be an expression that results in a **table**
- **filter** is a Boolean expression (*i.e.* something that may have only one of two values, such as 1 or 0, or yes / no) that is to be evaluated for each row of the table, *e.g.* **[Sales]** > 1000 or **[Country]** = "Australia".

I can use the **FILTER** function to reduce the number of rows in the table that I am working with and use only specific data in calculations. However, this function is not to be used independently, but rather as a function that is embedded in other functions that require a table as an argument.

Example

Imagine I have the following dataset (borrowed from the **DATEADD** example):

Date	Month Name	Sales
Sunday, 31 January 2021	January	*0*
Sunday, 28 February 2021	February	*50*
Wednesday, 31 March 2021	March	*60*
Friday, 30 April 2021	April	*73*
Monday, 31 May 2021	May	*87*
Wednesday, 30 June 2021	June	*94*
Saturday, 31 July 2021	July	*115*
Tuesday, 31 August 2021	August	*122*
Thursday, 30 September 2021	September	*116*
Sunday, 31 October 2021	October	*144*
Tuesday, 30 November 2021	November	*138*

From this dataset, I can create the following Card visualisation in Power BI that calculates the total sales in my dataset. I have borrowed the **Total sales** measure I created earlier in the **DATEADD** example to display on a Card visualisation:

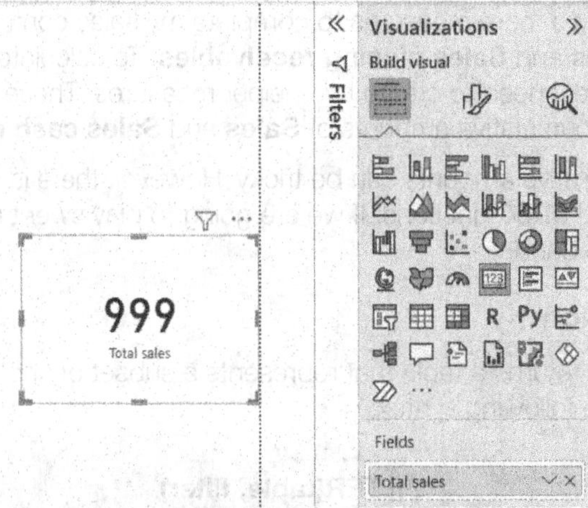

Up until extremely recently (as at the time of writing), I had to embed the **FILTER** function in the **CALCULATE** function to calculate the total sales in the month of June:

```
Total sales June =
CALCULATE([Total sales],
    FILTER(Sales,
    Sales[Month Name] = "June"
    )
)
```

```
Total sales June =
CALCULATE([Total sales],
 FILTER(Sales,
```

```
 Sales[Month Name] = "June"
 )
)
```

We needed **FILTER** here. You might be thinking, why can't I just use the condition

```
Sales[Month Name] = "June"
```

There were two reasons:

- **CALCULATE** is a great "starter" function in Power Query (Get & Transform) and Power BI. It has built-in "safety features" that allow formulae to be calculated quickly and stops many slow computations being formulated
- Filtering is one such feature that if constructed badly may slow down a model significantly. Therefore, raw filtering with **CALCULATE** is prevented in the code. To circumvent this, and switch off the safety features, you *had* to use **FILTER**. It's like driving with a seatbelt on.

Plotting this measure onto a card visualisation provides the following result:

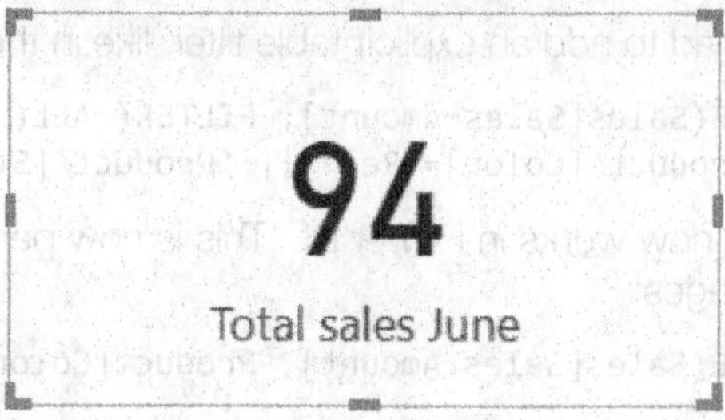

I can check that this is the sales amount in June, when comparing this result with the table:

Date	Total sales
Sunday, 31 January 2021	0
Sunday, 28 February 2021	50
Wednesday, 31 March 2021	60
Friday, 30 April 2021	73
Monday, 31 May 2021	87
Wednesday, 30 June 2021	94
Saturday, 31 July 2021	115
Tuesday, 31 August 2021	122
Thursday, 30 September 2021	116
Sunday, 31 October 2021	144
Tuesday, 30 November 2021	138
Total	**999**

Power BI – CALCULATE function update

Having mentioned this **FILTER** technique, Power BI has now updated the **CALCULATE** function. As an example, let's say you needed to calculate the sales amount for products that are either red or are part of a product line for women (style indicator 'W'). You already have a measure, **Sales Amount**, which is defined as:

```
Sales Amount := SUM(Sales[SalesAmount])
```

You might be tempted to try the following "old" Power BI DAX:

```
SalesRedW := CALCULATE(Sales[Sales Amount], Product[Color] = "Red" ||
Product[Style] = "W")
```

Unfortunately, this would not work:

```
SalesRedW := CALCULATE(Sales[Sales Amount],'Product'[Color]="Red"||'Product'[Style]="W")
```

The expression contains multiple columns, but only a single column can be used in a True/False expression that is used as a table filter expression.

To make this work, you had to add an explicit table filter, like in the following example:

```
SalesRedW := CALCULATE(Sales[Sales Amount], FILTER( ALL( 'Product'[Color],
'Product'[Style]), 'Product'[Color]="Red" || 'Product'[Style]="W"))
```

However, the first syntax now works in Power BI. This is now perfectly valid DAX and will work without error messages:

```
SalesRedW := CALCULATE(Sales[Sales Amount], Product[Color] = "Red" ||
Product[Style] = "W")
```

This makes it easier to build calculations that require multiple filters and complex combinations of conditions, such as **OR** (**||**) and **AND** (**&&**), as long as you are working in Power BI. If you are using **DAX** in Excel, presently, the **FILTER** technique must still be used. Even here, I will still employ **FILTER**, because I plan to use it to *remove* a filter.

The ALL function

The **ALL** function returns all the records in a table, or all the values in a column ignoring any filters that might have been applied for the field under scrutiny. This function is useful for clearing filters and creating calculations in all rows, in a given table.

The **ALL** function has the following syntax:

ALL(table or **column)**

where it accepts either a **table** or a **column** as an input.

Example

From my **FILTER** function example, I have the following table:

Date	Total sales
31-Jan-21	0
28-Feb-21	50
31-Mar-21	60
30-Apr-21	73
31-May-21	87
30-Jun-21	94
31-Jul-21	115
31-Aug-21	122
30-Sep-21	116
31-Oct-21	144
30-Nov-21	138
Total	**999**

If I include the **Total sales June** measure, I get the following result:

Date	Total sales	Total sales June
31-Jan-21	0	
28-Feb-21	50	
31-Mar-21	60	
30-Apr-21	73	
31-May-21	87	
30-Jun-21	94	94
31-Jul-21	115	
31-Aug-21	122	
30-Sep-21	116	
31-Oct-21	144	
30-Nov-21	138	
Total	**999**	**94**

If I wanted the total sales of June to be displayed on every row, I can modify the **Total sales June** function by adding an **ALL** function in it thus:

```
Total sales June =
CALCULATE([Total sales],
    FILTER(
        ALL(Sales),
        Sales[Month Name] = "June"
    )
)
```

```
Total sales June =
CALCULATE([Total sales],
 FILTER(
 ALL(Sales),
 Sales[Month Name] = "June"
 )
)
```

Do you see why **FILTER** is necessary here, even given the recent improvements in **CALCULATE**? The **FILTER** function is creating / ensuring I have a full set of **Sales** data, hence removing any filters that may cause issues for subsequent sales aggregation.

The measure will now return with the following result:

Date	Total sales	Total sales June
31-Jan-21	0	94
28-Feb-21	50	94
31-Mar-21	60	94
30-Apr-21	73	94
31-May-21	87	94
30-Jun-21	94	94
31-Jul-21	115	94
31-Aug-21	122	94
30-Sep-21	116	94
31-Oct-21	144	94
30-Nov-21	138	94

The **ALL** function ignores any filters. This includes the filters applied at each row and allows the measure to calculate the total sales for June for each row. This may be useful if I wanted to compare the sales of June to each month. However, that's not what I am going to do here.

The MAX function

The **MAX** function returns with the largest value in a column, or between two scalar expressions.

The **MAX** function has the following syntax:

MAX(column)

MAX(expression1, expression2)

- where **column** is a field in a table
- **expression1** and **expression2** are any **DAX** expressions that return with single values.

Example

I can write the following measure:

```
Max sales = MAX(Sales[Sales])
```

```
Max sales = MAX(Sales[Sales])
```

This measure will return with the highest sales value in the table:

Cumulative sales measures

Let's return to the model. Now that I have covered all the necessary functions, I can finally create the cumulative measures that I need.

```
Sales cum =
    CALCULATE([Sales],
        FILTER(
            ALL('Calendar'),
            'Calendar'[Date] <= MAX('Calendar'[Date])
            )
        )
```

```
Sales cum =
 CALCULATE([Sales],
 FILTER(
 ALL('Calendar'),
 'Calendar'[Date] <= MAX('Calendar'[Date])
 )
 )
```

This measure will calculate the cumulative amounts of sales. The **ALL('Calendar')** segment will allow the measure to look at the entire dataset's dates. The filter expression of **'Calendar'[Date] <= MAX('Calendar[Date])** says return with the rows where any of the calendar dates from the entire table is less than the maximum date in the current row context (current date in row or column).

Next, I will calculate the cumulative amount for the cash receipts:

```
Sales cash receipts cum =
    CALCULATE([Sales cash receipts],
        FILTER(
            ALL('Calendar'),
            'Calendar'[Date] <= MAX('Calendar'[Date])
            )
        )
```

```
Sales cash receipts cum =
 CALCULATE([Sales cash receipts],
 FILTER(
```

```
ALL('Calendar'),
'Calendar'[Date] <= MAX('Calendar'[Date])
)
)
```

Do you see the technique replicated? Just like the **Sales cum** measure, the **Sales cash receipts cum** measure will calculate the cumulative amounts for the cash receipts. I shall plot the **Sales cum** and **Sales cash receipts cum** measures into the visualisation as an example. Note I will not apply the formatting to them, as they will be removed in the completed control account:

Year	2021									
Qtr	Q1			Q2			Q3			Q4
	Jan	Feb	Mar	Apr	May	Jun	Jul	Aug	Sep	Oct
Sales	$599.40	$2,097.90	$2,447.55	$2,267.73	$2,297.70	$2,057.94	$2,267.73	$2,207.79	$1,918.08	$2,(
Sales cash receipts		($239.76)	($1,358.64)	($2,297.70)	($2,397.60)	($2,317.68)	($2,207.79)	($2,217.78)	($2,167.83)	($2.1
Sales cum	599.40	2,697.30	5,144.85	7,412.58	9,710.28	11,768.22	14,035.95	16,243.74	18,161.82	20.:
Sales cash receipts cum		-239.76	-1,598.40	-3,896.10	-6,293.70	-8,611.38	-10,819.17	-13,036.95	-15,204.78	-17.:

The **Sales opening receivables** measure is as follows:

```
Sales opening receivables =
    CALCULATE([Sales cum] + [Sales cash receipts cum],
        PREVIOUSDAY('Calendar'[Date])
    )
```

```
Sales opening receivables =
 CALCULATE([Sales cum] + [Sales cash receipts cum],
 PREVIOUSDAY('Calendar'[Date])
 )
```

Finally, the **Sales closing receivables** measure can be calculated as:

```
Sales closing receivables =
[Sales opening receivables] + [Sales] + [Sales cash receipts]
```

```
Sales closing receivables =
[Sales opening receivables] + [Sales] + [Sales cash receipts]
```

Sales control account

I can then place the **Sales closing receivables** and **Sales opening receivables** measures in the right order in the Values area, then apply the correct formatting. I have also removed the **Sales cum** and **Sales cash receipts cum** measures:

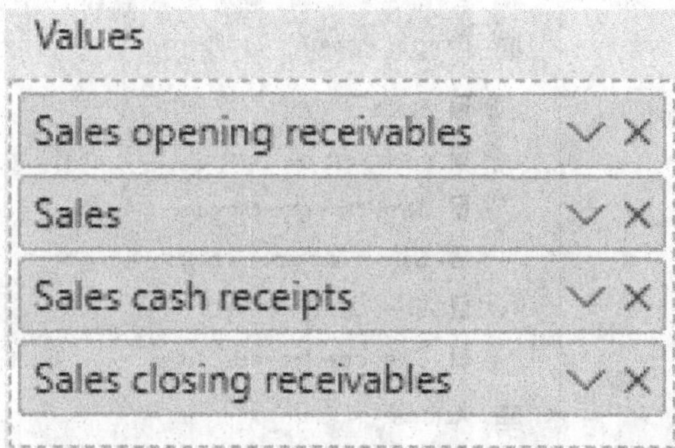

This will result in the visualisation:

Year	2021									
Qtr	Q1			Q2			Q3			Q4
	Jan	Feb	Mar	Apr	May	Jun	Jul	Aug	Sep	Oc
Sales opening receivables		$599.40	$2,457.54	$3,546.45	$3,516.48	$3,416.58	$3,156.84	$3,216.78	$3,206.79	$
Sales	$599.40	$2,097.90	$2,447.55	$2,267.73	$2,297.70	$2,057.94	$2,267.73	$2,207.79	$1,918.08	$
Sales cash receipts		($239.76)	($1,358.64)	($2,297.70)	($2,397.60)	($2,317.68)	($2,207.79)	($2,217.78)	($2,167.83)	($2
Sales closing receivables	$599.40	$2,457.54	$3,546.45	$3,516.48	$3,416.58	$3,156.84	$3,216.78	$3,206.79	$2,957.04	$

This method of calculating the opening and closing receivables allows us to drill into and out of the data while having the opening and closing receivables remain the same.

Notice the opening and closing receivables for quarters 1 and 2 in my data:

Year	2021									
Qtr	Q1			Q2			Q3			Q4
	Jan	Feb	Mar	Apr	May	Jun	Jul	Aug	Sep	Oc
Sales opening receivables		$599.40	$2,457.54	$3,546.45	$3,516.48	$3,416.58	$3,156.84	$3,216.78	$3,206.79	$
Sales	$599.40	$2,097.90	$2,447.55	$2,267.73	$2,297.70	$2,057.94	$2,267.73	$2,207.79	$1,918.08	$
Sales cash receipts		($239.76)	($1,358.64)	($2,297.70)	($2,397.60)	($2,317.68)	($2,207.79)	($2,217.78)	($2,167.83)	($2
Sales closing receivables	$599.40	$2,457.54	$3,546.45	$3,516.48	$3,416.58	$3,156.84	$3,216.78	$3,206.79	$2,957.04	$

If I use the drill up option, I will see the same opening and closing receivables, while the **Sales** and **Sales cash receipts** amounts will recalculate to the respective date level:

Year	2021			
	Qtr 1	Qtr 2	Qtr 3	Qtr 4
Sales opening receivables		$3,546.45	$3,156.84	$2,957.04
Sales	$5,144.85	$6,623.37	$6,393.60	$6,483.51
Sales cash receipts	($1,598.40)	($7,012.98)	($6,593.40)	($6,283.71)
Sales closing receivables	$3,546.45	$3,156.84	$2,957.04	$3,156.84

This method of calculating the control accounts will be adopted similarly for every control account. I have explained this in detail for the sales control account, but since the other accounts work in the same way I will not be repeating this explanation each time.

Before I move on, it is clear that as the model develops and I add more control accounts, I am going to have many measures. Although they are held in the same table, I want to keep the measures neatly organised within that table by grouping them into folders.

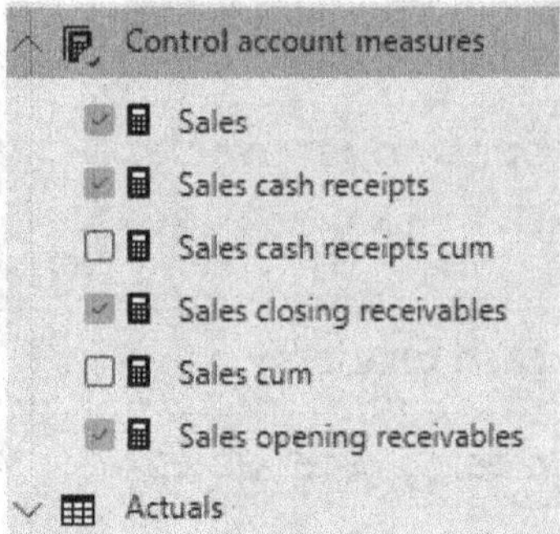

I navigate to the Model view on the left-hand side of the report. Note that:

- your tables will probably not be organised in the same way as the next image
- there are more tables that are not shown below: I have only shown the tables that are relevant to the current measures
- to organise them in the same way, simply click and drag and use the magnification settings as required.

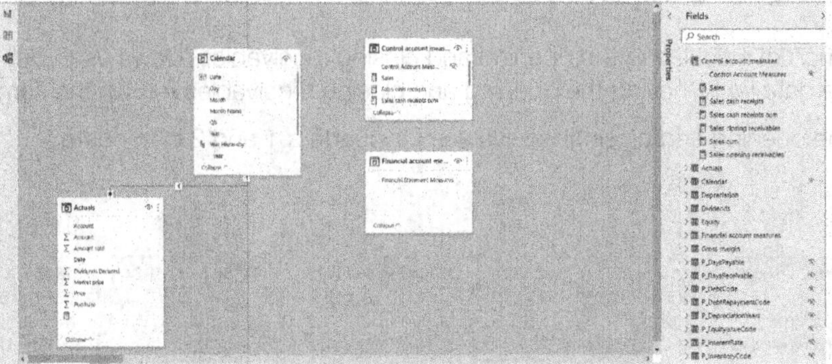

I can now group the Sales measures together in what is called a 'Display folder'. To do this, I highlight all the Sales measures in the Fields list.

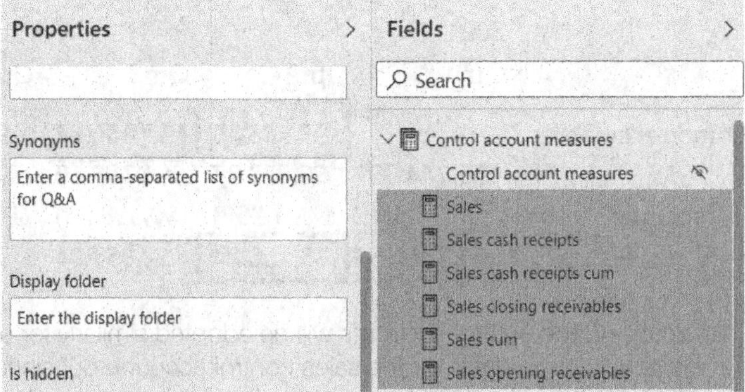

To create a 'Display folder', I enter a name for the folder where it says, 'Enter the display folder'.

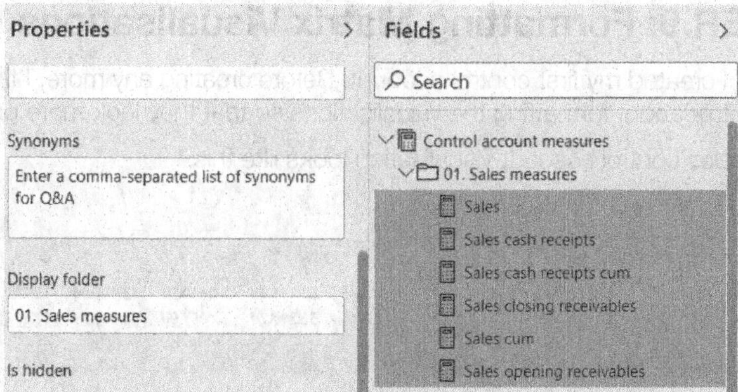

If I navigate back to the Report view, I can see that all my sales measures have been grouped into a display folder **01. Sales measures**.

Organising my measures into folders is extra work, but it's good practice, and will help me when I have lots of measures in one table. Please note that I will be creating display folders for each set of measures that belong to one control account in a similar fashion.

Next!

CHAPTER 9: Formatting Matrix Visualisations

Last chapter, I created my first control account. Before creating any more, I think it is a good time to talk about formatting the visualisations so that they look more presentable.

The current sales control account visualisation looks like this:

Year	2021								
Qtr	Q1			Q2			Q3		
	Jan	Feb	Mar	Apr	May	Jun	Jul	Aug	Sep
Sales opening receivables		$599.40	$2,457.54	$3,546.45	$3,516.48	$3,416.58	$3,156.84	$3,216.78	$3,206.79
Sales	$599.40	$2,097.90	$2,447.55	$2,267.73	$2,297.70	$2,057.94	$2,267.73	$2,207.79	$1,918.08
Sales cash receipts		($239.76)	($1,358.64)	($2,297.70)	($2,397.60)	($2,317.68)	($2,207.79)	($2,217.78)	($2,167.83)
Sales closing receivables	$599.40	$2,457.54	$3,546.45	$3,516.48	$3,416.58	$3,156.84	$3,216.78	$3,206.79	$2,957.04

I would like to colour the column headers to make the visualisation look more *appealing*.

With the visualisation selected, I head to the 'Format visual' pane on the Visualizations panel, then click on the 'Style presets' option. From the 'Style presets' dropdown, I select the 'Contrast alternating rows' option:

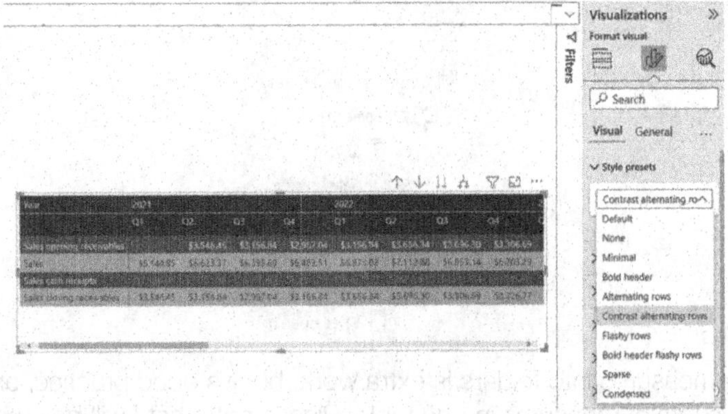

The latter colour settings make the visualisation more appealing already. However, I would like to make some changes. To begin with, I would like to use SumProduct's green colour (no harm in a bit of brand promotion, is there?). I click on the 'Column headers' option on the Visual panel, where I change the Background. I use the green identifiable with the following hex code: *#007033*

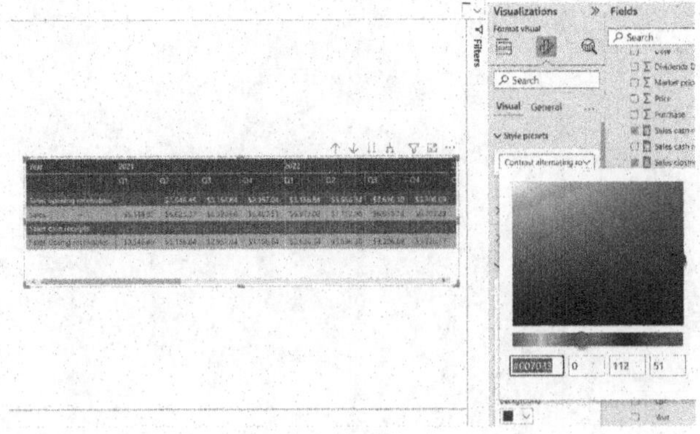

To change the colours of the rows, I click on the Values option on the Visualisations 'Format visual' panel:

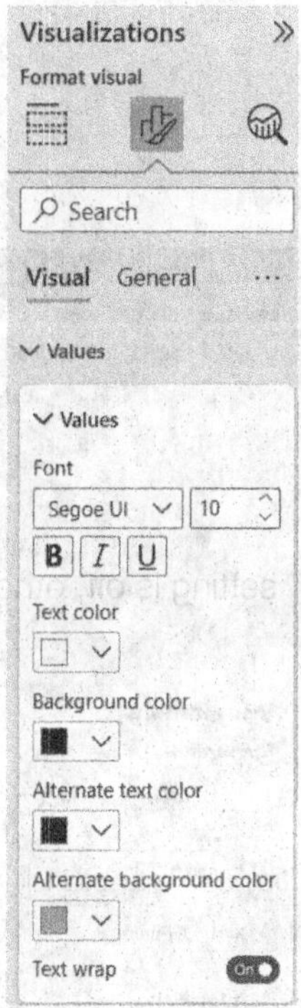

For my report, I have changed:

1. the 'Text' to black
2. the 'Background' to white
3. the 'Alternate text' to black
4. the 'Alternate background' to a lighter grey.

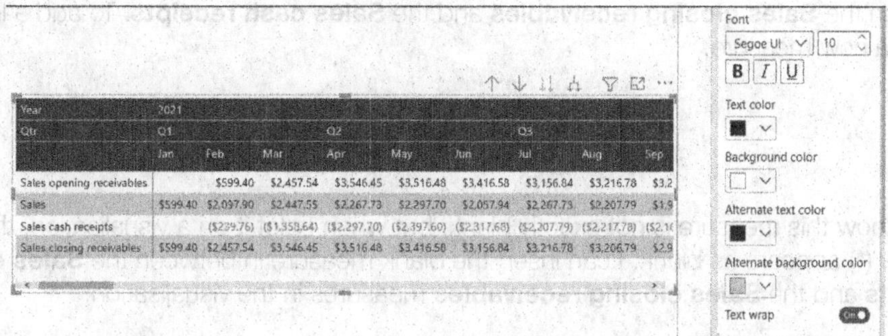

Year	2021								
Qtr	Q1			Q2			Q3		
	Jan	Feb	Mar	Apr	May	Jun	Jul	Aug	Sep
Sales opening receivables		$599.40	$2,457.54	$3,546.45	$3,516.48	$3,416.58	$3,156.84	$3,216.78	$3,2
Sales	$599.40	$2,097.90	$2,447.55	$2,267.73	$2,297.70	$2,057.94	$2,267.73	$2,207.79	$1,9
Sales cash receipts		($239.76)	($1,358.64)	($2,297.70)	($2,397.60)	($2,317.68)	($2,207.79)	($2,217.78)	($2.1
Sales closing receivables	$599.40	$2,457.54	$3,546.45	$3,516.48	$3,416.58	$3,156.84	$3,216.78	$3,206.79	$2,9

Then, I click on the Grid option, and change the 'Border' to a dark green colour:

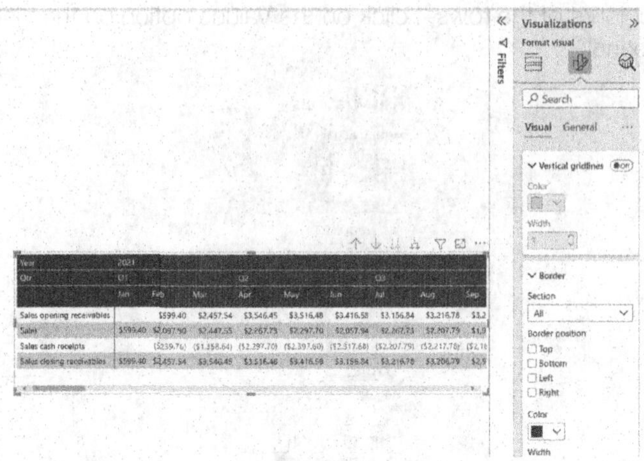

Also, I check the 'Horizontal gridli…' setting is off, otherwise I may have alignment issues as the matrix gets longer.

To make the last line in the control account stand out, I would like to darken the background of the **Sales closing receivables** (which I will look at shortly) and add a line between the **Sales closing receivables** and the **Sales cash receipts**. To add a line, I create a new measure.

```
* = " "
```

* = " "

Yes, I know this measure is not exactly blank, but when I plot it on a visualisation, the asterisk (*) appears as blank. I can insert the blank measure in between the **Sales cash receipts** and the **Sales closing receivables** measures in the visualisation:

Year	2021								
Qtr	Q1			Q2			Q3		
	Jan	Feb	Mar	Apr	May	Jun	Jul	Aug	Sep
Sales opening receivables		$599.40	$2,457.54	$3,546.45	$3,516.48	$3,416.58	$3,156.84	$3,216.78	$3,206.79
Sales	$599.40	$2,097.90	$2,447.55	$2,267.73	$2,297.70	$2,057.94	$2,267.73	$2,207.79	$1,918.08
Sales cash receipts		($239.76)	($1,358.64)	($2,297.70)	($2,397.60)	($2,317.68)	($2,207.79)	($2,217.78)	($2,167.83)
Sales closing receivables	$599.40	$2,457.54	$3,546.45	$3,516.48	$3,416.58	$3,156.84	$3,216.78	$3,206.79	$2,957.04

Values
Sales opening receivabl…
Sales
Sales cash receipts
*
Sales closing receivable…

In the 'Specific column' section on the formatting tab, I can change the background colour of the * measure to black. Also, I may toggle the 'Apply to header' option to On. It currently looks a little thick:

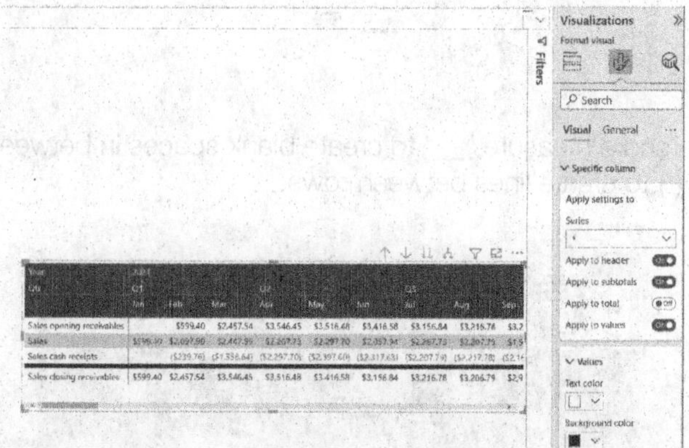

I can change this in the 'Options' section under the 'Grid' section in the 'Format visual' pane. Here, I set the 'Row padding' option to 1.

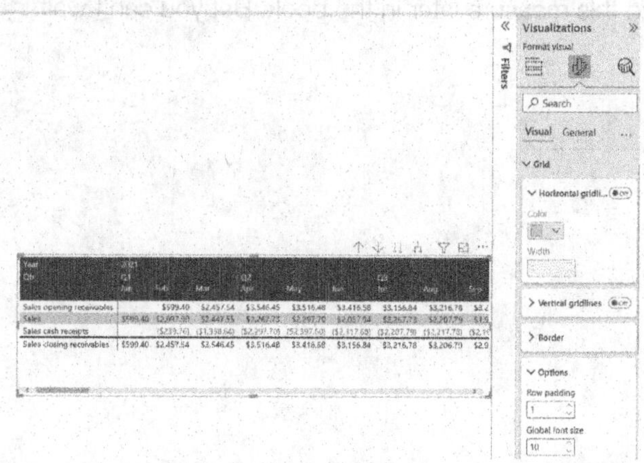

I would also like to give the **Sales closing receivables** measure a darker grey background relative to the other lines. This is done in the 'Specific column' section in the 'Format visual' pane. I should also toggle the 'Apply to header' option to On here:

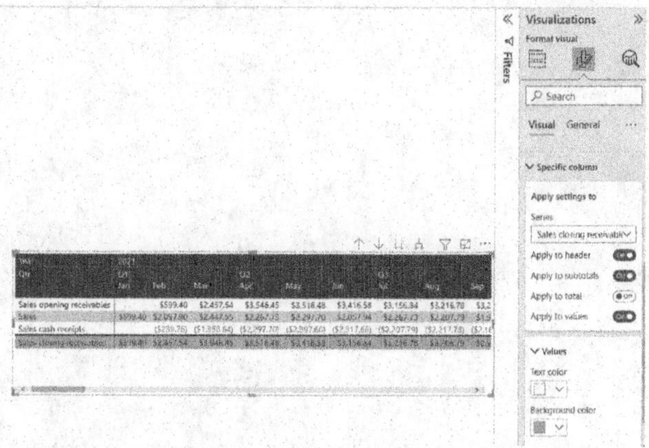

This will be the format that I will be using to style the subsequent control accounts.

I shall also create an additional measure that will serve as a blank row:

```
1 _ = ""
```

_ = ""

I will use the underscore measure "_" to create blank spaces in between rows, and the asterisk measure (*) to create lines between rows.

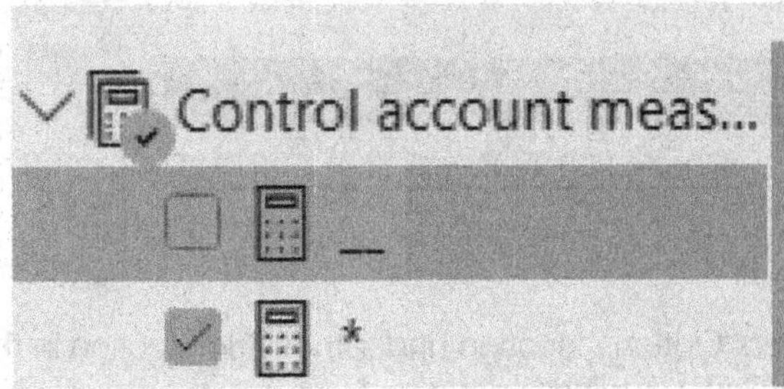

I will come back to this measure later in the book. Bet you can't wait.

CHAPTER 10: Calculating COGS (Part 1)

We are now at the next line of the Income Statement. Direct costs are those expenses that are immediately ("directly") attributable to a sale. If there is no sale, there is no cost. Examples of such expenses include direct labour costs (those involved in the sales process), and raw materials consumed in the creation of the sale. Do be careful here regarding the latter illustration: materials may be purchased at any time, but it is only when they have been sold that they are displayed on the Income Statement. Until then they are tucked away on the Balance Sheet – but more on that shortly.

As you may imagine, this complicates things.

Since I want to crawl before I walk before I run, this section introduces direct costs by assuming that Costs of Goods Sold (COGS) is just one expense item and that there is no "storage of costs" elsewhere first. In other words, this chapter ignores the direct costs of materials (*i.e.* the inventory consumed). However, if you think I am hardly going to talk about inventory, I will warn you, this book goes for overkill on the subject later!

With this borne in mind, I will again need to calculate the four line items that comprise the COGS control account:

1. COGS opening payables
2. COGS
3. COGS cash payments
4. COGS closing payables.

COGS opening and closing payables are simply functions of the COGS and COGS cash payments, analogous to the process adopted for **Sales**. These will be straightforward, but this time I do *not* begin with creating a measure for COGS. First, I actually need to calculate that number – and with the data from our example, I will begin by constructing a **Gross margin** measure.

The **Gross margin** measure is calculated as:

```
Gross margin = MAX('Gross margin'[Gross margin])
```

```
Gross margin = MAX('Gross margin'[Gross margin])
```

Now do be careful here: "margin" refers to a percentage or proportion, whereas "profit" is an absolute amount. For example, if sales were $200 and COGS were $140, then the Gross Profit would be $60 ($200 less $140), and the gross margin would be 30% (the $60 profit divided by the $200 sales achieved). Clearly, COGS may be calculated as the sales multiplied by (1 – gross margin) (*e.g.* $200 x (1 – 30%) = $140). This is how I will create my results here.

I use the **MAX** function so that I can select different gross margin amounts in a slicer, with the result that the **MAX** function will evaluate to whatever the maximum value is in my selection (*i.e.* it ensures no issue if more than one value is selected in the slicer).

For example, I can create a Slicer visualisation with the **Gross margin** column (note this is the *column*, not the measure I created a moment ago), by defining the Field in the Values area as follows (note the icon used):

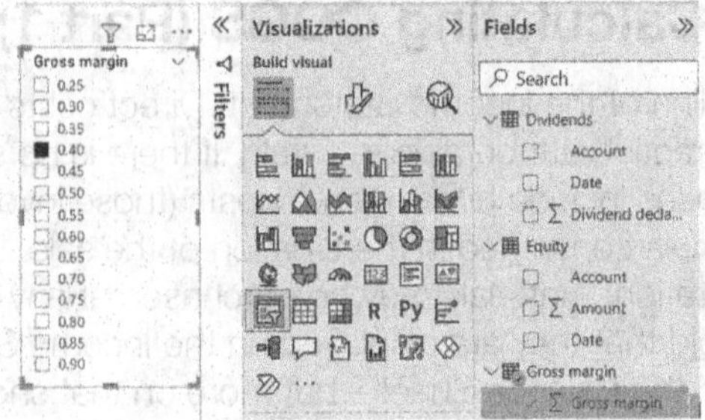

To get the Slicer in this format, choose ‘List’ from the Slicer dropdown:

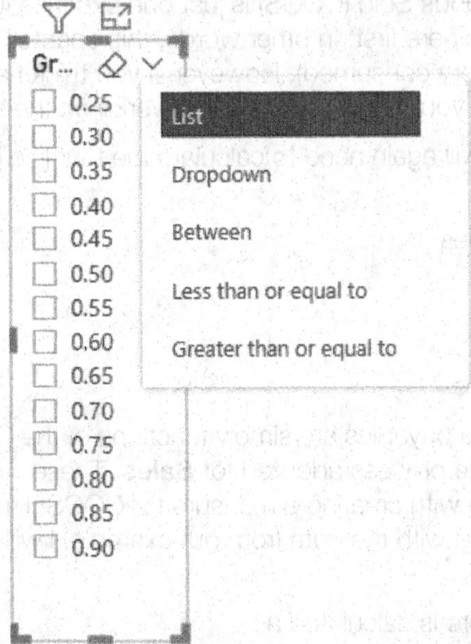

Selecting different gross margin column amounts will change the result of the **Gross margin** measure, which I have added as a card visualisation here *e.g.*

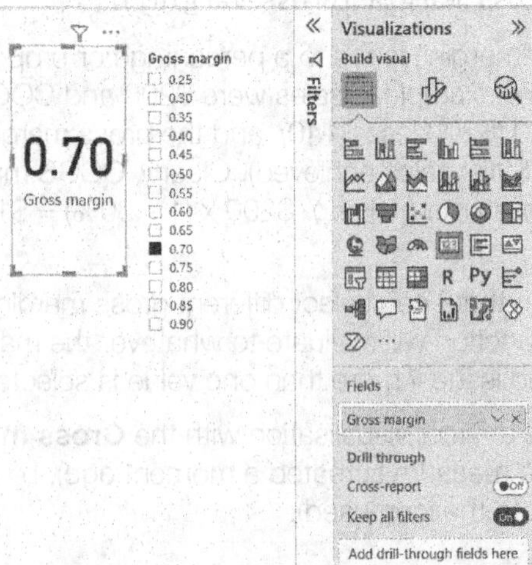

This will look better as a percentage, so I change the formatting on the measure **Gross margin** to percentage. I also change the formatting on the field Gross margin to percentage to make the slicer format match.

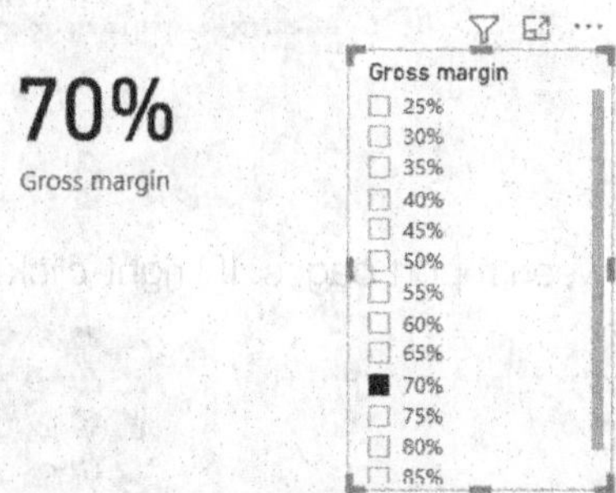

This will allow me to dynamically change the **Gross margin** value – and hence allows for built-in sensitivity analysis.

My next measure is **COGS** itself. This is calculated using the following **DAX** code:

```
COGS = [Sales] * (1 - [Gross margin])
```

COGS = [Sales] * (1 - [Gross margin])

If I plot this measure in a visualisation together with the above slicer, I can demonstrate how the **Gross margin** may be changed dynamically:

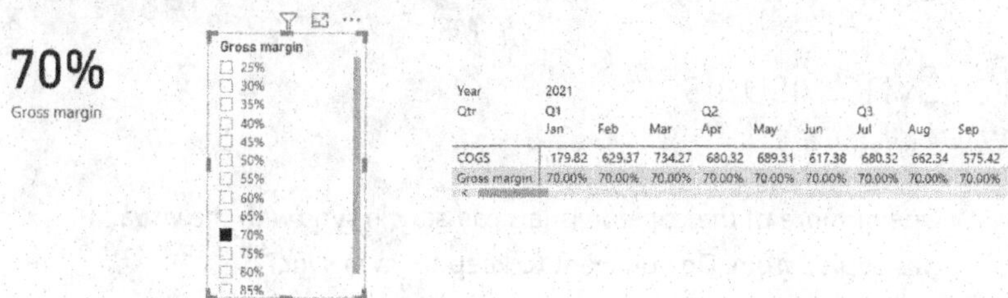

Year	2021								
Qtr	Q1			Q2			Q3		
	Jan	Feb	Mar	Apr	May	Jun	Jul	Aug	Sep
COGS	179.82	629.37	734.27	680.32	689.31	617.38	680.32	662.34	575.42
Gross margin	70.00%	70.00%	70.00%	70.00%	70.00%	70.00%	70.00%	70.00%	70.00%

I can change the **Gross margin** to 80% and dynamically calculate the new **COGS** values, *viz.*

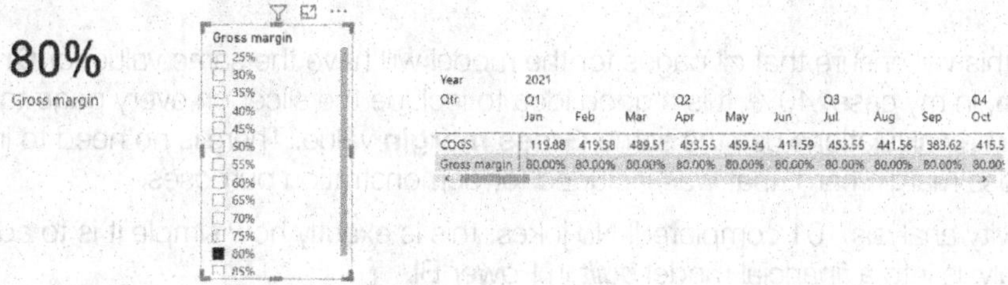

Year	2021									
Qtr	Q1			Q2			Q3			Q4
	Jan	Feb	Mar	Apr	May	Jun	Jul	Aug	Sep	Oct
COGS	119.88	419.58	489.51	453.55	459.54	411.59	453.55	441.56	383.62	415.5
Gross margin	80.00%	80.00%	80.00%	80.00%	80.00%	80.00%	80.00%	80.00%	80.00%	80.00

The **Gross margin** will now be set to 40% for illustration purposes in this model.

40%

Gross margin

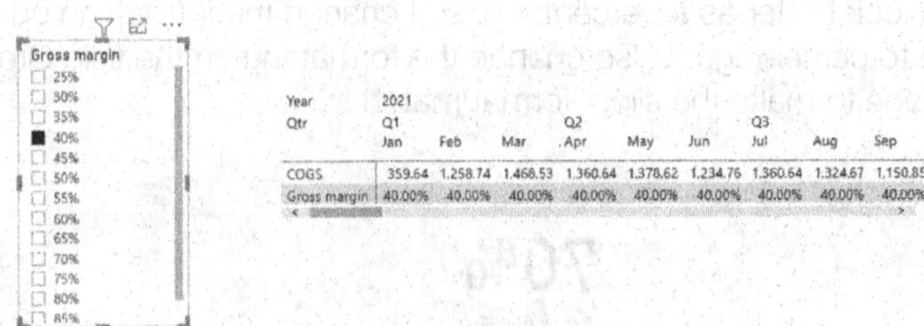

The slicer can be copied between report pages. If I right-click I have options:

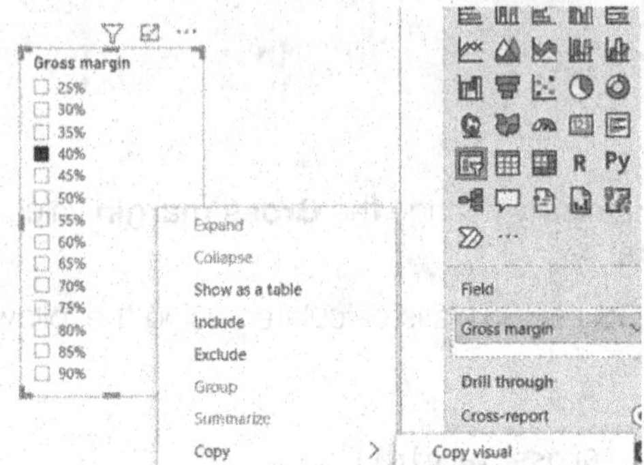

I can then use **CTRL** + **V** to paste onto another page. When I do this, I am given the option of synchronising the copied slicer with the original:

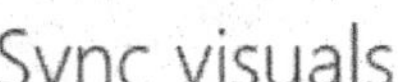

One or more of the copied visuals can stay in sync with the visual it was copied from. Do you want to keep them in sync?

Doing this will ensure that all pages for the model will have the same value for **Gross margin**, in my case, 40%. It is a good idea to include the slicer on every page to ensure that all the calculations use the same **Gross margin** value. There is no need to include the Gross margin card, that was included for demonstration purposes.

Sensitivity analysis 101 completed! No jokes: this is exactly how simple it is to add "what-if?" analysis into a financial model *built* in Power BI.

As the point of this book is to discuss and explore alternative approaches, I would like to introduce an alternative to the **DATEADD** method used for the **Sales cash receipts** measure earlier, when now defining the similar **COGS cash payments** calculation. This involves using the **USERELATIONSHIP** measure, mentioned earlier. Before I can do that though, I will need to set up the framework for this to work.

First, I go to the Data view of the model. I sort **Actuals** by ascending **Date**:

I check the format of the columns. I see that **Purchase** has format 'Whole Number', so I change this to General, which will allow for decimal places. This will help with later calculations.

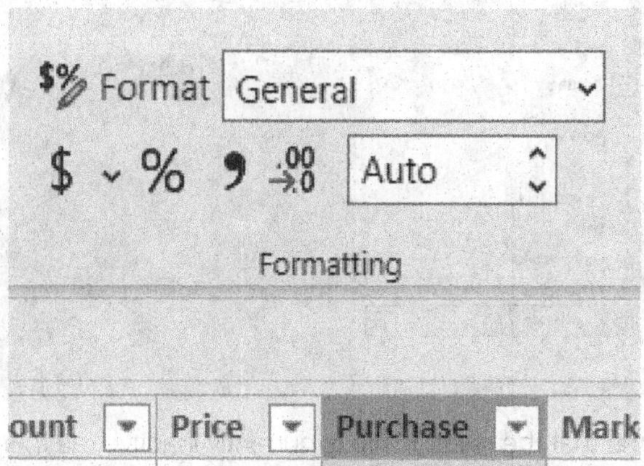

I need to create a calculated column in the **Actuals** table to replicate what **DATEADD** does in **DAX**, except I will compute it in the table. Note that I must be in the Data view to create a calculated column. On the Home tab on the Ribbon, I click on the 'New column' option:

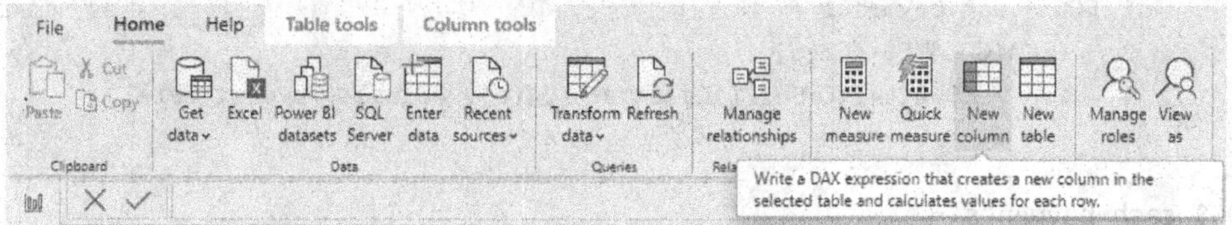

I create a **Payment date** column, where I will add the number of days payable to the current date of the transaction:

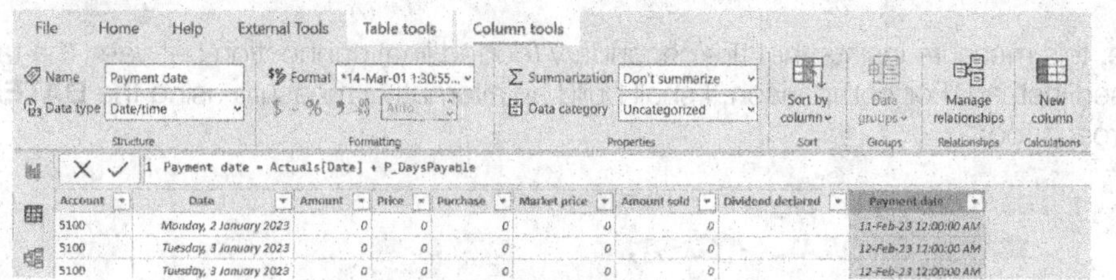

```
Payment date = Actuals[Date] + P_DaysPayable
```

This will mimic shifting the dates by the number of days payable in **DAX**. The data type defaults to Date/time, which I change to Date.

Next, I shall create a relationship between the **Actuals** table and the **Calendar** table using this newly defined **Payment date** column. In the Model view, I click on **Payment date** and drag it to **Date** on **Calendar**:

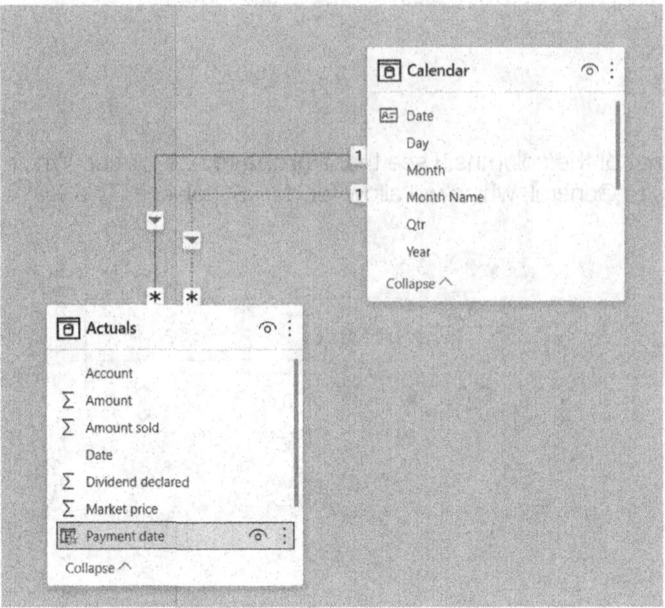

The dotted line means that the relationship is currently inactive, as there is already a relationship between the two tables (multiple relationships cannot be active at the same time).

This is where the **USERELATIONSHIP** function comes in handy as I go back to the Report view and create the **COGS cash payments** measure:

```
COGS cash payments =
    CALCULATE(-[COGS],
        USERELATIONSHIP('Calendar'[Date], Actuals[Payment date])
    )
```

```
COGS cash payments =
 CALCULATE(-[COGS],
 USERELATIONSHIP('Calendar'[Date], Actuals[Payment date])
 )
```

Here, this measure insists that the secondary (dotted line) connection between the tables is used instead. For comparison, I shall build an alternative measure using the **DATEADD** approach too:

```
COGS cash payments DATEADD =
    CALCULATE(-[COGS],
        DATEADD('Calendar'[Date], -P_DaysPayable, DAY)
    )
```

```
COGS cash payments DATEADD =
 CALCULATE(-[COGS],
 DATEADD('Calendar'[Date], -P_DaysPayable, DAY)
 )
```

Plotting both measures yield the following results:

Year	2021								
Qtr	Q1			Q2			Q3		
	Jan	Feb	Mar	Apr	May	Jun	Jul	Aug	Sep
COGS	359.64	1,258.74	1,468.53	1,360.64	1,378.62	1,234.76	1,360.64	1,324.67	1,150.85
COGS cash payments		-215.78	-959.04	-1,366.63	-1,534.46	-1,360.64	-1,222.78	-1,432.57	-1,246.75
COGS cash payments DATEADD		-215.78	-959.04	-1,366.63	-1,534.46	-1,360.64	-1,222.78	-1,432.57	-1,246.75

The next measures to create are the two cumulative measures for **COGS** and **COGS cash payments**, similar to the logic employed when I considered **Sales**. These are **COGS cum**:

```
COGS cum =
CALCULATE([COGS],
    FILTER(
        ALL('Calendar'),
        'Calendar'[Date] <= MAX('Calendar'[Date])
    )
)
```

```
COGS cum =
CALCULATE([COGS],
 FILTER(
 ALL('Calendar'),
 'Calendar'[Date] <= MAX('Calendar'[Date])
 )
)
```

and **COGS cash payments cum**:

```
COGS cash payments cum =
CALCULATE([COGS cash payments],
    FILTER(
        ALL('Calendar'),
        'Calendar'[Date] <= MAX('Calendar'[Date])
    )
)
```

```
COGS cash payments cum =
CALCULATE([COGS cash payments],
 FILTER(
 ALL('Calendar'),
 'Calendar'[Date] <= MAX('Calendar'[Date])
 )
)
```

I can now calculate the **COGS opening payables** measure:

```
COGS opening payables =
    CALCULATE([COGS cum] + [COGS cash payments cum],
        PREVIOUSDAY('Calendar'[Date])
    )
```

```
COGS opening payables =
 CALCULATE([COGS cum] + [COGS cash payments cum],
 PREVIOUSDAY('Calendar'[Date])
 )
```

and the **COGS closing payables**:

```
COGS closing payables =
[COGS opening payables] + [COGS] + [COGS cash payments]
```

```
COGS closing payables =
[COGS opening payables] + [COGS] + [COGS cash payments]
```

I am ready to construct the control account for **COGS.** I do not have to start from a blank matrix visualisation, instead I can copy the sales control account in the same way I copied the slicer (lazy modelling equals efficient modelling!). I click anywhere on the visual.

Year	2021								
Qtr	Q1			Q2			Q3		
	Jan	Feb	Mar	Apr	May	Jun	Jul	Aug	Sep
Sales opening receivables	-	$599.40	$2,457.54	$3,546.45	$3,516.48	$3,416.58	$3,156.84	$3,216.78	$3,206.79
Sales	$599.40	$2,097.90	$2,447.55	$2,267.73	$2,297.70	$2,057.94	$2,267.73	$2,207.79	$1,918.08
Sales cash receipts		($239.76)	($1,358.64)	($2,297.70)	($2,397.60)	($2,317.68)	($2,207.79)	($2,217.78)	($2,167.83)
Sales closing receivables	$599.40	$2,457.54	$3,546.45	$3,516.48	$3,416.58	$3,156.84	$3,216.78	$3,206.79	$2,957.04

I right-click and I have other options, including copy visual.

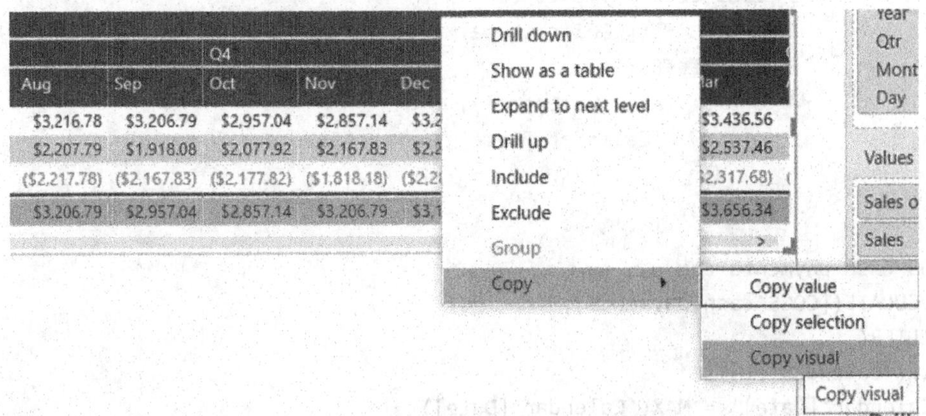

I can paste the visual using **CTRL** + **V** and move it where I want it on the sheet. I can then remove the **Sales** fields and use the **COGS** fields instead. After applying the formatting to the measures ("$#,##0.00;($#,##0.00);\- ; \-"), the control account for **COGS** is complete:

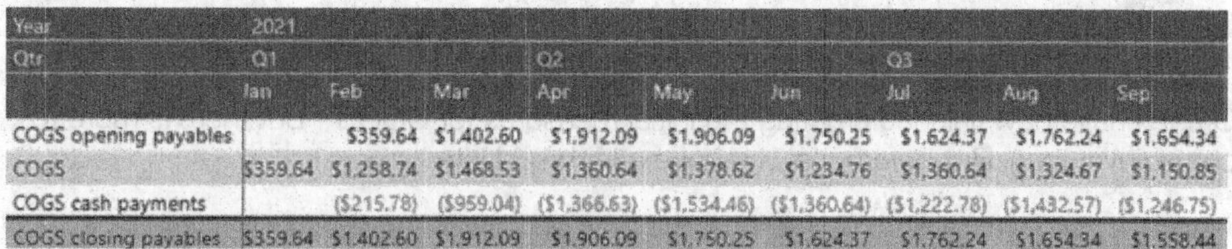

Year	2021								
Qtr	Q1			Q2			Q3		
	Jan	Feb	Mar	Apr	May	Jun	Jul	Aug	Sep
COGS opening payables		$359.64	$1,402.60	$1,912.09	$1,906.09	$1,750.25	$1,624.37	$1,762.24	$1,654.34
COGS	$359.64	$1,258.74	$1,468.53	$1,360.64	$1,378.62	$1,234.76	$1,360.64	$1,324.67	$1,150.85
COGS cash payments		($215.78)	($959.04)	($1,366.63)	($1,534.46)	($1,360.64)	($1,222.78)	($1,432.57)	($1,246.75)
COGS closing payables	$359.64	$1,402.60	$1,912.09	$1,906.09	$1,750.25	$1,624.37	$1,762.24	$1,654.34	$1,558.44

I should also remember to group my measures into a display folder:

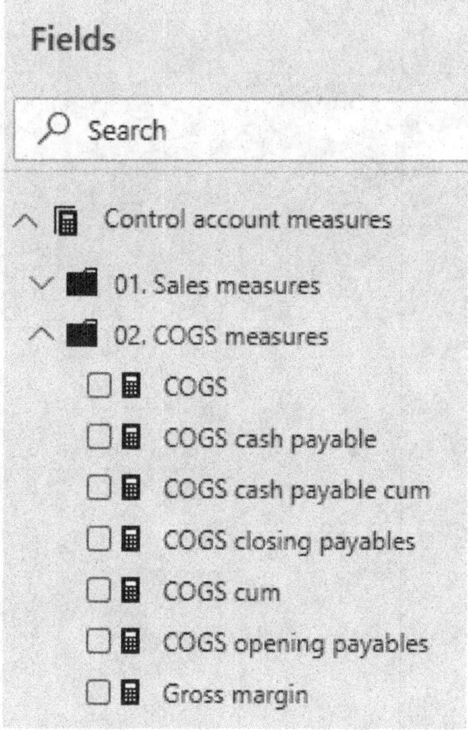

To organise the control accounts, I have grouped the **Sales** and **COGS** control accounts together on their own page. I have also included the **Gross margin** slicer, since the value of **Gross margin** impacts **COGS**:

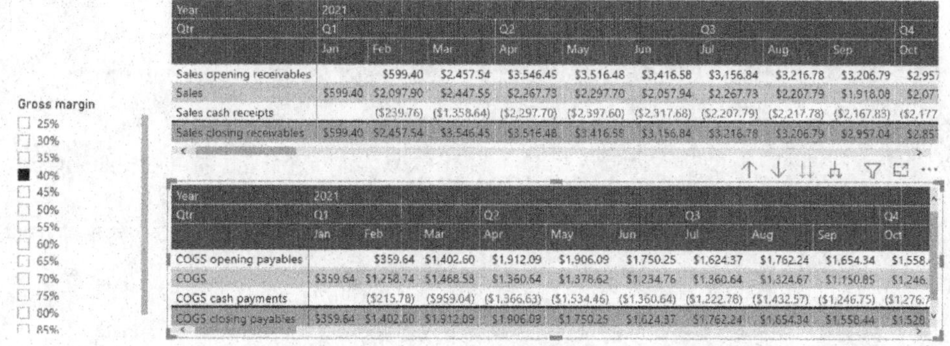

Year	2021									
Qtr	Q1			Q2			Q3			Q4
	Jan	Feb	Mar	Apr	May	Jun	Jul	Aug	Sep	Oct
Sales opening receivables		$599.40	$2,457.54	$3,546.45	$3,516.48	$3,416.58	$3,156.84	$3,216.78	$3,206.79	$2,957
Sales	$599.40	$2,097.90	$2,447.55	$2,267.73	$2,297.70	$2,057.94	$2,267.73	$2,207.79	$1,918.08	$2,07
Sales cash receipts		($239.76)	($1,358.64)	($2,297.70)	($2,397.60)	($2,317.68)	($2,207.79)	($2,217.78)	($2,167.83)	($2,177
Sales closing receivables	$599.40	$2,457.54	$3,546.45	$3,516.48	$3,416.58	$3,156.84	$3,216.78	$3,206.79	$2,957.04	$2,85

Year	2021									
Qtr	Q1			Q2			Q3			Q4
	Jan	Feb	Mar	Apr	May	Jun	Jul	Aug	Sep	Oct
COGS opening payables		$359.64	$1,402.60	$1,912.09	$1,906.09	$1,750.25	$1,624.37	$1,762.24	$1,654.34	$1,558.
COGS	$359.64	$1,258.74	$1,468.53	$1,360.64	$1,378.62	$1,234.76	$1,360.64	$1,324.67	$1,150.85	$1,246.
COGS cash payments		($215.78)	($959.04)	($1,366.63)	($1,534.46)	($1,360.64)	($1,222.78)	($1,432.57)	($1,246.75)	($1,276.7
COGS closing payables	$359.64	$1,402.60	$1,912.09	$1,906.09	$1,750.25	$1,624.37	$1,762.24	$1,654.34	$1,558.44	$1,528.

Grouping the control accounts separately does not make any material difference. All the model needs is for the measures to have been created.

Great; I have now finished creating the initial measures for COGS – but there is more to come (inventory). But before that, I require a technical interlude.

CHAPTER 11: VAR Variables

Let's take a breath. Before I move on to create the **DAX** columns in my **Inventory (FIFO)** table, I need to discuss the general concept of variables first.

In programming, variables are names that are used to hold one or more values. These are then stored locally (in **DAX** it is stored in the measure). Therefore, instead of repeating values in multiple places in the code, the variable will hold the result of the calculation, table or result of an evaluation and it may be referred to accordingly. I will explain with examples, which you do not need to create for the model.

The syntax to declare a variable in **DAX** is '**VAR**' followed by the name of the variable, *e.g.*

```
Variable example =
VAR VariableName = "June"
```

```
Variable example =
VAR VariableName = "June"
```

With the variable named I can specify the value of the variable with an equals (=) sign. The value of the variable may be a single value, parameter, evaluation or even a table. For this example, I will keep it simple and use the above single value, 'June'. She was always nice to me.

Let's revisit an earlier illustration. Do you remember the measure, **Total sales June**?

```
Total sales June =
CALCULATE([Total Sales],
    FILTER(
        ALL(Sales),
        Sales[Month name] = "June"
    )
)
```

```
Total sales June =
CALCULATE([Total sales],
 FILTER(
 ALL(Sales),
 Sales[Month name] = "June"
 )
)
```

I can define a variable and assign it with the value of 'June' as follows.

```
Total sales June =
VAR MonthVariable = "June"


CALCULATE([Total sales],
    FILTER(
        ALL(Sales),
        Sales[Month name] = MonthVariable
    )
)
```

Notice all the red underlines in the **DAX** measure? This means that there is something wrong with the syntax. This is because **DAX** expects the '**Return**' function to be issued after defining variables in a measure:

```
Total sales June =
VAR MonthVariable = "June"

Return
CALCULATE([Total sales],
    FILTER(
        ALL(Sales),
        Sales[Month name] = MonthVariable
    )
)
```

```
Total sales June =
VAR MonthVariable = "June"
Return
CALCULATE([Total Sales],
 FILTER(
 ALL(Sales),
 Sales[Month Name] = MonthVariable
 )
)
```

This will *return* with the same result as before:

Month	Total Sales	Total sales June
Sunday, 31 January 2021	0	94
Sunday, 28 February 2021	50	94
Wednesday, 31 March 2021	60	94
Friday, 30 April 2021	73	94
Monday, 31 May 2021	87	94
Wednesday, 30 June 2021	94	94
Saturday, 31 July 2021	115	94
Tuesday, 31 August 2021	122	94
Thursday, 30 September 2021	116	94
Sunday, 31 October 2021	144	94
Tuesday, 30 November 2021	138	94

I can also assign entire expressions as a variable, for example:

```
Monthly sales compared to June =
VAR MonthVariable = "June"
VAR MonthSales =
CALCULATE([Total sales],
    FILTER(
        ALL(Sales),
        Sales[Month name] = MonthVariable
    )
)

Return
( [Total Sales] / MonthSales ) - 1
```

```
Monthly sales compared to June =
VAR MonthVariable = "June"
VAR MonthSales =
CALCULATE([Total sales],
 FILTER(
 ALL(Sales),
 Sales[Month name] = MonthVariable
 )
)
Return
( [Total Sales] / MonthSales ) - 1
```

There are two things I want to highlight here:

1. I can assign an expression as a variable (**MonthSales**). For example, this variable is assigned with the June sales number, which is 94. This means that every time this variable is called, it will return with the value of 94
2. Variables can refer to each other. For example, notice that the filter condition in the **MonthSales** variable refers to the **MonthVariable** in the above image.

Plotting this in the table visualisation yields:

Month	Total Sales	Total sales June	Monthly sales compared to June
Sunday, 31 January 2021	0	94	-100.00%
Sunday, 28 February 2021	50	94	-46.81%
Wednesday, 31 March 2021	60	94	-36.17%
Friday, 30 April 2021	73	94	-22.34%
Monday, 31 May 2021	87	94	-7.45%
Wednesday, 30 June 2021	94	94	0.00%
Saturday, 31 July 2021	115	94	22.34%
Tuesday, 31 August 2021	122	94	29.79%
Thursday, 30 September 2021	116	94	23.40%
Sunday, 31 October 2021	144	94	53.19%
Tuesday, 30 November 2021	138	94	46.81%

With variables it is easy to know which part of the code I need to change should I wish to create a measure for another month, say, August:

```
Monthly sales compared to August =
VAR MonthVariable = "August"
VAR MonthSales =
CALCULATE([Total sales],
    FILTER(
        ALL(Sales),
        Sales[Month name] = MonthVariable
    )
)

Return
( [Total Sales] / MonthSales ) - 1
```

```
Monthly sales compared to August =
VAR MonthVariable = "August"
VAR MonthSales =
CALCULATE([Total sales],
 FILTER(
 ALL(Sales),
 Sales[Month name] = MonthVariable
 )
)

Return
( [Total Sales] / MonthSales ) - 1
```

Month	Total Sales	Total sales June	Monthly sales compared to June	Monthly sales compared to August
Sunday, 31 January 2021	0	94	-100.00%	-100.00%
Sunday, 28 February 2021	50	94	-46.81%	-59.02%
Wednesday, 31 March 2021	60	94	-36.17%	-50.82%
Friday, 30 April 2021	73	94	-22.34%	-40.16%
Monday, 31 May 2021	87	94	-7.45%	-28.69%
Wednesday, 30 June 2021	94	94	0.00%	-22.95%
Saturday, 31 July 2021	115	94	22.34%	-5.74%
Tuesday, 31 August 2021	122	94	29.79%	0.00%
Thursday, 30 September 2021	116	94	23.40%	-4.92%
Sunday, 31 October 2021	144	94	53.19%	18.03%
Tuesday, 30 November 2021	138	94	46.81%	13.11%

Considerations with variables

Variables are a very useful tool when writing **DAX** measures. However, it is important to understand how they work, otherwise they may become quite a hindrance.

In a **DAX** measure, variables are calculated the first time they are called upon. For example, looking at the following measure:

```
Total sales June VAR =
VAR TotalSales = SUM(Sales[Sales])
VAR MonthSales =
CALCULATE(TotalSales,
    FILTER(
        ALL(Sales),
        Sales[Month name] = "June"
    )
)

Return
MonthSales
```

```
Total sales June VAR =
VAR TotalSales = SUM(Sales[Sales])
VAR MonthSales =
CALCULATE(TotalSales,
 FILTER(
```

```
    ALL(Sales),
    Sales[Month name] = "June"
    )
)

Return
MonthSales
```

I have created a variable **TotalSales** which calculates the sum of the sales column. I then have a **MonthSales** variable that calculates the **TotalSales** and filters the **TotalSales** results to the month of June. I would expect this measure to return with the sales pertaining to the month of June. However, plotting this measure onto a matrix visualisation yields the following results:

Month Name	Total Sales	Total sales June	Total sales June VAR
January	0	94	0
February	50	94	50
March	60	94	60
April	73	94	73
May	87	94	87
June	94	94	94
July	115	94	115
August	122	94	122
September	116	94	116
October	144	94	144
November	138	94	138
Total	**999**	**94**	**999**

The **Total sales June VAR** variable evaluates to the total sales for each month in the dataset. This is in contrast the **Total sales June** measure, which is what I was expecting the **Total Sales June VAR** measure to evaluate to.

This is because the variable **TotalSales** is evaluated in the scope of *when* it is assigned. The value is then stored locally in the measure and called upon throughout the expression. In this example the **TotalSales** variable is calculated within the filter context of the visual. The variable is calculated at each month of the dataset. This value is then stored and used when the variable is called upon in the expression.

If I want to have the variable be calculated while considering both the visualisation and measure filters, I can write the following **DAX** code:

```
Total sales June VAR 2 =
VAR MonthSales =
CALCULATE(
    VAR TotalSales = SUM(Sales[Sales])
    Return
    TotalSales,
    FILTER(
        ALL(Sales),
        Sales[Month name] = "June"
    )
)

Return
MonthSales
```

```
Total sales June VAR 2 =
VAR MonthSales =
CALCULATE(
 VAR TotalSales = SUM(Sales[Sales])
 Return
 TotalSales,
 FILTER(
 ALL(Sales),
 Sales[Month name] = "June"
 )
)

Return
MonthSales
```

In **Total sales June VAR 2**, I have included the variable in the expression in the **CALCULATE** function. This will force the variable to be calculated within the measure's filter context. Plotting this measure into the same visualisation yields:

Month Name	Total Sales	Total sales June	Total sales June VAR	Total sales June VAR 2
January	0	94	0	94
February	50	94	50	94
March	60	94	60	94
April	73	94	73	94
May	87	94	87	94
June	94	94	94	94
July	115	94	115	94
August	122	94	122	94
September	116	94	116	94
October	144	94	144	94
November	138	94	138	94
Total	**999**	**94**	**999**	**94**

The measure is now evaluating as intended, returning the sales amounts in June for each month. Although this is an extraneous use of a variable, I felt that it was important to use a simple example to make an important point. It is imperative to consider where the variables are being created and evaluated in a **DAX** measure.

CHAPTER 12: Calculating Inventory (FIFO)

Let's return to the case study. So far, I have elected to consider COGS as an "amorphous blob" of direct costs. However, in reality, this is not usually the case. I may need to consider each direct cost separately. Most are simple and can use the Sales / COGS control account approaches detailed earlier, but alas, the calculations of inventory and direct materials costs are a little more involved. Therefore, I shall look at inventory in isolation for the purposes of this case study.

When raw materials are first purchased, the stock procured may not be immediately used in sales. For example, the company may make furniture and must buy wood that needs to be treated, then the furniture built and finally sold. The wood purchased at the beginning cannot be recognised immediately, as items in the Income Statement should be:

1. **matched:** costs are only recognised when the sale to which they relate is made
2. **accrued:** these costs are deducted from profit even if these items have not yet been paid for (discrepancies will be displayed in the Cash Flow Statement and what is owing in Trade Payables).

Therefore, before I model the direct materials costs, I should understand what inventory is on hand. This stock value is displayed in the Current Assets section of the Balance Sheet.

There are two methods that are commonly implemented to calculate inventory: First In First Out (FIFO) or Average Cost. Some readers may argue there are other approaches available too, but this a book on Financial Modelling in Power BI, not 1,001 Ways to Bore Your Readers to Death using Inventory Analysis – but it does give me an idea for my next book! *(Great: you're already three books in with your 1,001 Ways to Bore Your Readers to Death series – Ed.)*

For the purposes of this report, I will be using the FIFO method first – after all, it's First In, so it should be First Out. I will discuss why I am not starting with the alternative Average Cost method, but I will get to it later.

Unlike the other control account items, some of the inventory calculations are more complex than the control account calculations. Therefore, I have decided to off-load some calculations for Inventory into a table, via "**DAX** columns". This means I will need to prepare a separate inventory query table that will serve as the basis of further calculations.

Important side note

Do note you should never make arbitrary decisions about whether to perform calculations in **M** rather than **DAX**. As much as I hate **M** (I always thought it should be called **X** because it makes me say **X**-rated things when it doesn't work and makes me think my ex wrote it and my ex hates me!), the mashup language for Power Query is useful for extracting, loading and pertinently here, *transforming* your data.

The problem is, it performs calculations at the level called, so you cannot drill down below that level like you can with the aggregation syntax of **DAX**. However, since I am doing this on a record-by-record basis here, no granularity is lost. This is an important point and should always be borne in mind when deciding whether to calculate something in **M** or **DAX**.

If you're at all concerned about this seemingly arbitrary selection of which language to use to produce the main "engine" of the inventory calculations, think of it like this. The idea of **DAX** is that you may report on items in a given context and aggregate accordingly, whereas **M** performs calculations more at a record (or some transformation and / or aggregation of these records) level. If I am considering the analysis of purchased inventory, how can I allocate it to a given customer, location or time? Do I have a crystal ball? Yes, some inventory may be purchased specifically, but not all stock. Analysing inventory at the record level is not a cheat, it's more a pragmatic analysis, given many other allocations would be subjective and potentially arbitrary.

Creating the inventory query

To calculate inventory correctly, I need to create a separate table in Power Query:

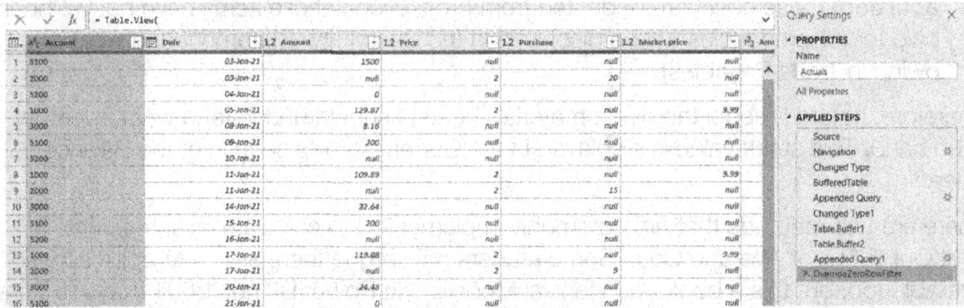

I make a reference of **Actuals**, which I rename **Inventory (FIFO)**.

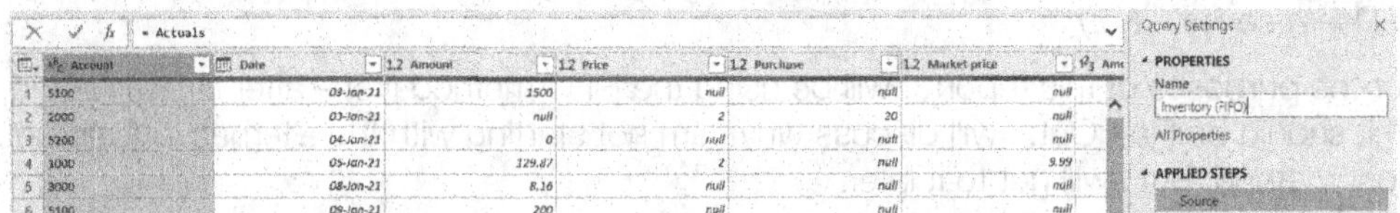

The next step is to transform the data so that I can calculate the inventory metrics. To ensure I only have the data I require, I filter the **Account** numbers. It is important to keep my tables short, so that they do not take up unnecessary processing time when I refresh the query. The account numbers I am interested in are "1000" and "2000"; these numbers relate to sales and purchases, respectively.

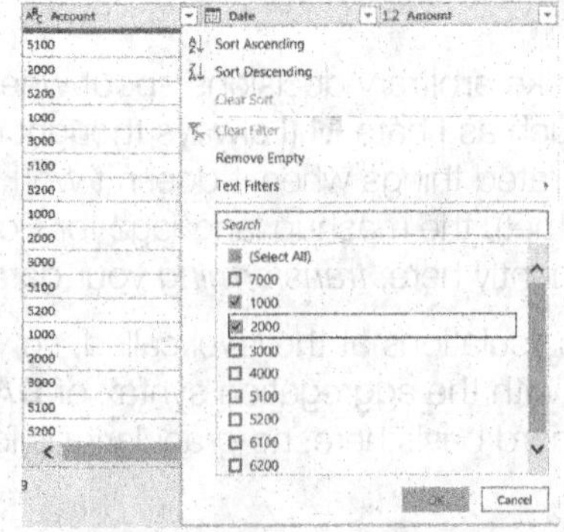

In the Formula Bar, I can see the **M** (Power Query) code that has been applied to my table:

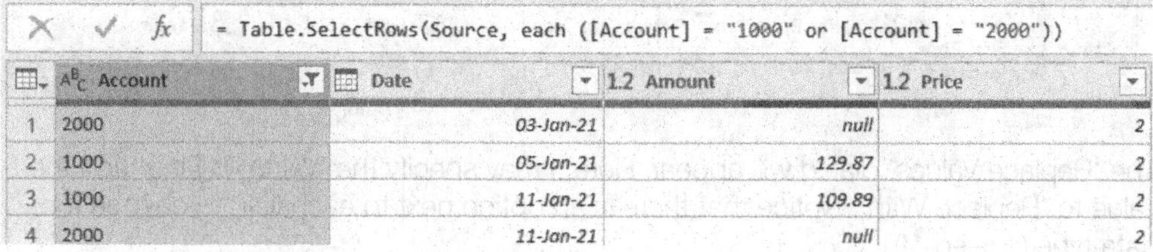

```
= Table.SelectRows(Source, each ([Account] = "1000" or [Account] = "2000"))
```

Remember the code parameters I created earlier? I can use them in **M** code as well. I can insert the **P_SalesCode** and **P_InventoryCode** parameters in place of "1000" and "2000":

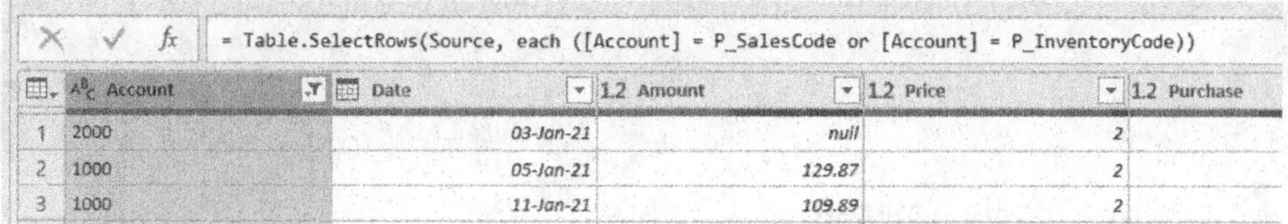

```
= Table.SelectRows(Source, each ([Account] = P_SalesCode or [Account] = P_
InventoryCode))
```

The next step is to sort the rows of the table in ascending order on the **Date** column. This is important as I will be creating an index later which has to be in chronological order. I click on the **Date** column's dropdown arrow, and select the 'Sort Ascending' option:

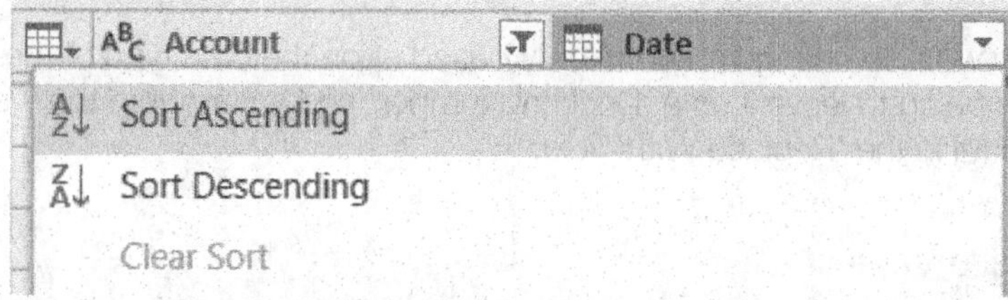

The next step is to replace the *null* values in the table with zero [0] so that calculations can be performed on the data. I highlight the **Amount**, **Price**, **Purchase**, **Market price** and **Amount sold** columns by holding down the **CTRL** button on the keyboard and clicking on each column header.

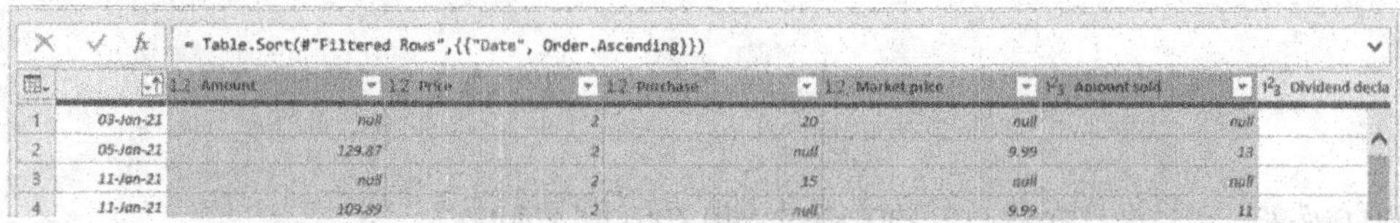

I navigate to the Transform tab on the Ribbon and click on the 'Replace Values' option.

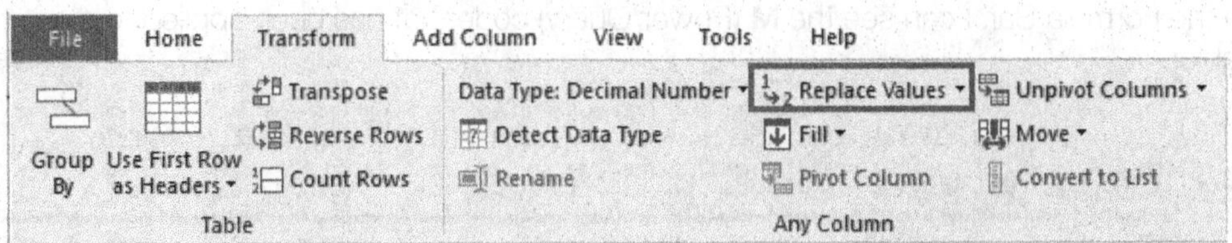

The 'Replace Values' dialog will appear. Here, I may specify the 'Value To Find' and the value to 'Replace With'. Notice that there is an option next to each field to change the data type (if needed).

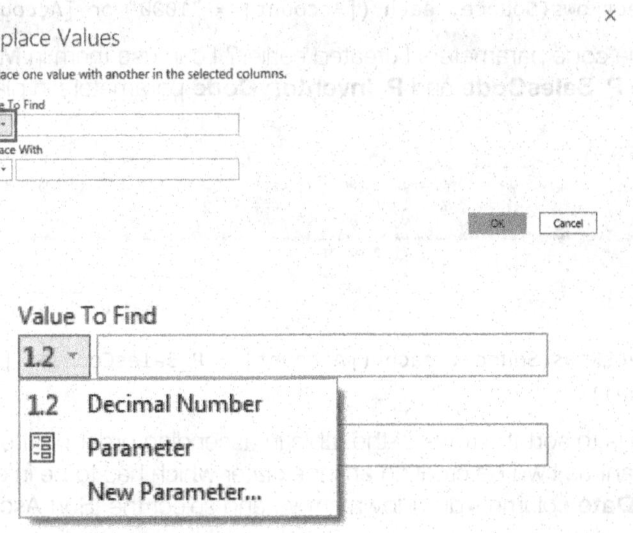

The data type will also change automatically based upon the data type of the column. For now, I am going to leave it as a 'Decimal Number' and enter *null* in the 'Value To Find' field and zero [0] in the 'Replace With' field:

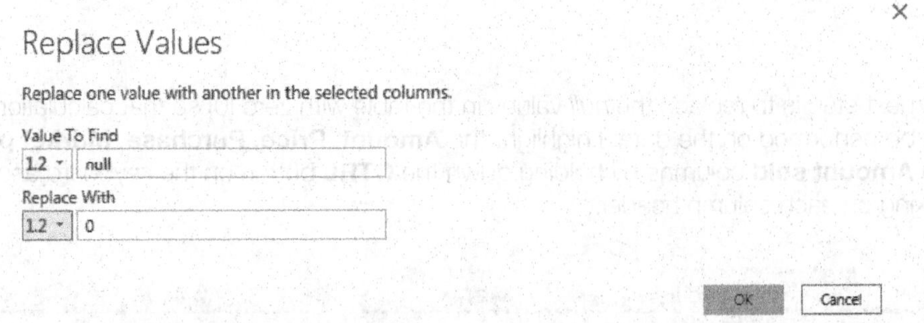

The *null* values have now been replaced with zero [0] values.

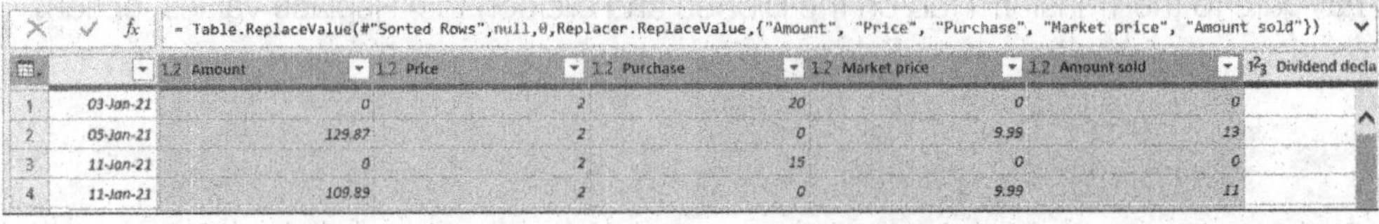

```
= Table.ReplaceValue(#"Sorted Rows",null,0,Replacer.ReplaceValue,{"Amount", "Price", "Purchase", "Market price", "Amount sold"})
```

		Amount	Price	Purchase	Market price	Amount sold	Dividend decla
1	03-Jan-21	0	2	20	0	0	
2	05-Jan-21	129.87	2	0	9.99	13	
3	11-Jan-21	0	2	15	0	0	
4	11-Jan-21	109.89	2	0	9.99	11	

The next step is optional but useful. I rename one of the columns (**Amount sold**) to **COGS**. To do this, I double-click on the **Amount sold** column header. This will allow me to type in the new name for the column:

Notice that the data currently contains multiple transactions per day. This is shown by having two or more rows for each date. The way I have designed the FIFO calculations to work (which will be discussed later) requires each row to correspond to one date.

To transform my data in Power Query, I will have to group these rows together. Therefore, I will navigate to the Home tab of the Ribbon and use the 'Group By' option:

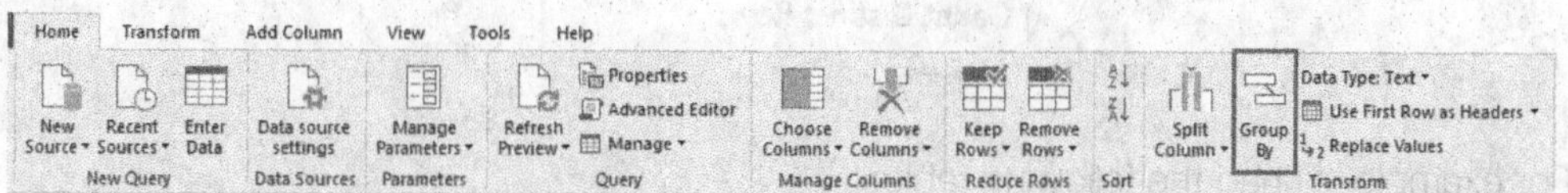

The 'Group By' dialog will appear. Before I group the data for this example, I will look at the options available on the 'Group By' dialog:

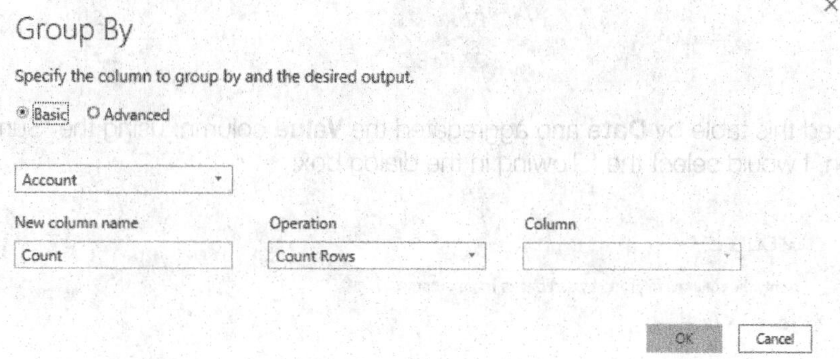

The Basic option only allows me to 'Group By' and aggregate a single column. However, I need to aggregate *several* columns. Therefore, I have changed it to the 'Advanced' setting:

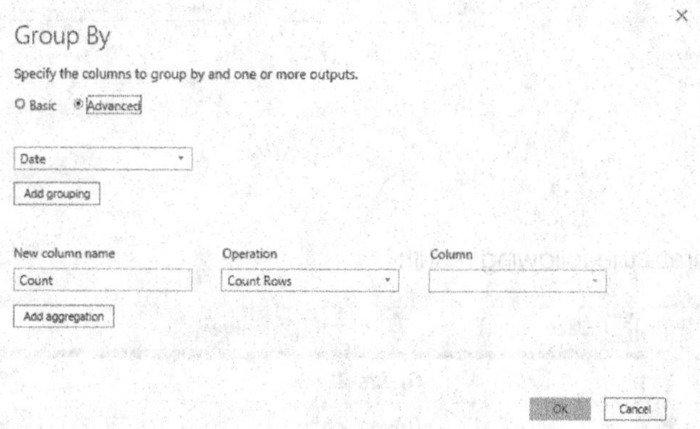

A grouping of a column means that Power BI will combine rows with the same value together in some form of aggregation. Power BI supports the following aggregations:

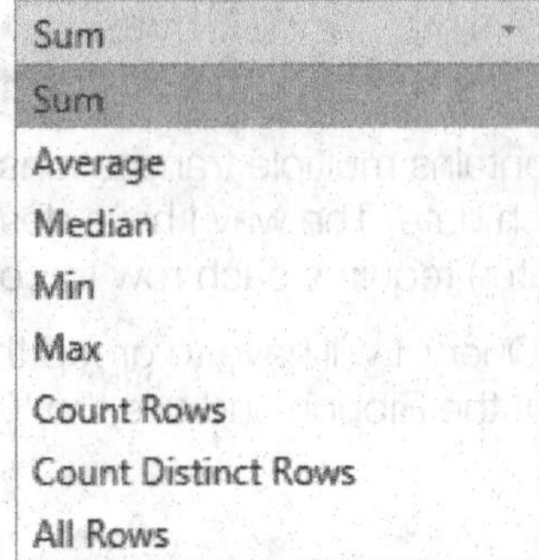

For example, if I had the following table:

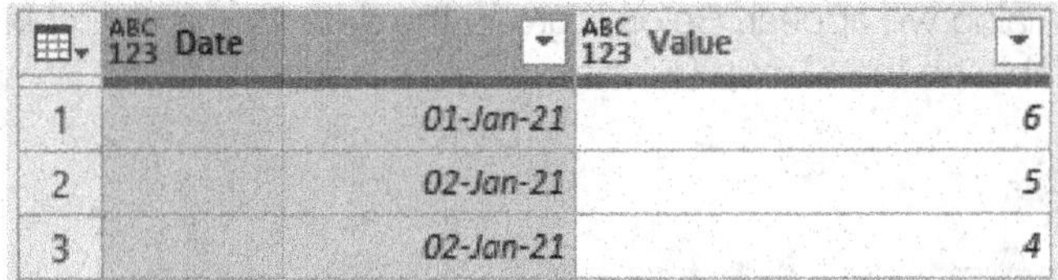

	ABC 123 Date	ABC 123 Value
1	01-Jan-21	6
2	02-Jan-21	5
3	02-Jan-21	4

If I grouped this table by **Date** and aggregated the **Value** column, using the 'Sum' operation, I would select the following in the dialog box:

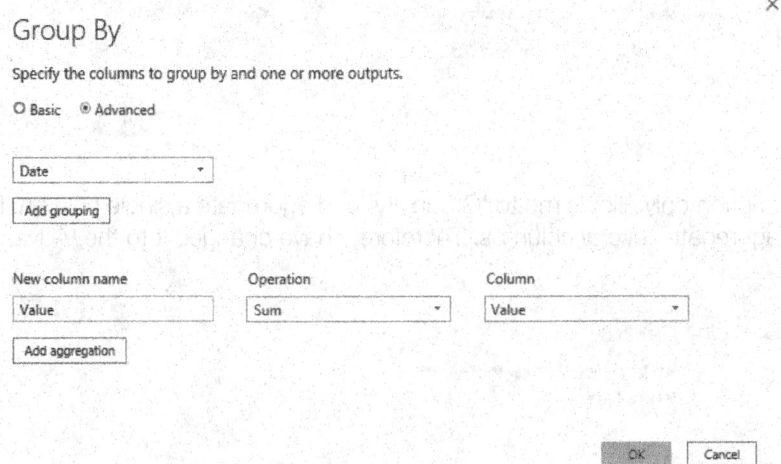

This would generate the following result:

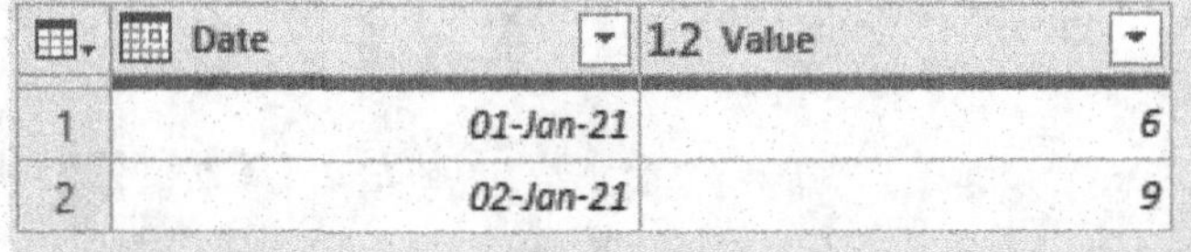

	Date	1.2 Value
1	01-Jan-21	6
2	02-Jan-21	9

The two 02-Jan-21 rows would be grouped into one row where the value has been summed.

Returning to our example, I can now add more groupings and aggregations to this step as follows:

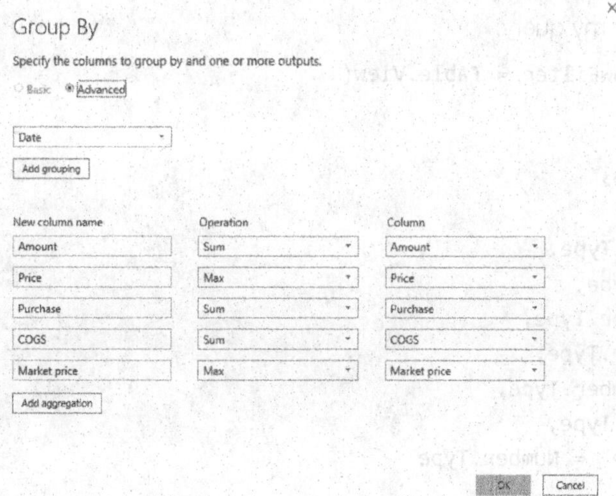

It is time to create the index I mentioned earlier. The index is essentially a counter to number the aggregated records. Please bear with me: I will explain why this is necessary later. To create the index, I select the 'Add Column' tab on the Ribbon, and in the 'Index Column' dropdown, I choose the 'From 1' option so that the counter commences from one [1].

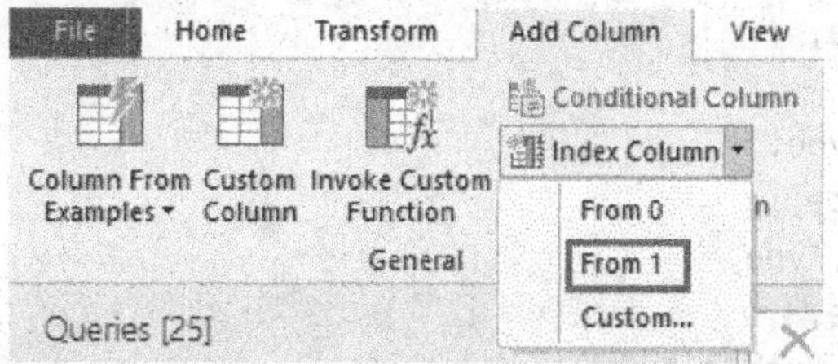

Power BI has now created an **Index** column, which numbers these grouped rows.

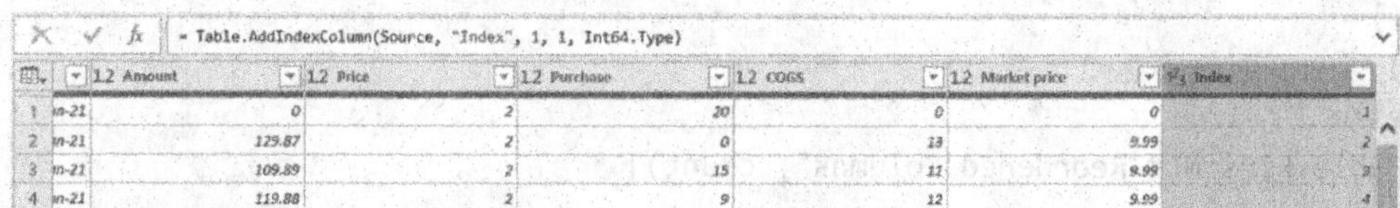
= Table.AddIndexColumn(Source, "Index", 1, 1, Int64.Type)

		1.2 Amount	1.2 Price	1.2 Purchase	1.2 COGS	1.2 Market price	Index
1	n-21	0	2	20	0	0	1
2	n-21	129.87	2	0	13	9.99	2
3	n-21	109.89	2	15	11	9.99	3
4	n-21	119.88	2	9	12	9.99	4

The last step is optional, but is good practice, allowing me to see all relevant data on screen at the same time. I move the **Index** column to the far-left side of the table:

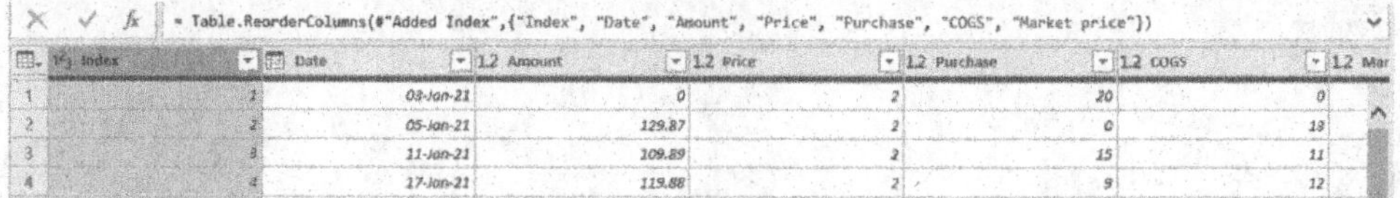
= Table.ReorderColumns(#"Added Index",{"Index", "Date", "Amount", "Price", "Purchase", "COGS", "Market price"})

	Index	Date	1.2 Amount	1.2 Price	1.2 Purchase	1.2 COGS	1.2 Mar
1	1	03-Jan-21	0	2	20	0	
2	2	05-Jan-21	129.87	2	0	13	
3	3	11-Jan-21	109.89	2	15	11	
4	4	17-Jan-21	119.88	2	9	12	

I shall add the **Table.View()** function into the **Inventory (FIFO)** query here to optimise load times. I open the Advanced Editor and add the following code to the last line. Please note, the previous step name, column name and type and column order must be correct for your query. The errors that can be encountered were described previously in Chapter 6, when I described how and why I can use **Table.View()** to improve efficiency.

This is correct for my query:

```
OverrideZeroRowFilter = Table.View(
null,
[
GetType = () =>
type table[
Index = Int64.Type,
Date = Date.Type,
Amount = Number.Type,
Price = Number.Type,
Purchase = Number.Type,
COGS = Number.Type,
#"Market price" = Number.Type
],
GetRows = () =>
#"Reordered Columns",
OnTake = (count as number) =>
if count = 0 then
#table(
type table[
Index = Int64.Type,
Date = Date.Type,
Amount = Number.Type,
Price = Number.Type,
Purchase = Number.Type,
COGS = Number.Type,
#"Market price" = Number.Type
],
{}
)
else
Table.FirstN(#"Reordered Columns", count)]
)
```

The code in the Advanced Editor for the **Inventory (FIFO)** query should now look something like this:

Advanced Editor

Inventory (FIFO)

Display Options

✓ No syntax errors have been detected.

Done Cancel

```
let
 Source = Actuals,
 #"Filtered Rows" = Table.SelectRows(Source, each ([Account] = P_SalesCode or [Account] = P_InventoryCode)),
 #"Sorted Rows" = Table.Sort(#"Filtered Rows",{{"Date", Order.Ascending}}),
 #"Replaced Value" = Table.ReplaceValue(#"Sorted Rows",null,0,Replacer.ReplaceValue,{"Amount", "Price", "Purchase", "Market price", "Amount sold"}),
 #"Renamed Columns" = Table.RenameColumns(#"Replaced Value",{{"Amount sold", "COGS"}}),
 #"Grouped Rows" = Table.Group(#"Renamed Columns", {"Date"}, {{"Amount", each List.Sum([Amount]), type number}, {"Price", each List.Max([Price]), type number}, {"Purchase", each List.Sum([Purchase]), type number}, {"COGS", each List.Sum([COGS]), type number}, {"Market price", each List.Max([Market price]), type number}}),
 #"Added Index" = Table.AddIndexColumn(#"Grouped Rows", "Index", 1, 1, Int64.Type),
 #"Reordered Columns" = Table.ReorderColumns(#"Added Index",{"Index", "Date", "Amount", "Price", "Purchase", "COGS", "Market price"}),
 OverrideZeroRowFilter = Table.View(
 null,
 [
 GetType = () =>
 type table[
 Index = Int64.Type,
 Date = Date.Type,
 Amount = Number.Type,
 Price = Number.Type,
 Purchase = Number.Type,
 COGS = Number.Type,
 #"Market price" = Number.Type
 ],
```

```
GetRows = () =>
#"Reordered Columns",
OnTake = (count as number) =>
if count = 0 then
#table(
type table[
Index = Int64.Type,
Date = Date.Type,
Amount = Number.Type,
Price = Number.Type,
Purchase = Number.Type,
COGS = Number.Type,
#"Market price" = Number.Type
],
{}
)
else
Table.FirstN(#"Reordered Columns", count)]
)

in
OverrideZeroRowFilter
```

Creating the inventory query (continued)

Now, I may click on the 'Close & Apply' option on the Ribbon to load my table into Power BI.

I can see the **Inventory (FIFO)** table on the Data view in my Power BI Desktop report. I sort the **Date** column into ascending order:

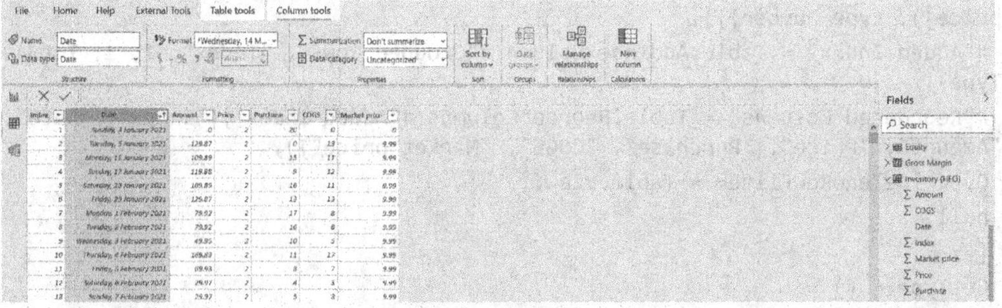

Before I add any new **Inventory (FIFO) DAX** columns, I should cover two more **DAX** functions that I will be using in the calculations, the **SUMX** and **MAXX** functions. Time for another detour. Note that the columns in the example are not in the same order as my current table.

The SUMX function

The **SUMX** function is similar to the **SUM** function, except it will return with the sum of an expression that is evaluated for each row in the table.

The **SUMX** function has the following syntax:

SUMX(table, expression)

where:

- **table** is the table that contains the rows for each the expression will be evaluated
- **expression** is what will be evaluated for each row of the **table**.

The **SUMX** function will take the first argument, a table or an expression that returns with a **table**. The second argument is a column (field) that contains the numbers that I want to sum, or an expression that evaluates to a column. It will ignore blanks, logical values and text.

For example, if I create the following calculated column:

```
SUMX example =
SUMX('Inventory (FIFO)',
'Inventory (FIFO)'[Purchase])
```

```
SUMX example =
SUMX('Inventory (FIFO)',
'Inventory (FIFO)'[Purchase])
```

This calculated column evaluates to 8,022, which is the total number of purchases for the entire dataset.

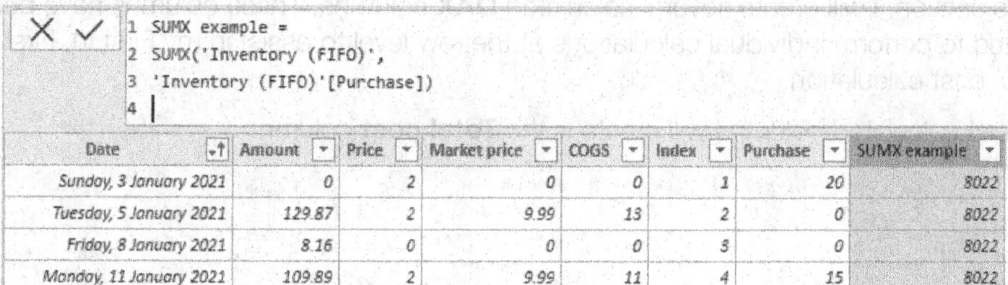

```
SUMX example =
SUMX('Inventory (FIFO)',
'Inventory (FIFO)'[Purchase])
```

Date	Amount	Price	Market price	COGS	Index	Purchase	SUMX example
Sunday, 3 January 2021	0	2	0	0	1	20	8022
Tuesday, 5 January 2021	129.87	2	9.99	13	2	0	8022
Friday, 8 January 2021	8.16	0	0	0	3	0	8022
Monday, 11 January 2021	109.89	2	9.99	11	4	15	8022

The MAXX function

The **MAXX** function evaluates an expression for each row in a table and returns the largest numerical value as a decimal number. The syntax of this function is:

MAXX (table, expression)

This means it is useful when you are trying to avoid creating an additional column in a **table** to calculate the interim calculations. Note:

- **table** is the table that contains the rows; for each row, the expression will be evaluated
- **expression** is what will be evaluated for each row of the **table**.

The **MAXX** function will take the first argument, a table or an expression that returns with a **table**. The second argument is a column that contains the numbers that I want to find the maximum of, or an expression that evaluates to a column.

For example, I can create the following calculated column:

```
MAXX example =
MAXX('Inventory (FIFO)',
'Inventory (FIFO)'[Amount])
```

```
MAXX example =
MAXX('Inventory (FIFO)',
'Inventory (FIFO)'[Amount])
```

It will return with the greatest sales amount throughout the entire dataset.

Date	Amount	Price	Market price	COGS	Index	Purchase	SUMX example	MAXX example
Sunday, 3 January 2021	0	2	0	0	1	20	8022	239.76
Tuesday, 5 January 2021	129.87	2	9.99	13	2	0	8022	239.76
Friday, 8 January 2021	8.16	0	0	0	3	0	8022	239.76
Monday, 11 January 2021	109.89	2	9.99	11	4	15	8022	239.76
Thursday, 14 January 2021	32.64	0	0	0	5	0	8022	239.76
Sunday, 17 January 2021	119.88	2	9.99	12	6	9	8022	239.76

Time to get back on the main highway…

Inventory (FIFO) DAX columns

In this section, I will create several calculated **DAX** columns. These columns have been created to perform individual calculations at the row level to assist in my First In, First Out (FIFO) cost calculation.

The first calculated column I will create is the **Total cost** column:

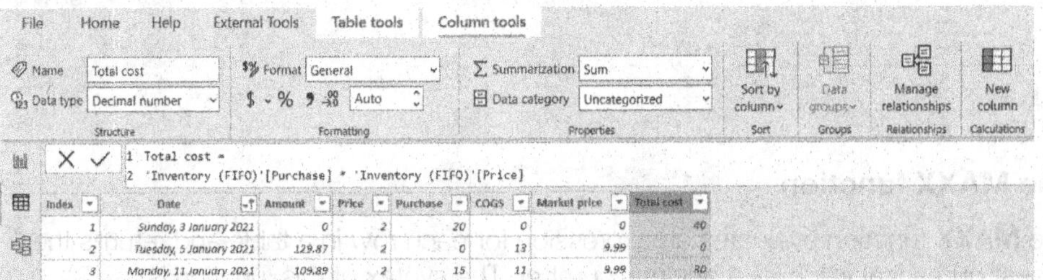

Index	Date	Amount	Price	Purchase	COGS	Market price	Total cost
1	Sunday, 3 January 2021	0	2	20	0	0	40
2	Tuesday, 5 January 2021	129.87	2	0	13	9.99	0
3	Monday, 11 January 2021	109.89	2	15	11	9.99	30

```
Total cost =
'Inventory (FIFO)'[Purchase] * 'Inventory (FIFO)'[Price]
```

I will now create cumulative columns for both the **Purchases** and **COGS** columns. This is so that I can track the amount of inventory I am forecast to have at each point in time. These two columns will also help me determine which time period's inventory figure I need to use for creating the calculations.

The cumulative purchases column is titled **Cumulative purch**:

```
Cumulative purch =
VAR MDate = 'Inventory (FIFO)'[Date]
VAR TFilter =
FILTER(
    'Inventory (FIFO)',
    'Inventory (FIFO)'[Date] <= MDate
)

RETURN
SUMX(
    TFilter,
    'Inventory (FIFO)'[Purchase]
)
```

```
Cumulative purch =
VAR MDate = ‘Inventory (FIFO)’[Date]
VAR TFilter =
FILTER(
 ‘Inventory (FIFO)’,
 ‘Inventory (FIFO)’[Date] <= MDate
)

RETURN
SUMX(
 TFilter,
 ‘Inventory (FIFO)’[Purchase]
)
```

Here, I have assigned the **TFilter** (abbreviated from table filter) variable to store a filtered table, where the current row's date **MDate** is greater than or equal to the **Date** column's dates. This will return with a table that looks backwards in time. The **SUMX** function will then sum all the rows in this **TFilter** generated table. Therefore, this will calculate the cumulative purchases on a row-by-row basis.

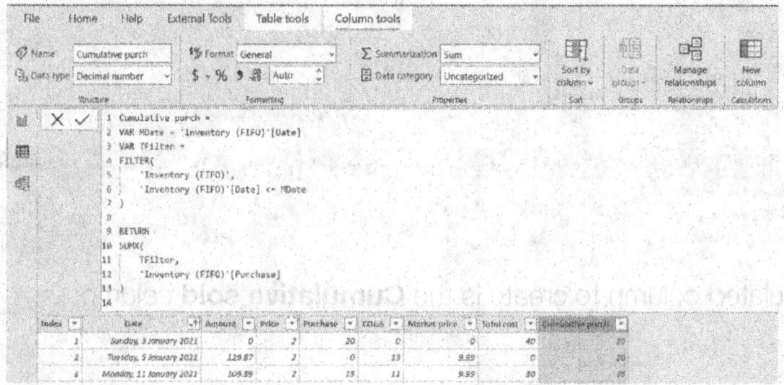

The **Cumulative cost** column follows a similar pattern:

```
Cumulative cost =
VAR MDate = 'Inventory (FIFO)'[Date]
VAR TFilter = FILTER(
    'Inventory (FIFO)',
    'Inventory (FIFO)'[Date] <= MDate
)

RETURN
SUMX(
    TFilter,
    'Inventory (FIFO)'[Total cost]
)
```


```
Cumulative cost =
VAR MDate = 'Inventory (FIFO)'[Date]
VAR TFilter = FILTER(
 'Inventory (FIFO)',
 'Inventory (FIFO)'[Date] <= MDate
)

RETURN
SUMX(
 TFilter,
 'Inventory (FIFO)'[Total cost]
)
```


File Home Help External Tools Table tools Column tools

Name: Cumulative cost | Data type: Decimal number | Format: General | Auto | Summarization: Sum | Data category: Uncategorized | Sort by column | Data groups | Manage relationships | New column

```
Cumulative cost =
VAR MDate = 'Inventory (FIFO)'[Date]
VAR TFilter = FILTER(
    'Inventory (FIFO)',
    'Inventory (FIFO)'[Date] <= MDate
)

RETURN
SUMX(
    TFilter,
    'Inventory (FIFO)'[Total cost]
)
```

Index	Date	Amount	Price	Purchase	COGS	Market price	Total cost	Cumulative purch	Cumulative cost
1	Sunday, 3 January 2021	0	2	20	0	0	40	20	40
2	Tuesday, 5 January 2021	129.87	2	0	13	9.99	0	20	40
3	Monday, 11 January 2021	109.89	2	15	11	9.99	30	35	70

The next calculated column to create is the **Cumulative sold** column:

```
Cumulative sold =
VAR MDate = 'Inventory (FIFO)'[Date]
VAR TFilter = FILTER(
    'Inventory (FIFO)',
    'Inventory (FIFO)'[Date] <= MDate
)

RETURN
SUMX(
    TFilter,
    'Inventory (FIFO)'[COGS]
)
```

```
Cumulative sold =
VAR MDate = 'Inventory (FIFO)'[Date]
VAR TFilter =
FILTER(
 'Inventory (FIFO)',
 'Inventory (FIFO)'[Date] <= MDate
)

RETURN
SUMX(
 TFilter,
 'Inventory (FIFO)'[COGS]
)
```

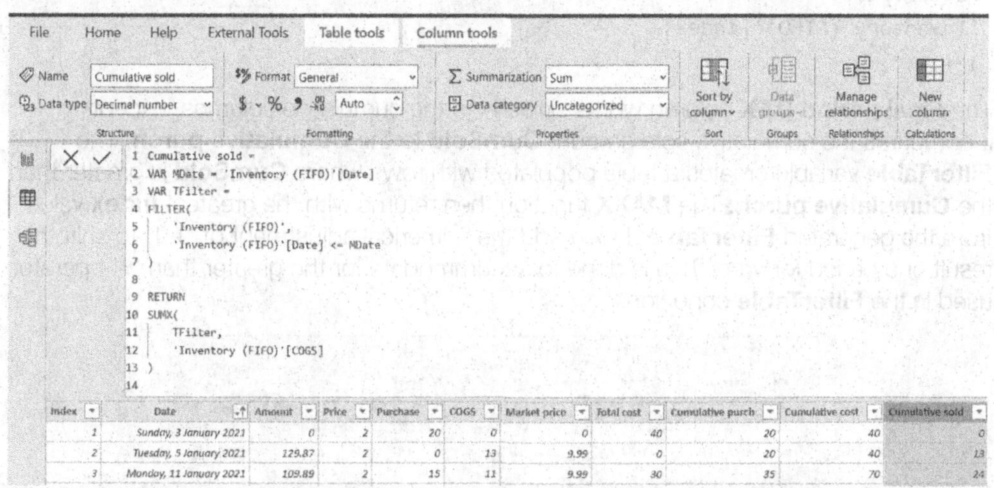

So far so good. Now, I must create an important column called **Final period**, which will use the numbers in the **Cumulative sold** and **Cumulative purch** columns to determine the final period. The final period is the period when stock was last bought to fulfil the current order.

For example, if I bought 10 units each month for periods 1 to 12 and in period 13 sold 25 units, I would use all the period 1 stock (First In, First Out), all of period 2 and half of period 3's inventory. Therefore, the **Final period** here would be period 3, and the proportion used in that period would be 50%.

The formula for this calculation is as follows:

```
Final period =
VAR CumSold = 'Inventory (FIFO)'[Cumulative Sold]

VAR FilterTable =
FILTER( 'Inventory (FIFO)',
    CumSold > 'Inventory (FIFO)'[Cumulative purch] )

RETURN
    MAXX(
        FilterTable,
        'Inventory (FIFO)'[Index]
    ) +1
```

```
Final period =
VAR CumSold = 'Inventory (FIFO)'[Cumulative sold]

VAR FilterTable =
FILTER(
 'Inventory (FIFO)',
 CumSold > 'Inventory (FIFO)'[Cumulative purch]
)

RETURN
 MAXX(
 FilterTable,
 'Inventory (FIFO)'[Index]
 ) + 1
```

The **Final period DAX** column works similarly to the cumulative columns, except it compares the cumulative sold amount **CumSold** to the **Cumulative purch**. The **FilterTable** variable creates a table populated with rows where **CumSold** is greater than the **Cumulative purch**. The **MAXX** function then returns with the greatest **Index** value from the generated **FilterTable**. I then add the numerical adjustment of '+ 1' to shift the result one period forward. This is done to accommodate for the greater than '>' operator used in the **FilterTable** condition.

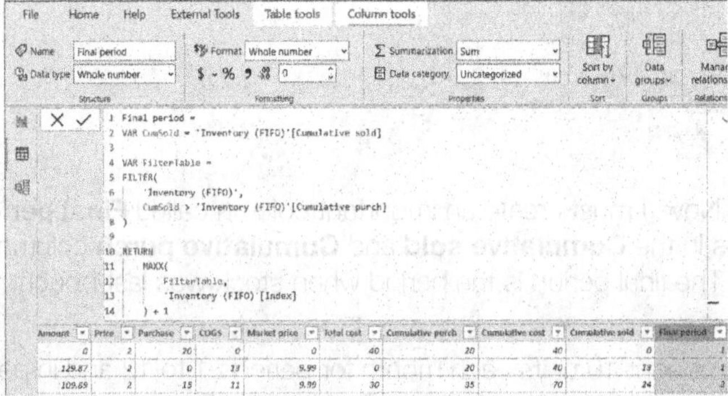

Based upon the logic in this table, each row represents a single period. This is uniquely identified by the **Index** column. Thus, if the row has an **Index** of 1, this translates to period one [1]; if the row has an **Index** value of 2, it translates to period two (2) and so on.

Cumulative purch	Cumulative cost	Cumulative sold	Final period
20	40	0	1
20	40	13	1
35	70	24	3

The first two periods there is a total cumulative sale of 13. Therefore, in each of these periods, I will be using the stock from period 1 to fulfil these orders. Once I move on to the third row, the cumulative sold is greater than the first two periods of cumulative purchases. Therefore, I will have to use the stock acquired in period 3 to fulfil the order in period 3.

The next step is to determine how much stock of the final period is being used to fulfil the current order. I have stepped this process out into two helper columns so that it is easier to understand. The two helper columns required are:

1. **Cum purch prev period** – cumulative purchases in previous period. This is not the previous period from the current row, but rather the previous period from the **Final period**
2. **Purch in final period** – purchases in final period. Essentially, this is a lookup column that returns with the number of purchases in the **Final period**.

The **Cum purch prev period** column uses the following code:

```
1 Cum purch prev period =
2 VAR Period = 'Inventory (FIFO)'[Final period]
3 VAR FilTable =
4 FILTER(
5     'Inventory (FIFO)',
6     'Inventory (FIFO)'[Index] = Period - 1
7 )
8
9 RETURN
10 MAXX(
11     FilTable,
12     'Inventory (FIFO)'[Cumulative purch]
13 )
```

```
Cum purch prev period =
VAR Period = 'Inventory (FIFO)'[Final period]
VAR FilTable =
FILTER(
 'Inventory (FIFO)',
 'Inventory (FIFO)'[Index] = Period - 1
)

RETURN
MAXX(
 FilTable,
 'Inventory (FIFO)'[Cumulative purch]
)
```

The **Cum purch prev period** looks at the previous period. I have adjusted this by first assigning the **Period** variable with the row context's **Final period** value. Then, in line six [6] of the code, I have adjusted the **Period** value by '- 1'. This will ensure that the calculation returns with the previous final period's **Index** value (hence why I needed to create this column earlier).

```
Purch in final period =
VAR Period = 'Inventory (FIFO)'[Final period]
VAR FilTable =
FILTER(
    'Inventory (FIFO)',
    'Inventory (FIFO)'[Index] = Period
)

RETURN
MAXX(
    FilTable,
    'Inventory (FIFO)'[Purchase]
)
```

```
Purch in final period =
VAR Period = 'Inventory (FIFO)'[Final period]
VAR FilTable =
FILTER(
 'Inventory (FIFO)',
 'Inventory (FIFO)'[Index] = Period
)

RETURN
MAXX(
 FilTable,
 'Inventory (FIFO)'[Purchase]
)
```

With these two columns now created, I may create the **% Final** column. This is the column that will calculate the percentage of stock that was acquired at the final period that will be used to fulfil the current period's order.

```
% Final =
('Inventory (FIFO)'[Cumulative sold] - 'Inventory (FIFO)'[Cum purch prev period]) /
'Inventory (FIFO)'[Purch in final period]
```

```
% Final =
('Inventory (FIFO)'[Cumulative Sold] - 'Inventory (FIFO)'[Cum purch prev
period]) / 'Inventory (FIFO)'[Purch in final period]
```

The **% Final** column works by subtracting the cumulative purchases in the previous period from the current period's cumulative sold, then dividing it by the purchases in the final period. I need to ensure that the Format is set to 'Decimal Number'.

The next column I need to calculate is the **Cum costs** of the stock I am selling. This requires two more helper columns, **Cum cost for prev period from final period** and **Total cost in period**.

```
Total cost in Period =
VAR Period = 'Inventory (FIFO)'[Final period]
VAR FilTable =
FILTER(
    'Inventory (FIFO)',
    'Inventory (FIFO)'[Index] = Period
)

RETURN
MAXX(
    FilTable,
    'Inventory (FIFO)'[Total Cost]
)
```

```
Total cost in period =
VAR Period = 'Inventory (FIFO)'[Final period]
VAR FilTable =
FILTER(
 'Inventory (FIFO)',
 'Inventory (FIFO)'[Index] = Period
)

RETURN
MAXX(
 FilTable,
 'Inventory (FIFO)'[Total cost]
)
```

The **Cum cost for prev period from final period** column will return with the cumulative cost from the previous period of the **Final period**. Clear as mud, yes?

```
Cum cost for prev period from final period =
VAR Period = 'Inventory (FIFO)'[Final period]
VAR FilTable =
FILTER(
    'Inventory (FIFO)',
    'Inventory (FIFO)'[Index] = Period -1
)

RETURN
MAXX(
    FilTable,
    'Inventory (FIFO)'[Cumulative Cost]
)
```

```
Cum cost for prev period from final period =
VAR Period = 'Inventory (FIFO)'[Final period]
VAR FilTable =
```

```
FILTER(
 'Inventory (FIFO)',
 'Inventory (FIFO)'[Index] = Period - 1
)

RETURN
MAXX(
 FilTable,
 'Inventory (FIFO)'[Cumulative Cost]
)
```

I have adopted a similar **DAX** structure to the **Cum purch prev period** column to calculate the **Cum cost for prev period from final period** column. This is where I shift the period filter back by one [1] period.

The next step here is to calculate the cumulative cost (**Cum costs**). This is easy with the help of the other two columns:

```
Cum costs =
('Inventory (FIFO)'[% Final] * 'Inventory (FIFO)'[Total cost in Period])
+ 'Inventory (FIFO)'[Cum cost for prev period from final period]
```

```
Cum costs =
('Inventory (FIFO)'[% Final] * 'Inventory (FIFO)'[Total cost in Period])
+ 'Inventory (FIFO)'[Cum cost for prev period from final period]
```

Using the cumulative costs **Cum costs** column, I can determine each period's '**FIFO cost**'.

```
FIFO cost =
VAR Period = 'Inventory (FIFO)'[Index]
VAR PrevCost =
    CALCULATE(MAX('Inventory (FIFO)'[Cum Costs]),
    FILTER('Inventory (FIFO)',
        'Inventory (FIFO)'[Index]= Period -1)
    )

RETURN
'Inventory (FIFO)'[Cum Costs] - PrevCost
```

```
FIFO cost =
VAR Period = 'Inventory (FIFO)'[Index]
VAR PrevCost =
 CALCULATE(
 MAX('Inventory (FIFO)'[Cum Costs]),
 FILTER('Inventory (FIFO)',
 'Inventory (FIFO)'[Index] = Period - 1
 )
 )
```

```
RETURN
'Inventory (FIFO)'[Cum Costs] - PrevCost
```

Here, I have used a similar methodology to the **Cum purch prev period** column to retrieve the previous period's cost. Once I have the previous period's cost, I simply subtract the previous period's cost from the current period's cost to calculate the **FIFO cost** for the current period. The new columns on **Inventory (FIFO)** should now look like this:

Cum purch prev period	Purch in final period	% Final	Total cost in period	Cum cost for prev period from final period	Cum costs	FIFO cost
	20	0.00	40		0	0
	20	0.65	40		26	26
20	15	0.27	30	40	48	22
35	9	0.11	18	70	72	24

Now that I've gone over the **DAX** columns and their logic, it is clear now that for this logic to work the **Inventory** table had to be grouped into one row per day, otherwise this logic would fall apart. It is just an important point to note if you are trying to replicate these results or build your own inventory table.

I can now move on to create the inventory and purchases control accounts.

Purchases control account

I will need to create two control accounts for inventory: a control account for purchases and a separate account for inventory costs.

The four measures items required in the purchases control account are:

1. Purchases opening payables ($)
2. Purchases ($)
3. Purchases cash payments ($)
4. Purchases closing payables ($).

This control account is keeping track of the purchases, insofar as what purchases have been contracted and how much has been paid, so that we know how much is still owed (*i.e.* payable). As always, the second and third line items are where the chief action happens. Therefore, I will begin with the **Purchases ($)** measure. This measure requires the purchases (dollar amount) to be calculated at the table level. I will create a new column in the **Actuals** table. This column will multiply the **Price** by the **Purchase** column. It should be noted that I have filtered out the irrelevant **Account** codes just for this screenshot:

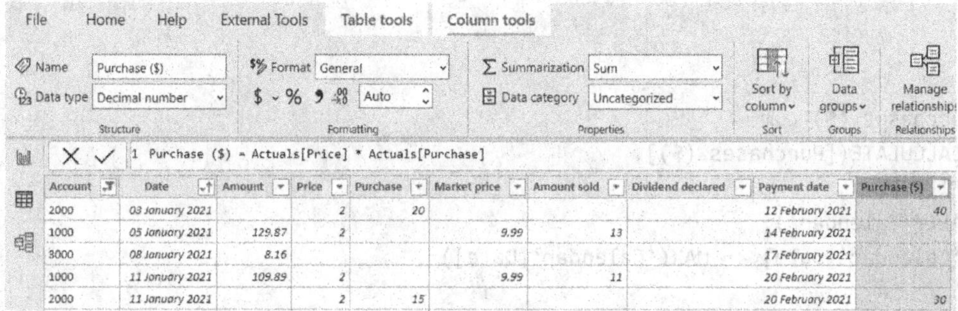

```
Purchase ($) = Actuals[Price] * Actuals[Purchase]
```

This step must be done at the table level, since if I try to do this with a measure, it will aggregate the price together based on the time period that is filtered. A row-by-row multiplication ensures the granularity of each time period's price and purchase amounts.

Moving back to the Report view, I can create the **Purchases ($)** measure:

```
Purchases ($) =
CALCULATE(
    SUM(Actuals[Purchase ($)]),
    Actuals[Account] = P_InventoryCode
)
```

```
Purchases ($) =
CALCULATE(
 SUM(Actuals[Purchase ($)]),
 Actuals[Account] = P_InventoryCode
)
```

Now I turn my attention to the **Purchases cash payments ($)** measure:

```
Purchases cash payments ($) =
CALCULATE(-[Purchases ($)],
    DATEADD('Calendar'[Date], -P_DaysPayable, DAY)
)
```

```
Purchases cash payments ($) =
CALCULATE(-[Purchases ($)],
 DATEADD('Calendar'[Date], -P_DaysPayable, DAY)
)
```

As with previous control accounts, I will need the cumulative measures to help calculate the opening and closing balances for purchases.

```
Purchases ($) cum =
    CALCULATE([Purchases ($)],
        FILTER(
            ALL('Calendar'),
            'Calendar'[Date] <= MAX('Calendar'[Date])
        )
    )
```

```
Purchases ($) cum =
 CALCULATE([Purchases ($)],
 FILTER(
 ALL('Calendar'),
 'Calendar'[Date] <= MAX('Calendar'[Date])
 )
 )
```

This is then followed by the **Purchases cash payments ($) cum**:

```
Purchases cash payments ($) cum =
    CALCULATE([Purchases cash payments ($)],
        FILTER(
            ALL('Calendar'),
            'Calendar'[Date] <= MAX('Calendar'[Date])
        )
    )
```

```
Purchases cash payments ($) cum =
 CALCULATE([Purchases cash payments ($)],
 FILTER(
 ALL('Calendar'),
 'Calendar'[Date] <= MAX('Calendar'[Date])
 )
 )
```

The **Purchases opening payables ($)** use similar logic to that previously discussed:

```
Purchases opening payables ($) =
CALCULATE([Purchases ($) cum] + [Purchases cash payments ($) cum],
    PREVIOUSDAY('Calendar'[Date])
)
```

```
Purchases opening payables ($) =
CALCULATE([Purchases ($) cum] + [Purchases cash payments ($) cum],
 PREVIOUSDAY('Calendar'[Date])
)
```

Similarly, I generate **Purchases closing payables ($)**:

```
Purchases closing payables ($) =
[Purchases opening payables ($)] + [Purchases ($)] + [Purchases cash payments ($)]
```

```
Purchases closing payables ($) =
[Purchases opening payables ($)] + [Purchases ($)] + [Purchases cash payments
($)]
```

Plotting these four measures into a matrix visualisation yields my purchases control account:

Year	2021								
Qtr	Q1			Q2			Q3		
	Jan	Feb	Mar	Apr	May	Jun	Jul	Aug	Sep
Purchases opening payables ($)		$146.00	$602.00	$1,266.00	$1,248.00	$1,196.00	$1,430.00	$1,724.00	$1,749.00
Purchases ($)	$146.00	$544.00	$1,026.00	$900.00	$904.00	$1,100.00	$1,374.00	$1,320.00	$1,215.00
Purchases cash payments ($)		($88.00)	($362.00)	($918.00)	($956.00)	($866.00)	($1,080.00)	($1,295.00)	($1,347.00)
Purchases closing payables ($)	$146.00	$602.00	$1,266.00	$1,248.00	$1,196.00	$1,430.00	$1,724.00	$1,749.00	$1,617.00

Next, I shall group the purchases measures into a display folder:

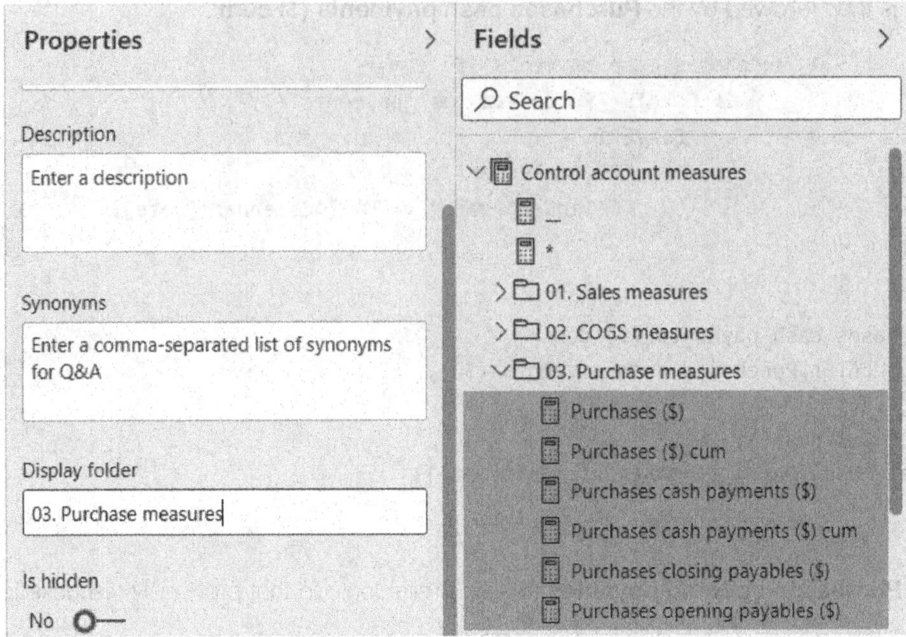

Given how many measures I am calculating, it is good practice to bundle measures together. This makes it easier for the model developer and for the end user alike, as clarity and transparency are enhanced.

Inventory control account

The inventory control account will also require four measures:

1. Inventory opening ($)
2. Inventory purchases ($)
3. Inventory cost ($)
4. Inventory closing ($)

This control account keeps track of the in's and out's of inventory, *i.e.* what has been purchased, and what had been consumed (sold). In our simple example, spoilage / wastage / theft are all ignored.

I start with the **Inventory purchases ($)** measure:

```
Inventory purchases ($) =
SUM('Inventory (FIFO)'[Total cost])
```

```
Inventory purchases ($) =
SUM('Inventory (FIFO)'[Total cost])
```

I do not need to apply any account filters in this measure, because that has already been performed at the query level, where I filtered the **Actuals** table to only give me the accounts related to the **P_SalesCode** and **P_InventoryCode**.

Plotting the **Inventory purchases** measure into the matrix visualisation:

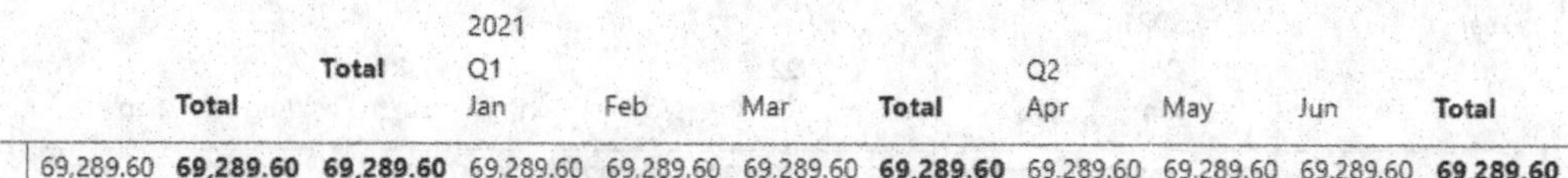

			2021							
		Total	Q1				Q2			
	Total		Jan	Feb	Mar	Total	Apr	May	Jun	Total
69,289.60	**69,289.60**	**69,289.60**	69,289.60	69,289.60	69,289.60	**69,289.60**	69,289.60	69,289.60	69,289.60	**69,289.60**

I notice that the purchase amounts are the same for each month throughout the dataset in the visualisation. This is because there is presently no relationship between the two tables **Inventory (FIFO)** and the **Calendar** table. I have used the dates from the **Calendar** table as the column headers in the visualisation, and the inventory purchases amounts from the **Inventory (FIFO)** table as the values. Since there is currently no relationship between the two tables, Power BI does not know how to break the purchases amounts by the respective months.

Therefore, I must create a relationship between the two tables in the Model view of the report:

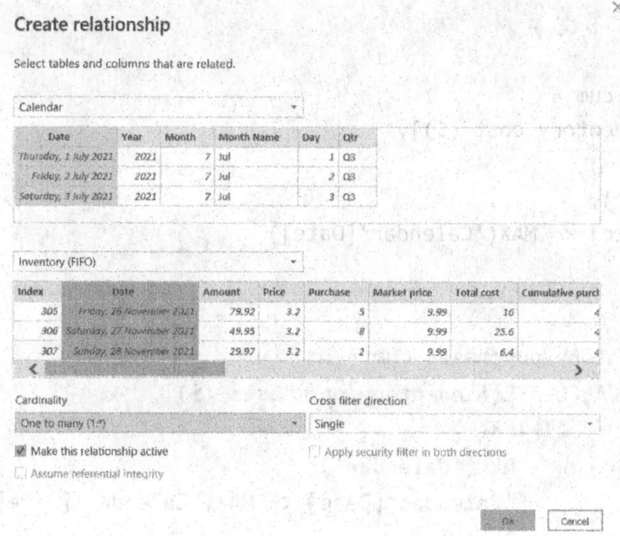

Going back to the Report view, the visualisation is now displaying the inventory amounts calculated properly:

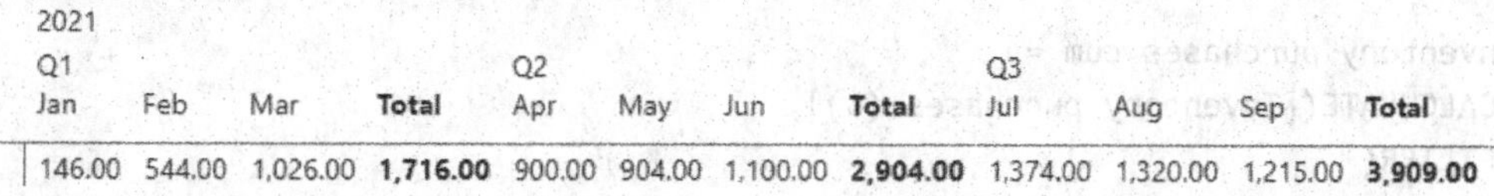

2021											
Q1				Q2				Q3			
Jan	Feb	Mar	Total	Apr	May	Jun	Total	Jul	Aug	Sep	Total
146.00	544.00	1,026.00	**1,716.00**	900.00	904.00	1,100.00	**2,904.00**	1,374.00	1,320.00	1,215.00	**3,909.00**

The **Inventory cost** measure is as follows:

```
Inventory cost ($) =
-SUM('Inventory (FIFO)'[FIFO Cost])
```

```
Inventory cost ($) =
-SUM('Inventory (FIFO)'[FIFO cost])
```

Year	2021								
Qtr	Q1			Q2			Q3		
	Jan	Feb	Mar	Apr	May	Jun	Jul	Aug	Sep
Inventory purchases ($)	146.00	544.00	1,026.00	900.00	904.00	1,100.00	1,374.00	1,320.00	1,215.00
Inventory cost ($)	-120.00	-420.00	-490.00	-454.00	-460.00	-412.00	-454.00	-442.00	-413.00

Just like before, I must create cumulative measures for the **Inventory cost** and the **Inventory purchases**.

```
Inventory cost cum =
    CALCULATE([Inventory cost ($)],
        FILTER(
            ALL('Calendar'),
            'Calendar'[Date] <= MAX('Calendar'[Date])
            )
        )
```

```
Inventory cost cum =
 CALCULATE([Inventory cost ($)],
 FILTER(
 ALL('Calendar'),
 'Calendar'[Date] <= MAX('Calendar'[Date])
 )
 )
```

```
Inventory purchases cum =
    CALCULATE([Inventory purchases ($)],
        FILTER(
            ALL('Calendar'),
            'Calendar'[Date] <= MAX('Calendar'[Date])
            )
        )
```

and

```
Inventory purchases cum =
 CALCULATE([Inventory purchases ($)],
 FILTER(
 ALL('Calendar'),
 'Calendar'[Date] <= MAX('Calendar'[Date])
 )
 )
```

With the cumulative measures done, I can calculate the opening inventory dollar amount:

```
Inventory opening ($) =
    CALCULATE([Inventory cost cum] + [Inventory purchases cum],
        PREVIOUSDAY('Calendar'[Date])
    )
```

```
Inventory opening ($) =
 CALCULATE([Inventory cost cum] + [Inventory purchases cum],
 PREVIOUSDAY('Calendar'[Date])
 )
```

Followed by the **Inventory closing ($)** measure:

```
Inventory closing ($) =
[Inventory opening ($)] + [Inventory purchases ($)] + [Inventory cost ($)]
```

```
Inventory closing ($) =
[Inventory opening ($)] + [Inventory purchases ($)] + [Inventory cost ($)]
```

The inventory control account is now complete and looks like this when plotted on a Matrix visualisation:

Year	2021								
Qtr	Q1			Q2			Q3		
	Jan	Feb	Mar	Apr	May	Jun	Jul	Aug	Sep
Inventory opening ($)	$0.00	$26.00	$150.00	$686.00	$1,132.00	$1,576.00	$2,264.00	$3,184.00	$4,062.00
Inventory purchases ($)	$146.00	$544.00	$1,026.00	$900.00	$904.00	$1,100.00	$1,374.00	$1,320.00	$1,215.00
Inventory cost ($)	($120.00)	($420.00)	($490.00)	($454.00)	($460.00)	($412.00)	($454.00)	($442.00)	($413.00)
Inventory closing ($)	$26.00	$150.00	$686.00	$1,132.00	$1,576.00	$2,264.00	$3,184.00	$4,062.00	$4,864.00

Before I move on, I should organise the **Inventory (FIFO) measures** together:

04. Inventory measures
- Inventory closing ($)
- Inventory cost ($)
- Inventory cost cum
- Inventory opening ($)
- Inventory purchases ($)
- Inventory purchases cum

CHAPTER 13: Average Inventory Calculation

In this section, I will calculate the cost of inventory using an alternative approach: the average cost method. As I mentioned earlier, average cost is a commonly used method of calculating the value of inventory, especially in areas where there are quite volatile costs of acquiring that inventory, such as the natural resources industry.

How it works

Average cost inventory brings in the latest cost of inventory and averages that cost across all of your other inventory items. If your latest lump of coal cost more to take out of the ground than all your earlier lumps of coal, then all of the rest of your coal in your stockpile is now considered to cost a little bit more, on average.

When we're calculating this in Excel, this is pretty easy because we can simply keep track of our inventory in a cell, and use that value in the next month's calculation. Power BI doesn't let us store those results in cells, so conceptually, we need to look back at the cost of every item that's ever gone into our inventory stockpile. Because we're taking averages, when we use our inventory, we never use up 100% of our very first purchase (unless we use up 100% of our inventory stock) – a very small fraction is always hanging around, averaged into and out of all of the future purchases and sales.

Suppose I buy 100 units at $1.00. Once that's done, I sell 60 units, and then buy 300 units at $1.50, then finally, sell a final 200 units. How does this all work?

Units

	Units	Closing value	Average inventory price
Buy 100 units at $1.00 = $100.00	100	$100.00	$1.00
Sell 60 units @ $1.00 per unit = $60.00	40	$40.00	$1.00
Buy 300 units at $1.50 = $450.00	340	$490.00	$1.44
Sell 200 units @ $1.44 per unit = $288.24	140	$201.76	$1.44

Another way of representing this might be:

	Units	Closing value	Average inventory price
Buy 100 units at $1.00 = $100.00	100	$100.00	$1.00
Sell 60 units @ $1.00 per unit = $60.00	40	$100.00 * (40 / 100)	$1.00
Buy 300 units at $1.50 = $450.00	340	$100.00 * (40 / 100) + $450.00	$1.44
Sell 200 units @ $1.44 per unit = $288.24	140	($100.00 * (40 / 100) + $450.00) * (140 / 340) **OR** $100.00 * (40 / 100) * (140 / 340) + $450 * (140 / 340)	$1.44

Looking at the closing value column above, do you see how that first purchase of $100 keeps hanging around? Even after more and more units get sold in the future, those first units purchased will still contribute to the value of your inventory, being the value of the purchase, multiplied by the proportion of inventory remaining each period, over and over again. Then, the second purchase amount gets reduced by the proportion of inventory sold in the second sale, and the third, and so on. This gives me a hint on how this needs to be calculated:

Purchases	Month 1	Month 2	Month 3	Month 4
Inv. Month 1 = $100	$100 * ($sold_1$/$stock_1$)	$100 * ($sold_1$/$stock_1$) * ($sold_2$/$stock_2$)	$100 * ($sold_1$/$stock_1$) * ($sold_2$/$stock_2$) * ($sold_3$/$stock_3$)	$100 * ($sold_1$/$stock_1$) * ($sold_2$/$stock_2$) * ($sold_3$/$stock_3$) * ($sold_4$/$stock_4$)
Inv. Month 2 = $200	n.a.	$200 * ($sold_2$/$stock_2$)	$200 * ($sold_2$/$stock_2$) * ($sold_3$/$stock_3$)	$200 * ($sold_2$/$stock_2$) * ($sold_3$/$stock_3$) * ($sold_4$/$stock_4$)
Inv. Month 3 = $300	n.a.	n.a.	$300 * ($sold_3$/$stock_3$)	$300 * ($sold_3$/$stock_3$) * ($sold_4$/$stock_4$)
Inv. Month 4 = $400	n.a.	n.a.	n.a.	$400 * ($sold_4$/$stock_4$)

Once I work this matrix out, I can sum down the column to work out what the total value of inventory remains in that month. So, the key calculation trick here is to work out, for each given purchase month / forecast month combination, what periods of inventory ins and outs it needs to use to calculate the closing value of the remaining inventory not sold. This is where the rest of this chapter will spend most of its time.

Why we aren't using this

Average inventory is a very common tool used in a lot of different industries, and as such, deserves a place in this book. However, due to the limitations of **DAX**, we are having to perform the heavy lifting calculations in far more inefficient **M**. This works well enough when we model on a monthly basis. However, once we start looking at a daily basis, we go from having a 12 x 12 matrix (144 cells, 78 meaningful ones) to having a 365 x 365 matrix (133,225 cells, 66,795 meaningful ones), which is nearly 1000 times more processor intensive. Extend a forecast to five years, and we have a 1,826 x 1,826 matrix, with 3.3m cells and 1.7m values that we actually need to calculate. This is a pretty trivial task in Excel that can be done in about four rows of calculations, but it's just not a feasible solution when we look at implementing this over a medium-term, daily forecast.

But just in case you still want to use Power BI, and are happy to deal with either the performance issues in refreshing your dataset, or are happy to calculate inventory on a less granular basis, then keep reading to see how it's done.

Similar to the **Inventory (FIFO)** calculation, the process of calculating the average cost requires creating a separate inventory table. It's strange; in Excel, this is the easier computation, but in Power BI, well, you make your own mind up…

It's easy to not see the wood for the trees in this comprehensive walkthrough. To surmise:

- I will demonstrate the concept only using a handful of dates (as the calculation is extremely resource hungry) – the dates I choose are entirely arbitrary
- Using Purchases – COGS and an index, I will generate a cumulative Net Movement
- Since my original opening balance is zero, this Net Movement total will be the closing balance of my Purchases control account (*i.e.* how many I have left in stock at any given time)
- The opening balance for any period may be deduced by calculating the Closing Balance less the Net Movement
- Thus, the COGS percentage will be given by COGS / (Opening Balance + Purchases)
- We use the "inverse" of this percentage (1-COGS%) to calculate as a percentage the proportion of inventory left
- This figure may be multiplied over time to work out the weighted average cost of the inventory, but to get this percentage we need to create a "triangle", as the second period calculation will use the first period, the third will require the first two, the third will require the first three, *etc.*

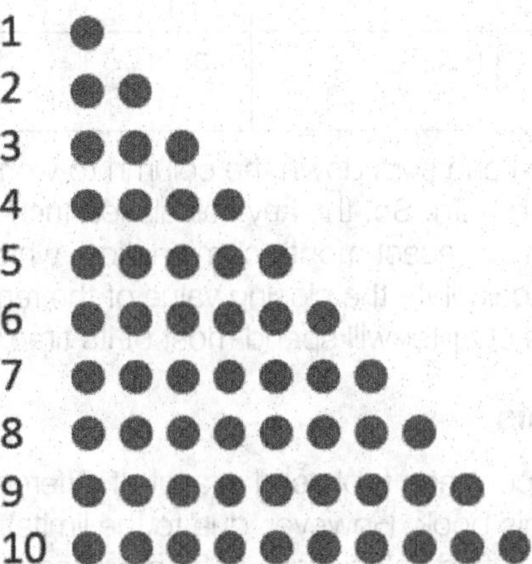

- To do this in Power BI, we will merge our calculated table with itself and then, with the assistance of a created custom function, perform the heavy lifting required.

Easy, yes? Maybe not. Quick and simple? Er, no. I am selling it well…

Average inventory table setup

First, I navigate to the Power Query editor, where I find the **Inventory (FIFO)** query. Here, I can steal some of the steps from this query and create a duplicate from it. The table I require for inventory consists of just the rows that are related to inventory. Therefore, I can look at the 'APPLIED STEPS' section and select the 'Added Index' step, right-click and select 'Extract Previous'.

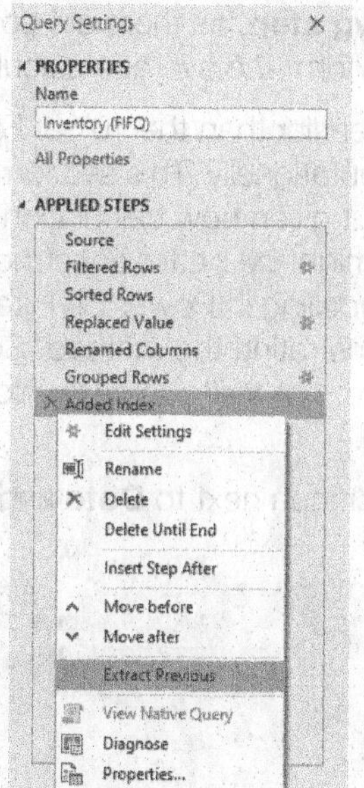

This brings up the 'Extract Steps' dialog, where I name the new query **Inventory data**.

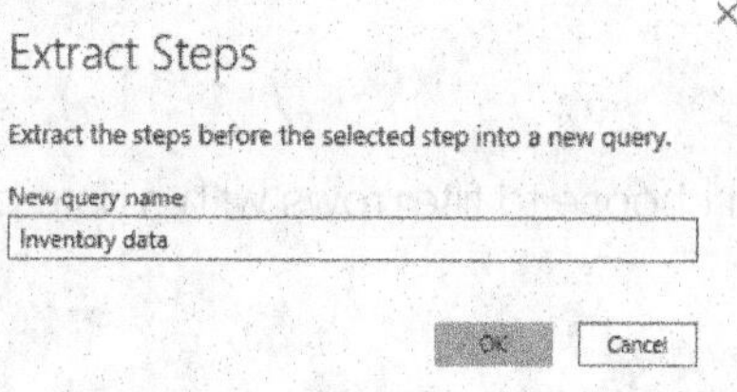

This will create the **Inventory data** query.

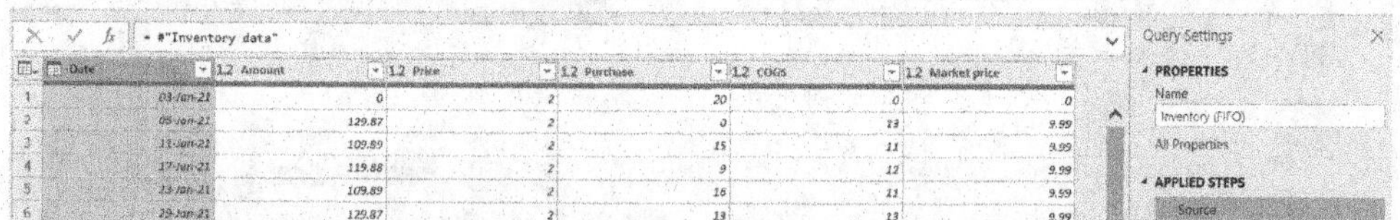

	Date	Amount	Price	Purchase	COGS	Market price
1	03-Jan-21	0	2	20	0	0
2	05-Jan-21	129.87	2	0	13	9.99
3	11-Jan-21	109.89	2	15	11	9.99
4	17-Jan-21	119.88	2	9	12	9.99
5	23-Jan-21	109.89	2	16	11	9.99
6	29-Jan-21	129.87	2	13	13	9.99

The **Inventory data** query will not be required in the report. Therefore, I have toggled it to not load to the report. I can now reference the **Inventory data** query and begin creating the table needed for the average inventory calculation.

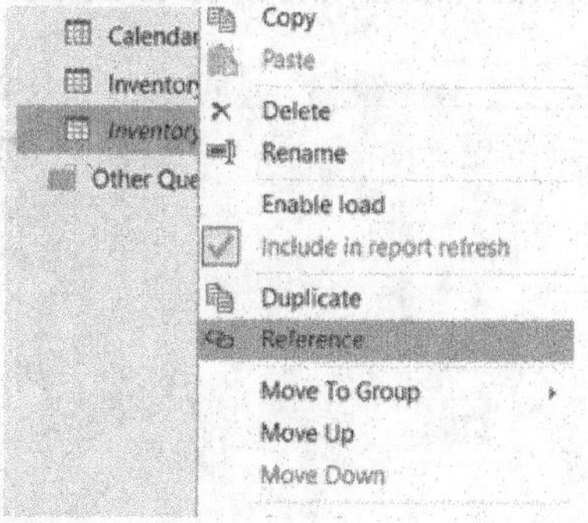

I shall call this table **Inventory avg step**, as there are some transformations I need to apply to the data before I can perform the average calculation.

The first step is to filter the rows earlier than the 10th of February. Unfortunately, this method is very demanding computationally. This section is meant to be an aside to show you how it can be done, but given how calculation intensive it is, I would not recommend it in Power BI. This might be better constructed in Excel in practice, but hey, this is a book about Financial Modelling in Power BI. Filtering the rows will reduce the processing needed, whilst demonstrating the method. So let's cheat and do that! We are demonstrating a concept here, not trying to see which reader has the most powerful computer.

To filter the rows, click on the filter icon next to **Date** and choose 'Date Filters', then 'Before…'

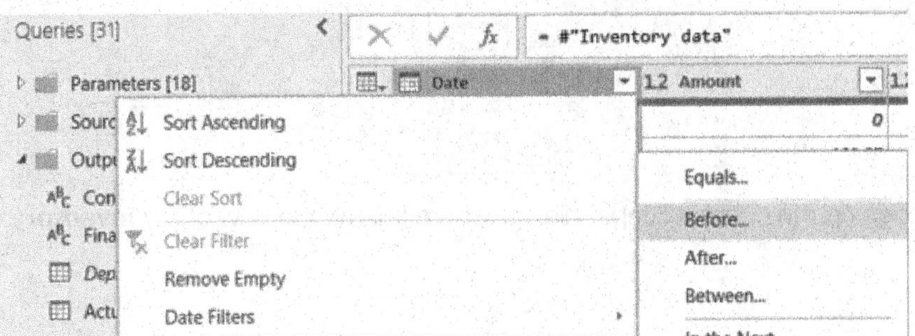

In the 'Filter Rows' dialog, I choose to filter rows with a date before 10th February.

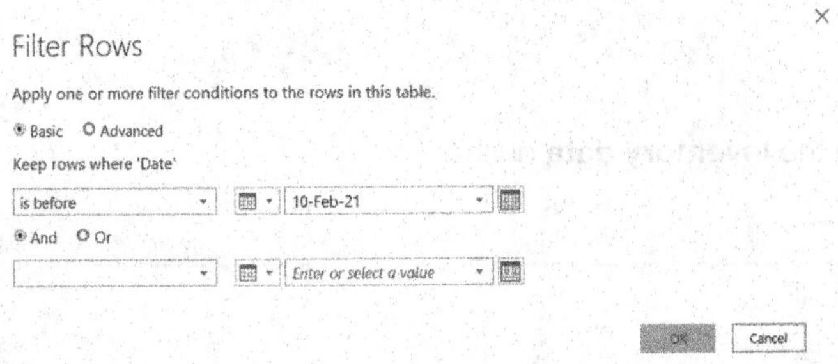

Next, I select the **Date, Price, Purchase** and **COGS** columns, right-click and select the 'Remove Other Columns' option. This is because I do not require the **Amount** or **Market** price columns, or any other columns that might emanate over time (it is usually safer to remove other columns rather than specify the ones to be discarded).

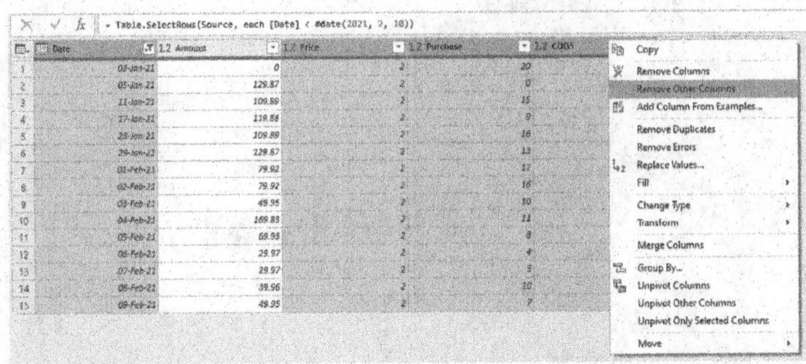

Next, I create the custom column **Net movement**:

Custom Column

Add a column that is computed from the other columns.

New column name

Net movement

Custom column formula

= [Purchase] - [COGS]

Available columns

Date
Price
Purchase
COGS

<< Insert

Learn about Power Query formulas

✓ No syntax errors have been detected.

OK Cancel

```
= [Purchase] - [COGS]
```

I change the type of the **Net movement** column to a decimal number and replace any *null* values with zero [0] as I will be using this number for calculations.

The next step is to create an **Index** column, starting from one [1].

`= Table.AddIndexColumn(#"Replaced Value", "Index", 1, 1, Int64.Type)`

	Date	1.2 Price	1.2 Purchase	1.2 COGS	1.2 Net movement	123 Index
1	03-Jan-21	2	20	0	20	1
2	05-Jan-21	2	0	13	-13	2
3	11-Jan-21	2	15	11	4	3
4	17-Jan-21	2	9	12	-3	4
5	23-Jan-21	2	16	11	5	5
6	29-Jan-21	2	13	13	0	6
7	01-Feb-21	2	17	8	9	7
8	02-Feb-21	2	16	8	8	8
9	03-Feb-21	2	10	5	5	9
10	04-Feb-21	2	11	17	-6	10
11	05-Feb-21	2	8	7	1	11
12	06-Feb-21	2	4	3	1	12
13	07-Feb-21	2	5	3	2	13
14	08-Feb-21	2	10	4	6	14
15	09-Feb-21	2	7	5	2	15

Using the **Index** column, I can create the **Closing balance** column. I use the following **M** code to create the **Closing balance** column as follows:

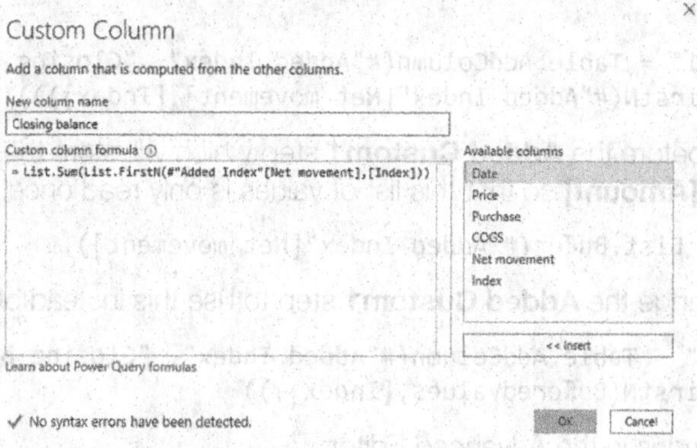


```
List.Sum(List.FirstN(#"Added Index"[Net movement],[Index]))
```

List.Buffer

The processing time to complete this step may be noticeable. This is because for each running total calculation, **List.Range()** creates a list of all the amounts to that point and then **List.Sum()** sums them. I can add another list function which will speed up the process. Like **Table.Buffer**, this function would prevent query folding, but since I am dealing with flat files, it's not relevant.

```
List.Buffer(list as list) as list
```

This buffers the **list** in memory, so that the result of this call *should* be a stable list. This basically means that the list does not need to be recalculated, and in this case, can be added to.

I look at the **M** code in the Advanced Editor:

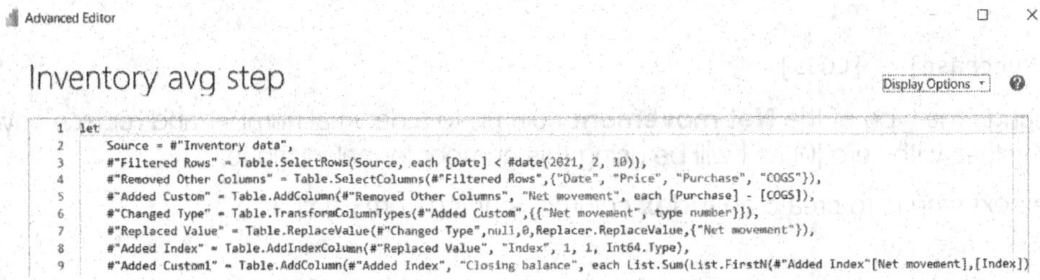

Advanced Editor

Inventory avg step

Display Options

```
let
    Source = #"Inventory data",
    #"Filtered Rows" = Table.SelectRows(Source, each [Date] < #date(2021, 2, 10)),
    #"Removed Other Columns" = Table.SelectColumns(#"Filtered Rows",{"Date", "Price", "Purchase", "COGS"}),
    #"Added Custom" = Table.AddColumn(#"Removed Other Columns", "Net movement", each [Purchase] - [COGS]),
    #"Changed Type" = Table.TransformColumnTypes(#"Added Custom",{{"Net movement", type number}}),
    #"Replaced Value" = Table.ReplaceValue(#"Changed Type",null,0,Replacer.ReplaceValue,{"Net movement"}),
    #"Added Index" = Table.AddIndexColumn(#"Replaced Value", "Index", 1, 1, Int64.Type),
    #"Added Custom1" = Table.AddColumn(#"Added Index", "Closing balance", each List.Sum(List.FirstN(#"Added Index"[Net movement],[Index])
```

```
let
 Source = #"Inventory data",
 #"Filtered Rows" = Table.SelectRows(Source, each [Date] < #date(2021, 2,
10)),
 #"Removed Other Columns" = Table.SelectColumns(#"Filtered Rows",{"Date",
"Price", "Purchase", "COGS"}),
 #"Added Custom" = Table.AddColumn(#"Removed Other Columns", "Net movement",
each [Purchase] - [COGS]),
 #"Changed Type" = Table.TransformColumnTypes(#"Added Custom",{{"Net move-
ment", type number}}),
 #"Replaced Value" = Table.ReplaceValue(#"Changed Type",null,0,Replacer.Re-
placeValue,{"Net movement"}),
 #"Added Index" = Table.AddIndexColumn(#"Replaced Value", "Index", 1, 1,
Int64.Type),
 #"Added Custom1" = Table.AddColumn(#"Added Index", "Closing balance", each
List.Sum(List.FirstN(#"Added Index"[Net movement],[Index])))
```

I can add a step before the **Added Custom1** step which will store the values for **#"Added Index"[Amount]** so that this list of values is only read once.

```
BufferedValues = List.Buffer(#"Added Index"[Net movement]),
```

I then need to change the **Added Custom1** step to use this instead of the values.

```
#"Added Custom1" = Table.AddColumn(#"Added Index", "Closing balance", each
List.Sum(List.FirstN(BufferedValues,[Index])))
```

I can see the changes in the Advanced Editor:

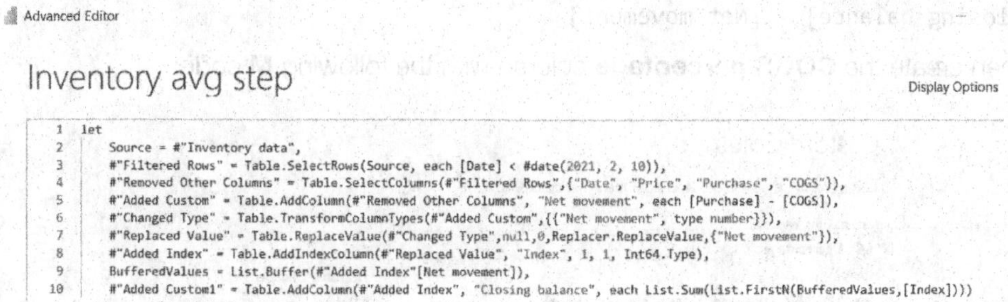

Advanced Editor

Inventory avg step

Display Options

```
let
    Source = #"Inventory data",
    #"Filtered Rows" = Table.SelectRows(Source, each [Date] < #date(2021, 2, 10)),
    #"Removed Other Columns" = Table.SelectColumns(#"Filtered Rows",{"Date", "Price", "Purchase", "COGS"}),
    #"Added Custom" = Table.AddColumn(#"Removed Other Columns", "Net movement", each [Purchase] - [COGS]),
    #"Changed Type" = Table.TransformColumnTypes(#"Added Custom",{{"Net movement", type number}}),
    #"Replaced Value" = Table.ReplaceValue(#"Changed Type",null,0,Replacer.ReplaceValue,{"Net movement"}),
    #"Added Index" = Table.AddIndexColumn(#"Replaced Value", "Index", 1, 1, Int64.Type),
    BufferedValues = List.Buffer(#"Added Index"[Net movement]),
    #"Added Custom1" = Table.AddColumn(#"Added Index", "Closing balance", each List.Sum(List.FirstN(BufferedValues,[Index])))
```

```
let
 Source = #"Inventory data",
 #"Filtered Rows" = Table.SelectRows(Source, each [Date] < #date(2021, 2,
10)),
 #"Removed Other Columns" = Table.SelectColumns(#"Filtered Rows",{"Date",
"Price", "Purchase", "COGS"}),
 #"Added Custom" = Table.AddColumn(#"Removed Other Columns", "Net movement",
each [Purchase] - [COGS]),
 #"Changed Type" = Table.TransformColumnTypes(#"Added Custom",{{"Net move-
ment", type number}}),
 #"Replaced Value" = Table.ReplaceValue(#"Changed Type",null,0,Replacer.Re-
placeValue,{"Net movement"}),
 #"Added Index" = Table.AddIndexColumn(#"Replaced Value", "Index", 1, 1,
Int64.Type),
 BufferedValues = List.Buffer(#"Added Index"[Net movement]),
 #"Added Custom1" = Table.AddColumn(#"Added Index", "Closing balance", each
List.Sum(List.FirstN(BufferedValues,[Index])))
```

This should make the running total more efficient. I will repeat this process later when I create the **Cumulative debt drawdown** (obviously not in this chapter!).

I can then create the **Opening balance** column with the following **M** code:

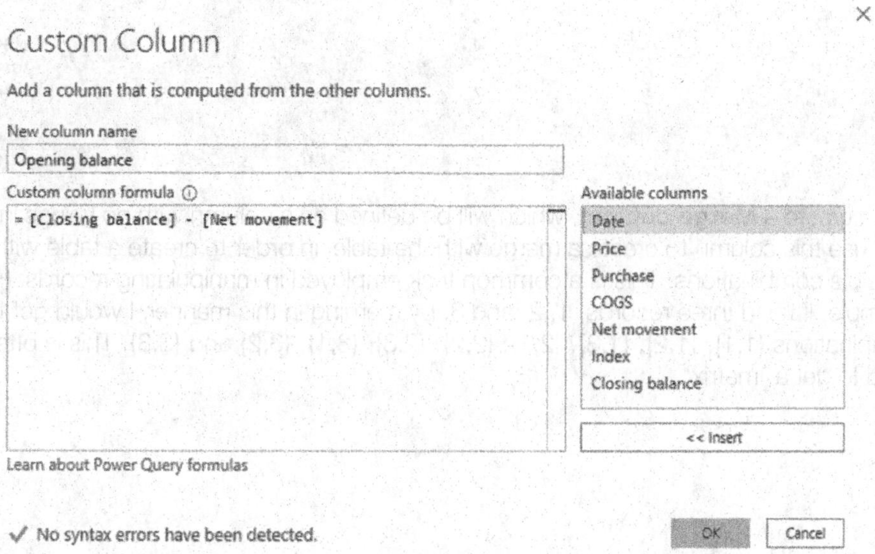

Custom Column

Add a column that is computed from the other columns.

New column name

Opening balance

Custom column formula

```
= [Closing balance] - [Net movement]
```

Available columns

Date
Price
Purchase
COGS
Net movement
Index
Closing balance

<< Insert

Learn about Power Query formulas

✓ No syntax errors have been detected.

OK Cancel

```
[Closing balance] - [Net movement]
```

I then create the **COGS percentage** column with the following **M** code:

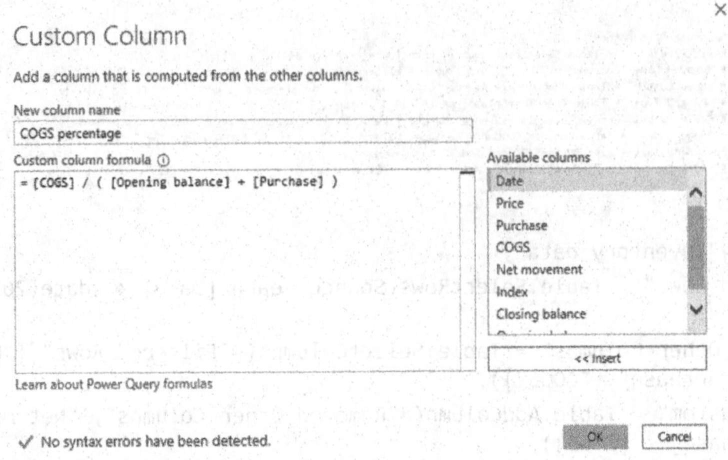


```
[COGS] / ( [Opening balance] + [Purchase] )
```

I then remove the **Net movement** column as that is no longer needed. Furthermore, I should also change the data types of the **Closing balance, Opening balance,** and **COGS percentage** columns to a decimal number.

`= Table.TransformColumnTypes(#"Added Custom3",{{"Closing balance", type number}, {"Opening balance", type numb`

		1.2 COGS	1²₃ Index	1.2 Closing balance	1.2 Opening balance	1.2 COGS percentage
1	20	0	1	20	0	0
2	0	13	2	7	20	0.65
3	15	11	3	11	7	0.5
4	9	12	4	8	11	0.6
5	16	11	5	13	8	0.458333333
6	13	13	6	13	13	0.5
7	17	8	7	22	13	0.266666667
8	16	8	8	30	22	0.210526316
9	10	5	9	35	30	0.125
10	11	17	10	29	35	0.369565217
11	8	7	11	30	29	0.189189189
12	4	3	12	31	30	0.088235294
13	5	3	13	33	31	0.083333333
14	10	4	14	39	33	0.093023256
15	7	5	15	41	39	0.108695652

I then create a **Merge column**, which will be defined as a column with no values in it. I will use this column to create a merge with the table, in order to create a table with all possible combinations. This is a common trick employed in manipulating records. For example, if I had three records, 1, 2, and 3, by merging in this manner, I would get the combinations {1,1}, {1,2}, {1,3}, {2,1}, {2,2}, {2,3}, {3,1}, {3,2} and {3,3}. This is often used to get a "matrix".

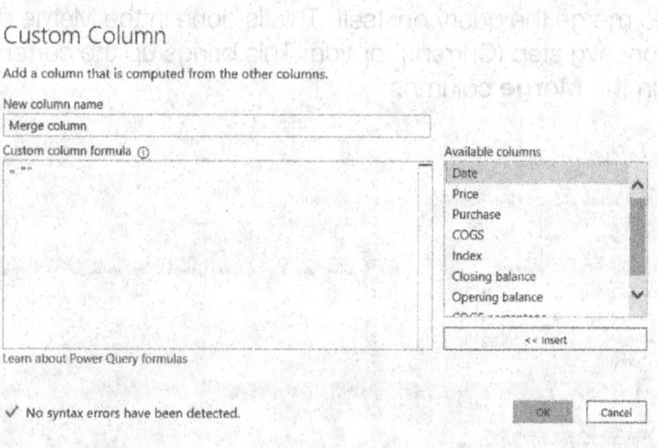

```
= ""
```

The next column is the remaining percentage after the **COGS percentage** has been deducted from 100%. I call this column 1 – [COGS percentage] as a working name to show how it has been calculated:

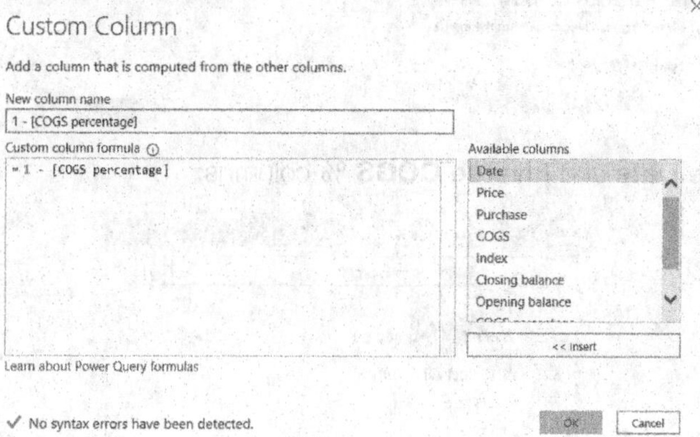

```
1 - [COGS percentage]
```

I can now delete the **COGS percentage** column as I no longer need it. I will also rename the **1 – [COGS percentage]** column to **Inverse COGS %**, as that will be easier to use in calculations. I should not forget to change the data type of the **Inverse COGS %** column to percentage:

		1.2 COGS	1²3 Index	1.2 Closing balance	1.2 Opening balance	ABC 123 Merge column	% Inverse COGS %
1	20	0	1	20	0		100.00%
2	0	15	2	7	20		55.00%
3	15	11	3	11	7		50.00%
4	9	12	4	8	11		40.00%
5	16	11	5	13	8		54.17%
6	13	13	6	13	13		50.00%
7	17	8	7	22	13		73.33%
8	16	8	8	30	22		78.95%
9	10	5	9	35	30		87.50%
10	11	17	10	29	35		63.04%
11	8	7	11	30	29		81.08%
12	4	3	12	31	30		91.18%
13	5	3	13	33	31		91.67%
14	10	4	14	39	33		90.70%
15	7	5	15	41	39		89.13%

The next step is to merge the query on itself. This is done in the Merge dialog, where I select the 'Inventory avg step (Current)' option. This brings up the current table. Then I select to merge on the **Merge** columns.

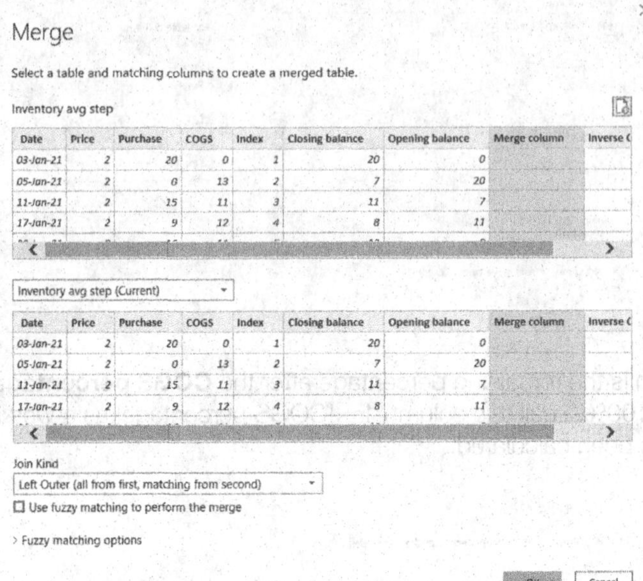

I expand only the **Date** and **Inverse COGS %** columns:

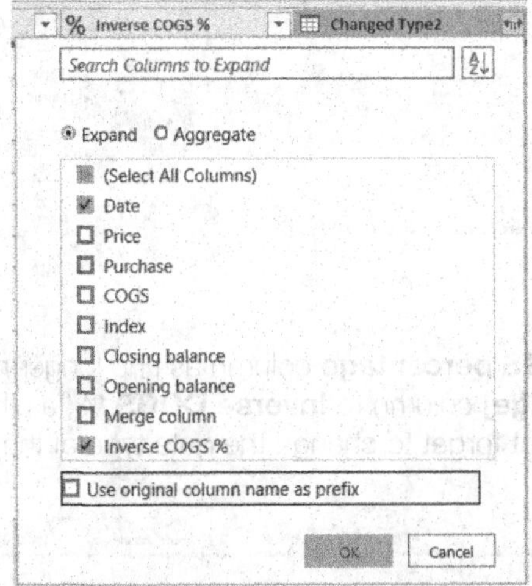

The resulting table has two more columns added to it:

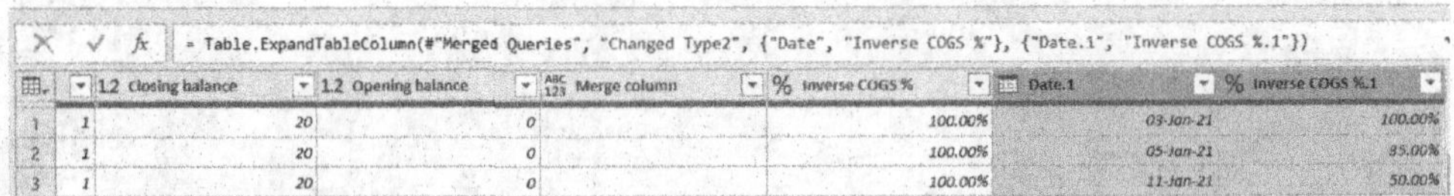

To make it more legible, I have renamed the **Date.1** and **Inverse COGS %.1** columns to **Merged date** and **Merged inverse COGS %** respectively.

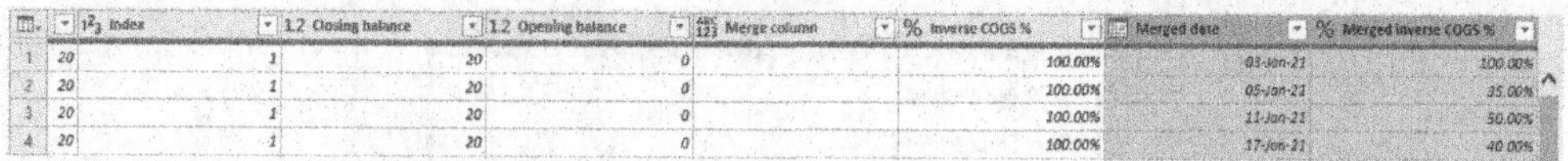

		Index	Closing balance	Opening balance	Merge column	Inverse COGS %	Merged date	Merged inverse COGS %
1	20	1	20	0		100.00%	03-Jan-21	100.00%
2	20	1	20	0		100.00%	05-Jan-21	35.00%
3	20	1	20	0		100.00%	11-Jan-21	50.00%
4	20	1	20	0		100.00%	17-Jan-21	40.00%

I need to add a **Table.Buffer** line before the merge step:

```
BufferedTable = Table.Buffer(#"Changed Type2"),
```

Note that #"Changed Type2" is the step before the merge. If you have done the steps in a different order this should be changed to whatever the step <u>before</u> the merge is called.

I also need to change the 'Merged Queries' step from this:

```
= Table.NestedJoin(#"Changed Type2", {"Merge column"}, #"Changed Type2",
{"Merge column"}, "Changed Type2", JoinKind.LeftOuter)
```

to this

```
= Table.NestedJoin(BufferedTable, {"Merge column"}, BufferedTable, {"Merge
column"}, "Changed Type2", JoinKind.LeftOuter)
```

This will make the merge more efficient.

I need to add another helper column I will call the **Triangle flag**. This column determines which rows I use in the inventory calculation. The **Triangle flag** column uses the following **M** code:

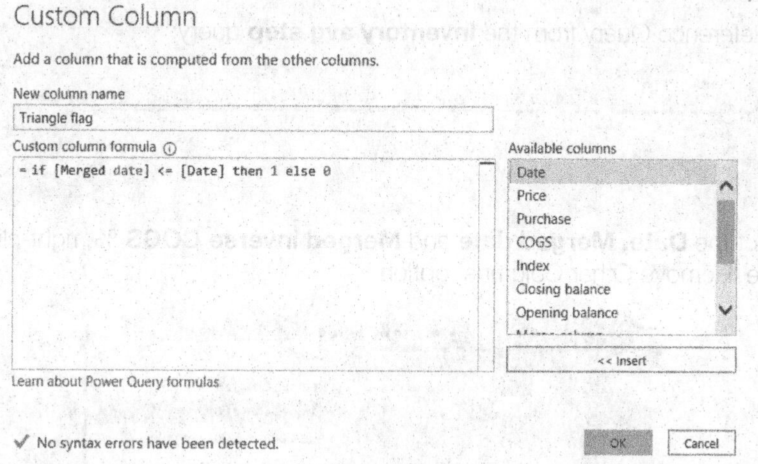


```
if [Merged date] <= [Date] then 1 else 0
```

I then filter the **Triangle flag** column to keep values of one [1]. Effectively, my matrix created by merging on a blank column has been "halved" along the leading diagonal using the condition

```
[Merged date] <= [Date]
```

Hence the "Triangle" name.

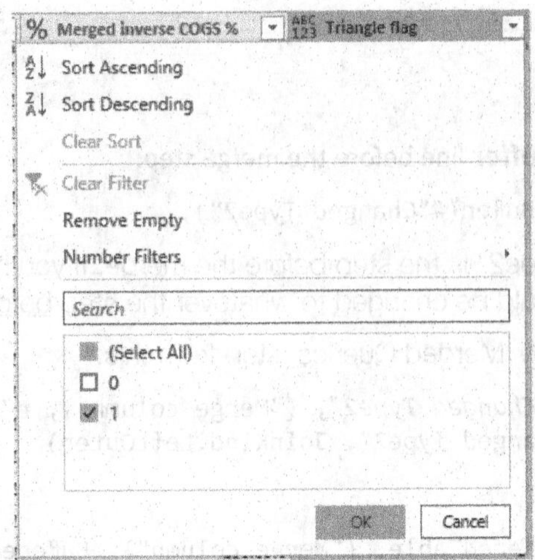

Average inventory custom function

I can now create the custom function required to calculate the average inventory cost. Sometimes it is useful to create custom functions in Power Query. These are essentially queries that are created to perform certain steps for a specified set of inputs.

It may be easier to understand if I build one.

I make a Reference Query from the **Inventory avg step** query:

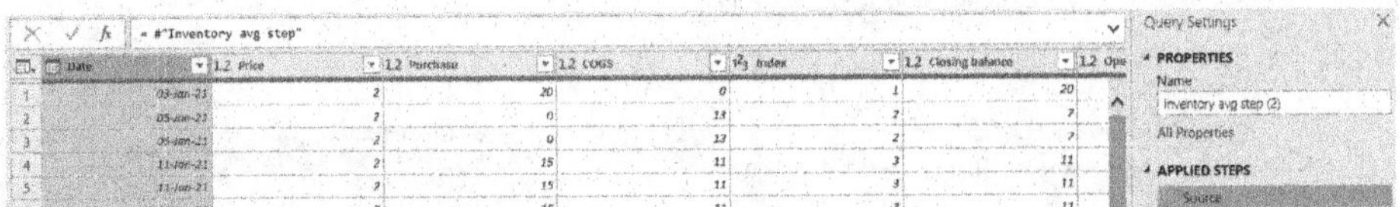

I then select the **Date, Merged date** and **Merged inverse COGS %**, right-click and choose the 'Remove Other Columns' option:

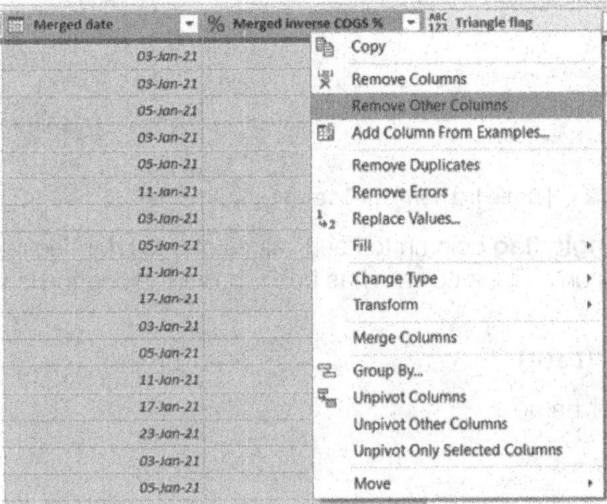

To simulate looking back from a future date, I will have to create a filter on **Date** here, with a date as a placeholder. For this example, I will use the 5th Jan 2021 as a placeholder. I will then change the input of this filter into a parameter that will determine how many dates the function should look back in time:

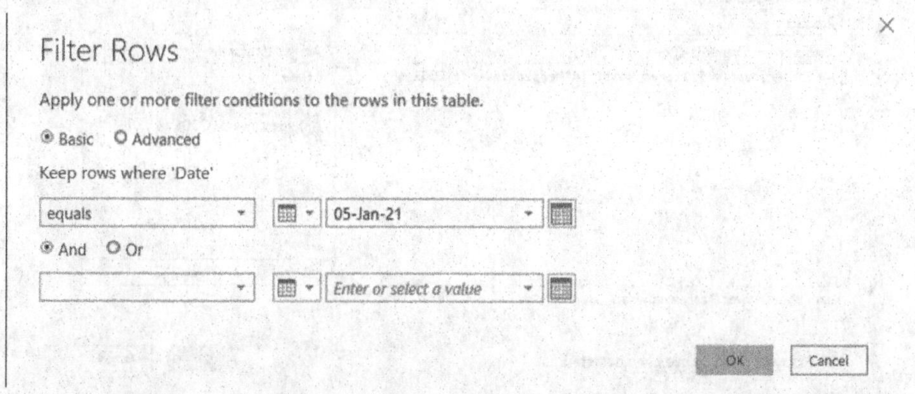

The next step is to filter the **Merged date** column on dates that are greater than or equal to the first date of the dataset. Again, I am using the first date of the dataset as a placeholder. I will replace this date with a parameter later.

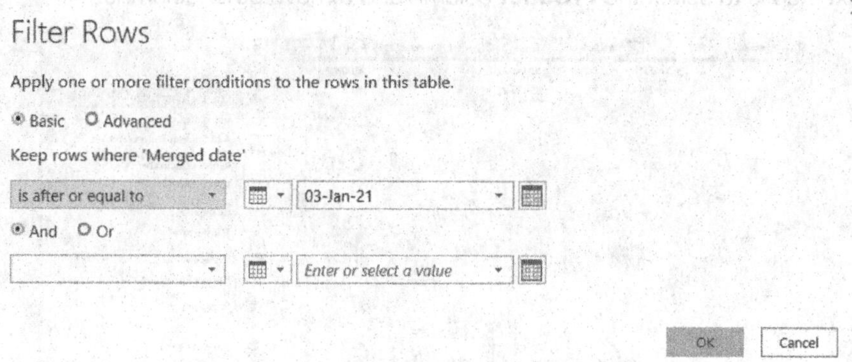

This will result in no significant change to the table for now:

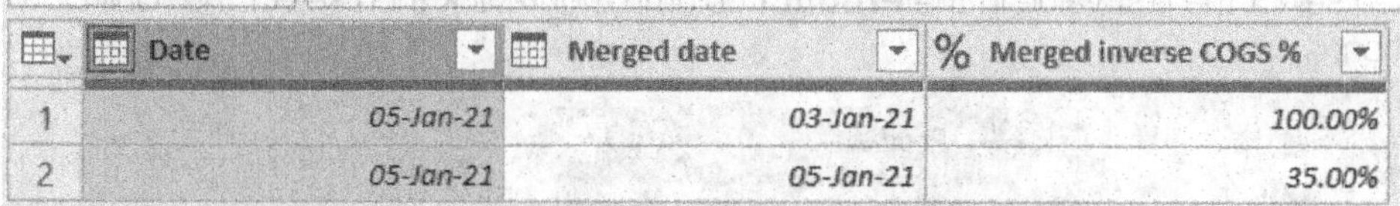

	Date	Merged date	Merged inverse COGS %
1	05-Jan-21	03-Jan-21	100.00%
2	05-Jan-21	05-Jan-21	35.00%

I must create one more custom column here, called the **Product** column. This column will create a product of every percentage in the **Merged inverse COGS %** column. I will use the following **M** code:

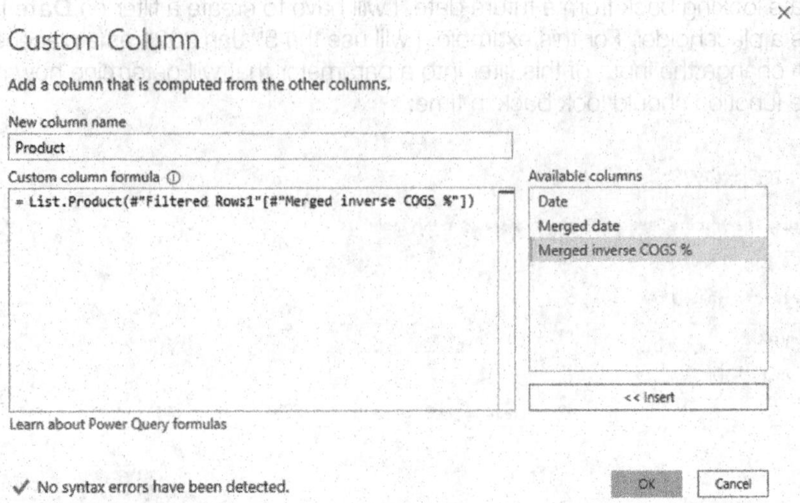


```
List.Product(#"Filtered Rows1"[#"Merged inverse COGS %"])
```

'**Filtered Rows1**' comes up as the previous step where I filtered rows in the **M** code.

The next step is to select the **Product** column and remove other columns:

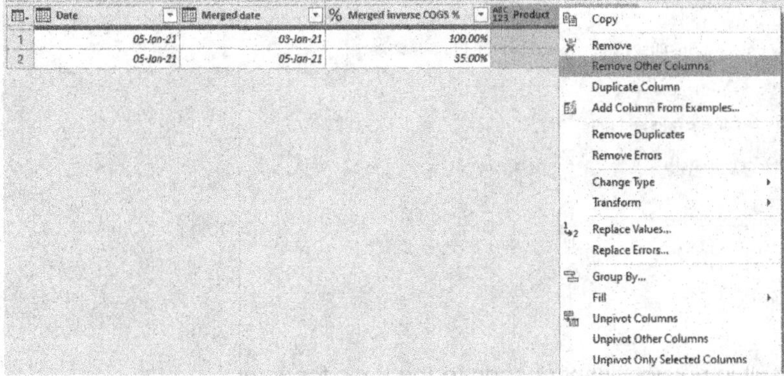

I then select the first value in the **Product** column, right-click then select the 'Drill Down' option:

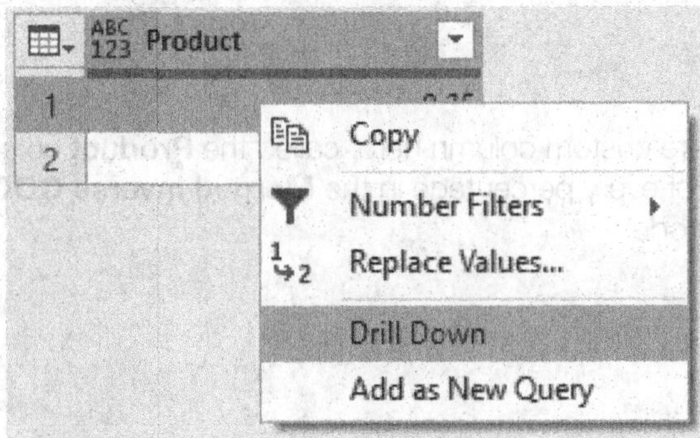

This results in the query returning with a single value:

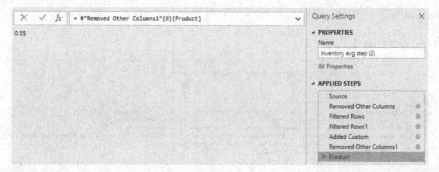

The next step is turning this query into a function. With the query selected (**Inventory avg step (2)**). I open the Advanced Editor, and I enclose the existing code with the following start and end lines:

Start line:

```
let
 GridCalc = (currentdate as date, lookback as date, tablename as table) =>
```

End line:

```
in
 GridCalc
```

I also make changes to the following segments of code:

Advanced Editor

Inventory avg step (2)

```

let
    GridCalc = (currentdate as date, lookback as date, tablename as table) =>


let
    Source = #"Inventory avg step",
    #"Removed Other Columns" = Table.SelectColumns(Source,{"Date", "Merged date", "Merged inverse COGS %"}),
    #"Filtered Rows" = Table.SelectRows(#"Removed Other Columns", each [Date] = #date(2021, 1, 5)),
    #"Filtered Rows1" = Table.SelectRows(#"Filtered Rows", each [Merged date] >= #date(2021, 1, 3)),
    #"Added Custom" = Table.AddColumn(#"Filtered Rows1", "Product", each List.Product(#"Filtered Rows1"[#"Merged inverse COGS %"])),
    #"Removed Other Columns1" = Table.SelectColumns(#"Added Custom",{"Product"}),
    Product = #"Removed Other Columns1"{0}[Product]
in
    Product

in
    GridCalc
```

The changes are summarised here:

- **#"Inventory avg step"** is changed to **tablename**
- **#date(2021, 1, 5)** is changed to **currentdate**
- **#date(2021, 1, 3)** is changed to **lookback**

Advanced Editor

Inventory avg step (2)

```
let
    GridCalc = (currentdate as date, lookback as date, tablename as table) =>


let
    Source = tablename,
    #"Removed Other Columns" = Table.SelectColumns(Source,{"Date", "Merged date", "Merged inverse COGS %"}),
    #"Filtered Rows" = Table.SelectRows(#"Removed Other Columns", each [Date] = currentdate),
    #"Filtered Rows1" = Table.SelectRows(#"Filtered Rows", each [Merged date] >= lookback),
    #"Added Custom" = Table.AddColumn(#"Filtered Rows1", "Product", each List.Product(#"Filtered Rows1"[#"Merged inverse COGS %"])),
    #"Removed Other Columns1" = Table.SelectColumns(#"Added Custom",{"Product"}),
    Product = #"Removed Other Columns1"{0}[Product]
in
    Product

in
    GridCalc
```

```
let
 GridCalc = (currentdate as date, lookback as date, tablename as table) =>

let
 Source = tablename,
 #"Removed Other Columns" = Table.SelectColumns(Source,{"Date", "Merged
date", "Merged inverse COGS %"}),
 #"Filtered Rows" = Table.SelectRows(#"Removed Other Columns", each [Date] =
currentdate),
 #"Filtered Rows1" = Table.SelectRows(#"Filtered Rows", each [Merged date] >=
lookback),
 #"Added Custom" = Table.AddColumn(#"Filtered Rows1", "Product", each List.
Product(#"Filtered Rows1"[#"Merged inverse COGS %"])),
 #"Removed Other Columns1" = Table.SelectColumns(#"Added Custom",{"Prod-
uct"}),
 Product = #"Removed Other Columns1"{0}[Product]
in
 Product

in
 GridCalc
```

I then rename the function to **FN_InventoryAverage** and disable the load for the **Inventory avg step** query.

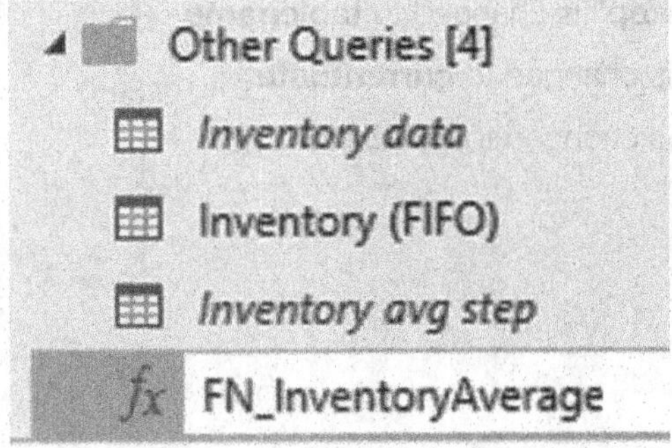

Inventory cost table query

I need to create one more table to aid in the average cost calculation. This table will contain the inventory costs at each date there is a transaction. I will call this table the **Inventory cost table**.

To create this table, I reference the **Inventory data** table.

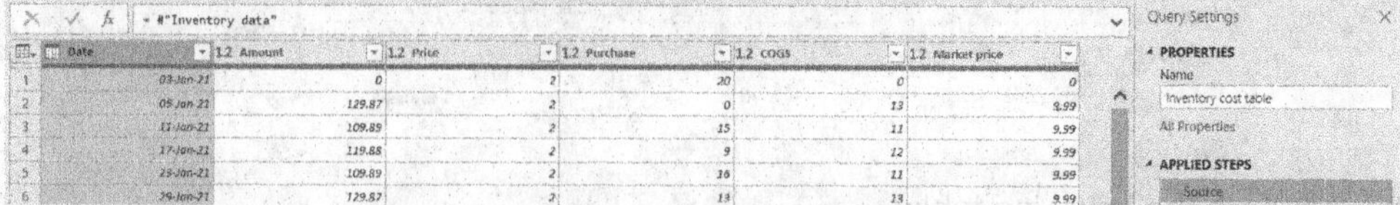

The first step here is to select the **Date, Price** and **Purchase** columns, right-click then select the 'Remove Other Columns' option:

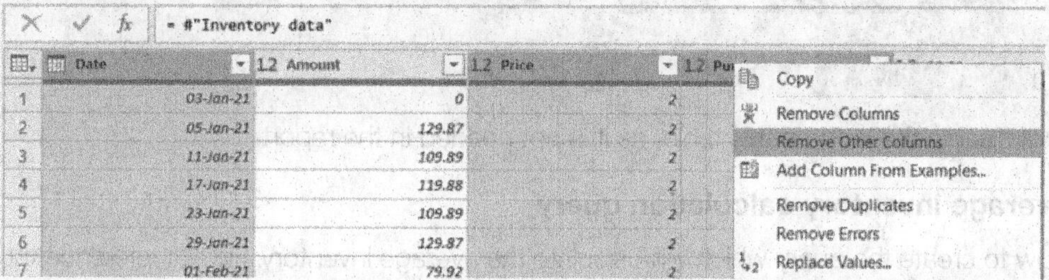

I create a custom column **Purchase price**, which uses the following **M** code:

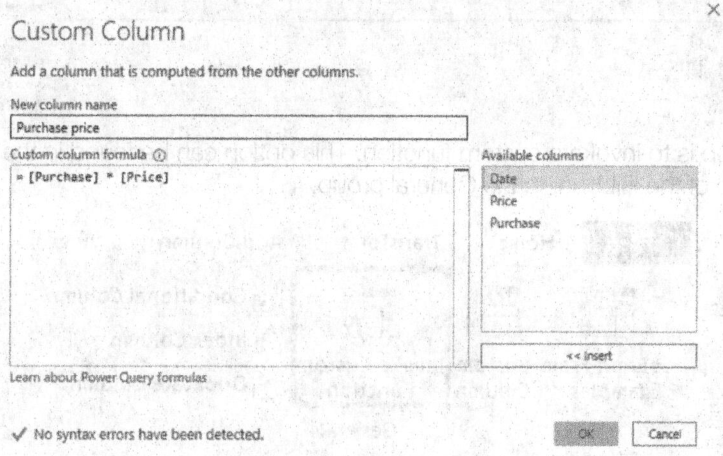


```
[Purchase]* [Price]
```

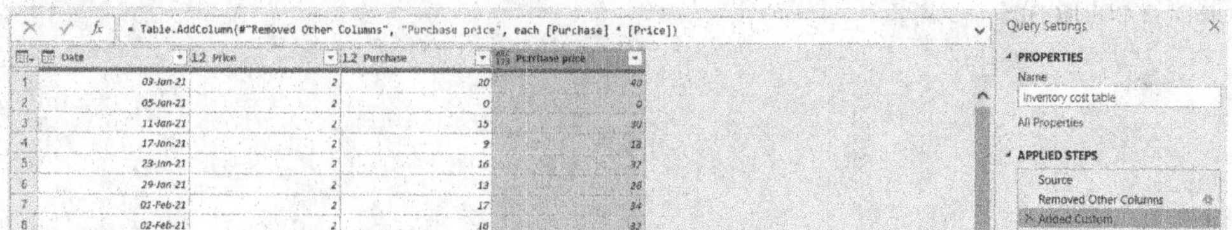

The next step here is to group the **Purchase price** column by the date.

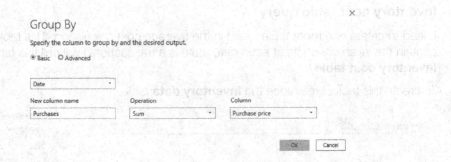

Group By

Specify the column to group by and the desired output.

Basic   Advanced

Date

New column name	Operation	Column
Purchases	Sum	Purchase price

OK   Cancel

This results in the following table:

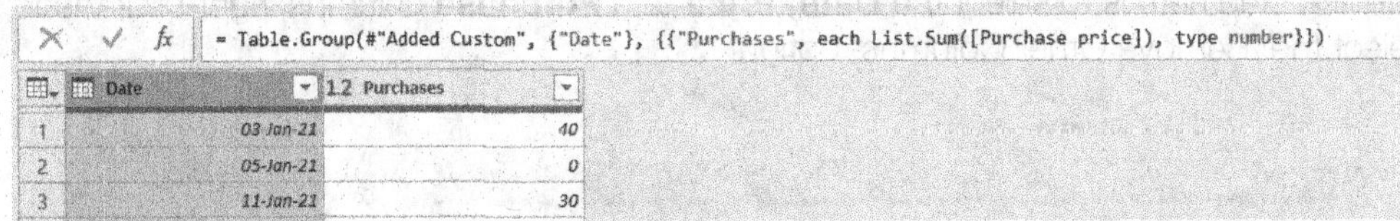

= Table.Group(#"Added Custom", {"Date"}, {{"Purchases", each List.Sum([Purchase price]), type number}})

	Date	1.2 Purchases
1	03-Jan-21	40
2	05-Jan-21	0
3	11-Jan-21	30

I will disable the load on this table, as it is not needed in the report.

Average inventory calculation query

Now to create the query which will calculate the average inventory. Here, I reference the **Inventory avg step** query. I rename it to **Inventory avg calc**.

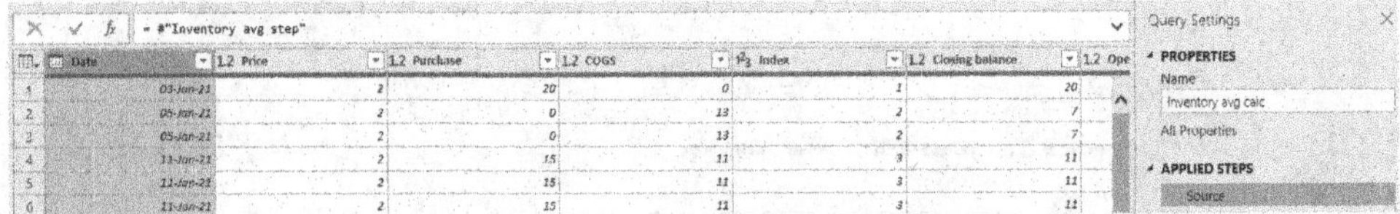

= #"Inventory avg step"

	Date	1.2 Price	1.2 Purchase	1.2 COGS	1²3 Index	1.2 Closing balance	1.2 Ope
1	03-Jan-21	2	20	0	1	20	
2	05-Jan-21	2	0	13	2	7	
3	05-Jan-21	2	0	13	2	7	
4	11-Jan-21	2	15	11	3	11	
5	11-Jan-21	2	15	11	3	11	
6	11-Jan-21	2	15	11	3	11	

The next step is to invoke a custom function. This option can be found in the 'Add Column' tab of the Ribbon, in the General group.

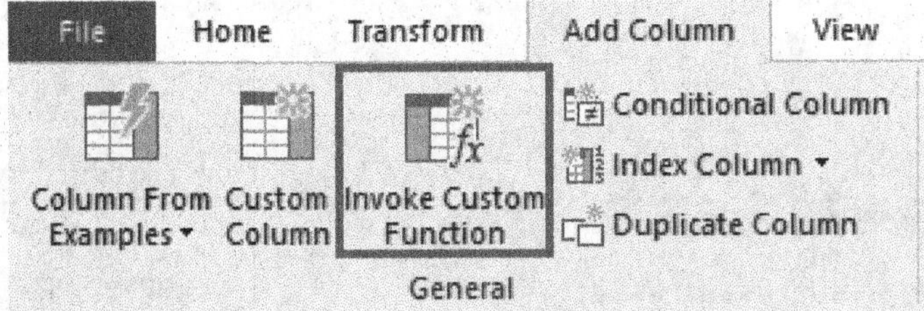

This will bring up the 'Invoke Custom Function' dialog, where I have used the following options (note that I have used the dropdowns under **currentdate** and **lookback** to select a column):

Invoke Custom Function

Invoke a custom function defined in this file for each row.

New column name

ProductBack%

Function query

FN_InventoryAverage

currentdate

Date

lookback

Merged date

tablename

Inventory avg step

OK Cancel

This will begin the process. However, I need to make a change: the table name needs to be the **Source** step in the same query. If I look at the Formula Bar, can see that the third parameter that requires a table is currently set to '#"Inventory avg step"'. I can change it directly in the Formula Bar to 'Source'.

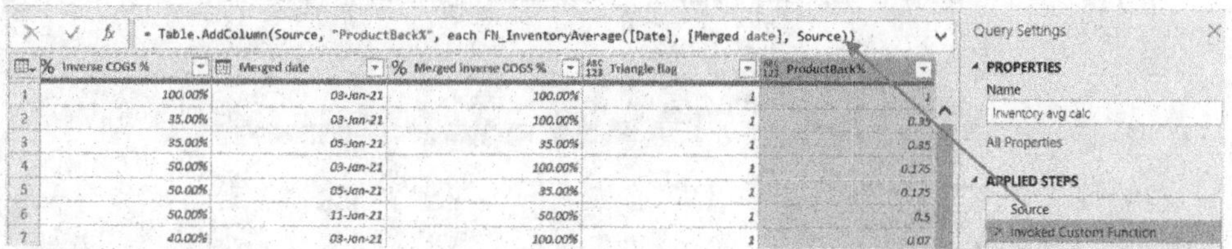

This will ensure that I am referring to the previous step in the query. Applying the function involves substantial processing which might take time to load.

I now have to merge this query with the purchase data from the **Inventory cost table**. The 'Merge Queries' option is located on the Home tab of the Ribbon in the Combine group.

The Merge dialog will appear. Here is where I specify the merge to occur on the **Date** column in both tables:

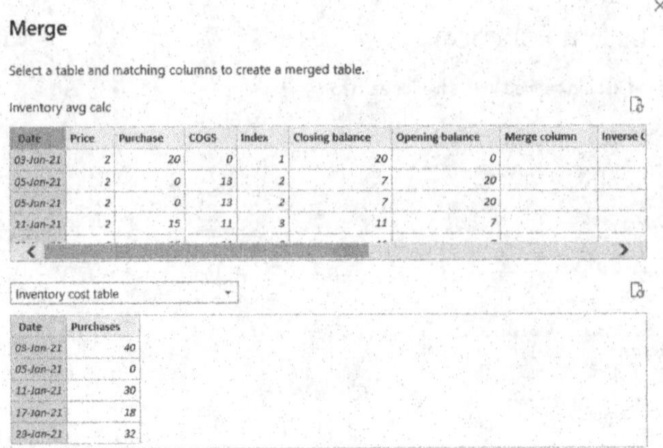

I need to perform a second merge. However, this time, I use the **Merge date** column instead of the **Date** column in the **Inventory avg calc** table:

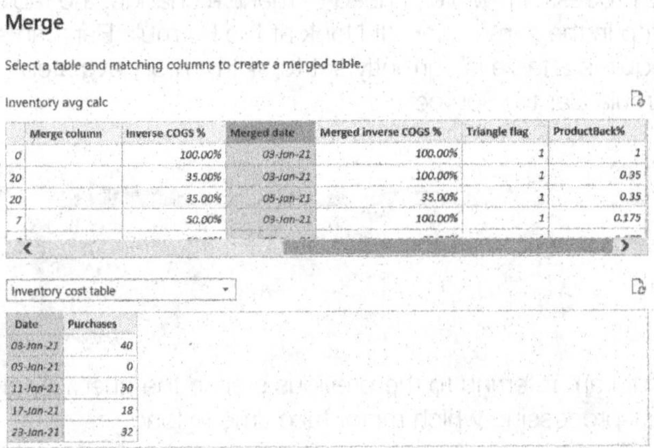

I expand both merge columns now, bringing in the **Purchases** amounts for both.

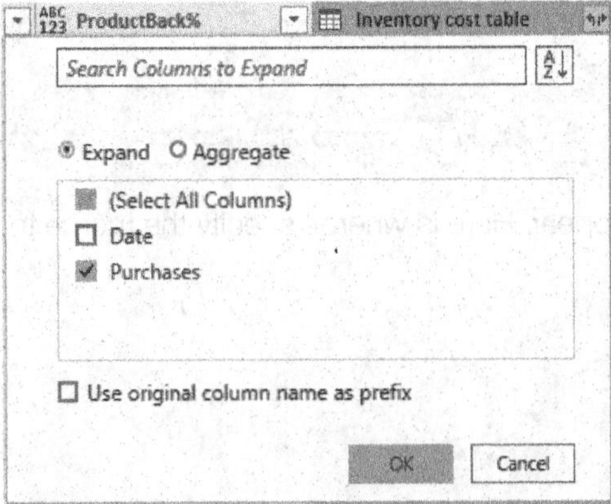

Merging with **Inventory cost table** uses considerable memory, and I have done this twice. I am going to look at a way to reduce the memory involved, which will involve an excursion into the topic of joining tables.

Table.NestedJoin vs. Table.Join

When I merge with **Inventory cost table**, the **M** code generated is:

```
= Table.NestedJoin(#"Invoked Custom Function", {"Date"}, #"Inventory cost
table", {"Date"}, "Inventory cost table", JoinKind.LeftOuter)
```

The function used is **Table.NestedJoin()**:

Table.NestedJoin(table1 as table, **key1** as any, **table2** as any, **key2** as any, **newColumnName** as text, optional **joinKind** as nullable number, optional **keyEqualityComparers** as nullable list) as table.

This joins the rows of **table1** with the rows of **table2**, based upon the equality of the values of the key columns selected by **key1** (for **table1**) and **key2** (for **table2**). The results are entered into the column named **newColumnName**.

The optional **joinKind** specifies the kind of join to perform. By default, a left outer join is performed if a **joinKind** is not specified. An optional set of **keyEqualityComparers** may be included to specify how to compare the key columns. This feature is currently intended for what is known as "internal use only".

There is another way to join tables called **Table.Join()**. The description for this function sounds very similar, with one noticeable difference:

Table.Join(table1 as table, **key1** as any, **table2** as table, **key2** as any, optional **joinKind** as nullable number, optional **joinAlgorithm** as nullable number, optional **keyEqualityComparers** as nullable list) as table

This joins the rows of **table1** with the rows of **table2**, based upon the equality of the values of the key columns selected by **key1** (for **table1**) and **key2** (for **table2**). By default, an inner join is performed, however an optional **joinKind** may be included to specify the type of join. Options include:

- JoinKind.Inner
- JoinKind.LeftOuter
- JoinKind.RightOuter
- JoinKind.FullOuter
- JoinKind.LeftAnti
- JoinKind.RightAnti.

An optional set of **keyEqualityComparers** may be included to specify how to compare the key columns. This feature is currently intended for internal use only.

There is no column name specified, but more importantly, there is an option to use **joinAlgorithm**. Both differences will affect the way I plan to join to **Inventory cost table.**

I am not going to look at all the possible values for **joinAlgorithm** here, suffice to say, the one that is useful to me is **JoinAlgorithm.SortMerge**. The reason it is useful is because I am working with flat files and not a relational database. Both tables are therefore held in memory in order to perform the merge. If my data is already in ascending order, I can use the **SortMerge** join algorithm to merge my data without holding it all in memory first. Therefore, I amend the 'Merged Queries' step in my merged data from

```
= Table.NestedJoin(#"Invoked Custom Function", {"Date"}, #"Inventory cost table", {"Date"}, "Inventory cost table", JoinKind.LeftOuter)
```

to

```
= Table.Join(#"Invoked Custom Function", {"Date"}, #"Inventory cost table", {"Date"}, JoinKind.LeftOuter, JoinAlgorithm.SortMerge)
```

This soon reveals another change I need to make!

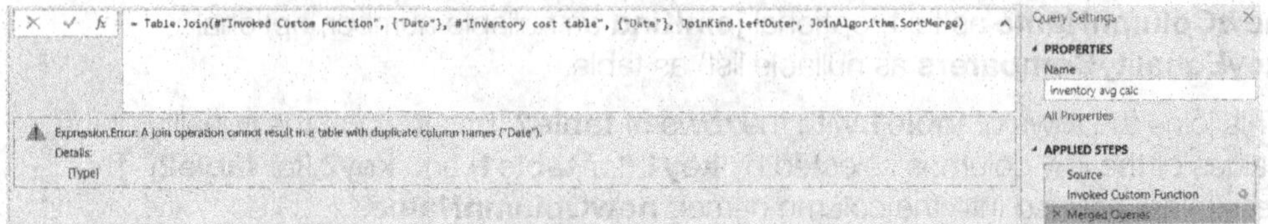

This way of joining tables immediately pulls in the data, which means two things here. The good news is, I will not need the step to expand the data from the table. The bad news is, I must go and change the column in **Inventory cost table** from **Date** to something that will be unique in this join, *e.g.* **Purchase Date**.

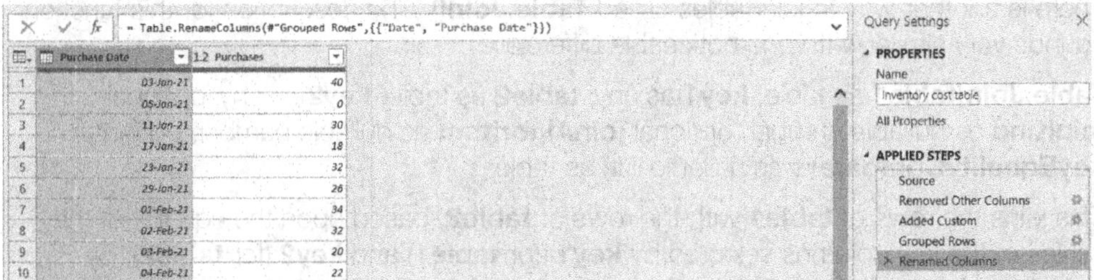

Now I can go back and amend the Merged Queries step again to

```
= Table.Join(#"Invoked Custom Function", {"Date"}, #"Inventory cost table", {"Purchase Date"}, JoinKind.LeftOuter, JoinAlgorithm.SortMerge)
```

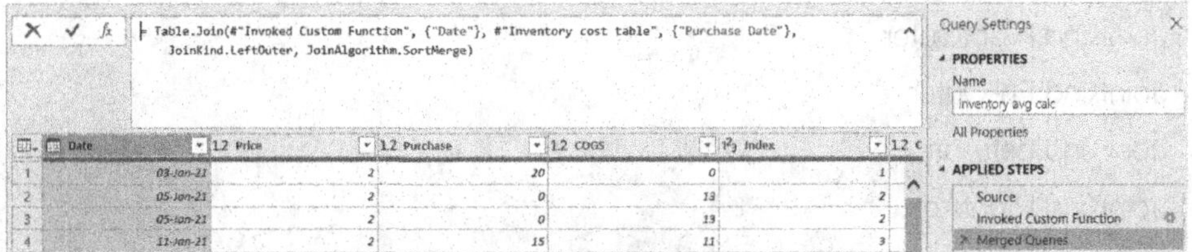

I do not want to keep the **Purchase Date** column, so I can delete that. Bearing in mind that I am going to repeat this merge using the **Merge Date**, it's important that I rename the **Purchases** column, as it will cause a problem when I merge again. I rename it to **Purchases item period**. I will get warnings about inserting steps before 'Merged Queries1', but I may ignore them. There are still errors on the subsequent steps, but I will fix them next.

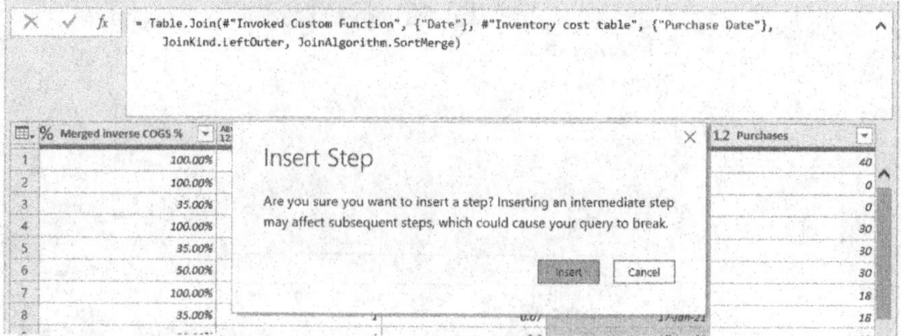

I move on to 'Merged Queries1', and make a similar change from

```
= Table.NestedJoin(#"Renamed Columns", {"Merged date"}, #"Inventory cost ta-
ble", {"Date"}, "Inventory cost table.1", JoinKind.LeftOuter)
```

to

```
= Table.Join(#"Renamed Columns", {"Merged date"}, #"Inventory cost table",
{"Purchase Date"}, JoinKind.LeftOuter, JoinAlgorithm.SortMerge)
```

Note that #"Renamed Columns" refers to the previous step. If your step has a different name, then use this instead.

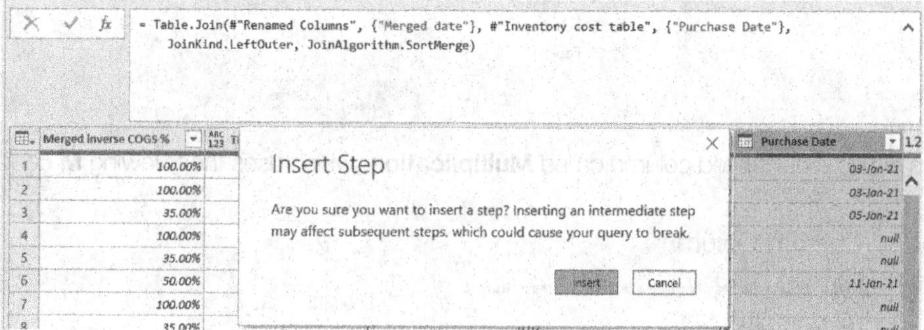

I remove the **Purchase Date** column and rename the **Purchases** column **Purchases historical period**, ignoring any inserted step warnings. I can then remove both of the 'Expand…' steps by clicking on the cross icon next to them.

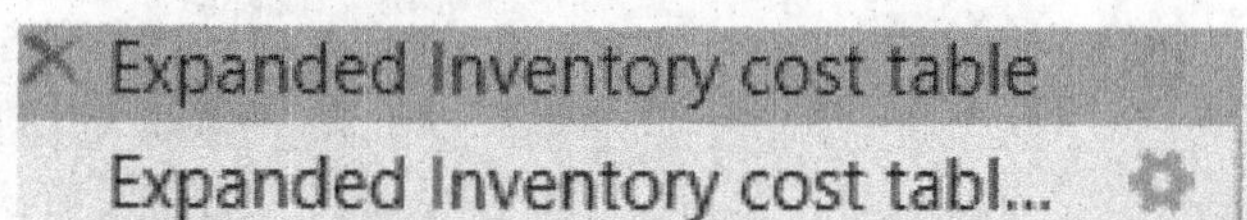

I will get a warning again, but I can continue.

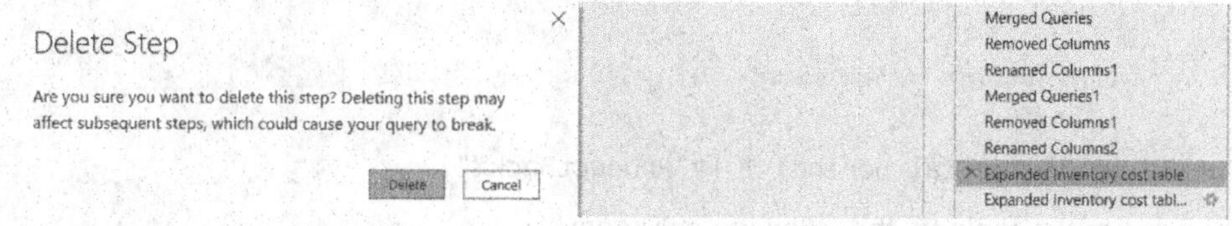

I sort the **Date** column into ascending values:

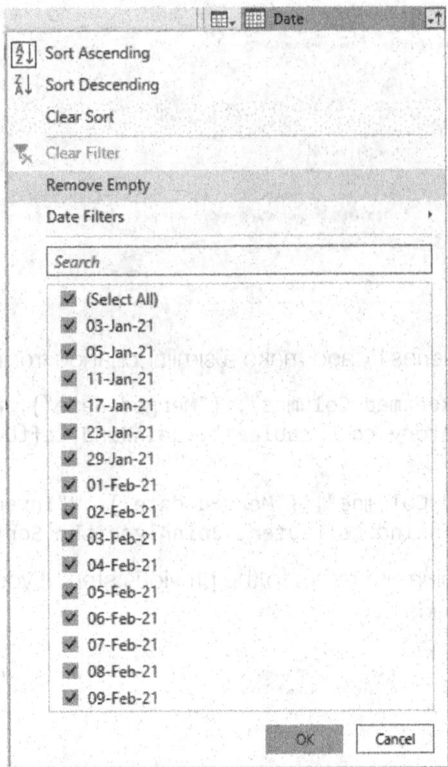

I then create a calculated column called **Multiplication**, which uses the following **M** code:

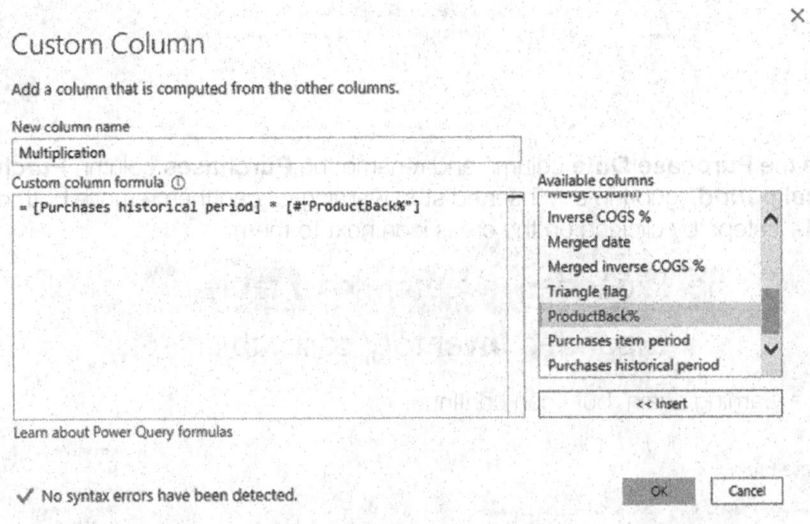


```
[Purchases historical period] * [#"ProductBack%"]
```

I then group the table by the following columns:

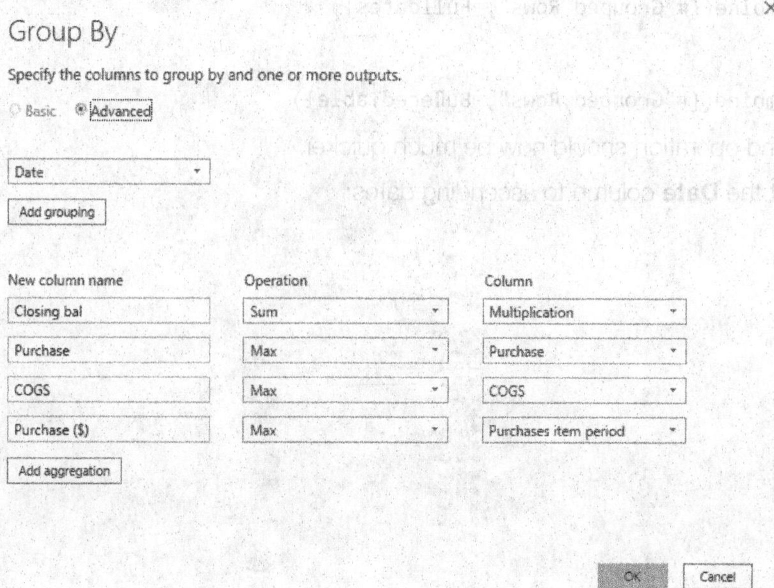

The resulting table will have calculated the **Closing bal** (short for closing balance) at each row or date:

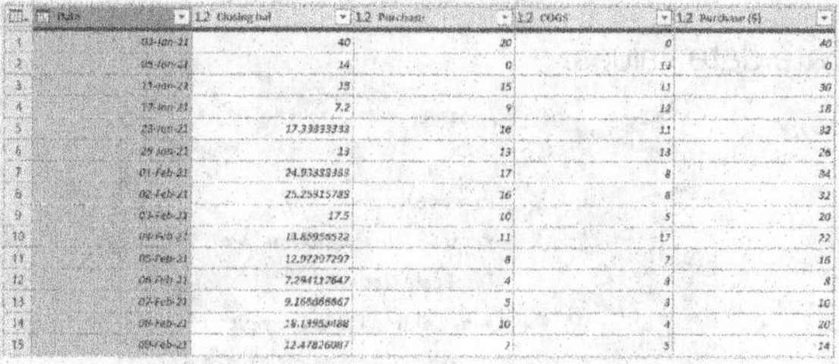

	Date	1.2 Closing bal	1.2 Purchase	1.2 COGS	1.2 Purchase ($)
1	03-Jan-21	40	20	0	40
2	05-Jan-21	14	0	14	0
3	11-Jan-21	15	15	11	30
4	17-Jan-21	7.2	9	12	18
5	23-Jan-21	17.33333333	16	11	32
6	29-Jan-21	13	13	13	26
7	01-Feb-21	24.93333333	17	8	34
8	02-Feb-21	25.25815789	16	8	32
9	03-Feb-21	17.5	10	5	20
10	04-Feb-21	13.85955522	11	17	22
11	05-Feb-21	12.97297297	8	7	16
12	06-Feb-21	7.294117647	4	8	8
13	07-Feb-21	9.166666667	5	3	10
14	08-Feb-21	18.13953488	10	4	20
15	09-Feb-21	12.47826087	7	5	14

I must perform one last transformation so that the table can easily be read in **DAX**. I will append this query with the **Fulldates** query, which we set up back in Chapter 6.

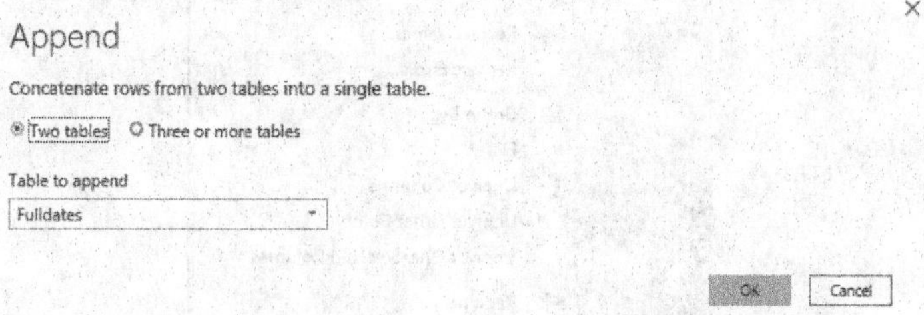

I can make this append step more efficient by adding a **Table.Buffer()** step. As I did previously, I will do this in the Advanced Editor. The line I will add is before the 'Appended Query' step:

```
BufferedTable = Table.Buffer(Fulldates),
```

I also need to change the 'Appended Queries' step from this:

```
Table.Combine({#"Grouped Rows", Fulldates})
```

to this:

```
Table.Combine({#"Grouped Rows", BufferedTable})
```

The append operation should now be much quicker.

I then sort the **Date** column to ascending dates:

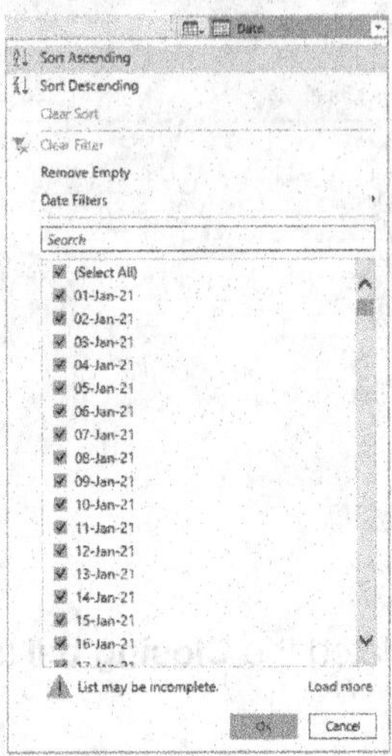

Now I remove duplicate date values:

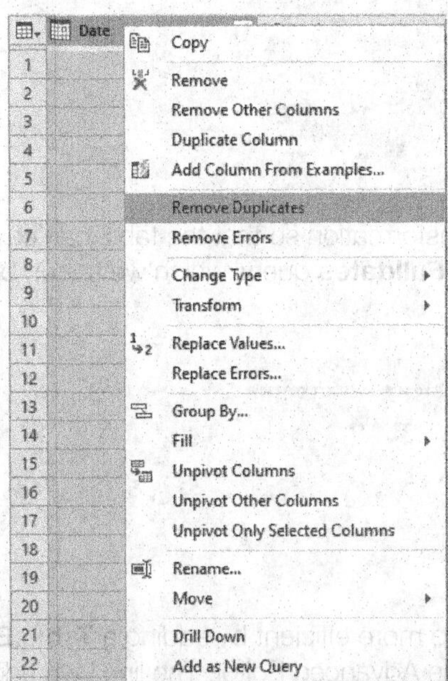

Then, I select the **Closing bal** column and select the 'Fill down' option. This option is located on the Transform tab on the Ribbon in the 'Any Column' group.

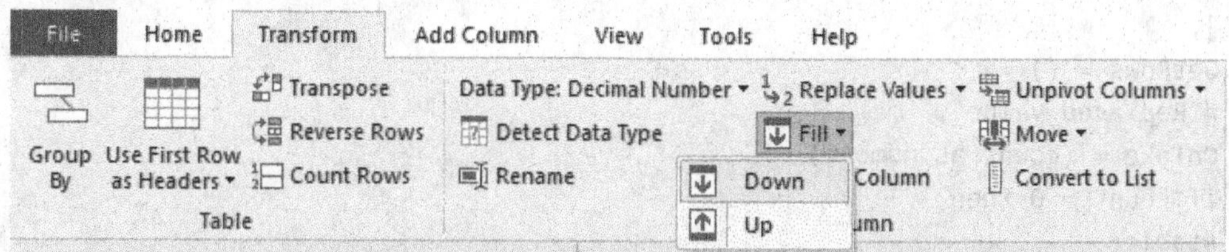

I shall then replace *null* values in the **Closing bal, Purchase, COGS** and **Purchase ($)** columns to zero [0].

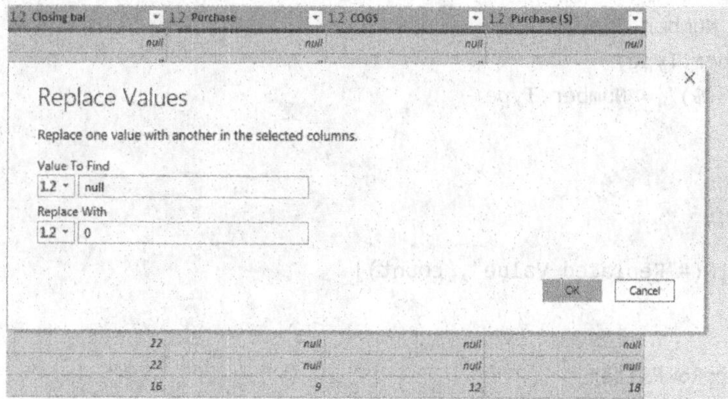

The **Inventory avg calc** table should now look like this:

	Date	Closing bal	Purchase	COGS	Purchase ($)
1	01-Jan-21	0	0	0	0
2	02-Jan-21	0	0	0	0
3	03-Jan-21	40	20	0	40
4	04-Jan-21	40	0	0	0
5	05-Jan-21	14	0	13	0
6	06-Jan-21	14	0	0	0
7	07-Jan-21	14	0	0	0
8	08-Jan-21	14	0	0	0
9	09-Jan-21	14	0	0	0
10	10-Jan-21	14	0	0	0

Since this table will be loaded to the model, I add the table view step to the end of the code in the Advanced Editor.

```
#"Replaced Value" = Table.ReplaceValue(#"Filled Down",null,0,Replacer.
ReplaceValue,{"Closing bal", "Purchase", "COGS", "Purchase ($)"}),
 OverrideZeroRowFilter = Table.View(
 null,
 [
 GetType = () =>
 type table[
 Date = Date.Type,
 Closing bal = Number.Type,
 Purchase = Number.Type,
 COGS = Number.Type,
 #"Purchase ($)" = Number.Type
```

```
],
GetRows = () =>
#"Replaced Value",
OnTake = (count as number) =>
if count = 0 then
#table(
type table[
Date = Date.Type,
Closing bal = Number.Type,
Purchase = Number.Type,
COGS = Number.Type,
#"Purchase ($)" = Number.Type
],
{}
)
else
Table.FirstN(#"Replaced Value", count)]
)
in
OverrideZeroRowFilter
```

I can now close and apply this table.

Average inventory cost control account

Before any measures, I must create the relationship between the **Inventory avg calc** table and the **Calendar** table:

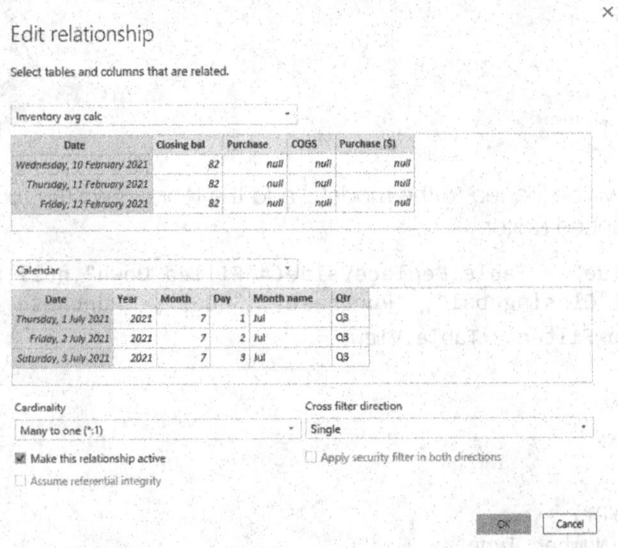

The order is slightly different for this control account. I have calculated the closing balance amount for each time period in the table.

Before I create the **Inventory closing balance (avg)** measure, I shall introduce a function that I will use. That function is called the **LASTDATE** function.

The **LASTDATE** function uses the following syntax to operate:

LASTDATE(dates)

The **dates** parameter is a column that contains date values.

This function will evaluate to the last date found in the **Date** column in the current filter context.

I will now start with the **Inventory closing balance (avg)** measure.

```
Inventory closing balance (avg) =
IF(
    SUM(
        'Inventory avg calc'[Closing Bal]) = BLANK(),
        0,
    CALCULATE(
        SUM('Inventory avg calc'[Closing Bal]),
        LASTDATE('Inventory avg calc'[Date])
    )
)
```

```
Inventory closing balance (avg) =
IF(
 SUM(
 'Inventory avg calc'[Closing Bal]) = BLANK(),
 0,
 CALCULATE(
 SUM('Inventory avg calc'[Closing Bal]),
 LASTDATE('Inventory avg calc'[Date])
 )
)
```

The next measure is the **Inventory purchases (avg)** measure, it uses the following **DAX** code:

```
Inventory purchases (avg) =
    IF(
        SUM(
            'Inventory avg calc'[Purchase ($)]) = BLANK(),
            0,
        SUM(
            'Inventory avg calc'[Purchase ($)]
        )
    )
```

```
Inventory purchases (avg) =
 IF(
 SUM(
 'Inventory avg calc'[Purchase ($)]) = BLANK(),
 0,
 SUM(
 'Inventory avg calc'[Purchase ($)]
```

```
  )
)
```

Next, I can calculate the **Inventory opening balance (avg)**:

```
Inventory opening balance (avg) =
    CALCULATE( [Inventory closing balance (avg)],
        PREVIOUSDAY('Calendar'[Date])
    )
```

```
Inventory opening balance (avg) =
 CALCULATE( [Inventory closing balance (avg)],
 PREVIOUSDAY('Calendar'[Date])
 )
```

I then work backwards here to calculate the amount of inventory sold in the **Inventory cost (avg) $** measure:

```
Inventory cost (avg) $ =
    IF(
        [Inventory closing balance (avg)] = 0 ,
        0,
        [Inventory closing balance (avg)] - ([Inventory opening balance (avg)]
        + [Inventory purchases (avg)]
        )
    )
```

```
Inventory cost (avg) $ =
 IF(
 [Inventory closing balance (avg)] = 0 ,
 0,
 [Inventory closing balance (avg)] - ([Inventory opening balance (avg)]
 + [Inventory purchases (avg)]
 )
 )
```

After applying the appropriate formatting, plotting the four measures into a visualisation results in:

Year	2021								
Qtr	Q1			Q2			Q3		
	Jan	Feb	Mar	Apr	May	Jun	Jul	Aug	Sep
Inventory opening balance (avg)	-	$13.00	$12.48	$12.48	$12.48	$12.48	$12.48	$12.48	$12.48
Inventory purchases (avg)	$146.00	$176.00	-	-	-	-	-	-	-
Inventory cost (avg) $	($133.00)	($176.52)	-	-	-	-	-	-	-
Inventory closing balance (avg)	$13.00	$12.48	$12.48	$12.48	$12.48	$12.48	$12.48	$12.48	$12.48

I now group the measures into the **Inventory** display folder:

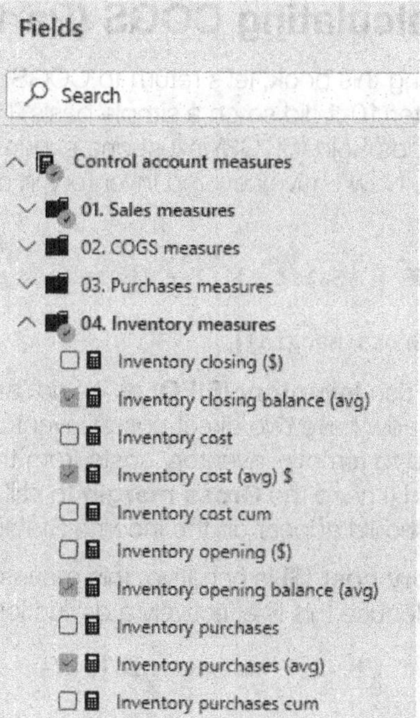

All very easy, yes..? Be honest: who has skipped most of this chapter? If you have, make sure you have looked at the way I appended the **Fulldates** query! You will need that later.

CHAPTER 14: Calculating COGS (Part 2)

Assuming you are still reading this book, let's return to COGS. You will recall, that when I calculated COGS in Chapter 10, I did so on a simple basis. I introduced direct costs by assuming that Costs of Goods Sold (COGS) is just one expense item. I ignored the direct costs of the inventory used. Now I have covered Inventory in detail, allow me to return to the **COGS** measure.

```
COGS = [Sales] * (1 - [Gross margin])
```

```
COGS = [Sales] * (1 - [Gross margin])
```

In the model, I am going to use **Inventory (FIFO)** as it's not as resource hungry as its weighted average sibling. I now have two direct costs: inventory costs and everything else. This means that I need to remove Inventory costs from the **COGS** calculation so they are not double counted (I need the **Gross margin** to still work as intended). I will revisit how the COGS line should appear on the Income Statement later!

Since the measure **Inventory cost ($)** is negative, this means I need to add this measure to **COGS** (*i.e.* you should deduce this is effectively a deduction):

```
COGS = ([Sales] * (1 - [Gross margin])) + [Inventory cost ($)]
```

```
COGS = ([Sales] * (1 - [Gross margin])) + [Inventory cost ($)]
```

Making this change updates the values on the COGS control account:

Year	2021								
Qtr	Q1			Q2			Q3		
	Jan	Feb	Mar	Apr	May	Jun	Jul	Aug	Sep
COGS opening payables		$359.64	$1,402.60	$1,912.09	$1,906.09	$1,750.25	$1,624.37	$1,762.24	$1,654.34
COGS	$239.64	$838.74	$978.53	$906.64	$918.62	$822.76	$906.64	$882.67	$737.85
COGS cash payments	$120.00	$204.22	($469.04)	($912.63)	($1,074.46)	($948.64)	($768.78)	($990.57)	($833.75)
COGS closing payables	$359.64	$1,402.60	$1,912.09	$1,906.09	$1,750.25	$1,624.37	$1,762.24	$1,654.34	$1,558.44

This creates an issue, as my control account no longer balances. The way I have calculated **COGS cash payments** is not working. You will recall that I created two measures in order to demonstrate **USERELATIONSHIP,** and the way it gave the same result as **DATEADD**:

```
COGS cash payments =
    CALCULATE(-[COGS],
        USERELATIONSHIP('Calendar'[Date], Actuals[Payment date])
    )
```

```
COGS cash payments =
 CALCULATE(-[COGS],
 USERELATIONSHIP('Calendar'[Date], Actuals[Payment date])
 )
```

```
COGS cash payments DATEADD =
    CALCULATE(-[COGS],
        DATEADD('Calendar'[Date], -P_DaysPayable, DAY)
    )
```

```
COGS cash payments DATEADD =
 CALCULATE(-[COGS],
 DATEADD('Calendar'[Date], -P_DaysPayable, DAY)
 )
```

I employed the **USERELATIONSHIP** version of **COGS cash payments** so far in the model, but this will no longer work. This is because **COGS cash payments** is currently using an alternative link to **Calendar** using **Payment date** of **Actuals**. However, to calculate **Inventory cost ($)** I need to use **Sales date** of **Actuals** to link to Calendar. **COGS cash payments** is calculated from **COGS,** which in turn uses **Inventory cost ($)**, so by using **USERELATIONSHIP** I am trying to use the wrong link to **Calendar** for **Inventory cost ($)**. There are two ways I could resolve this:

1. I could change the **Invoice cost ($)** calculation to use **USERELATIONSHIP** too. I would not recommend this, since I think you will agree, I am already using signification memory to calculate inventory, and using another **USERELATIONSHIP** will only add to that.

2. I could change **COGS cash payments** to have the same formula as **COGS cash payments DATEADD**. This is the simple solution.

```
COGS cash payments =
    CALCULATE(-[COGS],
        DATEADD('Calendar'[Date], -P_DaysPayable, DAY)
    )
```

```
COGS cash payments =
 CALCULATE(-[COGS],
 DATEADD('Calendar'[Date], -P_DaysPayable, DAY)
```

This changes the control account to the correct values:

Year	2021								
Qtr	Q1			Q2			Q3		
	Jan	Feb	Mar	Apr	May	Jun	Jul	Aug	Sep
COGS opening payables		$239.64	$934.60	$1,274.09	$1,270.09	$1,166.25	$1,082.37	$1,174.24	$1,102.34
COGS	$239.64	$838.74	$978.53	$906.64	$918.62	$822.76	$906.64	$882.67	$737.85
COGS cash payments		($143.78)	($639.04)	($910.63)	($1,022.46)	($906.64)	($814.78)	($954.57)	($830.75)
COGS closing payables	$239.64	$934.60	$1,274.09	$1,270.09	$1,166.25	$1,082.37	$1,174.24	$1,102.34	$1,009.44

If you have chosen a different value for **Gross margin**, you might get different results:

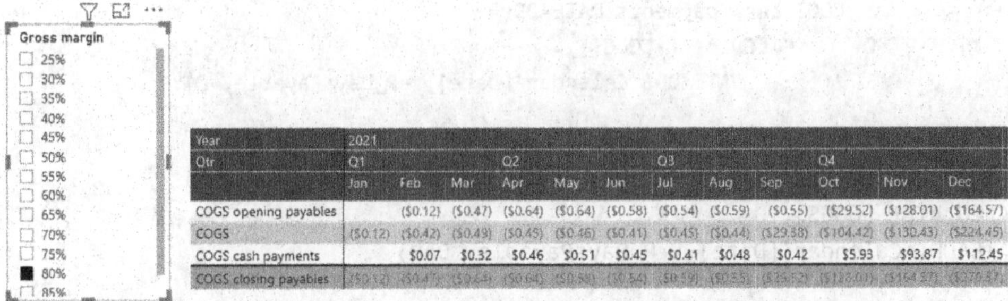

Year	2021											
Qtr	Q1			Q2			Q3			Q4		
	Jan	Feb	Mar	Apr	May	Jun	Jul	Aug	Sep	Oct	Nov	Dec
COGS opening payables		($0.12)	($0.47)	($0.64)	($0.64)	($0.58)	($0.54)	($0.59)	($0.55)	($29.52)	($128.01)	($164.57)
COGS	($0.12)	($0.42)	($0.49)	($0.45)	($0.46)	($0.41)	($0.45)	($0.44)	($29.38)	($104.42)	($130.43)	($224.45)
COGS cash payments		$0.07	$0.32	$0.46	$0.51	$0.45	$0.41	$0.48	$0.42	$5.93	$93.87	$112.45
COGS closing payables	($0.12)	($0.47)	($0.64)	($0.64)	($0.58)	($0.54)	($0.59)	($0.55)	($29.52)	($128.01)	($164.57)	[illegible]

The negative values in **COGS closing payables** do not indicate a problem with the calculations; it is a problem with the data being used in the what-if? analysis. When we have **Gross margin** set to 40%, then the values make sense:

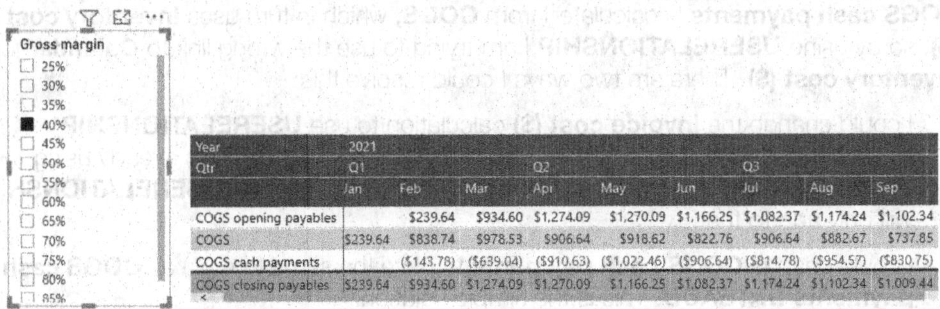

Year	2021								
Qtr	Q1			Q2			Q3		
	Jan	Feb	Mar	Apr	May	Jun	Jul	Aug	Sep
COGS opening payables		$239.64	$934.60	$1,274.09	$1,270.09	$1,166.25	$1,082.37	$1,174.24	$1,102.34
COGS	$239.64	$838.74	$978.53	$906.64	$918.62	$822.76	$906.64	$882.67	$737.85
COGS cash payments		($143.78)	($639.04)	($910.63)	($1,022.46)	($906.64)	($814.78)	($954.57)	($830.75)
COGS closing payables	$239.64	$934.60	$1,274.09	$1,270.09	$1,166.25	$1,082.37	$1,174.24	$1,102.34	$1,009.44

I get negative values for a **Gross margin** of 80% because the inventory amounts are large, and the direct costs are only 20% in total. **COGS** must be the balancing figure, and therefore it becomes a negative cost in order to maintain the 20% restriction. Keep in mind that this is a figure which can be adjusted to suit your scenario. It's not the calculation that's wrong; it's the assumption used. I will keep **Gross margin** at 40% for the purposes of this model.

Having adjusted **COGS** to allow for inventory costs, let's move on.

CHAPTER 15: Calculating Operating Expenditure (Opex)

Having finally navigated through the choppy waters of COGS, the next line item in the Income Statement should be smooth sailing. In this section, I will calculate the Operating Expenditure, affectionately known as 'Opex'. These are the indirect costs, *i.e.* those costs that will be incurred in the short term whether or not any sales are made.

I can begin with the measure:

```
Opex =
CALCULATE(
    SUM(Actuals[Amount]),
    'Actuals'[Account] = P_OpexCode
)
```

```
Opex =
CALCULATE(
 SUM(Actuals[Amount]),
 'Actuals'[Account] = P_OpexCode
)
```

It should be noted that since I have parameterised the account codes earlier, one great benefit is that I no longer need to type in the filter text value, but rather I may directly use the previously defined parameter instead.

I will revert to the **DATEADD** method of calculating the cash payables here, similar to the approach taken with **Sales**:

```
Opex cash payments =
    CALCULATE(-[Opex],
        DATEADD('Calendar'[Date], -P_DaysReceivable, DAY)
    )
```

```
Opex cash payments =
 CALCULATE(-[Opex],
 DATEADD('Calendar'[Date],-P_DaysReceivable, DAY)
 )
```

The pattern should be becoming familiar by this stage. I must construct the cumulative functions **Opex cum** and **Opex cash payments cum.**

```
Opex cum =
CALCULATE([Opex],
    FILTER(
        ALL('Calendar'),
        'Calendar'[Date] <= MAX('Calendar'[Date])
    )
)
```

```
Opex cum =
```

```
CALCULATE([Opex],
 FILTER(
 ALL('Calendar'),
 'Calendar'[Date] <= MAX('Calendar'[Date])
 )
)
```

```
Opex cash payments cum =
CALCULATE(
    [Opex cash payments],
    FILTER(
        ALL('Calendar'),
        'Calendar'[Date] <= MAX('Calendar'[Date])
    )
)
```

```
Opex cash payments cum =
CALCULATE(
 [Opex cash payments],
 FILTER(
 ALL('Calendar'),
 'Calendar'[Date] <= MAX('Calendar'[Date])
 )
)
```

Before I calculate the opening and closing payables for **Opex**, I would like to introduce an alternative method of calculation. Instead of calculating the opening payables first, this time I will develop the closing payables:

```
Opex closing payables =
[Opex cum] + [Opex cash payments cum]
```

```
Opex closing payables =
[Opex cum] + [Opex cash payments cum]
```

This is followed by the **Opex opening payables**:

```
Opex opening payables =
    CALCULATE([Opex closing payables],
        PREVIOUSDAY('Calendar'[Date])
    )
```

```
Opex opening payables =
 CALCULATE([Opex closing payables],
 PREVIOUSDAY('Calendar'[Date])
 )
```

With the six measures complete, I can now populate my matrix visualisation:

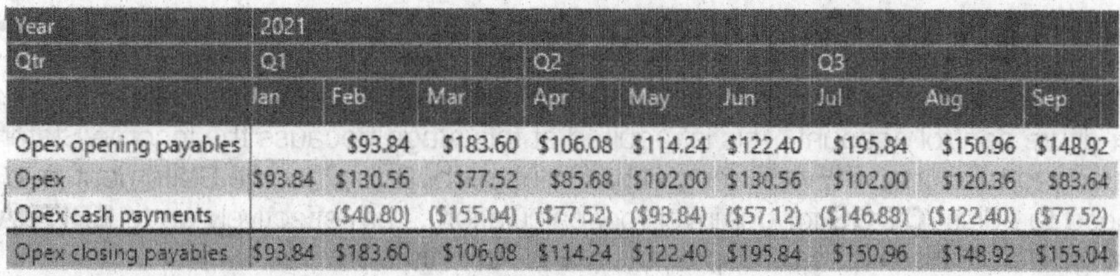

Year	2021								
Qtr	Q1			Q2			Q3		
	Jan	Feb	Mar	Apr	May	Jun	Jul	Aug	Sep
Opex opening payables		$93.84	$183.60	$106.08	$114.24	$122.40	$195.84	$150.96	$148.92
Opex	$93.84	$130.56	$77.52	$85.68	$102.00	$130.56	$102.00	$120.36	$83.64
Opex cash payments		($40.80)	($155.04)	($77.52)	($93.84)	($57.12)	($146.88)	($122.40)	($77.52)
Opex closing payables	$93.84	$183.60	$106.08	$114.24	$122.40	$195.84	$150.96	$148.92	$155.04

Of course, when I am finished creating the measures required for **Opex** I should group them into their own display folder:

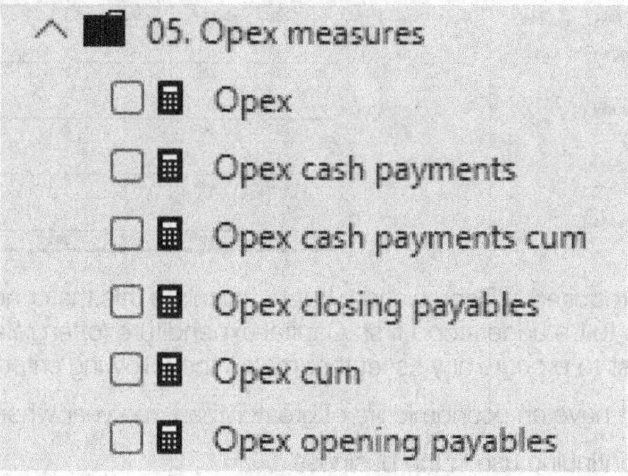

CHAPTER 16: Calculating Capital Expenditure (Capex)

Following through our order discussed earlier, I now need to derive the capital expenditure control account. This is required at this stage because the Income Statement is starting to take shape. Even though I have not yet built the Income Statement (and still need to adjust **COGS** for our inventory calculation), I am effectively up to **EBITDA** (Earnings Before Interest, Tax, Depreciation and Amortisation):

1. Income Statement						
Revenue	US$'000	400	448	493	532	559
COGS	US$'000	(120)	(134)	(148)	(160)	(168)
Gross Profit	US$'000	280	314	345	373	391
Operating Expenditure	US$'000	(60)	(65)	(68)	(70)	(71)
EBITDA	US$'000	220	249	277	303	320
Depreciation	US$'000					
EBIT	US$'000	220	249	277	303	320
Interest Expense	US$'000					
NPBT	US$'000	220	249	277	303	320
Tax Expense	US$'000					
NPAT	US$'000	220	249	277	303	320

The next line item required is Depreciation, but to calculate this the concept of capital expenditure needs to be understood first. Capital expenditure (often referred to as "Capex") is the cost to procure any asset that meets the following criteria:

- the asset must have an economic life of greater than one year when purchased
- it is held for continuing use in the business
- the asset must generate an accounting profit / economic return
- the value of the asset when purchased must exceed a *de minimis* limit which varies from geographic region / accounting jurisdiction.

The idea is that capital expenditure tends to be expensive (*e.g.* acquiring a building, purchasing a fleet of cars) and expensing all these costs in any one period would lead to an horrific loss and go against the accruals concept. The intention is to match the costs over the life of the profits they generate (hence the test for profitability).

There are four common methods of depreciation. They are based on the **depreciable amount**, which is defined as the original price of the asset less its estimated resale price (**residual** or **salvage value**):

1. **Straight Line:** By far the most common method, this approach linearly apportions the depreciable amount evenly over the remainder of its useable life. Favoured by accountants and statutory reporting, for many industries and sectors it is the simplest and least contentious approach. This gets its name as plotting time against an asset's remaining value (known as **Net Book Value**) will generate a straight line on a chart.

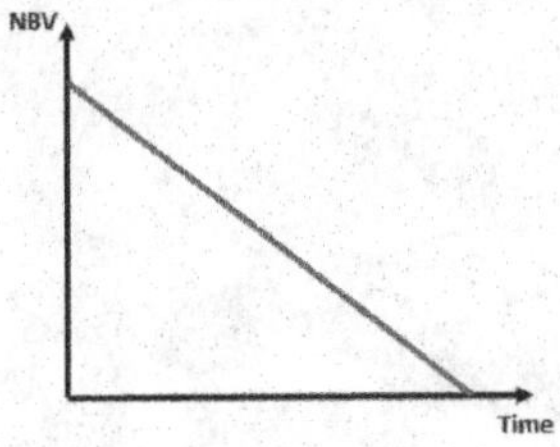

2. **Diminishing Value or Declining Balance:** This approach calculates a proportion of the remaining value to depreciate each year, based on the initial purchase price, not the depreciable amount. The rate is usually a function of the economic life and a multiplier.

   For example, consider an asset purchased for $1,000 that has a depreciable amount of $1,000 also. The asset has a four-year life and a multiplier of 2.0x (this is known as **Double Declining Balance**). This would give a depreciation rate of 2.0 / 4 = 50% on the remaining balance:

	$
	1,000.00
Depn: P1	(500.00)
	500.00
Depn: P2	(250.00)
	250.00
Depn: P3	(125.00)
	125.00
Depn: P4	(62.50)
	62.50

   It should be noted that the depreciation rate can never be above 100%, that only the depreciable amount can be depreciated and that in some jurisdictions, the remainder of the depreciable amount is written off in the final economic period.

   This method is frequently used in many jurisdictions / territories for tax computations.

3. **Sum Of Digits (SOD):** This method considers the economic life but apportions on an increasing or decreasing proportion each year. For example, a four-year economic life might depreciate the depreciable amount by 1/10 in Year 1, 2/10 in Year 2, 3/10 in Year 3 and 4/10 in Year 4, where the common denominator 10 = 1 + 2 + 3 + 4. (This can be decreasing as well as increasing.) This approach is becoming less and less common.

4. **Usage Basis:** This amortises the depreciable amount based on what proportion of the asset is estimated to have been used in a particular year. This is quite common in the mining and resources industries.

Typically, 21st century modelling tends to assume no residual value so that generally the depreciable amount is the initial purchase price. To keep things simple, I will use straight line depreciation here.

Like the Inventory control account, calculating this accurately in Power BI requires an additional calculated table. I must consider each capital expenditure amount separately and be able to depreciate it at a daily level over its asset life.

I have two depreciation calculations to construct: one for accounting and one for tax. This is because tax authorities often decree how costs will be amortised over time (and will thus be needed for their calculations), whereas accounting is all about matching costs with the benefits they produce ("matching") and is included in the financial statements. The latter is seen as a "true and fair approach", but hey, when was tax ever true or fair? But more on that later.

At this stage, let's construct the accounting depreciation using a straight line approach (and we will calculate the tax counterpart with a declining balance approach when discussing tax in Chapter 20).

Accounting depreciation

I reference the **Depreciation** query to create a new query where I will perform the grouping. I have renamed this **Depreciation straight line**.

For my depreciation calculation to work, I will need a table with all the dates when the company is operating. Going back to my **Depreciation straight line** table, I can append it with the **Fulldates** table.

I select the **Fulldates** table as the Table to append:

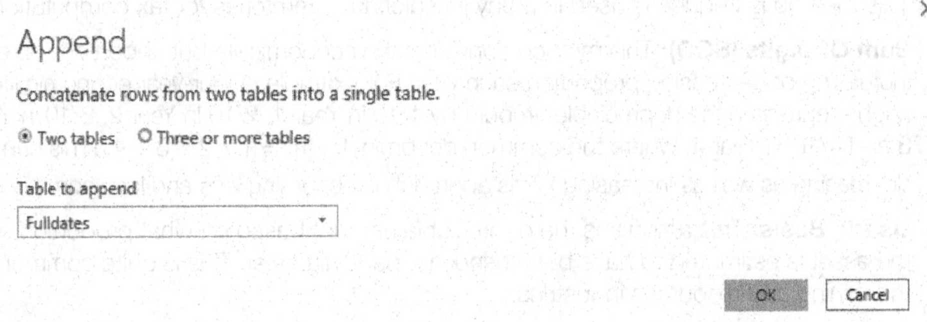

Before I continue, I shall add a **Table.Buffer()** step before the append query step. To do this, I shall open the Advanced Editor and add the following code:

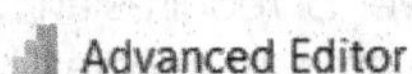

Depreciation straight line

```
let
    Source = Depreciation,
    BufferedTable = Table.Buffer(Fulldates),
    #"Appended Query" = Table.Combine({Source, BufferedTable}),
```

```
let
```

```
Source = Depreciation,
BufferedTable = Table.Buffer(Fulldates),
#"Appended Query" = Table.Combine({Source, BufferedTable})
```

The next step here is to sort the rows of the table in ascending date order:

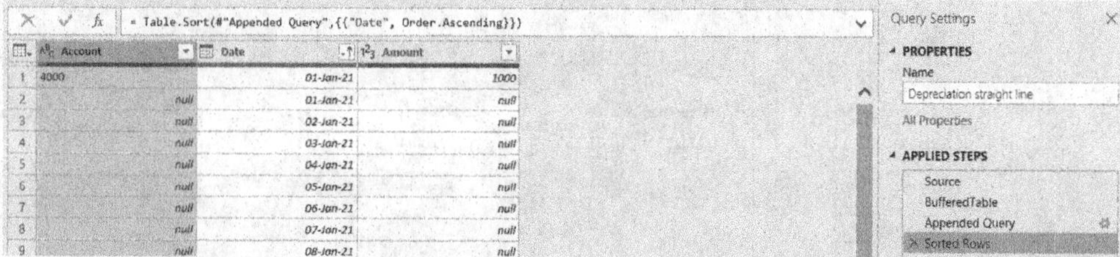

I then remove the **Date** column's duplicate values. I could just right-click and choose to remove duplicates, but this could potentially delete valid **Amount** data:

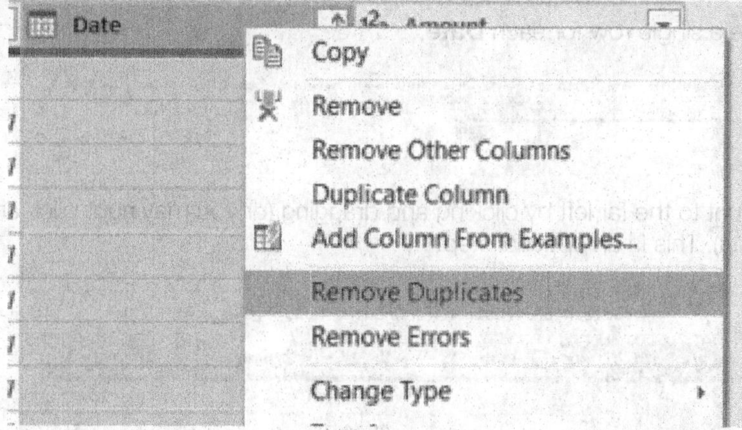

Instead, I will group the data using the 'Group By' option from the Home tab (this option also appears on the Transform tab, and has exactly the same functionality).

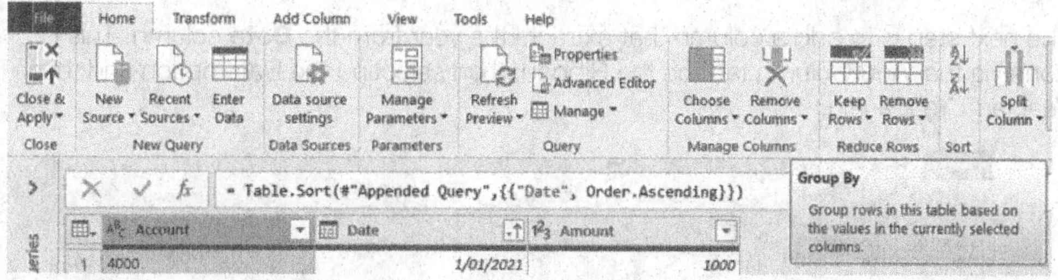

I choose the Advanced grouping options so that I can have more than one aggregation. I Group by **Date** and then select the Maximum of **Account** and the Sum of **Amount**.

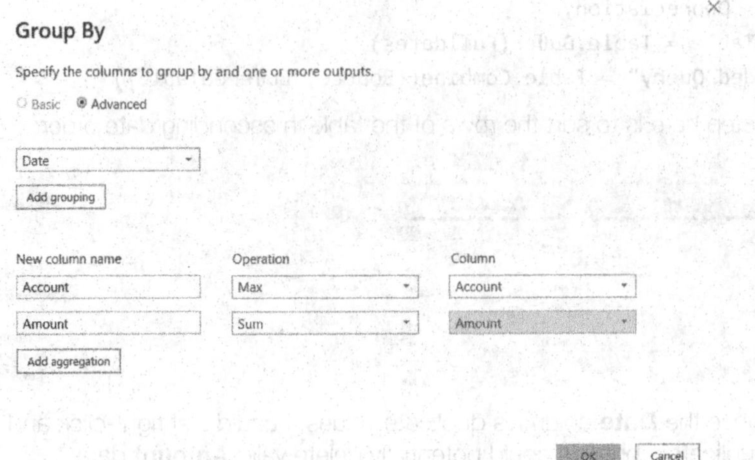

This gives me a single row for each **Date**.

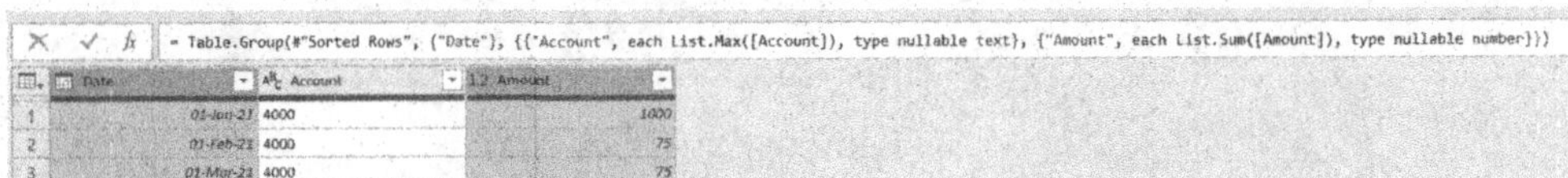

I move Account to the far left by clicking and dragging (or you may right-click and use the shortcut menu). This is an optional step.

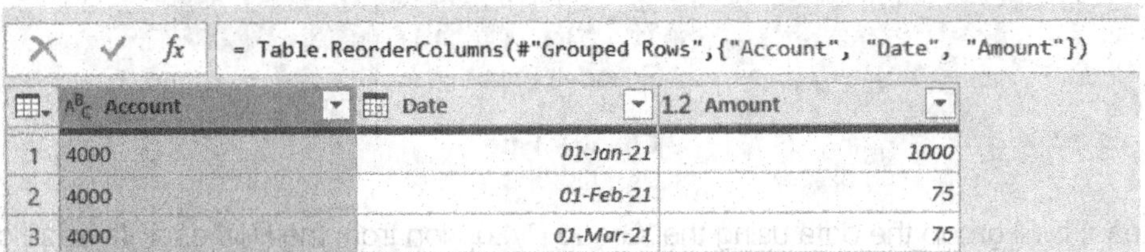

I also need to sort the data into ascending **Date** order, just as I did earlier.

The next step is to add a column that extracts the year from the **Date** column. This is done via the 'Add Column tab' on the Ribbon, then selecting the Date option and then Year, and Year again:

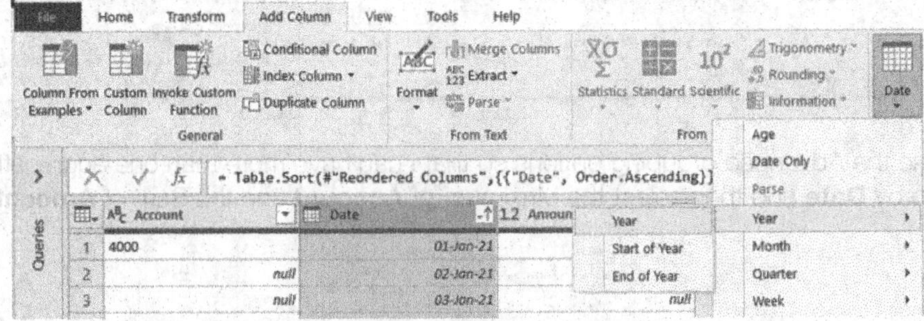

Now I add a custom column that will calculate the depreciation window:

Custom Column

Add a column that is computed from the other columns.

New column name

DepWindow

Custom column formula

```
= Date.AddYears([Date], -P_DepreciationYears)
```

Available columns

Account
Date
Amount
Year

<< Insert

Learn about Power Query formulas

✓ No syntax errors have been detected.

OK Cancel

```
Date.AddYears([Date], -P_DepreciationYears)
```

P_DepreciationYears is currently equal to five [5], so this function subtracts five years from the current date. I will use this column to look back five years and name it **DepWindow**.

I then ensure that the columns have been assigned the following data types (the reason why this is critical will become clear shortly):

- **Account:** Whole Number
- **Date:** Date
- **Amount:** Whole Number
- **Year:** Whole Number
- **DepWindow:** Date.

I should create a group for **Depreciation straight line**, as calculating the straight-line depreciation requires several queries. They can all be housed nicely in a group. I have given the group the appropriate name of **DepreciationSL** short for depreciation straight-line:

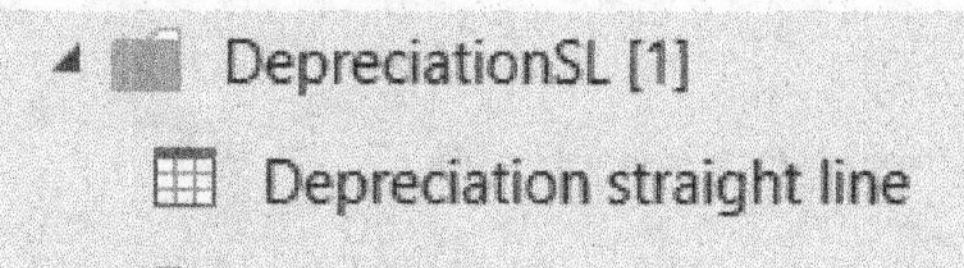

Creating the depreciation function

To begin, I will create a Reference Query from the **Depreciation straight line** query. From here, I need to create a function that looks back five [5] years or as far as the value in the **DepWindow** column allows. For example, at the row that contains the 31st Dec 2023 in the **Date** column, the function will look back five years, so that would be 31st Dec 2018 or the value in the **DepWindow** column.

Let me explain what I am doing here. To calculate the daily depreciation rate of any **Capex** item, I use the following formula:

Capex amount * Depreciation rate / Days in current year = Daily rate of depreciation

For example:

- If the **Capex amount** is 1,000
- The **Depreciation rate** is 20%
  - derived from (1 / 5), five [5] being the depreciation years. Therefore, assuming a straight line depreciation approach, the asset will depreciate 20% of its original value every year
- the **Days in current year** is 365

  1000 * 20% / 365 = 0.547945...

To calculate the depreciation at any point in time, I need a table that will return with the assets that are still active and depreciating. I can derive this by looking a certain number of years back in time. With this borne in mind, I shall apply two filters on the date column. This is achieved with applying a 'Between…' filter on the date column:

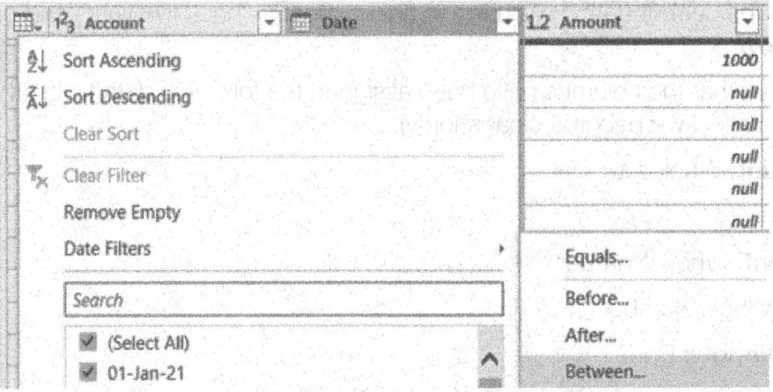

The 'Filter Rows' dialog will appear. I shall apply placeholder dates 1-Jan-21 and 2-Jan-21. This way, I can illustrate a single day's worth of depreciation. The conditions that I use are 'is after or equal to' and 'is before':

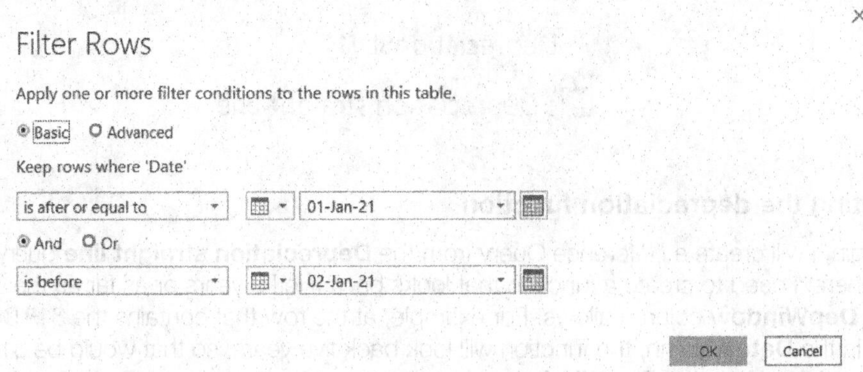

The function will also require the current date's value in the table. This is to determine the **Days in current year**. To do this, I create a custom column called **CurrDate**, to "simulate" what the function will see on the 2-Jan-21.

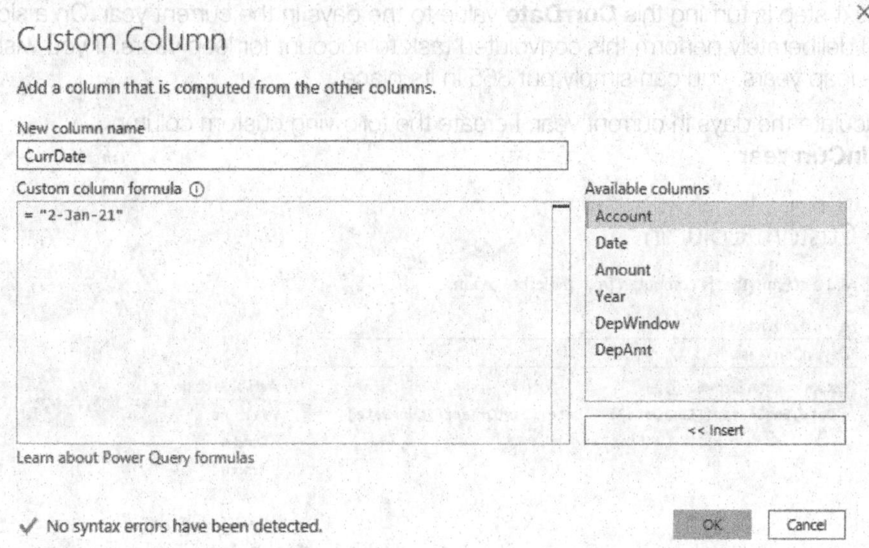

Now, I will change the data type to Date.

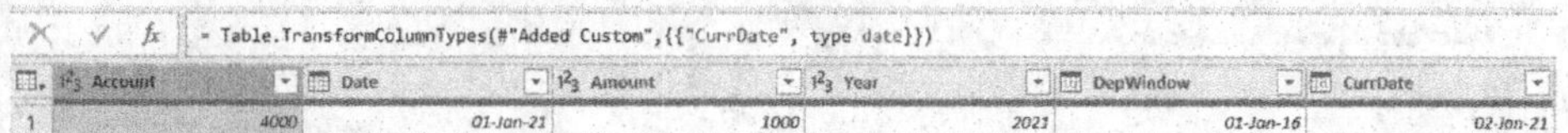

Next, I apply a step to filter out **Amounts** in the dataset that this function is applied to that do not have a value or are currently *null*. I click on the arrow icon next to the title on the **Amount** column and select 'Remove Empty':

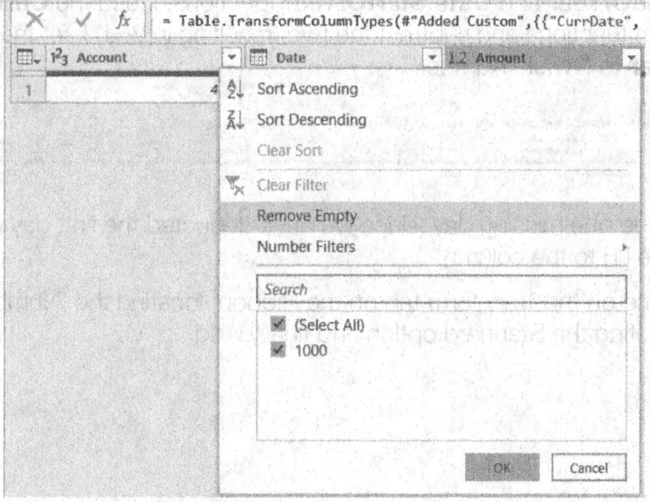

This has no impact on the current query:

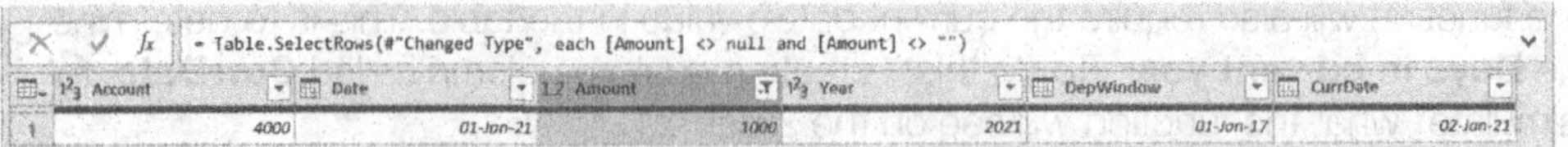

The next step is turning this **CurrDate** value to the days in the current year. On a side note, I deliberately perform this convoluted task to account for leap years. If you wish to ignore leap years, you can simply put 365 in its place.

To calculate the days in current year, I create the following custom column **DaysInCurrYear**:

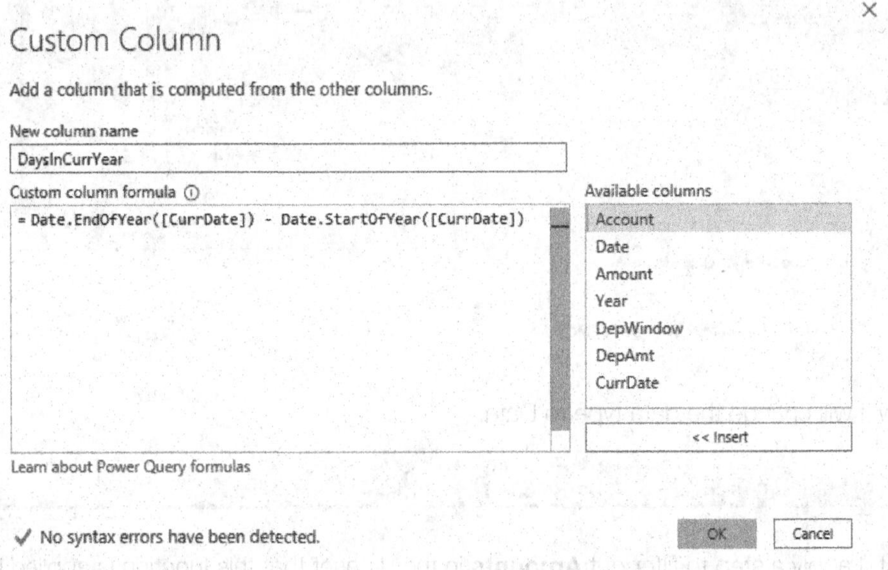


```
Date.EndOfYear([CurrDate]) - Date.StartOfYear([CurrDate])
```

M has **Date.EndOfYear** and **Date.StartOfYear** functions. I feed the **CurrDate** column into both functions and subtract the two, resulting in 364. I set the data type of **DaysInCurrYear** to 'Whole Number'.

To account for the one missing day (since we have deducted the first day of the period), I need to add one [1] to the column.

This may be done on the Transform tab on the Ribbon, locating the 'Number Column' group then selecting the Standard option and finally Add.

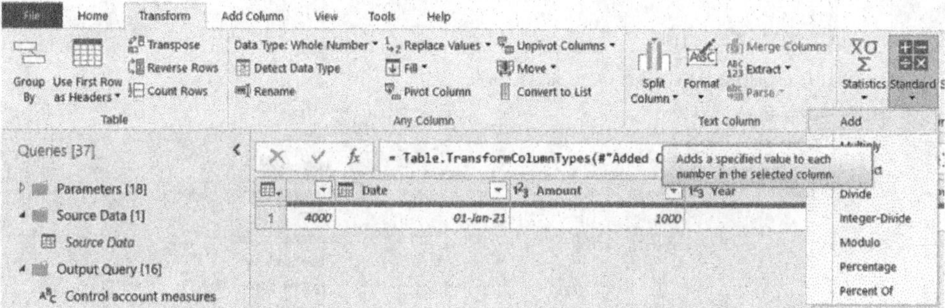

This brings up the Add dialog:

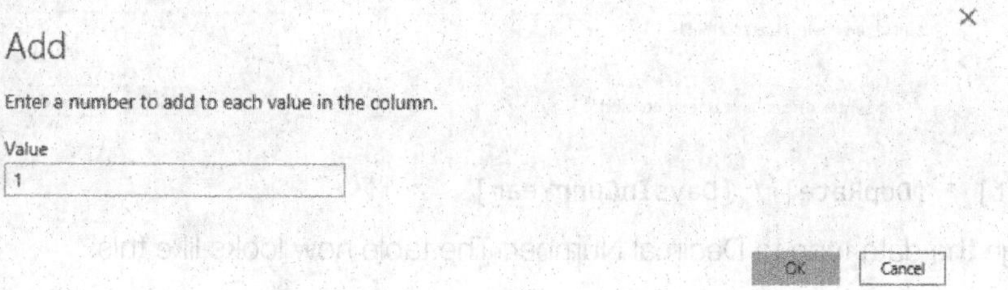

The penultimate column I need to create is the **Depreciation rate** column or (**DepRate**). This is a simple custom column:

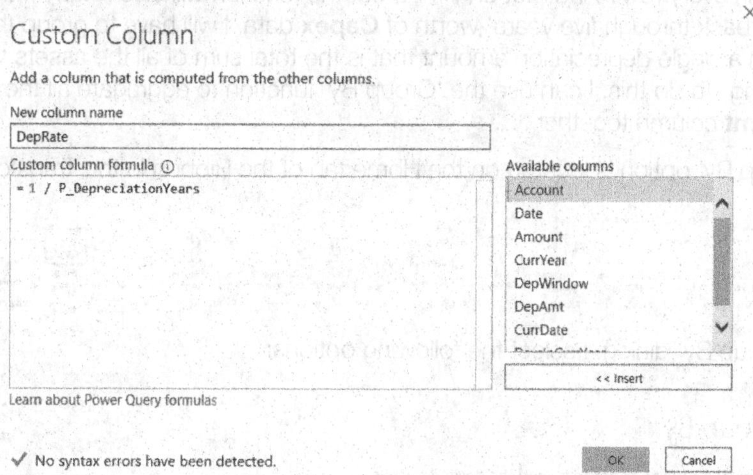


```
1 / P_DepreciationYears
```

I assign the decimal number data type to the **DepRate** column. The next custom column is the depreciation amount column **DepAmt**.

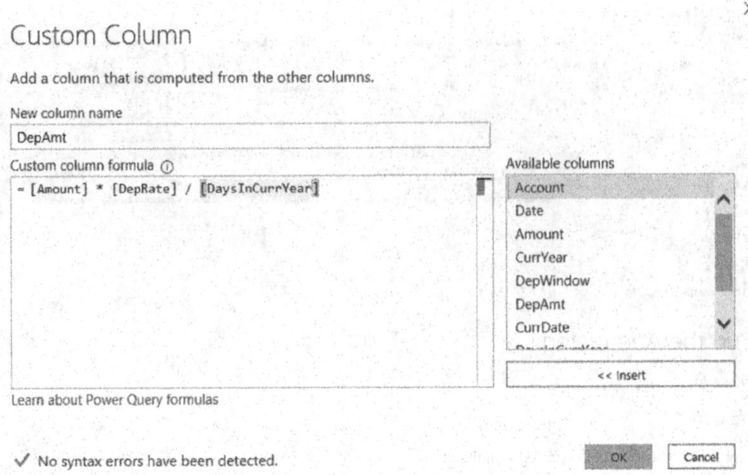


```
[Amount] * [DepRate] / [DaysInCurrYear]
```

I change the data type to Decimal Number. The table now looks like this:

	...	Year	DepWindow	CurrDate	DaysInCurrYear	DepRate	DepAmt
1	000	2021	01-Jan-17	02-Jan-21	365	0.2	0.547945205

Almost there! However, do you remember that this will be a function that would be evaluated in every row? And, not only that, but the function will also return with a table that looks back through five years' worth of **Capex** data. I will have to group the rows to return with a single depreciation amount that is the total sum of all the assets that are still depreciating. To do this, I can use the 'Group By' function to aggregate all the values in the **DepAmt** column together.

The 'Group By' option is located on the Home tab of the Ribbon in the Transform group:

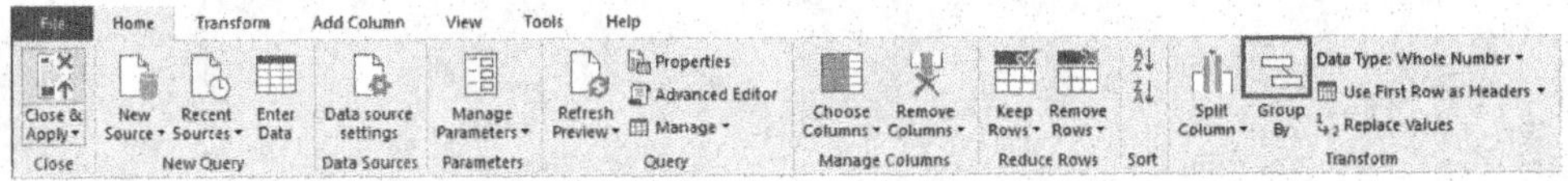

In the 'Group By' dialog, I select the following options:

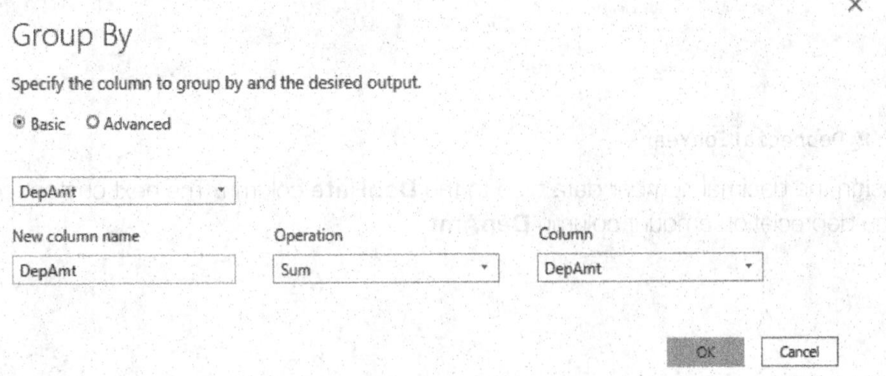

The resulting table now looks like this:

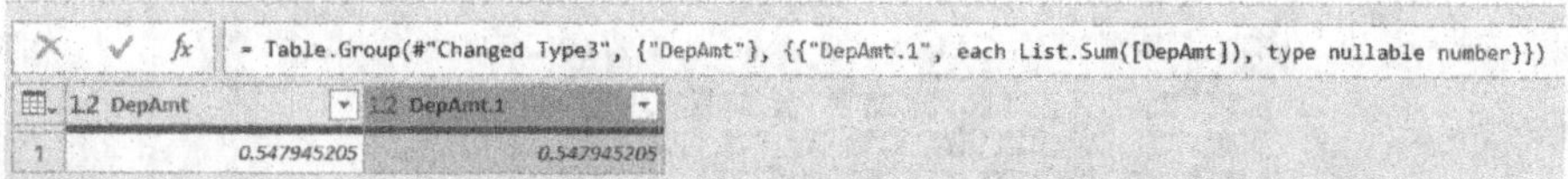

The table currently returns with two values. Power BI will not be able to evaluate two column values into one. A little trick I will employ is to delete the **DepAmt** in the code in the Formula Bar:

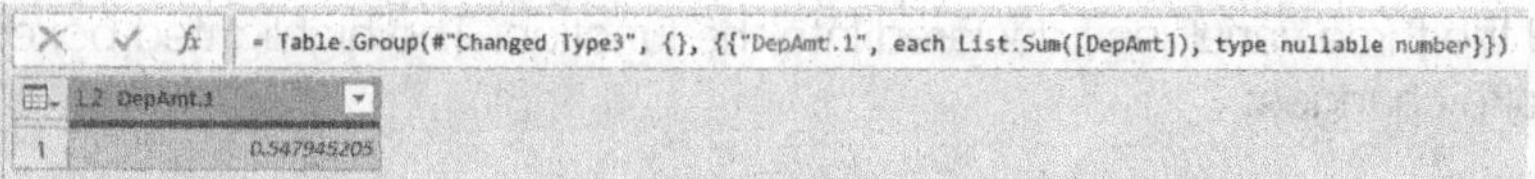

I can now turn this query into a function. To do so, I navigate to the Advanced Editor. Here, the Advanced Editor dialog looks like this:

Advanced Editor

Depreciation straight line (2)

Display Options

```
let
    Source = #"Depreciation straight line",
    #"Filtered Rows" = Table.SelectRows(Source, each [Date] >= #date(2021, 1, 1) and [Date] < #date(2021, 1, 2)),
    #"Added Custom" = Table.AddColumn(#"Filtered Rows", "CurrDate", each "2-Jan-21"),
    #"Changed Type" = Table.TransformColumnTypes(#"Added Custom",{{"CurrDate", type date}}),
    #"Filtered Rows1" = Table.SelectRows(#"Changed Type", each [Amount] <> null and [Amount] <> ""),
    #"Added Custom1" = Table.AddColumn(#"Filtered Rows1", "DaysInCurrYear", each Date.EndOfYear([CurrDate]) - Date.StartOfYear([CurrDate]
    #"Changed Type1" = Table.TransformColumnTypes(#"Added Custom1",{{"DaysInCurrYear", Int64.Type}}),
    #"Added to Column" = Table.TransformColumns(#"Changed Type1", {{"DaysInCurrYear", each _ + 1, type number}}),
    #"Added Custom2" = Table.AddColumn(#"Added to Column", "DepRate", each 1 / P_DepreciationYears),
    #"Changed Type2" = Table.TransformColumnTypes(#"Added Custom2",{{"DepRate", type number}}),
    #"Added Custom3" = Table.AddColumn(#"Changed Type2", "DepAmt", each [Amount] * [DepRate] / [DaysInCurrYear]),
    #"Changed Type3" = Table.TransformColumnTypes(#"Added Custom3",{{"DepAmt", type number}}),
    #"Grouped Rows" = Table.Group(#"Changed Type3", {}, {{"DepAmt.1", each List.Sum([DepAmt]), type nullable number}})
in
    #"Grouped Rows"
```

To declare that I want to use this query as a function, I shall insert the following code at the beginning:

```
let
 DepCalc = (Tbl as table, LookBackDate as date, CurrDate as date) =>
```

This defines the function as **DepCalc**, and it has three variables, **Tbl**, **LookBackDate** and **CurrDate**. Each variable has its Data Type then defined right after it after the delimiter 'as'. The **'=>'** delimiter tells Power BI that this is where the function begins.

To close off the function, I shall insert the following code to the end of this section:

```
in
 DepCalc
```

```
1  let
2      DepCalc = (Tbl as table, LookBackDate as date, CurrDate as date) =>
3
4
5  let
6      Source = #"Depreciation straight line",
7      #"Filtered Rows" = Table.SelectRows(Source, each [Date] >= #date(2021, 1, 1) and [Date] < #date(2021, 1, 2)),
8      #"Added Custom" = Table.AddColumn(#"Filtered Rows", "CurrDate", each "2-Jan-21"),
9      #"Changed Type" = Table.TransformColumnTypes(#"Added Custom",{{"CurrDate", type date}}),
10     #"Filtered Rows1" = Table.SelectRows(#"Changed Type", each [Amount] <> null and [Amount] <> ""),
11     #"Added Custom1" = Table.AddColumn(#"Filtered Rows1", "DaysInCurrYear", each Date.EndOfYear([CurrDate]) - Date.StartOfYear([CurrDate
12     #"Changed Type1" = Table.TransformColumnTypes(#"Added Custom1",{{"DaysInCurrYear", Int64.Type}}),
13     #"Added to Column" = Table.TransformColumns(#"Changed Type1", {{"DaysInCurrYear", each _ + 1, type number}}),
14     #"Added Custom2" = Table.AddColumn(#"Added to Column", "DepRate", each 1 / P_DepreciationYears),
15     #"Changed Type2" = Table.TransformColumnTypes(#"Added Custom2",{{"DepRate", type number}}),
16     #"Added Custom3" = Table.AddColumn(#"Changed Type2", "DepAmt", each [Amount] * [DepRate] / [DaysInCurrYear]),
17     #"Changed Type3" = Table.TransformColumnTypes(#"Added Custom3",{{"DepAmt", type number}}),
18     #"Grouped Rows" = Table.Group(#"Changed Type3", {}, {{"DepAmt.1", each List.Sum([DepAmt]), type nullable number}})
19 in
20     #"Grouped Rows"
21
22 in
23     DepCalc
```

I now feed the three variables I declared into the function. The highlighted boxes are where I make changes:

```
1  let
2      DepCalc = (Tbl as table, LookBackDate as date, CurrDate as date) =>
3
4
5  let
6      Source = #"Depreciation straight line",
7      #"Filtered Rows" = Table.SelectRows(Source, each [Date] >= #date(2021, 1, 1) and [Date] < #date(2021, 1, 2)),
8      #"Added Custom" = Table.AddColumn(#"Filtered Rows", "CurrDate", each "2-Jan-21"),
9      #"Changed Type" = Table.TransformColumnTypes(#"Added Custom",{{"CurrDate", type date}}),
```

I shall make the following changes:

1. **#"Depreciation straight line"** to **Tbl**
2. **#date(2021, 1, 1)** to **LookBackDate**
3. **#date(2021, 1, 2)** to **CurrDate**
4. **"2-Jan-21"** to **CurrDate**

I also need to make a small change to the way the data is filtered. The current filter was constructed this way to allow me to work with one row whilst I was building the function, now I need to change the equal sign around too.

Line 7 will be changed from:

```
#"Filtered Rows" = Table.SelectRows(Source, each [Date] >= LookBackDate and [Date] < CurrDate),
```

to

```
#"Filtered Rows" = Table.SelectRows(Source, each [Date] > LookBackDate and [Date] <= CurrDate),
```

```
1  let
2      DepCalc = (Tbl as table, LookBackDate as date, CurrDate as date) =>
3
4
5  let
6      Source = Table.Buffer,
7      #"Filtered Rows" = Table.SelectRows(Source, each [Date] > LookBackDate and [Date] <= CurrDate),
8      #"Added Custom" = Table.AddColumn(#"Filtered Rows", "CurrDate", each CurrDate),
9      #"Changed Type" = Table.TransformColumnTypes(#"Added Custom",{{"CurrDate", type date}}),
10     #"Filtered Rows1" = Table.SelectRows(#"Changed Type", each [Amount] <> null and [Amount] <> ""),
11     #"Added Custom1" = Table.AddColumn(#"Filtered Rows1", "DaysInCurrYear", each Date.EndOfYear([CurrDate]) - Date.StartOfYear([CurrDate
12     #"Changed Type1" = Table.TransformColumnTypes(#"Added Custom1",{{"DaysInCurrYear", Int64.Type}}),
13     #"Added to Column" = Table.TransformColumns(#"Changed Type1", {{"DaysInCurrYear", each _ + 1, type number}}),
14     #"Added Custom2" = Table.AddColumn(#"Added to Column", "DepRate", each 1 / P_DepreciationYears),
15     #"Changed Type2" = Table.TransformColumnTypes(#"Added Custom2",{{"DepRate", type number}}),
16     #"Added Custom3" = Table.AddColumn(#"Changed Type2", "DepAmt", each [Amount] * [DepRate] / [DaysInCurrYear]),
17     #"Changed Type3" = Table.TransformColumnTypes(#"Added Custom3",{{"DepAmt", type number}}),
18     #"Grouped Rows" = Table.Group(#"Changed Type3", {}, {{"DepAmt.1", each List.Sum([DepAmt]), type nullable number}})
19 in
20     #"Grouped Rows"
21
22 in
23     DepCalc
```

I rename the function in the Queries area; I give it the name of **FN_DepStraightLine**.

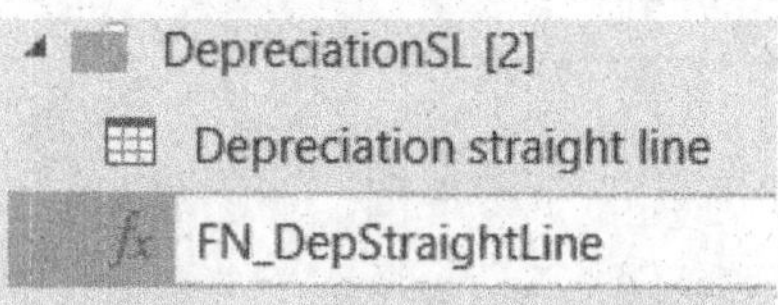

Creating the depreciation table

Let's return to the **Depreciation Straight Line** table. I can now invoke a custom function. The 'Invoke Custom Function' option is located on the 'Add Column' tab on the Ribbon in the General group, *viz*.

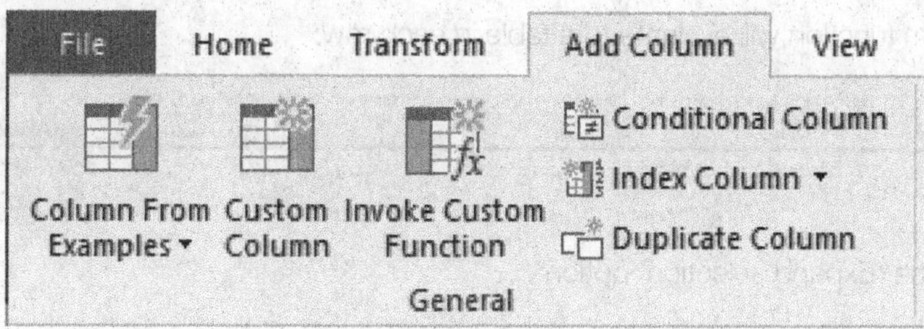

This brings up the 'Invoke Custom Function' dialog, where I input the following options:

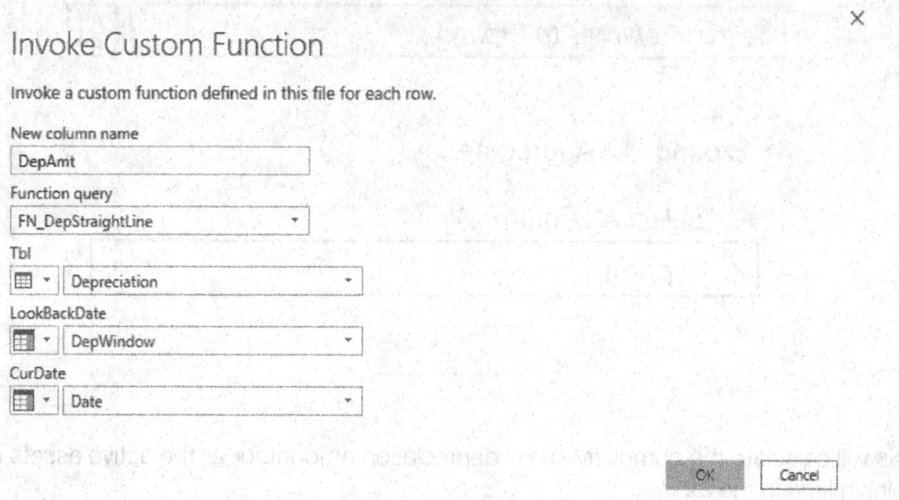

Note that to select a column instead of specifying a value, I use the dropdown next to each parameter:

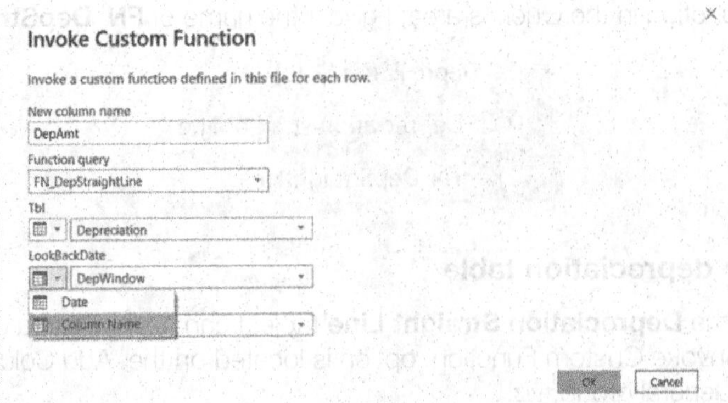

The custom function will evaluate to a table in each row:

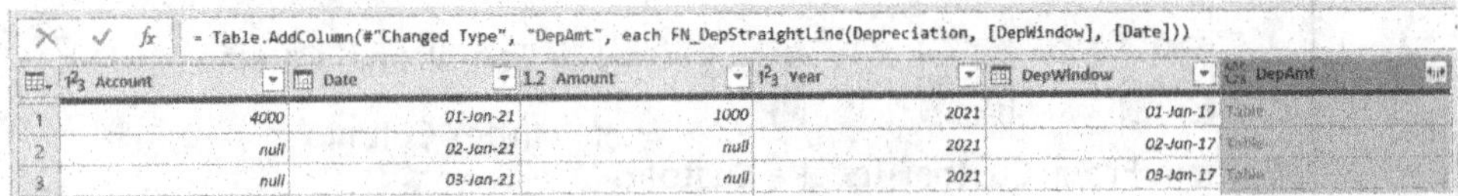

	Account	Date	Amount	Year	DepWindow	DepAmt
1	4000	01-Jan-21	1000	2021	01-Jan-17	Table
2	null	02-Jan-21	null	2021	02-Jan-17	Table
3	null	03-Jan-21	null	2021	03-Jan-17	Table

I click on the 'Expand selection' option:

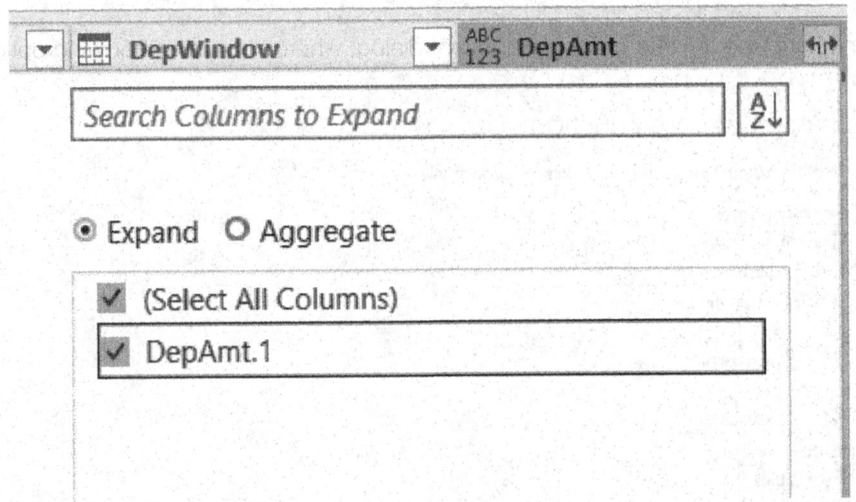

This will calculate the cumulative daily depreciation amount for <u>all</u> the active assets at any point in time in the table:

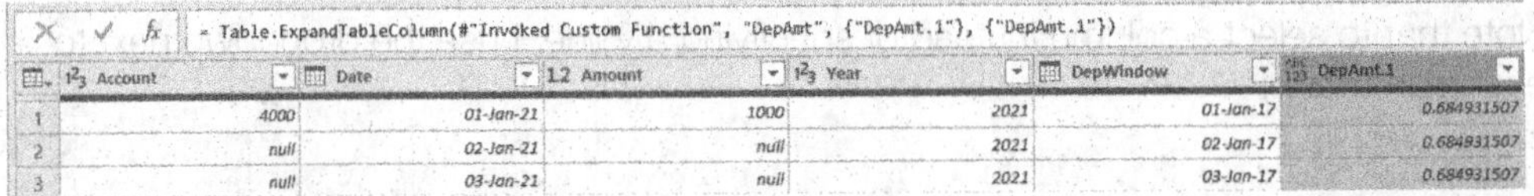

	Account	Date	Amount	Year	DepWindow	DepAmt.1
1	4000	01-Jan-21	1000	2021	01-Jan-17	0.684931507
2	null	02-Jan-21	null	2021	02-Jan-17	0.684931507
3	null	03-Jan-21	null	2021	03-Jan-17	0.684931507

Calculating the **Capex** control account measures will become much easier now when I just sum the amounts in the **DepAmt.1** column. Although I should rename the column from **DepAmt.1** to **DepAmt** and assign it the decimal number data type:

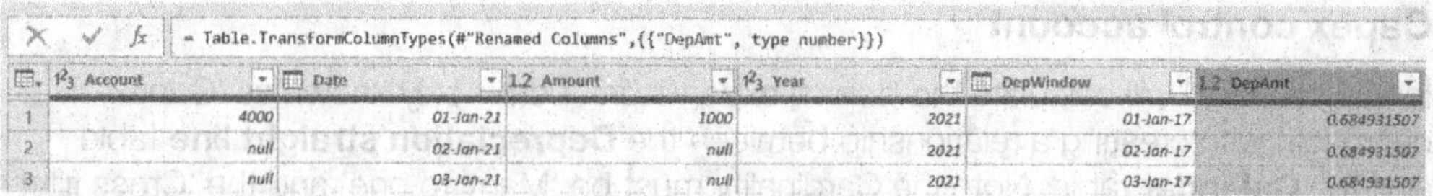

= Table.TransformColumnTypes(#"Renamed Columns",{{"DepAmt", type number}})

	Account	Date	Amount	Year	DepWindow	DepAmt
1	4000	01-Jan-21	1000	2021	01-Jan-17	0.684931507
2	null	02-Jan-21	null	2021	02-Jan-17	0.684931507
3	null	03-Jan-21	null	2021	03-Jan-17	0.684931507

I am now in a position to calculate the **Capex DAX** measures. The *null* values may be left in the table.

Since this is the end of the query, I can add a **Table.View** step at the end of the code:

```
 #"Changed Type1" = Table.TransformColumnTypes(#"Renamed Columns",{{"DepAmt",
type number}}),
 OverrideZeroRowFilter = Table.View(
 null,
 [
 GetType = () =>
 type table[
 Account = Int64.Type,
 Date = Date.Type,
 Amount = Int64.Type,
 Year = Int64.Type,
 DepWindow = Date.Type,
 DepAmt = Number.Type
 ],
 GetRows = () =>
 #"Changed Type1",
 OnTake = (count as number) =>
 if count = 0 then
 #table(
 type table[
 Account = Int64.Type,
 Date = Date.Type,
 Amount = Int64.Type,
 Year = Int64.Type,
 DepWindow = Date.Type,
 DepAmt = Number.Type
 ],
 {}
 )
 else
 Table.FirstN(#"Changed Type1", count)]
 )
in
 OverrideZeroRowFilter
```

I now 'Close & Apply' this table to the model.

Capex control account

In this section, I will calculate the Capital expenditure, commonly known as 'Capex'. I can begin with creating a relationship between the **Depreciation straight line** table and the **Calendar** table. Note the Cardinality must be 'Many to one' and the 'Cross filter direction' is single.

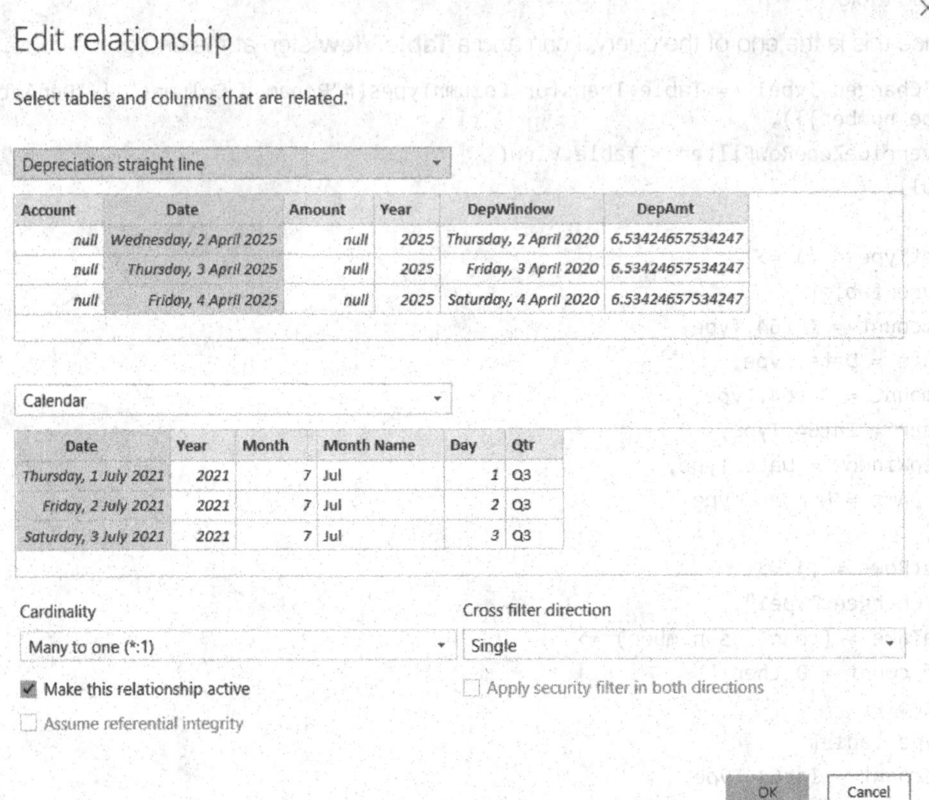

The first measure I will create is the **Capex** measure:

```
Capex =
    SUM('Depreciation straight line'[Amount])
```

```
Capex =
 SUM('Depreciation straight line'[Amount])
```

The **Capex depreciation** measure is as follows:

```
Capex depreciation =
    -SUM('Depreciation straight line'[DepAmt])
```

```
Capex depreciation =
 -SUM('Depreciation straight line'[DepAmt])
```

The difference here, is I have already calculated the daily depreciation amounts in the table. Therefore, a simple **Sum** function will suffice.

The pattern should be becoming familiar by this stage. I now construct the cumulative functions **Capex cum** and **Capex depreciation cum.**

```
Capex cum =
CALCULATE([Capex],
    FILTER(
        ALL('Calendar'),
        'Calendar'[Date] <= MAX('Calendar'[Date])
    )
)
```

```
Capex cum =
CALCULATE([Capex],
 FILTER(
 ALL('Calendar'),
 'Calendar'[Date] <= MAX('Calendar'[Date])
 )
)
```

```
Capex depreciation cum =
CALCULATE([Capex depreciation],
    FILTER(
        ALL('Calendar'),
        'Calendar'[Date] <= MAX('Calendar'[Date])
    )
)
```

```
Capex depreciation cum =
CALCULATE([Capex depreciation],
 FILTER(
 ALL('Calendar'),
 'Calendar'[Date] <= MAX('Calendar'[Date])
 )
)
```

Now I can calculate the Capex opening and closing net book value measures:

```
Capex opening net book value =
    IF(
        PREVIOUSDAY('Calendar'[Date]) = BLANK(),
        0,
        CALCULATE([Capex cum] + [Capex depreciation cum],
        PREVIOUSDAY('Calendar'[Date])
        )
    )
```

```
Capex opening net book value =
 IF(
 PREVIOUSDAY('Calendar'[Date]) = BLANK(),
 0,
 CALCULATE([Capex cum] + [Capex depreciation cum],
```

```
PREVIOUSDAY('Calendar'[Date])
)
)
```

This is followed by the **Capex closing net book value**:

```
Capex closing net book value =
[Capex opening net book value] + [Capex] + [Capex depreciation]
```

```
Capex closing net book value =
[Capex opening net book value] + [Capex] + [Capex depreciation]
```

With the six measures complete, I can now populate my matrix visualisation:

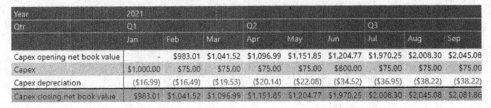

Year	2021								
Qtr	Q1			Q2			Q3		
	Jan	Feb	Mar	Apr	May	Jun	Jul	Aug	Sep
Capex opening net book value	-	$983.01	$1,041.52	$1,096.99	$1,151.85	$1,204.77	$1,970.25	$2,008.30	$2,045.08
Capex	$1,000.00	$75.00	$75.00	$75.00	$75.00	$800.00	$75.00	$75.00	$75.00
Capex depreciation	($16.99)	($16.49)	($19.53)	($20.14)	($22.08)	($34.52)	($36.95)	($38.22)	($38.22)
Capex closing net book value	$983.01	$1,041.52	$1,096.99	$1,151.85	$1,204.77	$1,970.25	$2,008.30	$2,045.08	$2,081.86

Of course, when I am finished creating the measures required for **Capex**, I should group them into their own display folder:

Fields

Search

Control account measures

01. Sales measures

02. COGS measures

03. Purchases measures

04. Inventory measures

05. Opex measures

06. Capex measures

Capex

Capex closing net book value

Capex cum

Capex depreciation

Capex depreciation cum

Capex opening net book value

CHAPTER 17: Calculating Debt

If I am continuing the journey down the Income Statement, then the next line item is Interest Expense. However, I cannot calculate this until I consider debt.

Over the years, I have seen various forms of business and project financing, including equity, shareholder loans, senior debt, mezzanine finance, hire purchase, bonds, convertibles, warrants and so on. *Prima facie*, this myriad of financial instruments can obfuscate the uninitiated, but like this last phrase, the jargon can be simplified.

No matter what the financial instrument, the mechanics essentially boil down to two key elements:

- **Return *on* finance:** the yield to investors or the costs of capital to the recipient of capital (*e.g.* interest, dividends); *and*
- **Return *of* finance:** repayments (or conversion) of original capital issued / drawn down.

And it really is as simple as that. The logic behind how the calculations may vary, such as when capital and returns are paid or rolled up, what order it is paid in and so on, but the computations may be summarised by two control accounts (*i.e.* summaries that show / reconcile how the Balance Sheet varies from one period to the next):

Returns of Finance

Opening Balance (e.g. Debt / Equity) b/f	XX	*Previous period Balance Sheet item*
Additions (e.g. drawdowns / issuances / conversions)	X	*Typically in Cash Flow Statement*
Returns on finance rolled up (e.g. "interest capitalised")	X	*Usually a Balance Sheet movement*
Deductions (e.g. repayments / buybacks / conversions)	(X)	*Typically in Cash Flow Statement*
Closing Balance (e.g. Debt / Equity) c/f	**XX**	*Current period Balance Sheet item*

Returns on Finance

Opening Return Payable (e.g. Interest Payable) b/f	XX	*Previous period Balance Sheet item*
Return Accrued (e.g. Interest Expense)	X	*Income Statement or Balance Sheet movement*
Return Paid (e.g. Interest Paid)	(X)	*Cash Flow Statement*
Closing Return Payable (e.g. Interest Payable) c/f	**XX**	*Current period Balance Sheet item*

The 3 R's of debt modelling

When both businesses and lenders consider debt, they look at two key aspects: risk and return. These are important for credit risk modelling / portfolio analysis, etc. However, when undertaking financial modelling, it is the third 'R' that is often the most important.

In a financial model, risk and return are usually modelled via simple inputs and occasional what-if analysis. Ranking, on the other hand, affects the entire financial structure of the model:

1. Debt Cascade

	Date 1	Date 2	Date 3	Date 4	Date 5	Date 6	Date 7	Date 8	Date 9	Date 10	Date 11	Date 12
Cashflow Before Funding	(16.0)	(0.2)	(0.5)	(0.5)	(0.5)	4.3	6.7	6.8	6.8	7.1	7.3	7.4
Funding	16.0	-	-	-	-	-	-	-	-	-	-	-
Cashflow After Funding	-	(0.2)	(0.5)	(0.5)	(0.5)	4.3	6.7	6.8	6.8	7.1	7.3	7.4
Tax	-	-	-	-	-	-	-	-	-	-	-	-
Cashflow Available before WC Funding	-	(0.2)	(0.5)	(0.5)	(0.5)	4.3	6.7	6.8	6.8	7.1	7.3	7.4
Working Capital Facility Funding	-	0.2	0.5	0.5	0.5	-	-	-	-	-	-	-
Cash Flow Available for Debt Service (CFADS)	-	-	-	-	-	4.3	6.7	6.8	6.8	7.1	7.3	7.4
Senior Debt Service	-	(0.4)	(0.4)	(0.4)	(0.4)	(1.7)	(1.7)	(1.7)	(1.7)	(1.7)	(1.7)	(1.7)
Cashflow Available for Debt Service Reserve Account	-	(0.4)	(0.4)	(0.4)	(0.4)	2.6	5.0	5.1	5.1	5.4	5.6	5.7
Debt Service Reserve Account	-	4.0	0.0	-	-	(2.6)	(0.8)	0.0	0.0	(0.0)	(0.0)	0.0
Cashflow Available for Mezzanine	-	3.6	(0.4)	(0.4)	(0.4)	-	4.2	5.1	5.1	5.4	5.6	5.7
Mezzanine Debt Service	-	(2.7)	-	-	-	-	(3.1)	(3.8)	(3.8)	(4.1)	(4.2)	(4.3)
Cashflow Available for WC Facility	-	0.9	(0.4)	(0.4)	(0.4)	-	1.0	1.3	1.3	1.4	1.4	1.4
Working Capital Facility	-	(0.2)	(0.0)	(0.0)	(0.0)	-	(1.0)	(0.5)	-	-	-	-
Cashflow Available for Equity	-	0.7	(0.4)	(0.4)	(0.5)	-	-	0.7	1.3	1.4	1.4	1.4
Dividends	-	5.3	5.2	5.2	5.3	(2.0)	(2.0)	(2.2)	(2.3)	(3.0)	(3.1)	(3.4)
Net Cashflow	-	5.9	4.7	4.8	4.8	(2.0)	(2.0)	(1.4)	(1.0)	(1.6)	(1.7)	(1.9)
Cash Balance B/f	-	-	5.9	10.7	15.4	20.2	18.3	16.2	14.8	13.8	12.1	10.4
Cash Balance C/f	-	5.9	10.7	15.4	20.2	18.3	16.2	14.8	13.8	12.1	10.4	8.4

As the above graphic shows, if the order of service repaying capital changes, the entire logic will change. This may affect interest / debt service cover ratios (see below). It is important in scoping any such model that the order is understood and how it will be affected by such factors as:

- Conversion of financial instruments
- Breach of covenants or other ratios
- Liquidation / insolvency.

It is not correct to assume that the order of financing will never change, but that is out of scope here (as is the whole idea of order of financing to be honest!). But simplified case studies apart, do be mindful of this key consideration.

Returning to the case study

The debt control account is comprised of four line items:

1. Debt opening payables
2. Debt drawdown
3. Debt repayment
4. Debt closing payables.

I shall begin with the **Debt drawdown** measure. This uses the following **DAX** code:

```
Debt drawdown =
    CALCULATE(
        SUM(Actuals[Amount]),
        Actuals[Account] =  P_DebtCode
    )
```

```
Debt drawdown =
 CALCULATE(
```

```
SUM(Actuals[Amount]),
Actuals[Account] = P_DebtCode
)
```

Followed by the **Debt repayment calc** measure, this measure will sum the debt repayment amounts in my **Actuals** table:

```
Debt repayment calc =
    CALCULATE(
        SUM(Actuals[Amount]),
        Actuals[Account] =  P_DebtRepaymentCode
    )
```

```
Debt repayment calc =
 CALCULATE(
 SUM(Actuals[Amount]),
 Actuals[Account] = P_DebtRepaymentCode
 )
```

I will then use the **Debt repayment** measure to accommodate for days payable:

```
Debt repayment =
    CALCULATE(-[Debt repayment calc],
        DATEADD('Calendar'[Date], -P_DaysPayable, DAY)
    )
```

```
Debt repayment =
 CALCULATE(-[Debt repayment calc],
 DATEADD(‘Calendar’[Date], -P_DaysPayable, DAY)
 )
```

Now, I calculate the cumulative measures for both the drawdowns and repayments:

```
Debt drawdown cum =
CALCULATE([Debt drawdown],
    FILTER(
        ALL('Calendar'),
        'Calendar'[Date] <= MAX('Calendar'[Date])
    )
)
```

```
Debt drawdown cum =
CALCULATE([Debt drawdown],
 FILTER(
 ALL(‘Calendar’),
 ‘Calendar’[Date] <= MAX(‘Calendar’[Date])
 )
)
```

```
Debt repayment cum =
CALCULATE([Debt repayment],
    FILTER(
        ALL('Calendar'),
        'Calendar'[Date] <= MAX('Calendar'[Date])
    )
)
```

```
Debt repayment cum =
CALCULATE([Debt repayment],
 FILTER(
 ALL('Calendar'),
 'Calendar'[Date] <= MAX('Calendar'[Date])
 )
)
```

The **Debt opening payables** measure is calculated with the following **DAX** code:

```
Debt opening payables =
    IF(
        PREVIOUSDAY('Calendar'[Date]) = BLANK(),
        0,
        CALCULATE([Debt drawdown cum] + [Debt repayment cum],
        PREVIOUSDAY('Calendar'[Date])
        )
    )
```

```
Debt opening payables =
 IF(
 PREVIOUSDAY('Calendar'[Date]) = BLANK(),
 0,
 CALCULATE([Debt drawdown cum] + [Debt repayment cum],
 PREVIOUSDAY('Calendar'[Date])
 )
 )
```

The **Debt closing payables** measure is calculated with the following **DAX** code:

```
Debt closing payables =
[Debt opening payables] + [Debt drawdown] + [Debt repayment]
```

```
Debt closing payables =
[Debt opening payables] + [Debt drawdown] + [Debt repayment]
```

After applying the appropriate formatting and plotting the four measures into a matrix visualisation, I get the following result:

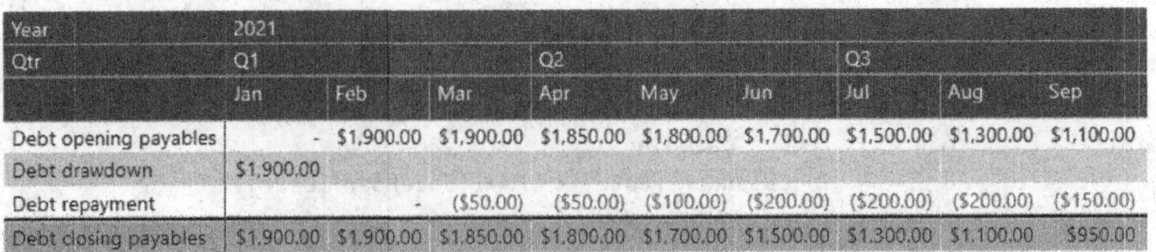

Year	2021								
Qtr	Q1			Q2			Q3		
	Jan	Feb	Mar	Apr	May	Jun	Jul	Aug	Sep
Debt opening payables	-	$1,900.00	$1,900.00	$1,850.00	$1,800.00	$1,700.00	$1,500.00	$1,300.00	$1,100.00
Debt drawdown	$1,900.00								
Debt repayment		-	($50.00)	($50.00)	($100.00)	($200.00)	($200.00)	($200.00)	($150.00)
Debt closing payables	$1,900.00	$1,900.00	$1,850.00	$1,800.00	$1,700.00	$1,500.00	$1,300.00	$1,100.00	$950.00

This is my return **OF** finance.

And before I forget, good practice dictates I should group my measures into a display folder:

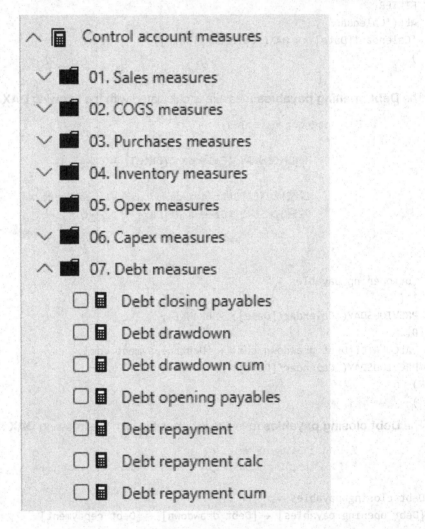

Control account measures
- 01. Sales measures
- 02. COGS measures
- 03. Purchases measures
- 04. Inventory measures
- 05. Opex measures
- 06. Capex measures
- 07. Debt measures
  - Debt closing payables
  - Debt drawdown
  - Debt drawdown cum
  - Debt opening payables
  - Debt repayment
  - Debt repayment calc
  - Debt repayment cum

CHAPTER 18: Calculating Interest

Continuing the discussion of the last chapter, interest represents the return **ON** finance. There are a couple of issues to consider here, namely getting the jargon right and avoiding circularities. Therefore, before I start modelling in Power BI, allow me to clear these points up first.

Capitalised vs. rolled up

There is confusion between the jargon used by the banking industry and accountants when considering debt mechanics:

Scenario	Banking term	Accounting term
Interest is not paid (either by agreement or due to insufficient funds) and is added to the outstanding principal for future interest calculations	Interest capitalised	Interest rolled-up
Interest is not added to the balance but is paid (although there may be a slight timing issue)	Interest amortised (principal is amortised similarly)	When accrued: interest expense When paid: interest paid
Regardless of whether paid or not in reality, interest meets the criteria specified in the relevant accounting standards to be held in the Balance Sheet	n/a	Interest capitalised
When capitalised under accounting rules, the interest charge is released to the P&L over the life of a project on some agreed equitable basis	n/a	Interest amortised

When holding conversations with financiers, be sure you are on the same page before building interest into a financial model. Debt term sheets can be difficult enough to understand without unnecessarily adding to the complexity.

Avoiding circularity

This is a key issue in Excel:

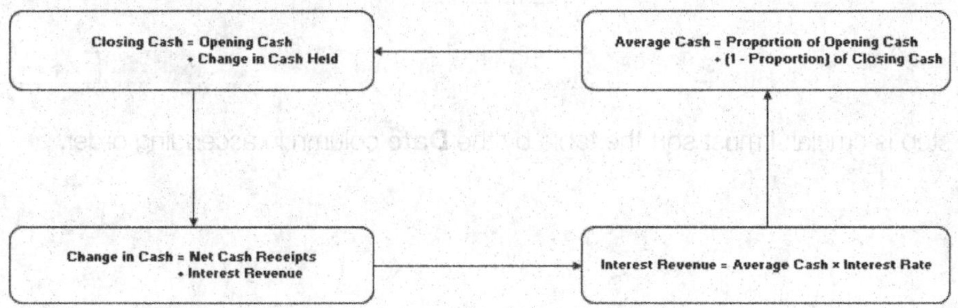

This is not so pertinent for Power BI, as I can calculate interest on a daily basis if necessary – so I am always calculating interest on an "opening balance approach". I just need to ensure – as I need the values to reconcile at whatever level I view them – that they reconcile. Hence, **interest must be calculated on a daily basis**.

Returning to the case study

Bearing all of the above in mind, calculating interest is a slightly trickier control account. The way I have decided to tackle this is to calculate interest at a daily level in the table. This avoids the circularity issue and will ensure reconciliation of interest over whatever period of time I choose to analyse.

To break this problem down, this will require two helper tables:

1. one helper table is used to return the cumulative debt drawdown
2. the other helper table is required to return the cumulative debt repayment amounts.

I shall begin with creating the helper table to calculate the cumulative debt drawdown amount.

Calculating the cumulative debt drawdown

To begin, I create a Reference Query from the **Actuals** table.

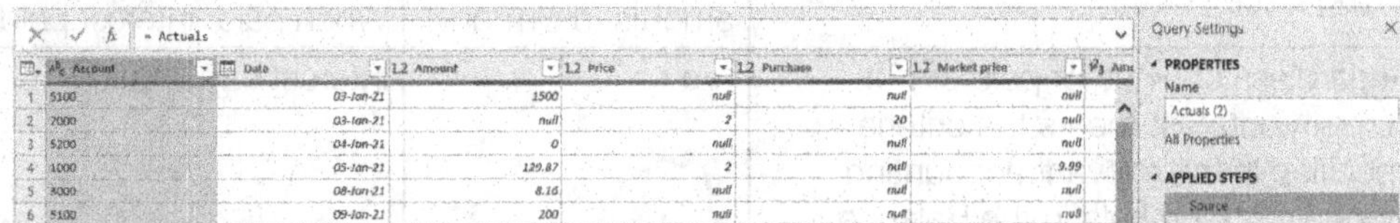

I call this table **Cumulative debt drawdown**.

Next, I can filter the **Account** column by the **P_DebtCode** parameter:

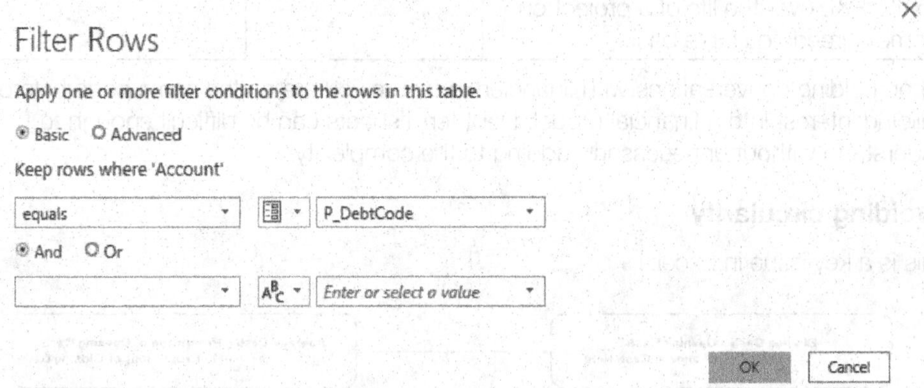

This step is crucial: I must sort the table by the **Date** column in ascending order.

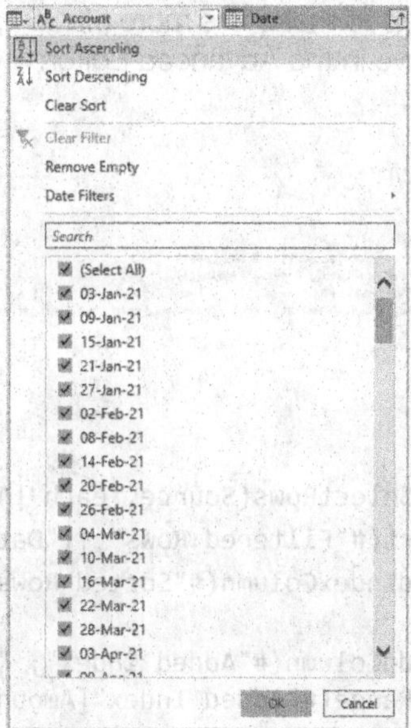

Next, I add an index column that starts from one [1] into the table. As a reminder, the option to add an index column is located on the 'Add Column' tab on the Ribbon, in the General group:

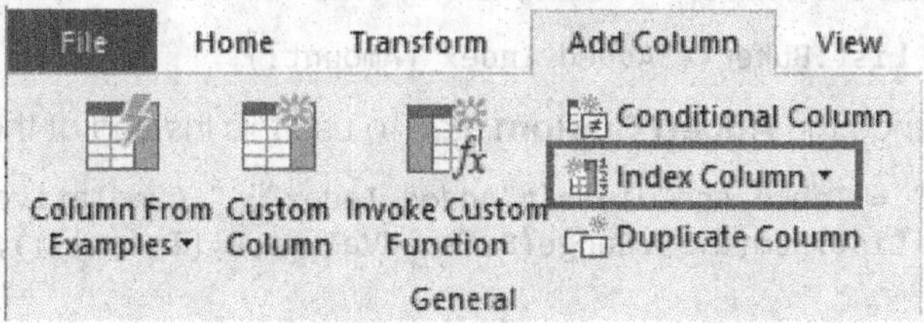

With the **Index** column, I can create the **Cumulative debt drawdown** column using the following **M** code:

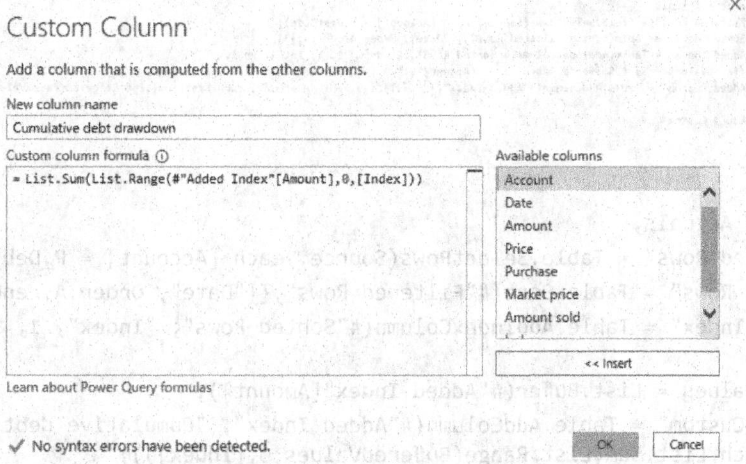


```
List.Sum(List.Range(#"Added Index"[Amount],0,[Index]))
```

I need to add a **List.Buffer** step to make this more efficient, as I did for **Inventory avg step**. I look at the **M** code I have in the Advanced Editor:

Advanced Editor

Cumulative debt drawdown

```
let
    Source = Actuals,
    #"Filtered Rows" = Table.SelectRows(Source, each [Account] = P_DebtCode),
    #"Sorted Rows" = Table.Sort(#"Filtered Rows",{{"Date", Order.Ascending}}),
    #"Added Index" = Table.AddIndexColumn(#"Sorted Rows", "Index", 1, 1, Int64.Type),
    #"Added Custom" = Table.AddColumn(#"Added Index", "Cumulative debt drawdown", each List.Sum(List.Range(#"Added Index"[Amount],0,[Index])))
in
    #"Added Custom"
```

```
let
 Source = Actuals,
 #"Filtered Rows" = Table.SelectRows(Source, each [Account] = P_DebtCode),
 #"Sorted Rows" = Table.Sort(#"Filtered Rows",{{"Date", Order.Ascending}}),
 #"Added Index" = Table.AddIndexColumn(#"Sorted Rows", "Index", 1, 1, Int64.
Type),
 #"Added Custom" = Table.AddColumn(#"Added Index", "Cumulative debt draw-
down", each List.Sum(List.Range(#"Added Index"[Amount],0,[Index])))
in
 #"Added Custom"
```

I can add a step before the **Added Custom** step which will store the values for **#"Added Index"[Amount]** so that this list of values is only read once.

```
BufferedValues = List.Buffer(#"Added Index"[Amount]),
```

I then need to change the **Added Custom** step to use this instead of the values.

```
 #"Added Custom" = Table.AddColumn(#"Added Index", " Cumulative debt
drawdown", each List.Sum(List.Range(BufferedValues,0,[Index]))),
```

Advanced Editor

Cumulative debt drawdown

```
let
    Source = Actuals,
    #"Filtered Rows" = Table.SelectRows(Source, each [Account] = P_DebtCode),
    #"Sorted Rows" = Table.Sort(#"Filtered Rows",{{"Date", Order.Ascending}}),
    #"Added Index" = Table.AddIndexColumn(#"Sorted Rows", "Index", 1, 1, Int64.Type),
    BufferedValues = List.Buffer(#"Added Index"[Amount]),
    #"Added Custom" = Table.AddColumn(#"Added Index", "Cumulative debt drawdown", each List.Sum(List.Range(BufferedValues,0,[Index])))
in
    #"Added Custom"
```

```
let
 Source = Actuals,
 #"Filtered Rows" = Table.SelectRows(Source, each [Account] = P_DebtCode),
 #"Sorted Rows" = Table.Sort(#"Filtered Rows",{{"Date", Order.Ascending}}),
 #"Added Index" = Table.AddIndexColumn(#"Sorted Rows", "Index", 1, 1, Int64.
Type),
 BufferedValues = List.Buffer(#"Added Index"[Amount]),
 #"Added Custom" = Table.AddColumn(#"Added Index", "Cumulative debt draw-
down", each List.Sum(List.Range(BufferedValues,0,[Index])))
in
 #"Added Custom"
```

My query should now run more efficiently, and I can move on to the next step.

I change the data type of **Cumulative debt drawdown** to a decimal number. Then I select **Account, Date,** and **Cumulative debt drawdown**, right-click and select to 'Remove Other Columns':

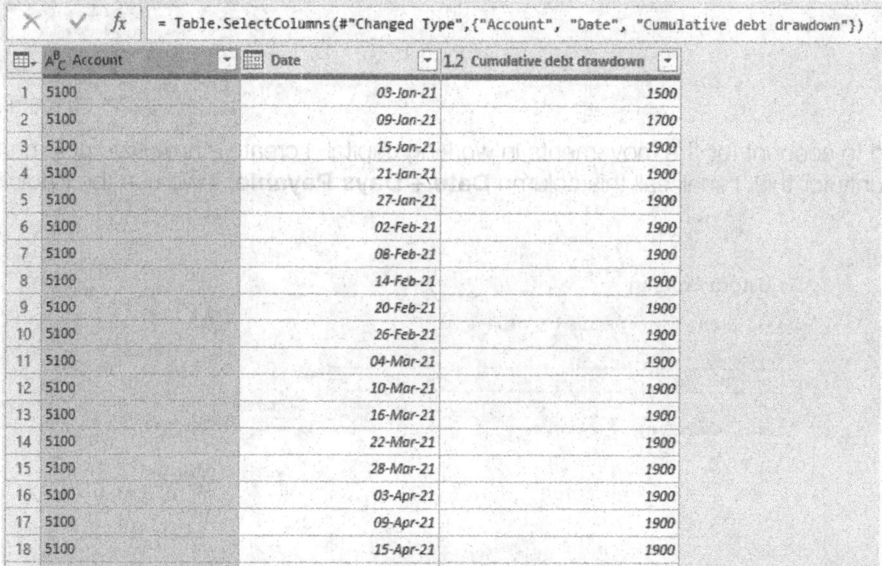

```
= Table.SelectColumns(#"Changed Type",{"Account", "Date", "Cumulative debt drawdown"})
```

	Account	Date	Cumulative debt drawdown
1	5100	03-Jan-21	1500
2	5100	09-Jan-21	1700
3	5100	15-Jan-21	1900
4	5100	21-Jan-21	1900
5	5100	27-Jan-21	1900
6	5100	02-Feb-21	1900
7	5100	08-Feb-21	1900
8	5100	14-Feb-21	1900
9	5100	20-Feb-21	1900
10	5100	26-Feb-21	1900
11	5100	04-Mar-21	1900
12	5100	10-Mar-21	1900
13	5100	16-Mar-21	1900
14	5100	22-Mar-21	1900
15	5100	28-Mar-21	1900
16	5100	03-Apr-21	1900
17	5100	09-Apr-21	1900
18	5100	15-Apr-21	1900

Now, I may move on to the **Cumulative debt repayments** table. I can duplicate this query and make some alterations. I am using a duplicate rather than a reference because I am going to use the **Cumulative debt drawdown** as a template and change a step later.

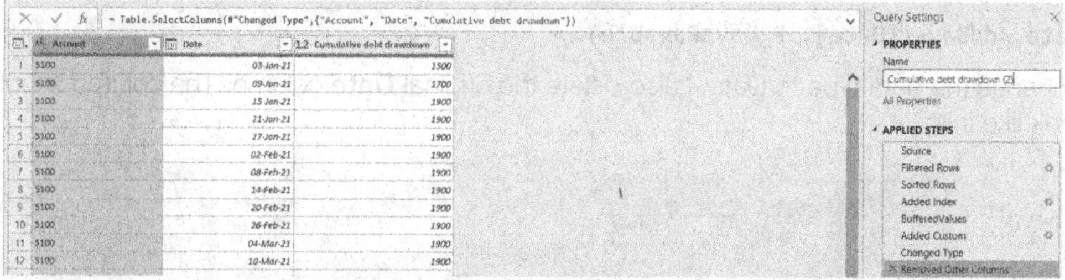

```
= Table.SelectColumns(#"Changed Type",{"Account", "Date", "Cumulative debt drawdown"})
```

	Account	Date	Cumulative debt drawdown
1	5100	03-Jan-21	1500
2	5100	09-Jan-21	1700
3	5100	15-Jan-21	1900
4	5100	21-Jan-21	1900
5	5100	27-Jan-21	1900
6	5100	02-Feb-21	1900
7	5100	08-Feb-21	1900
8	5100	14-Feb-21	1900
9	5100	20-Feb-21	1900
10	5100	26-Feb-21	1900
11	5100	04-Mar-21	1900
12	5100	10-Mar-21	1900

I rename the table to **Cumulative debt repayments**.

Looking at the 'APPLIED STEPS' section, I can navigate to the 'Filtered Rows' step and change the filter from **P_DebtCode** to **P_DebtRepaymentCode**.

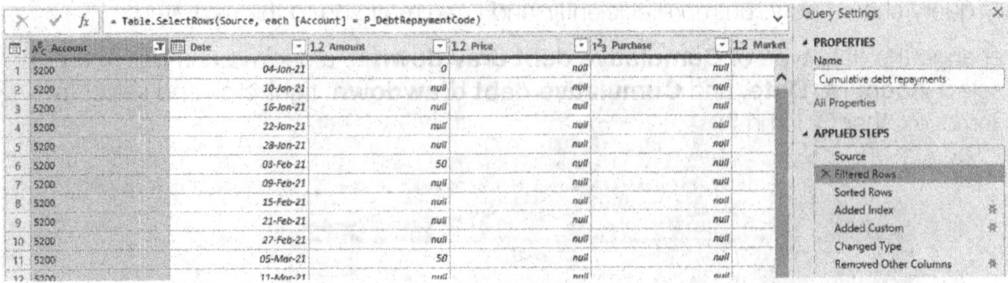

I need to account for the movements in working capital. I create a new date column that accounts for this. I shall call this column **Date + Days Payable**, it will use the following code:

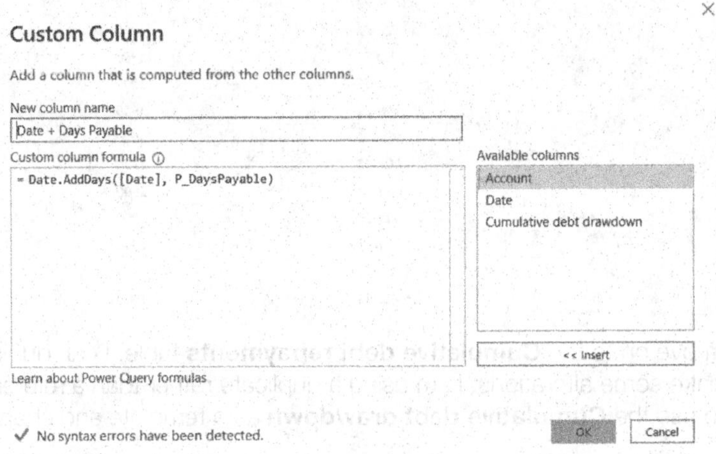


```
Date.AddDays([Date], P_DaysPayable)
```

I change the data type to Date. I also delete the original **Date** column. The column should look like this:

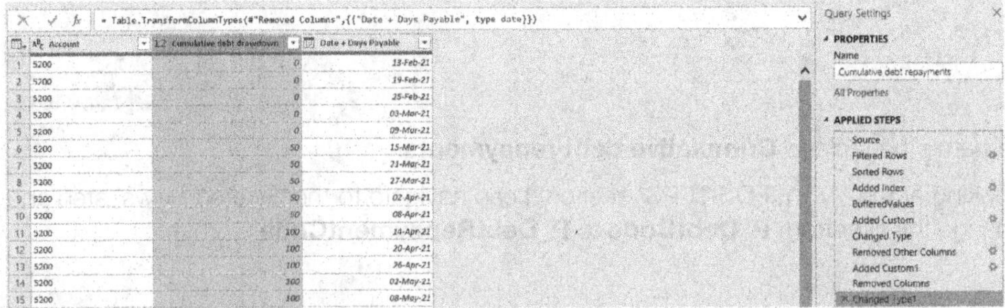

The final step is to rename **Date + Days Payable** to **Date**, and **Cumulative debt drawdown** to **Cumulative debt repayments**. This is to ensure the tables will be appended properly.

I then append the two tables, together with the **Fulldates** table. This is done by navigating to the **Cumulative debt drawdown** table and then clicking on the 'Append Queries' option, which is located on the Home tab of the Ribbon in the Combine group.

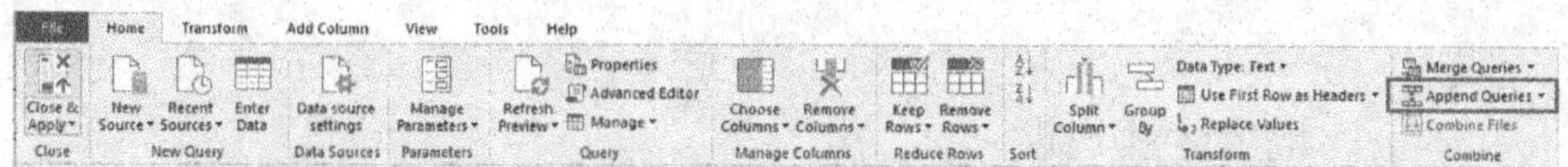

I select the 'Append Queries as New' option, bringing up the Append dialog:

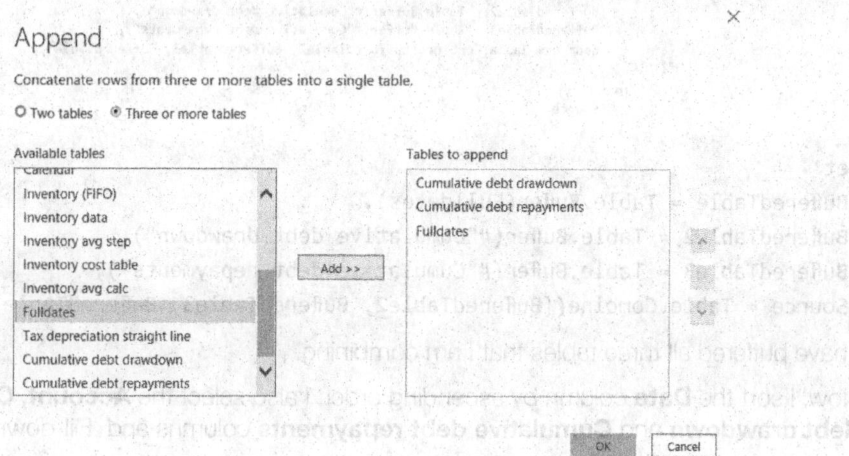

Here, I select the 'Three or more tables' option, then pick from the list of 'Available tables': **Cumulative debt drawdown, Cumulative debt repayments** and **Fulldates.** I call the resulting query **Interest calc**.

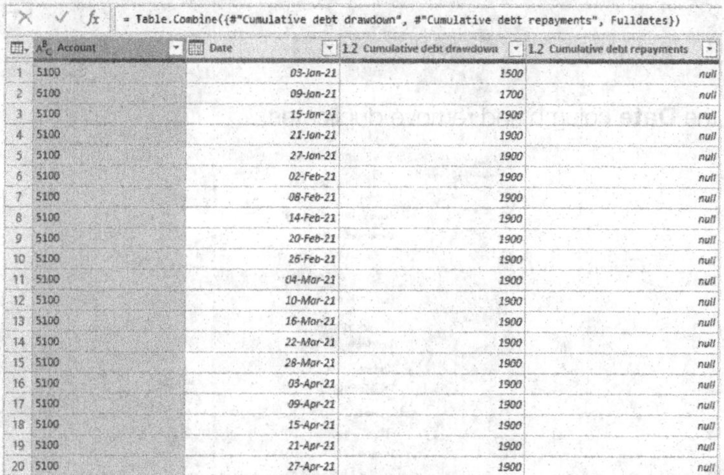

```
= Table.Combine({#"Cumulative debt drawdown", #"Cumulative debt repayments", Fulldates})
```

	Account	Date	Cumulative debt drawdown	Cumulative debt repayments
1	5100	03-Jan-21	1500	null
2	5100	09-Jan-21	1700	null
3	5100	15-Jan-21	1900	null
4	5100	21-Jan-21	1900	null
5	5100	27-Jan-21	1900	null
6	5100	02-Feb-21	1900	null
7	5100	08-Feb-21	1900	null
8	5100	14-Feb-21	1900	null
9	5100	20-Feb-21	1900	null
10	5100	26-Feb-21	1900	null
11	5100	04-Mar-21	1900	null
12	5100	10-Mar-21	1900	null
13	5100	16-Mar-21	1900	null
14	5100	22-Mar-21	1900	null
15	5100	28-Mar-21	1900	null
16	5100	03-Apr-21	1900	null
17	5100	09-Apr-21	1900	null
18	5100	15-Apr-21	1900	null
19	5100	21-Apr-21	1900	null
20	5100	27-Apr-21	1900	null

I should take this opportunity to add a **Table.Buffer** line to allow for a faster evaluation. This is done by entering the following code before the merge occurs:

Advanced Editor

Interest calc

```
let
    BufferedTable = Table.Buffer(Fulldates),
    BufferedTable2 = Table.Buffer(#"Cumulative debt drawdown"),
    BufferedTable3 = Table.Buffer(#"Cumulative debt repayments"),
    Source = Table.Combine({BufferedTable2, BufferedTable3, BufferedTable})

in
    Source
```

```
let
 BufferedTable = Table.Buffer(Fulldates),
 BufferedTable2 = Table.Buffer(#"Cumulative debt drawdown"),
 BufferedTable3 = Table.Buffer(#"Cumulative debt repayments"),
 Source = Table.Combine({BufferedTable2, BufferedTable3, BufferedTable})
```

I have buffered all three tables that I am combining.

Now, I sort the **Date** column by ascending order. I also select the **Account, Cumulative debt drawdown** and **Cumulative debt repayments** columns and 'Fill-down'.

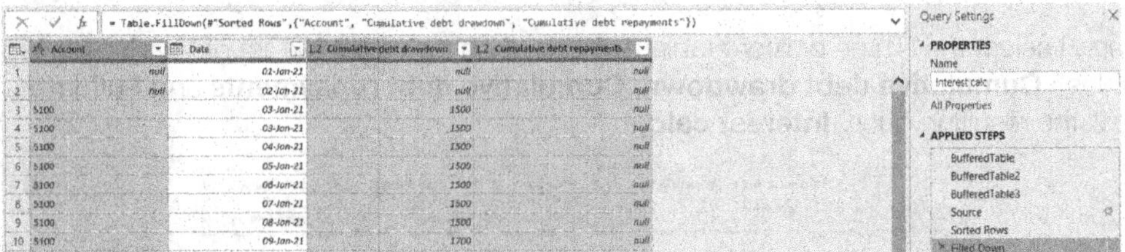

I then select the **Date** column and remove duplicates.

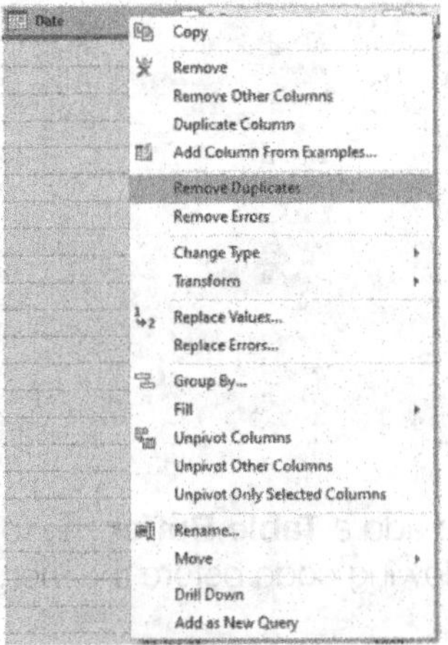

The next thing to do is to replace *null* values with zero [0] in the **Cumulative debt drawdown** and **Cumulative debt repayments**. This is because I am about to insert calculated columns, and they do not recognise *null* as a numerical value. Therefore, an evaluation with *null* will result in an error.

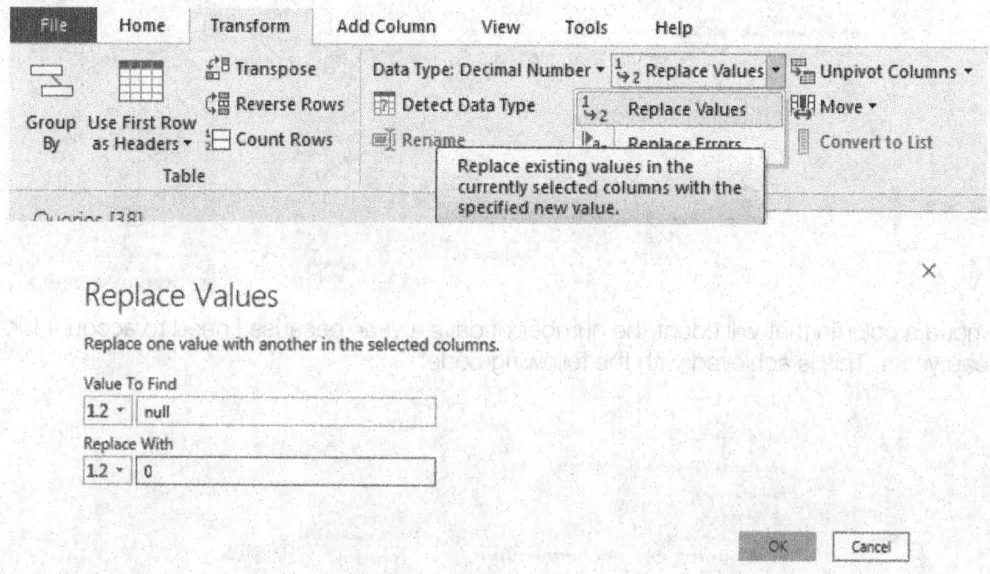

Now, I can add a custom column to calculate the **Debt closing balance**. This is achieved with the following **M** code:

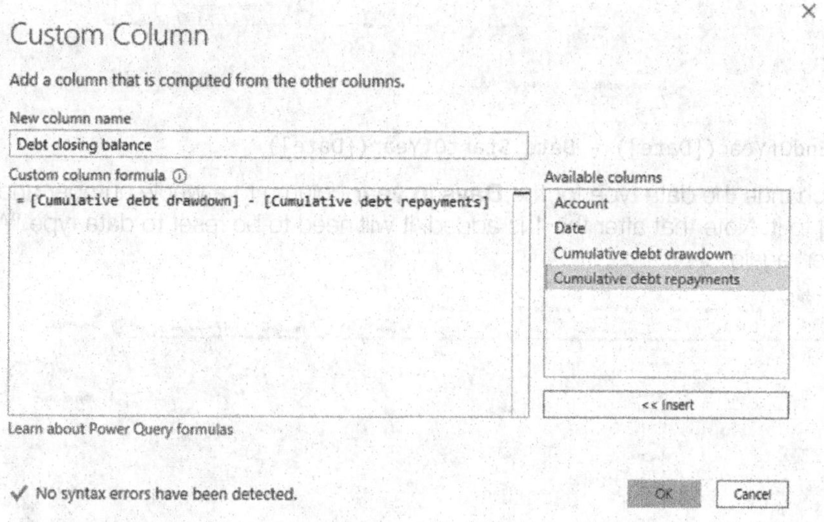


```
[Cumulative debt drawdown] - [Cumulative debt repayments]
```

I change the data type of the **Debt closing balance** column to a decimal number.

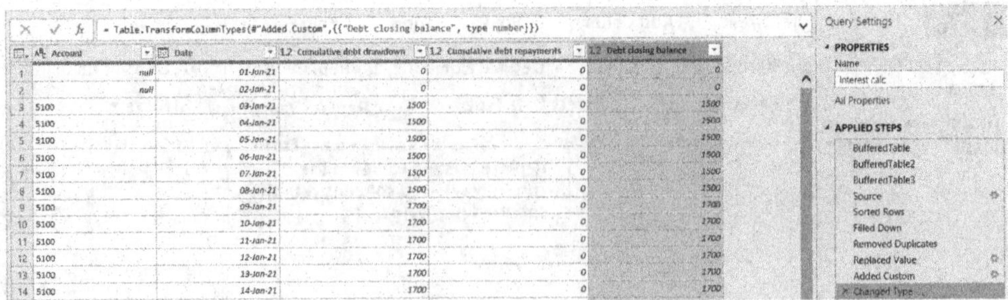

I need a column that will count the number of days a year, because I need to account for leap years. This is achieved with the following code:

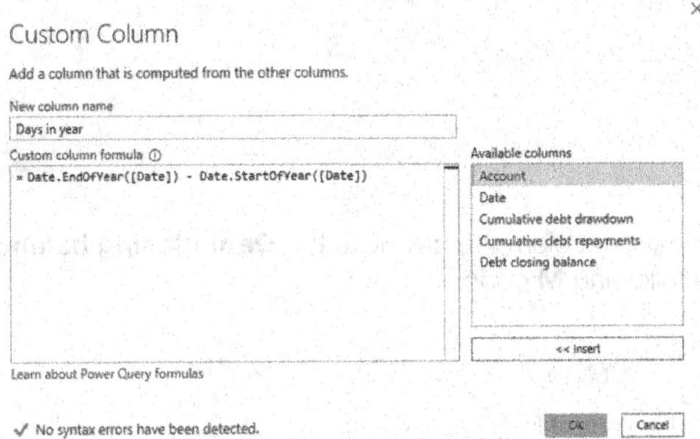


```
Date.EndOfYear([Date]) - Date.StartOfYear([Date])
```

I then change the data type for the **Days in year** column to a whole number and add one [1] to it. Note that after the 1 is added, it will need to be reset to data type 'Whole Number' again.

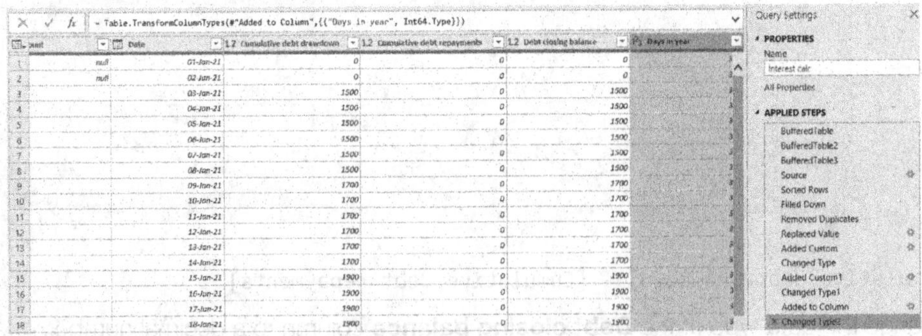

Now I can create the column that will calculate the daily interest expense, I shall call this column **Interest expense daily**. This is done with the following **M** code:

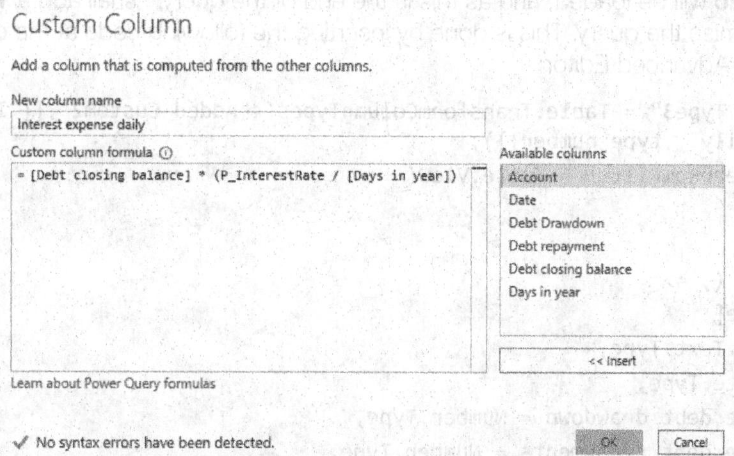

```
[Debt closing balance] * (P_InterestRate / [Days in year])
```

Obviously, if you have a debt term sheet that calculates always on 365 days (say), then clearly, change this formula accordingly.

I must change the data type of the **Interest expense daily** column to a decimal number.

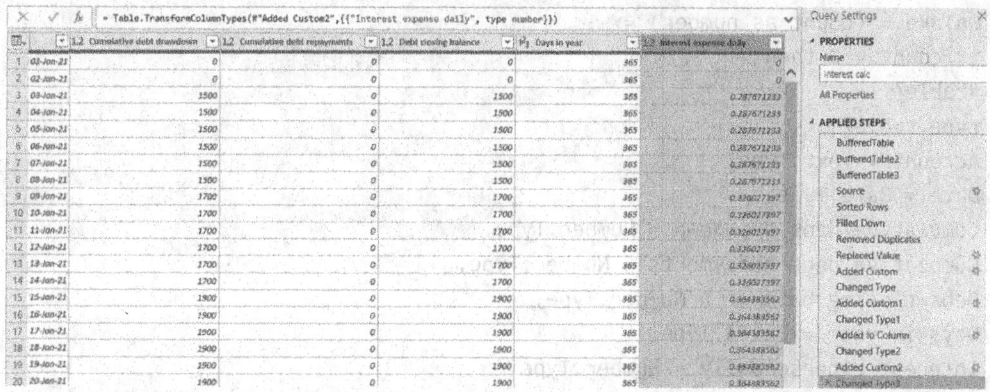

I need to disable the load for the **Cumulative debt drawdown** and **Cumulative debt repayments** tables. I do not want to unnecessarily populate the fields list on the report.

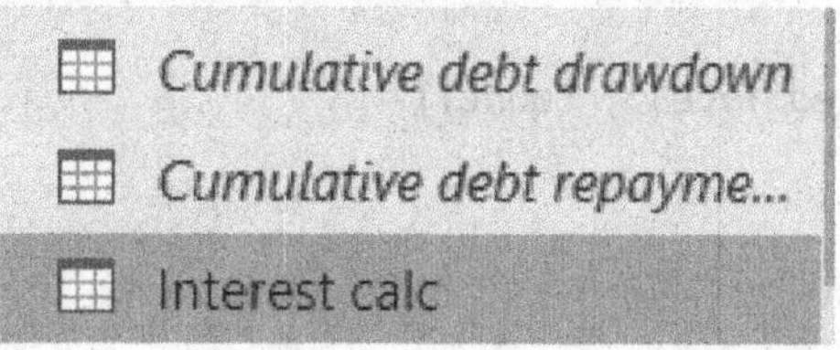

Interest calc will be loaded, and as this is the end of the query, I shall add a **Table.View** step to optimise the query. This is done by inserting the following code at the end of the query in the Advanced Editor:

```
#"Changed Type3" = Table.TransformColumnTypes(#"Added Custom2",{{"Interest
expense daily", type number}}),
OverrideZeroRowFilter = Table.View(
null,
[
GetType = () =>
type table[
Account = Text.Type,
Date = Date.Type,
Cumulative debt drawdown = Number.Type,
Cumulative debt repayments = Number.Type,
Debt closing balance = Number.Type,
Days in year = Int64.Type,
Interest expense daily = Number.Type
],
GetRows = () =>
#"Changed Type3",
OnTake = (count as number) =>
if count = 0 then
#table(
type table[
Account = Text.Type,
Date = Date.Type,
Cumulative debt drawdown = Number.Type,
Cumulative debt repayments = Number.Type,
Debt closing balance = Number.Type,
Days in year = Int64.Type,
Interest expense daily = Number.Type
],
{}
)
else
Table.FirstN(#"Changed Type3", count)]
)
in
OverrideZeroRowFilter
```

I then simply 'Close & Apply'.

Calculating the interest control account

As the interest data is housed in a separate table, I must create a relationship between the **Interest calc** table and the **Calendar** table.

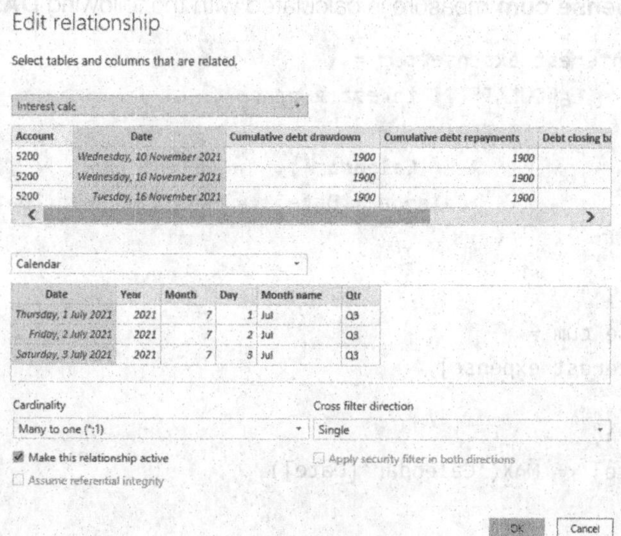

The interest control account is comprised of four line items:

1. Interest opening payables
2. Interest expense
3. Interest cash paid
4. Interest closing payables.

I shall start with the **Interest expense** measure. It is calculated with the following **DAX** code:

```
Interest expense =
SUM('Interest calc'[Interest expense daily])
```

```
Interest expense =
SUM('Interest calc'[Interest expense daily])
```

You should know the drill by now. Next, I construct the **Interest cash paid** measure:

```
Interest cash paid =
    CALCULATE(-[Interest expense],
        DATEADD('Calendar'[Date], -P_DaysPayable, DAY)
    )
```

```
Interest cash paid =
 CALCULATE(-[Interest expense],
 DATEADD('Calendar'[Date], -P_DaysPayable, DAY)
 )
```

I then create the cumulative measures to facilitate the calculation of the opening and closing payables measures.

The **Interest expense cum** measure is calculated with the following **DAX** code:

```
Interest expense cum =
    CALCULATE([Interest expense],
        FILTER(
            ALL('Calendar'),
            'Calendar'[Date] <= MAX('Calendar'[Date])
            )
        )
```

```
Interest expense cum =
 CALCULATE([Interest expense],
 FILTER(
 ALL('Calendar'),
 'Calendar'[Date] <= MAX('Calendar'[Date])
 )
 )
```

The **Interest cash paid cum** measure is calculated with the following **DAX** code:

```
Interest cash paid cum =
    CALCULATE([Interest cash paid],
        FILTER(
            ALL('Calendar'),
            'Calendar'[Date] <= MAX('Calendar'[Date])
            )
        )
```

```
Interest cash paid cum =
 CALCULATE([Interest cash paid],
 FILTER(
 ALL('Calendar'),
 'Calendar'[Date] <= MAX('Calendar'[Date])
 )
 )
```

This is followed by the **Interest opening payables** measure. This measure is calculated by the following **DAX** code:

```
Interest opening payables =
    IF(
        PREVIOUSDAY('Calendar'[Date]) = BLANK(),
        0,
        CALCULATE([Interest cash paid cum] + [Interest expense cum],
        PREVIOUSDAY('Calendar'[Date])
        )
    )
```

```
Interest opening payables =
 IF(
 PREVIOUSDAY('Calendar'[Date]) = BLANK(),
 0,
 CALCULATE([Interest cash paid cum] + [Interest expense cum],
 PREVIOUSDAY('Calendar'[Date])
 )
 )
```

Finally, the **Interest closing payables** measure uses the following **DAX** code:

```
Interest closing payables =
[Interest opening payables] + [Interest expense] + [Interest cash paid]
```


```
Interest closing payables =
[Interest opening payables] + [Interest expense] + [Interest cash paid]
```


After applying the appropriate formatting to the measures and applying the standardised formatting to the visualisation, I get the following result:

Year	2021								
Qtr	Q1			Q2			Q3		
	Jan	Feb	Mar	Apr	May	Jun	Jul	Aug	Sep
Interest opening payables	-	$9.88	$14.58	$14.41	$14.03	$13.46	$12.35	$10.78	$9.21
Interest expense	$9.88	$10.20	$11.13	$10.48	$10.36	$9.09	$8.19	$6.96	$5.75
Interest cash paid		($5.50)	($11.30)	($10.86)	($10.92)	($10.20)	($9.76)	($8.53)	($7.10)
Interest closing payables	$9.88	$14.58	$14.41	$14.03	$13.46	$12.35	$10.78	$9.21	$7.86

If it is getting repetitive, then it means you are following the methodology well!

I create a folder for the **Interest measures**.

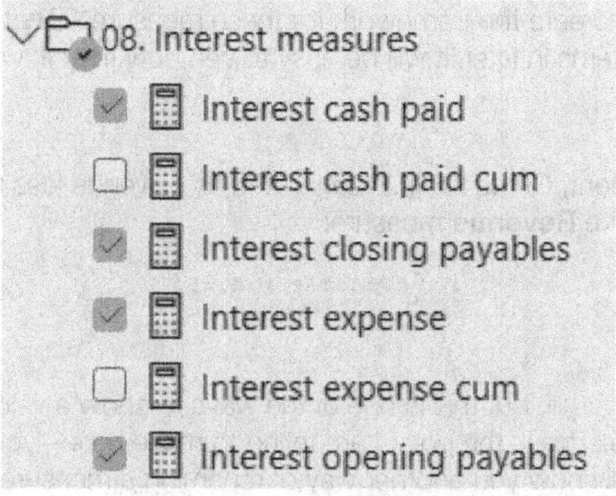

CHAPTER 19: Income Statement (Part 1)

You are probably expecting that the next control account to be calculated should be for tax. However, the key driver of tax is the Net Profit Before Tax line or **NPBT**. This line item is calculated near the end of the Income Statement. Therefore, I must calculate the Income Statement before I can create any tax measures.

The Income Statement is the one of the three financial statements I will construct. Coincidentally, it is *conceptually* the smallest financial statement of the three, as you may recall from earlier:

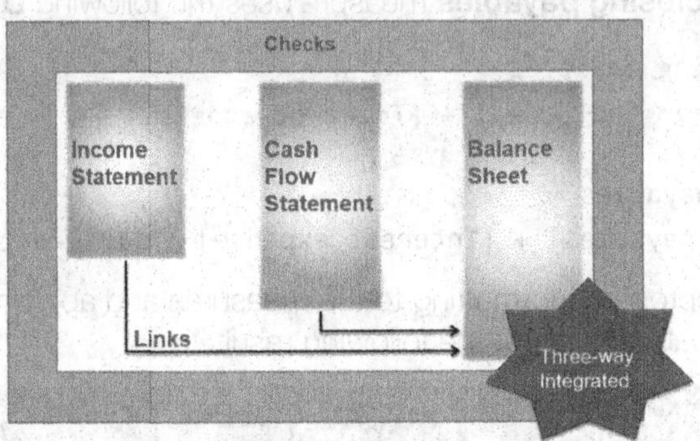

The Income Statement is comprised of five key line items:

1. Gross Profit
2. **E**arnings **B**efore **I**nterest, **T**axes, **D**epreciation and **A**mortisation (**EBITDA**)
3. **E**arnings **B**efore **I**nterest and **T**axes (**EBIT**)
4. **N**et **P**rofit **B**efore **T**ax (**NPBT**)
5. **N**et **P**rofit **A**fter **T**ax (**NPAT**)

I will describe how to create the framework for these measures. That way, when I add the control account line items in later, it will be easy to see how they flow through.

Gross Profit

In the Income Statement, Gross Profit is calculated as Revenue less COGS and Inventory costs. First, I create the **Revenue** measure:

```
Revenue = [Sales]
```

```
Revenue = [Sales]
```

This may seem like overkill, but this is one of the ways to show a value with more than one descriptive name. This is the point I am trying to make here – you could just use **Sales** otherwise! I will show you another way of renaming a measure *very* shortly...

Now that I am creating measures for the Income Statement, the 'Home table' should be **Financial account measures**.

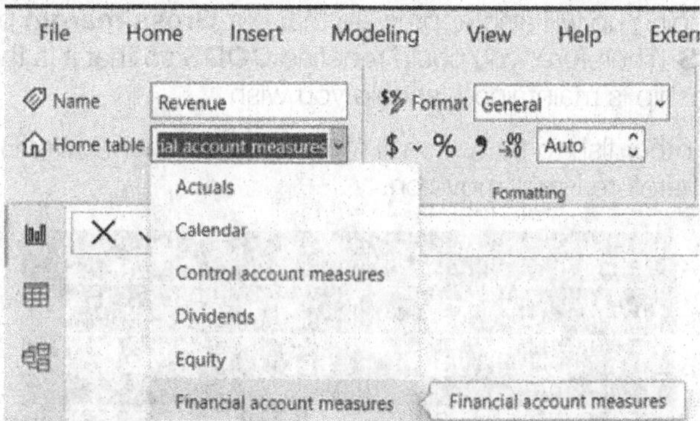

Now I have a measure in **Financial account measures**, I can hide the column which has the same name as the table, which will make Power BI recognise it as a Measures Folder, changing the icon and moving it up the list in the Fields pane. The next image is in the Model view.

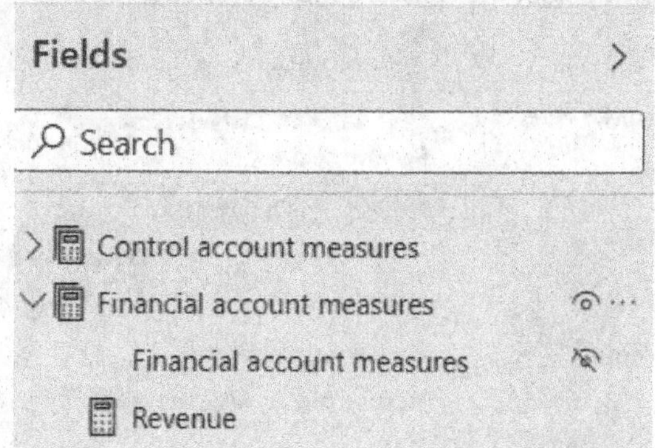

The next line item in the Income Statement is the **COGS** line. It should be presented as a negative number. However, COGS is currently evaluated as a positive number in our control account. Therefore, to display it correctly on the Income Statement I shall create a measure to flip the sign.

```
COGS IS =
-[COGS] + [Inventory cost ($)]
```


```
COGS IS =
-[COGS] + [Inventory cost ($)]
```


This effectively aggregates the two direct costs, COGS and inventory, together as negative values. The signage is a little confusing, but this is down to how these measures were necessarily defined earlier.

Also, do note that I have called this measure **COGS IS**, 'IS' short for Income Statement. When plotting this onto the visualisation it will initially appear as **COGS IS,** but, of course, I can rename it.

Those that are keeping up will also appreciate that our **Gross margin** parameter will not fully drive **COGS IS**. Therefore, you could redefine **COGS** so that it is the balancing item, so that the relationship is maintained, should you wish.

But for me, I have other fish to fry so I shall move on and other Power BI features I wish to demonstrate. Therefore I shall move on.

Year	2021		
Qtr	Q1		
	Jan	Feb	Mar
COGS IS	-359.64	-1,258.74	-1,468.53

Note that since **COGS IS** driven by the **Gross margin**, the values above are using the **Gross margin** value of 40% that I decided on earlier. With the above visualisation selected, I can navigate to the Values section. I find the **COGS IS** measure, then click on the down arrow icon and select the 'Rename for this visual' option:

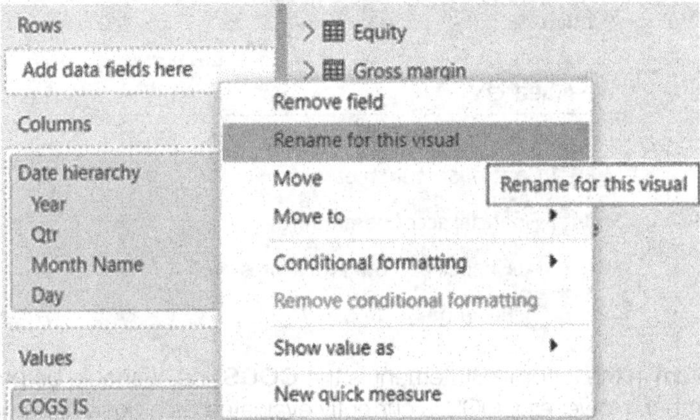

I can remove the 'IS' from the name of the measure, and it now appears as **COGS** in the visualisation:

Year	2021		
Qtr	Q1		
	Jan	Feb	Mar
COGS	-359.64	-1,258.74	-1,468.53

I can now create the **Gross profit** measure. The **Gross profit** measure (not to be confused with our earlier **Gross margin** measure) uses the following **DAX** code:

```
Gross profit =
[Revenue] + [COGS IS]
```


```
Gross profit =
[Revenue] + [COGS IS]
```

Note that the signs for **COGS IS** and **Inventory cost** are negative, therefore, I shall just sum the measures together to calculate **Gross Profit**.

Before moving on to the next line item, I think it might be a good time to cover the creation of blank lines in Power BI.

Creating blank lines

Remember the "__ = "" " measure? I can insert a copy of it into the visualisation:

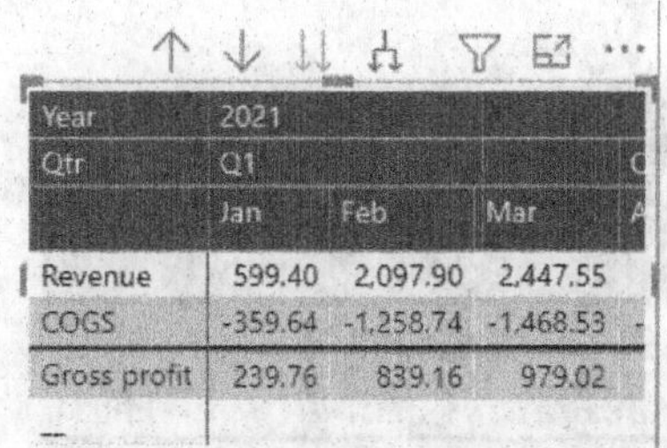

Year	2021		
Qtr	Q1		
	Jan	Feb	Mar
Revenue	599.40	2,097.90	2,447.55
COGS	-359.64	-1,258.74	-1,468.53
Gross profit	239.76	839.16	979.02
__			

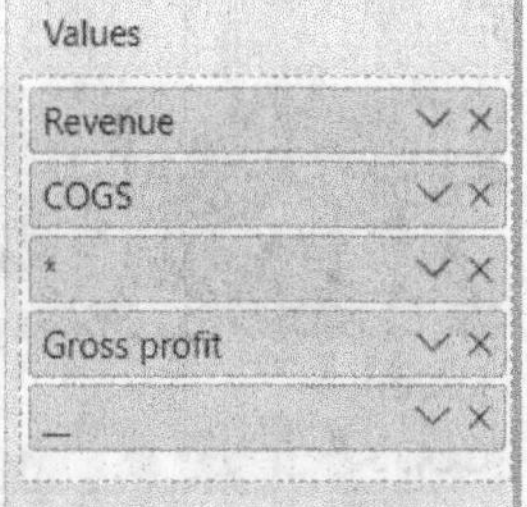

It's almost a blank line, I just need to make a small tweak. In the 'Specific column' section for the blank line measure, I set the 'Text' to white (even if the setting is already white) and 'Apply to header':

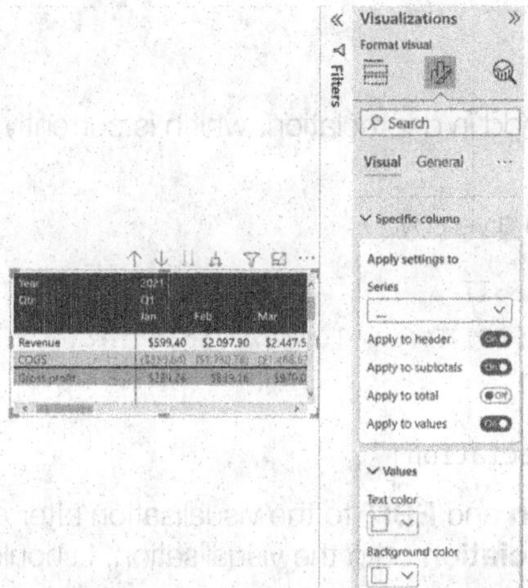

This process must be repeated in every visualisation to turn this field blank (though do remember visualisations can be copied). Multiple copies of the '__' measure can be used in the same visualisation, and will have the same formatting as the original.

EBITDA

Moving on to the **EBITDA** line. **EBITDA** is calculated as **Gross Profit** less **Operating expenditure**. Therefore, I shall create an **Operating expenditure** measure first, where I flip the sign of the **Opex** measure:

```
Operating expenditure = -[Opex]
```

Operating expenditure = -[Opex]

The **EBITDA** measure is then calculated with the following **DAX** code:

```
EBITDA =
[Gross profit] + [Operating expenditure]
```

```
EBITDA =
[Gross Profit] + [Operating expenditure]
```

I can then plot these two measures into the visualisation with a blank line in between, and apply formatting:

Year	2021		
Qtr	Q1		
	Jan	Feb	Mar
Revenue	$599.40	$2,097.90	$2,447.55
COGS	($359.64)	($1,258.74)	($1,468.53)
Gross profit	$239.76	$839.16	$979.02
Operating expenditure	($93.84)	($130.56)	($77.52)
EBITDA	$145.92	$708.60	$901.50

EBIT

To calculate **EBIT** I must add in depreciation, which is currently calculated in the **Capex depreciation** measure.

The **EBIT** measure is then given by:

```
EBIT =
[EBITDA] + [Capex depreciation]
```

```
EBIT =
[EBITDA] + [Capex depreciation]
```

I add **Capex depreciation** and **EBIT** to the visualisation after another blank line. After plotting the **Capex depreciation** onto the visualisation, I should also rename it to '**Depreciation**':

Year	2021		
Qtr	Q1		
	Jan	Feb	Mar
Revenue	$599.40	$2,097.90	$2,447.55
COGS	($359.64)	($1,258.74)	($1,468.53)
Gross profit	$239.76	$839.16	$979.02
Operating expenditure	($93.84)	($130.56)	($77.52)
EBITDA	$145.92	$708.60	$901.50
Depreciation	($16.99)	($16.49)	($19.53)
EBIT	$128.93	$692.11	$881.97

NPBT

The next line item in the Income Statement is the Net Profit Before Tax or NPBT. It is calculated by **EBIT** less interest expense. The interest control account currently evaluates **Interest expense** as a positive number. Therefore, to be consistent with the rest of the financial statements, I shall create a measure that will flip the sign:

```
Interest expense IS = - [Interest expense]
```



```
Interest expense IS = - [Interest expense]
```


I can then calculate the **NPBT** measure with the following **DAX** code:

```
NPBT =
[EBIT] + [Interest expense IS]
```



```
NPBT =
[EBIT] + [Interest expense IS]
```


The final measure is **NPAT**. Note that this measure requires the tax calculation to be complete. Therefore, although I have included it in this section, I will revisit this measure later after completing the Tax control account, so consider this a work in progress!

The **NPAT** measure is calculated with the following **DAX** code:

```
NPAT =
[NPBT]
```



```
NPAT =
[NPBT]
```


Clearly, this is not correct, but I have created a placeholder for now.

After applying the formatting and appropriate data types to the measures, I get the following result when plotting them into a matrix visualisation:

Year	2021		
Qtr	Q1		
	Jan	Feb	Mar
Revenue	$599.40	$2,097.90	$2,447.55
COGS	($359.64)	($1,258.74)	($1,468.53)
Gross profit	$239.76	$839.16	$979.02
Operating expenditure	($93.84)	($130.56)	($77.52)
EBITDA	$145.92	$708.60	$901.50
Depreciation	($16.99)	($16.49)	($19.53)
EBIT	$128.93	$692.11	$881.97
Interest expense	($9.88)	($10.20)	($11.13)
NPBT	$119.06	$681.90	$870.83
NPAT	$119.06	$681.90	$870.83

The final step is to group all the measures into a display folder:

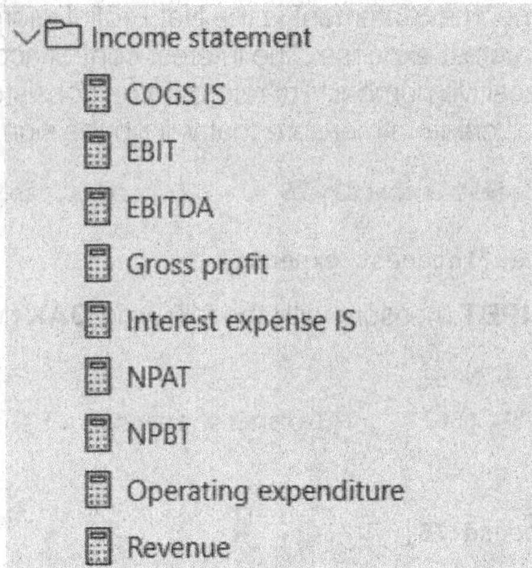

Now I can move on to tax. I will revisit the Income Statement – hence there is a Part 2! – later and complete it.

The Income Statement is the largest matrix I have created so far, and you may have noticed that each time a measure is updated, the matrix is recalculated. The page is irrelevant to the measure creation, so to avoid waiting for the matrix to be redrawn, measures can be created whilst on a new blank page and then I can return to the appropriate page to position the measures in the relevant matrix. Just a tip to help keep things moving as we enter a more taxing chapter…

CHAPTER 20: Calculating Tax (Part 1)

Before going full tilt into taxation, I will address (amongst other topics) the difference between the accounting and tax depreciation, which makes up part of the tax calculation.

To be clear, this section is only going to cover company (income) tax. Indirect taxes such as Goods and Services Tax (GST) or Value Added Tax (VAT) vary too much from territory to territory and are not usually included in a model as essentially the company is collecting taxes on behalf of the State. Similarly, state and federal taxes, capital gains taxes, mining resources tax, "need a new tax" tax *etc.* are to be ignored as the rules for how they are calculated varies under different circumstances. For the purposes of simplification, I am going to assume a very simple income tax with a flat tax rate of 30%.

Now this tax may be a simple or a complex calculation. Let me revert to first principles. Consider the following Interest Expense control account:

Opening Interest Payable	**10**
Interest Expense	**20**
Interest Paid	**(10)**
Closing Interest Payable	**20**

This all makes sense, now let me change it to Tax:

Opening Tax Payable	**10**
Tax Expense	**20**
Tax Paid	**(10)**
Closing Tax Payable	**97**

Pardon? What happened there? Welcome to the wonderful world of **Accounting v. Taxation**. Accounting is all about producing a true and fair view of the world (although the terms "true" and "fair" are never actually defined anywhere), whereas you could say that the Tax authorities do not give two figs for true and fair. *You* could say that. I won't. I might get taxed.

To be "fair", there are many more accounting auditors than their tax counterparts. It is important for shareholders and stakeholders to have a true and fair view of a company's accounts in order to form a view for the basis of making future decisions. Tax authorities, by and large, tend to look for a simple prescriptive rule book, *e.g.* if companies A and B both make the same profit from the same sources with similar cost and financing structures, they should pay a similar level of tax. Therefore, there tend to be simplifying rules.

Accounting works on an accruals basis, dealing with revenue and cost recognition which may differ from tax. This will give rise to **timing differences**, often referred to as **temporary differences**. But there are other types of difference too. If I choose not to pay tax, get taken to court and I am fined, that would be a legitimate expense to me and would have to be shown in my Income Statement. However, I can't claim this as a tax deduction – how cool would that be..?

This would be an example of a **permanent difference**, that is, an amount that will never reconcile between accounting and taxation. Any income or expenditure derived from breaking the law is usually excluded from a tax calculation. Other examples may be costs or income assessable to a different type of tax, and so on.

It is not always bad news. It usually is though. You might wish to consider **Liam's Law of Tax**:

> **Liam's Law of Tax**
>
> Often in tax legislation, rules may be ambiguous. If this occurs, calculate the tax to be paid under the different possibilities. Whichever is the worst for you is the one that was meant.

I have yet to find an exception to this rule.

Most of the time, expenses are disallowed, but sometimes revenue is non-assessable. For example, if you are creating a forecast of worldwide revenues for all subsidiaries of a group of companies, all external income must be included for accounting purposes. That may not be the case for tax: Tax treaties, double taxation relief and other rulings may be in place that permanently exclude some income from the tax calculation.

Permanent differences need to be recognised in a model as these must be adjusted for in calculating the Tax Expense. For example,

	$	$
Net Profit Before Tax		1,000
Adjustments:		
Deduct: Non-Assessable Revenue	(100)	
Add Back: Disallowable Expenses	200	
Accounting Taxable Profit	1,100	
Tax Expense (@ 30%)		(330)
Net Profit After Tax		670

The permanent differences are adjusted for to derive an **Accounting Taxable Profit** of $1,100. The tax rate of 30% is applied to this to generate a Tax Expense of $330, leaving a Net Profit After Tax (NPAT) of $670. The effective tax rate here is 33%, being 330 / 1,000.

Timing differences on the other hand lead to **deferred tax** issues instead as these differences will eventually reconcile. The most common cause of a timing difference is depreciation, *e.g.*

Assumptions

Economic Life	4 years
Tax Life	4 years

	Accounting	Tax	Difference	Tax Effect
Multiplier	n/a	2.0x		
Depreciation Rate	25%	50%		
	$	$	$	$
Capex	1,000	1,000		
Depn: Yr 1	(250)	(500)	250	75
	750	500		
Depn: Yr 2	(250)	(250)	-	-
	500	250		
Depn: Yr 3	(250)	(125)	(125)	(38)
	250	125		
Depn: Yr 4	(250)	(125)	(125)	(38)
	-	-	-	-

In this example, the $1,000 non-current asset in question has both an economic life and a tax life of four years. There is absolutely no reason why these values should coincide, but I am keeping it simple for this example.

No residual value is assumed. For accounting purposes, depreciation is calculated on a straight line basis of 25% p.a. For tax purposes, I am assuming a double declining balance method, which would be 50% of the remaining balance. Assuming the asset is disposed of at the end of four years, the final year's tax balance is written down to zero [0].

Let me compare the differences (the first of the two shaded columns in the figure above). In the first year, more depreciation may be claimed for the tax calculation than under the comparable accounting calculation. This will lead to a lower taxable profit, meaning less tax to pay. This is usually what happens in the early years of tax depreciation: companies benefit from these **accelerated capital allowances**, sometimes referred to as **ACAs**.

In our example, the profit in the first period would be $250 higher. With a tax rate of 30%, this would mean the tax to pay would be $75 less. This is real money. Whilst it all balances out in the end (*i.e.* the total differences for the actual amount and the tax effected amounts sum to zero), considering the time value of money, this would be of benefit to a company.

Why would a Tax authority do this? Remember, Tax authorities work for the government of the territory to which they pertain and they want to encourage economic investment. By providing beneficial capital allowances, companies may be encouraged to spend more in a territory, providing more jobs, economic growth and ultimately more taxable income.

The tax effect shows what the benefit is worth – measurements of worth are shown in the Balance Sheet at their tax effected (*i.e.* after tax) amounts. If we receive a benefit of $75 now and the differences eventually sum to zero, in the future we will have to pay $75 more than accounting forecasts will show. Since it is in the future, this will be a **tax deferred liability**.

This all ties up with the patented ***Liam Theory of Smiley Faces***:

Who would have equated tax with smiley faces? Only a madman, I suspect. A deferred tax liability provides a benefit now, but will cause a greater cost later. Deferred tax assets create bad news now, but good news later.

The most common cause of a deferred tax asset occurs when losses are made. If I make a $1m loss this year, will the Tax authority reimburse me 30%? No. In most jurisdictions (if not all), the Tax authority will not provide any sort of "refund". However, most territories will allow you to memorialise the loss to use against future profits. Some countries may allow you to use the loss to offset profits in earlier periods. Some may restrict their use (so they may only be carried forward several years and / or against similar activities that caused the loss and / or assume the majority of owners remain the same). This is not a discussion on the intricacies of taxation. I will be keeping it very simple.

If you make a loss of $1m, the Tax Credit for the period (assuming a 30% tax rate) would be 30%. That is correct as it is associated with the period. However, you will not receive any cash back. Assume you make $3m profit the following year. Normally, you would have to pay $900,000 tax on this. However, in many territories you can offset the loss against this profit and pay tax on only $2m, *i.e.* $600,000. The loss is worth $300,000 as this is the amount it has saved. This could have been calculated in the first instance as $1m x 30%, which is the tax effected amount. Even though there is pain now, you could recognise this as a **deferred tax asset** on the Balance Sheet – as long as it may be assumed you will make a profit in future years / before the tax credit expires, if applicable.

Accounting regulations suggest you discount this amount to consider the time value of money, but nowhere can you find guidance on how this might be calculated. It doesn't really matter though. For financial modelling and management accounts, deferred tax assets are calculated, but you will seldom see one in statutory accounts.

The reason for this is that auditors have to sign off on statutory accounts. If they acknowledge a deferred tax asset on the face of the Balance Sheet, they are signing off that the company that has just made a loss will make a profit again in the future. Would you be prepared to bet everything you own that this would be the case? No? Neither would auditors. There have been case law precedents where investors have successfully sued auditors for displaying deferred tax assets on a company that subsequently went into liquidation. The investors argued that they could infer auditors were signing off that the company would be profitable again in the future and relied upon this inference in making their investment decisions. Courts have agreed. Hence deferred tax assets are unlikely to be seen on the face of statutory accounts.

Deferred tax is a definite Friday afternoon accounting rule. I say this because:

- Deferred tax assets and deferred tax liabilities are always non-current even if they will crystallise immediately.
- They should be netted off in the accounts (why would you net depreciation differences against tax losses?).

There are other causes of deferred tax, such as revaluations, but that is for another time. I think we have more than enough to go on with. I can now revisit the tax control account from earlier:

Opening Tax Payable	**10**
Tax Expense	**20**
Tax Paid	**(10)**
Movement in Deferred Tax Assets	**(15)**
Movement in Deferred Tax Liabilities	**92**
Closing Tax Payable	**97**

The reason the control account didn't balance was because we hadn't completed it. There were line items missing, namely the **Movement** in Deferred Tax Assets and the **Movement** in Deferred Tax Liabilities. I have stressed **Movement** because Deferred Tax Assets and Deferred Tax Liabilities are to be found in the Balance Sheet and amounts in this financial statement must be shown cumulatively. We will need to keep a running total (*i.e.* more control accounts) of these balances.

For the purposes of this exercise, I will only consider swapping out the accounting depreciation for the tax depreciation. The other adjustments may be modelled using the techniques already described.

Thus, similar to the straight line depreciation developed earlier, I calculate the tax depreciation in a table with a custom function in Power Query.

This time, I will be constructing depreciation on a declining balance basis, *i.e.* the amount deducted each year will be a constant proportion of the opening balance at the beginning of the period.

Creating the tax depreciation table

To begin I open the 'Power Query editor'. Here, I reference the **Depreciation** table I created earlier:

I create a separate group for this table and rename it to **Tax depreciation.**

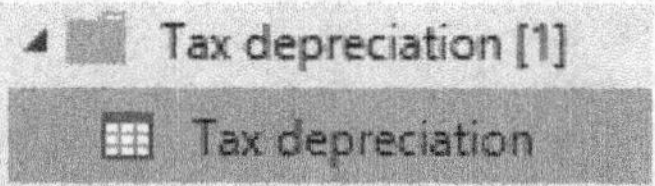

I will now append the **Tax depreciation** table with the **Fulldates** query:

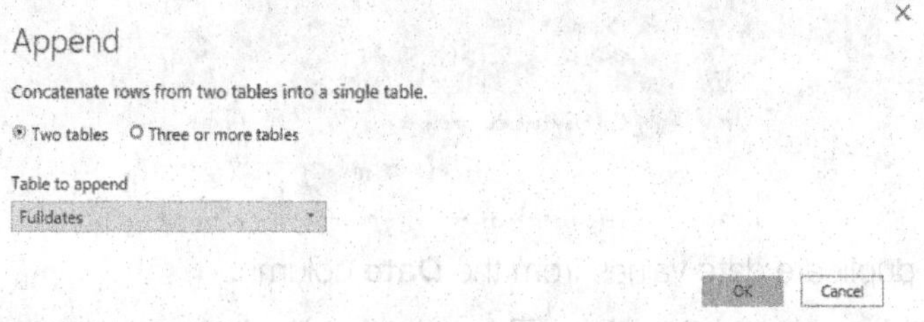

Here is an opportunity for me to add a **Table.Buffer** step. To do this, I navigate to Advanced Editor, and add this line before the **Appended Query** step:

```
BufferedTable = Table.Buffer(Fulldates),
```

I should also replace the

Fulldates reference in **#"Appended Query"** to **BufferedTable**.

The code should be:

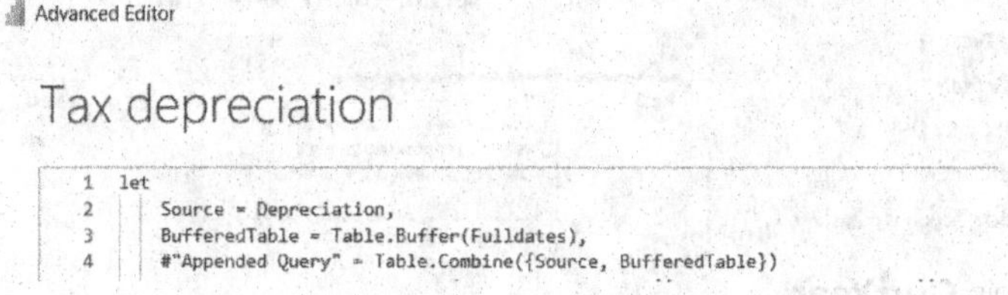

```
let
 Source = Depreciation,
 BufferedTable = Table.Buffer(Fulldates),
 #"Appended Query" = Table.Combine({Source, BufferedTable})
```

The next step is to sort the **Date** column in the table by ascending order:

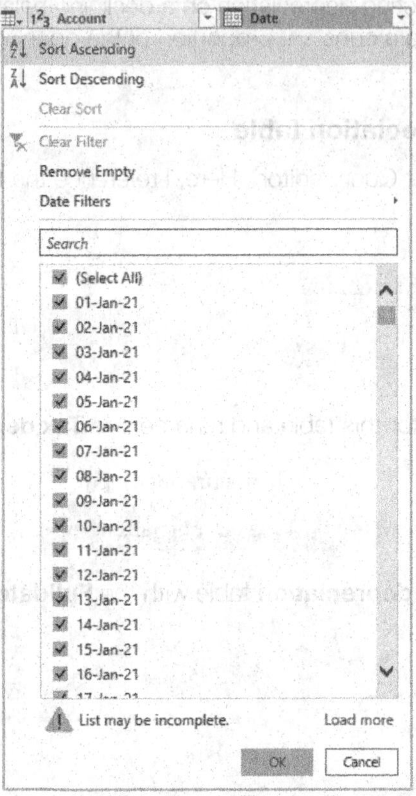

I then remove duplicate date values from the **Date** column.

Next, I add a column called **CurrYear**. This column will return with the current year of that row. I click on the **Date** column, then from the 'Add Column' tab, I select the Date option from the 'From Date & Time' group. I can then select Year and Year again on the dropdown menu:

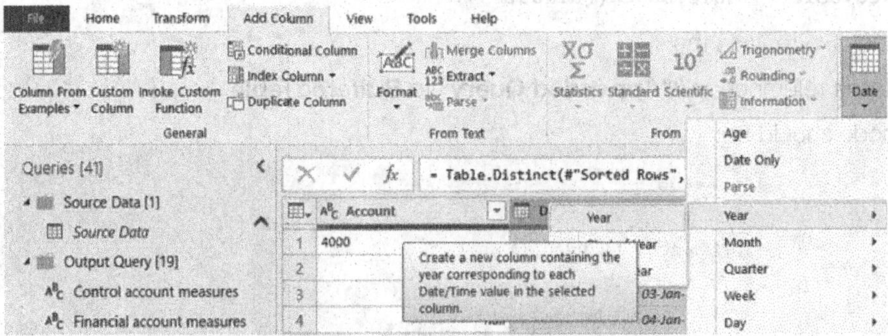

I will rename this **CurrYear**.

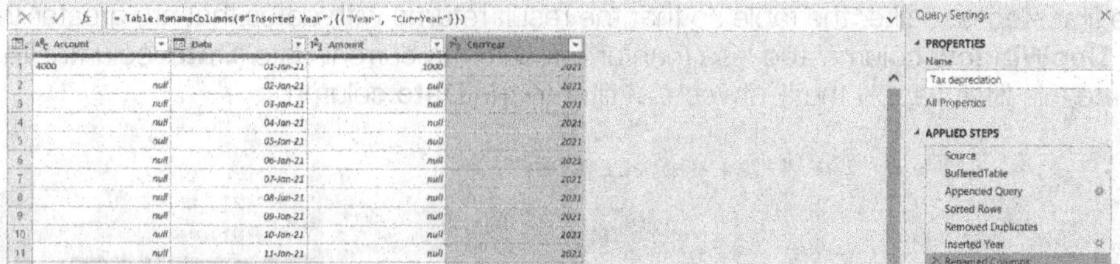

The next field to create is the **DepWindow** column, which is short for depreciation window. This column returns a date, which determines how far back to look when considering depreciation.

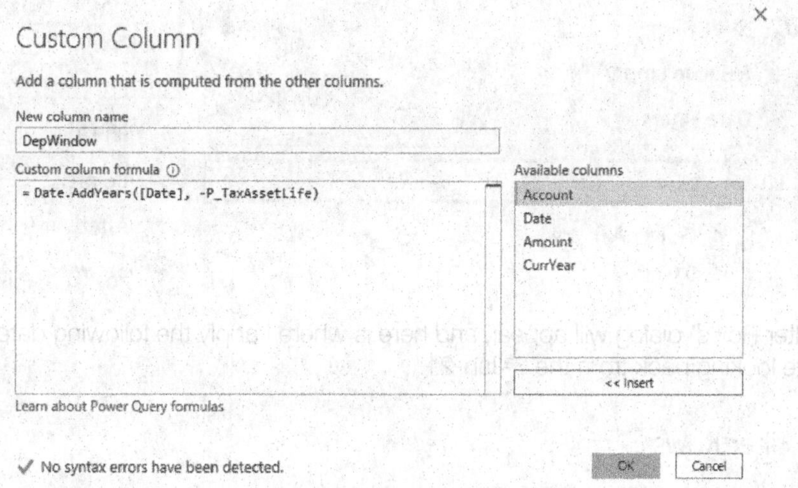


```
Date.AddYears([Date], -P_TaxAssetLife)
```

I change the data type of the **DepWindow** column to a date:

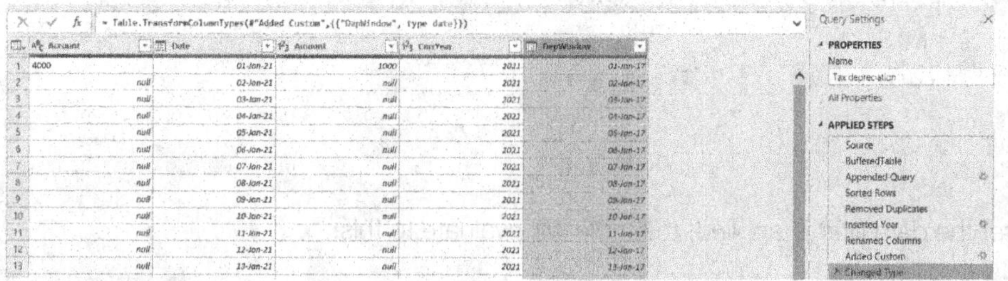

I now have all the columns needed to create my custom function.

Creating the custom function for tax depreciation

I make a Reference Query from the **Tax depreciation** query:

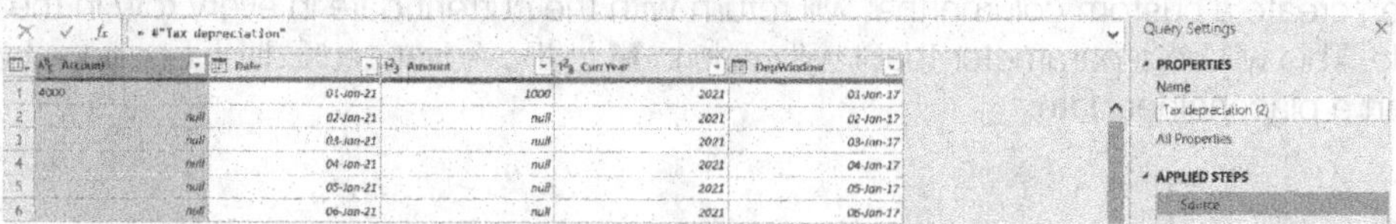

The first step is to filter the table so that the result returns with dates that are greater than the **DepWindow** column and less than or equal to the current date (**Date**) column. To create this filter, I apply the 'Between…' filter to the **Date** column:

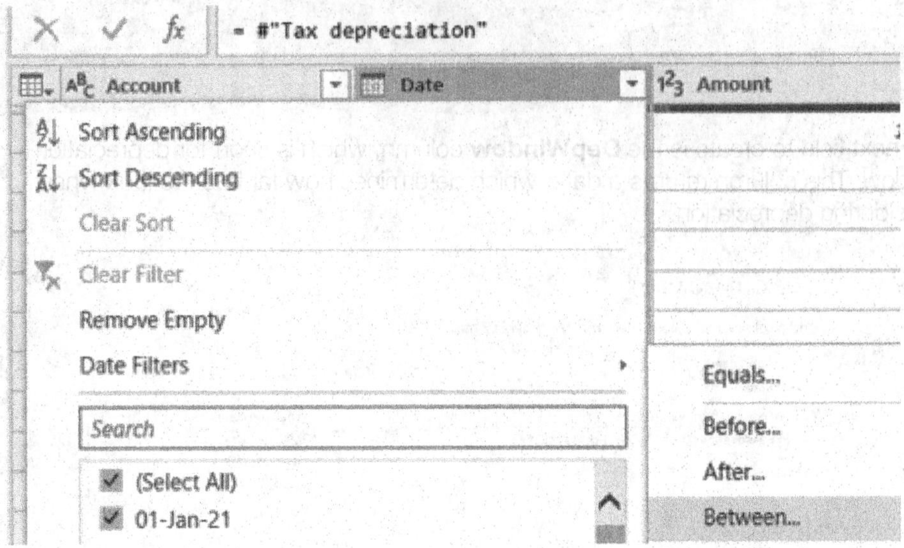

The 'Filter Rows' dialog will appear, and here is where I apply the following date filters to simulate looking back from the 3-Jan-21:

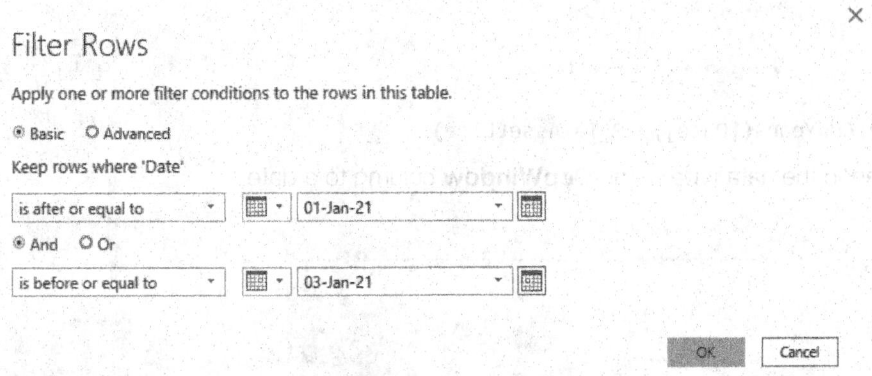

After the date filter is applied, the table will evaluate to this:

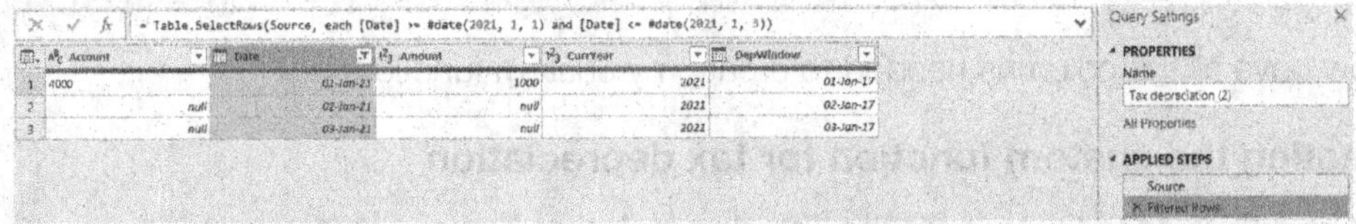

I then create a custom column that will return with the current date in every row in the table. This will be a parameter that I will code in **M** in the Advanced Editor. For now, I will insert a placeholder date:

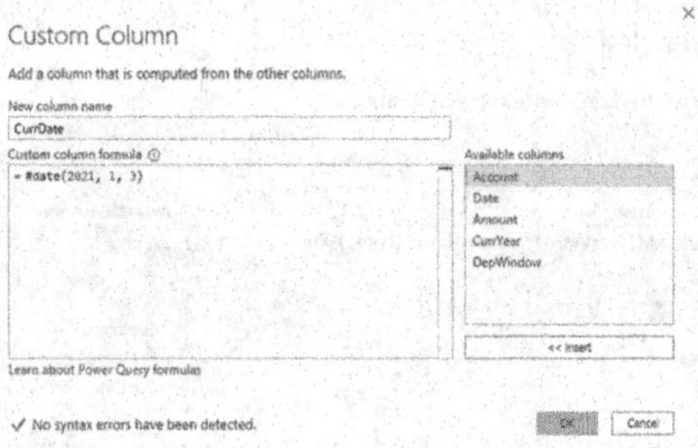

```
#date(2021, 1, 3)
```

CurrDate should be changed to data type Date.

In an effort to lessen the calculation load, I use the 'Number Filters' dropdown to filter out null values in the **Amount** column (note that unselecting '(null)' is not sufficient):

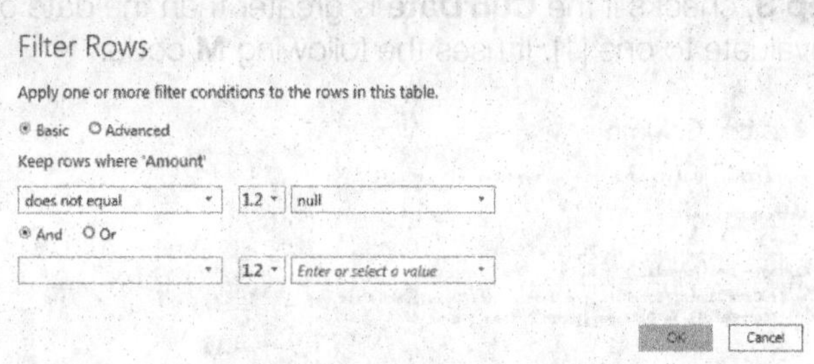

The next three columns work together to help me to determine which depreciation year the asset is currently being reported in. The depreciation year is important, because I will use that to drive the depreciation amount later. The calculation may seem convoluted, but this is to ensure that I account for leap years.

The first column, which I call **Step 1** uses the following **M** code. It checks if there is a difference between the two years:

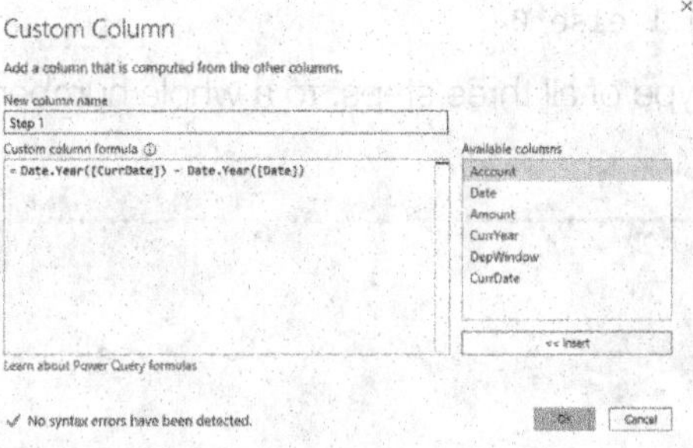

```
Date.Year([CurrDate]) - Date.Year([Date])
```

The second column will check if the month of the current date is later than the date of asset purchase. **Step 2** uses the following **M** code:

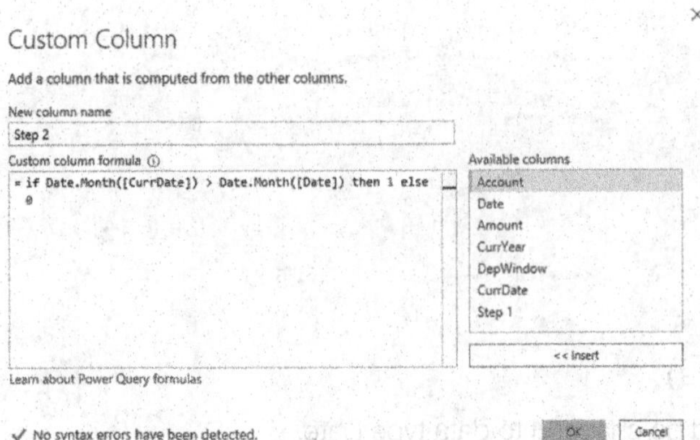


```
if Date.Month([CurrDate]) > Date.Month([Date]) then 1 else 0
```

The final step, **Step 3**, checks if the **CurrDate** is greater than the date of asset purchase. If it is, then it will evaluate to one [1]. It uses the following **M** code:

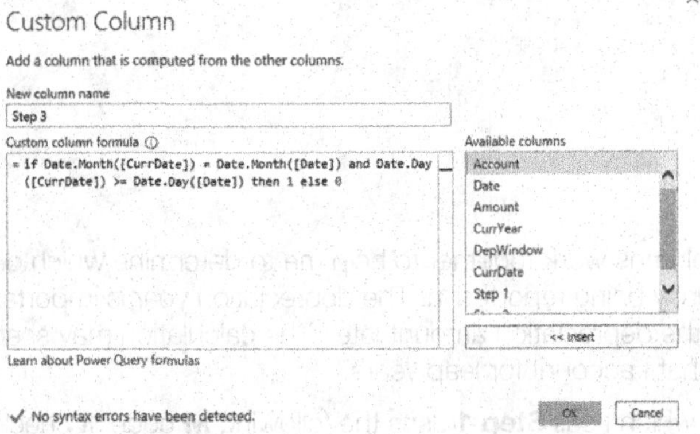


```
if Date.Month([CurrDate]) = Date.Month([Date]) and Date.Day([CurrDate]) >=
Date.Day([Date]) then 1 else 0
```

I shall now change the type of all three steps, to a whole number:

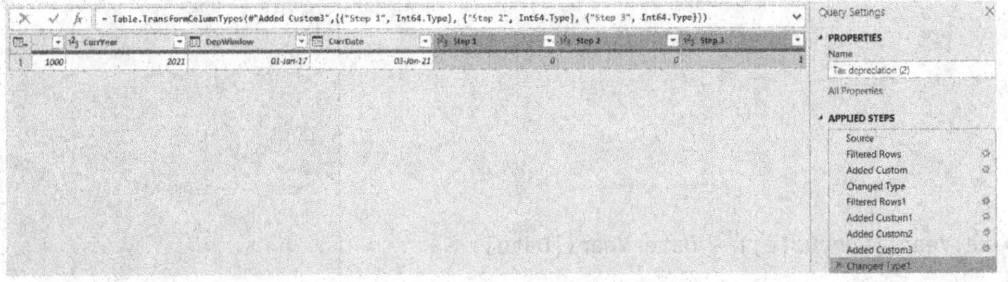

I then highlight all three steps, right-click and select the Sum option:

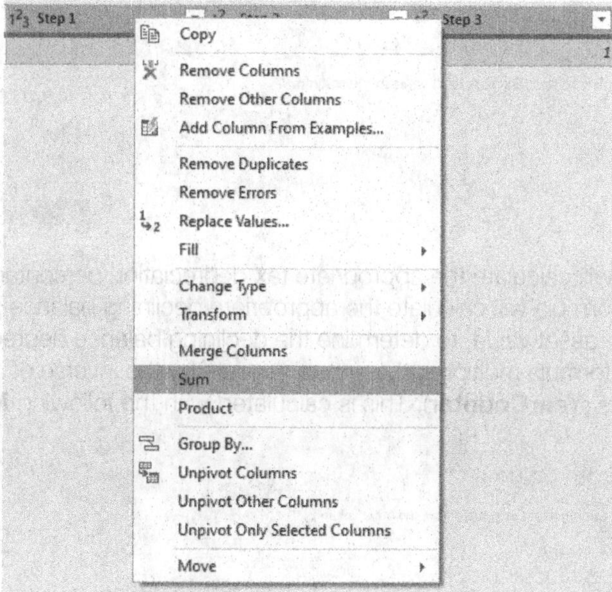

This will create a new column called **Addition** that is the sum of all three steps. I shall rename this column **YearCounter**.

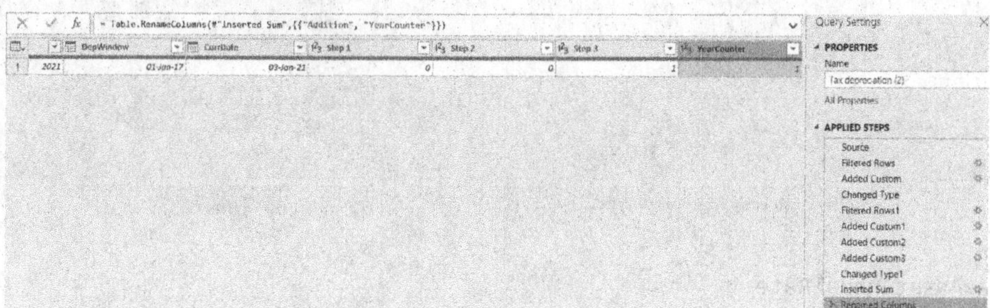

I then subtract the value of one [1] from the **YearCounter** column. My calculation requires the first year to be recognised as zero [0]. This is because the formula to determine the declining balance percentage will use exponents, and hence requires the first year to be zero [0]. This is ensured by selecting the **YearCounter** column, by navigating to the Transform tab on the Ribbon and then selecting the Subtract option from the Standard dropdown option located in the 'Number Column' group.

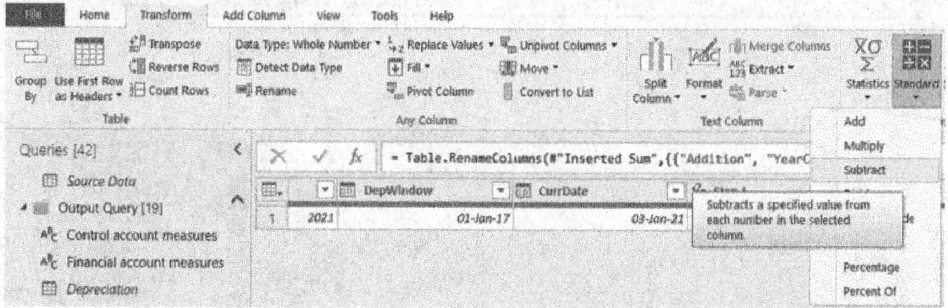

I then enter one [1] into the Subtract value:

Subtract

Enter a number to subtract from each value in the column.

Value

1

OK Cancel

The next column will calculate the appropriate tax depreciation percentage to apply to the asset value. The formula will calculate the appropriate declining balance percentage to be multiplied with the asset value, to determine the declining balance depreciation amount for that year. The formula multiplies the annual tax rate by the inverse of itself, raised to the power of years (**YearCounter**). This is calculated with the following **M** code:

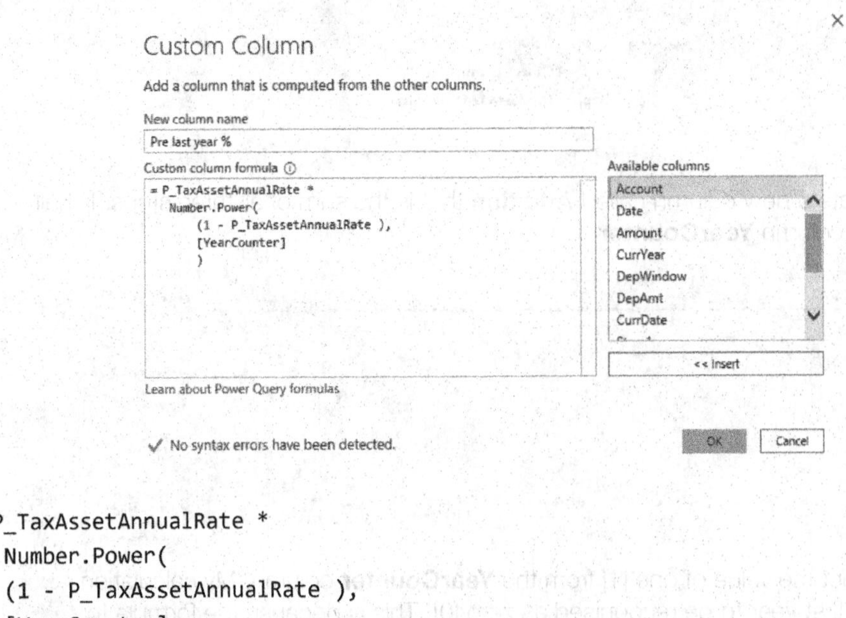


```
P_TaxAssetAnnualRate *
 Number.Power(
 (1 - P_TaxAssetAnnualRate ),
 [YearCounter]
 )
```

I then change the data type of **Pre last year %** to a percentage.

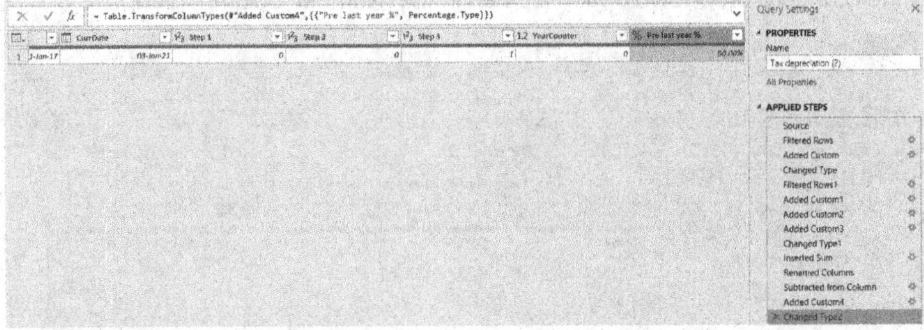

This is the percentage that will be used for assets that have not reached their final year of declining rate of depreciation. The final year is determined by a separate column.

The percentage for the final year is calculated slightly differently. It is calculated by raising the inverse tax asset annual rate by the power of the number of years. It calculated with the following **M** code:

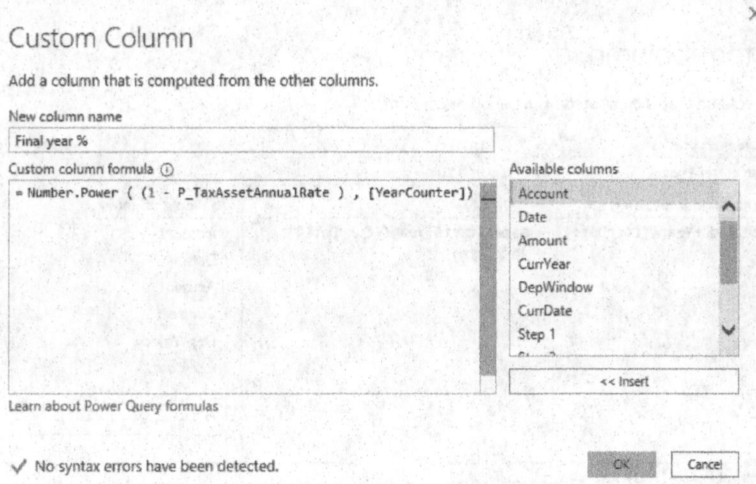


```
Number.Power ( (1 - P_TaxAssetAnnualRate ) , [YearCounter])
```

This column uses the value in the **YearCounter** column as the exponent. This method will allow me to calculate the percentage of depreciation in the final year. Then, I change the data type for the **Final year %** column to a percentage:

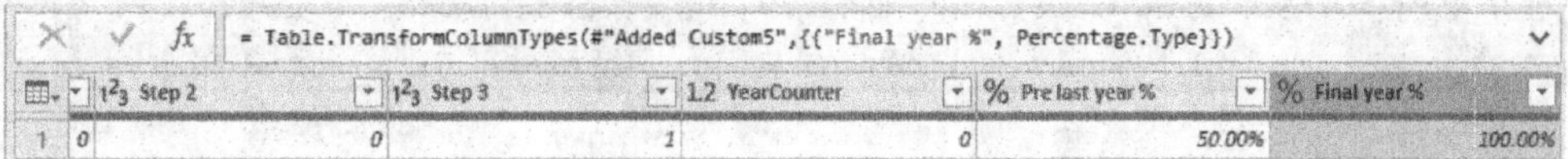

The next custom column is a conditional column that will determine which percentage to use, either **Pre last year %** or **Final year %**. I will call this column the **Percentage** column, it will use the following **M** code:

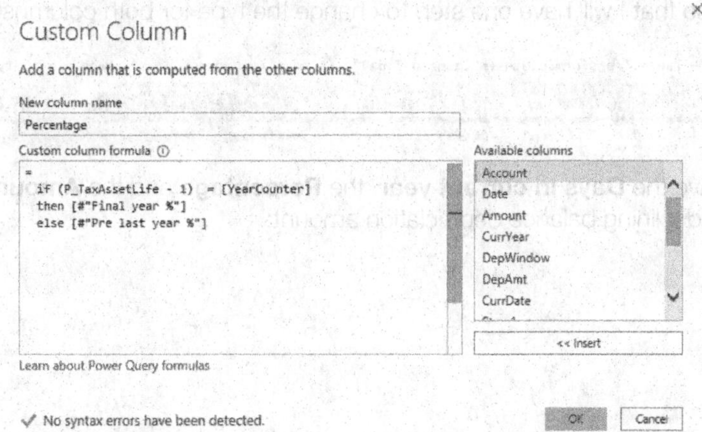

```
if (P_TaxAssetLife - 1) = [YearCounter]
then [#"Final year %"]
else [#"Pre last year %"]
```

There is one more piece of the puzzle to add. I also have to calculate the number of days in the current year. I will call this column **Days in current year** it will use the following **M** code:

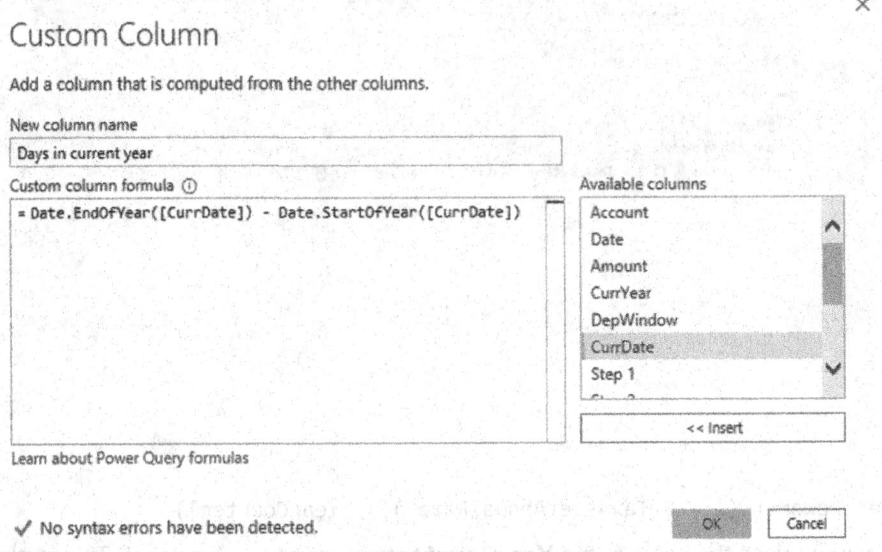


```
Date.EndOfYear([CurrDate]) - Date.StartOfYear([CurrDate])
```

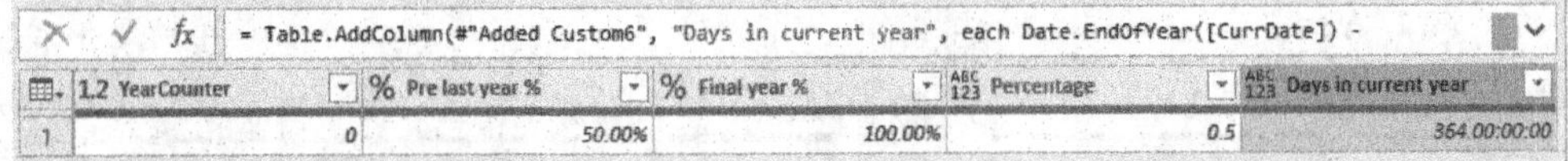

Just like other columns with similar **M** code, I will have to change the data type to a whole number before adding one [1] to accommodate for the subtraction of dates (otherwise the start of the year date is not counted). Before I add one [1] to **Days in current year**, I should also change the data type of the **Percentage** column to a percentage, so that I will have one step to change the type for both columns:

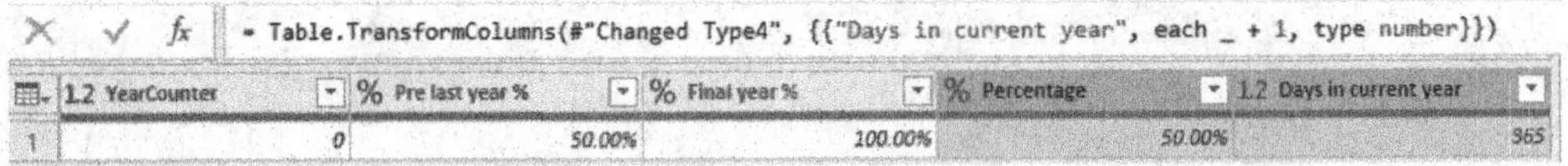

Now that I have the **Days in current year**, the **Percentage** and the **Amounts**, I can calculate the declining balance depreciation amount:

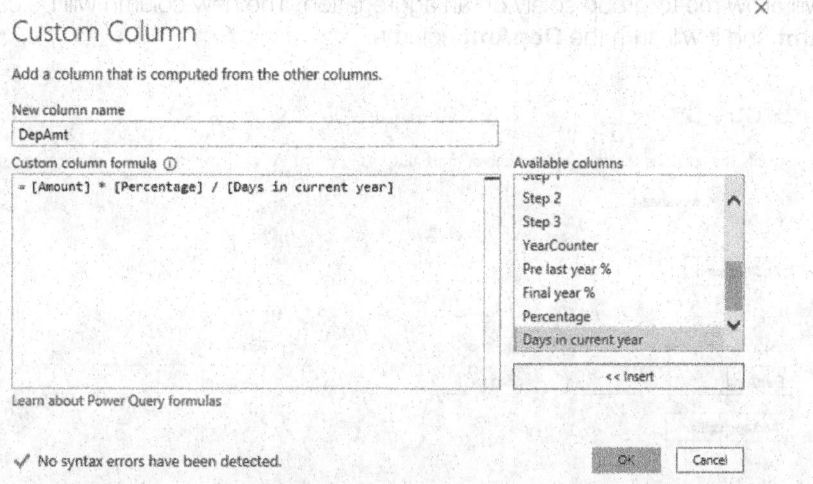


```
[Amount] * [Percentage] / [Days in current year]
```

I then use the 'Group By' option to group the **DepAmt** column together. This will ensure that I capture the depreciation amounts for all assets that are currently live, into a single value.

The 'Group By' option is located on the Transform tab on the Ribbon, in the Table group:

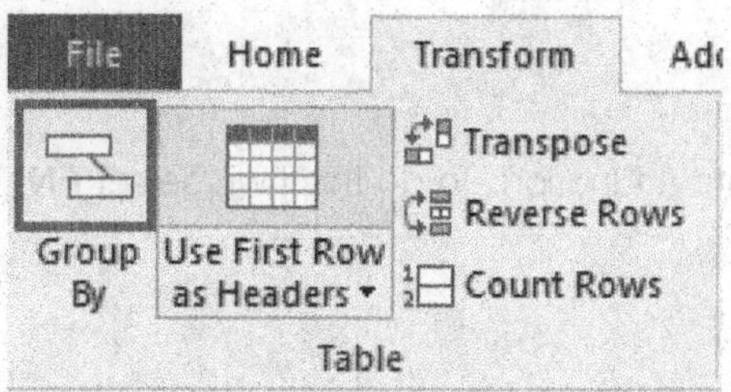

I select the Advanced option, which allows me to group solely on a new column. Power BI will attempt to group on a column by default. To circumvent this, I can hover the mouse next to the **Account** column, and click on the ellipsis ("**...**"), and then select the Delete option.

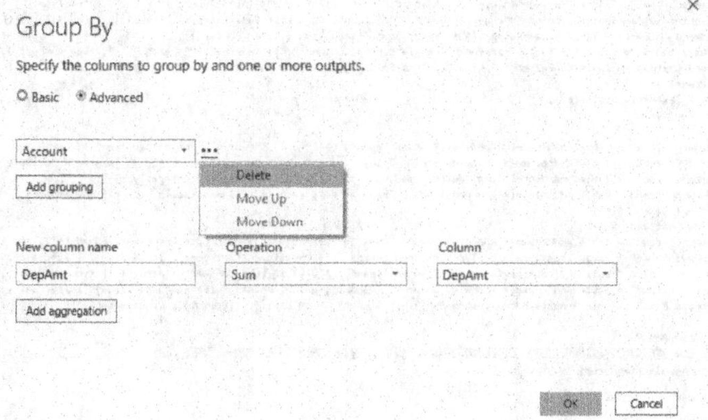

This will allow me to group solely on an aggregation. The new column will be called **DepAmt** and it will sum the **DepAmt** column.

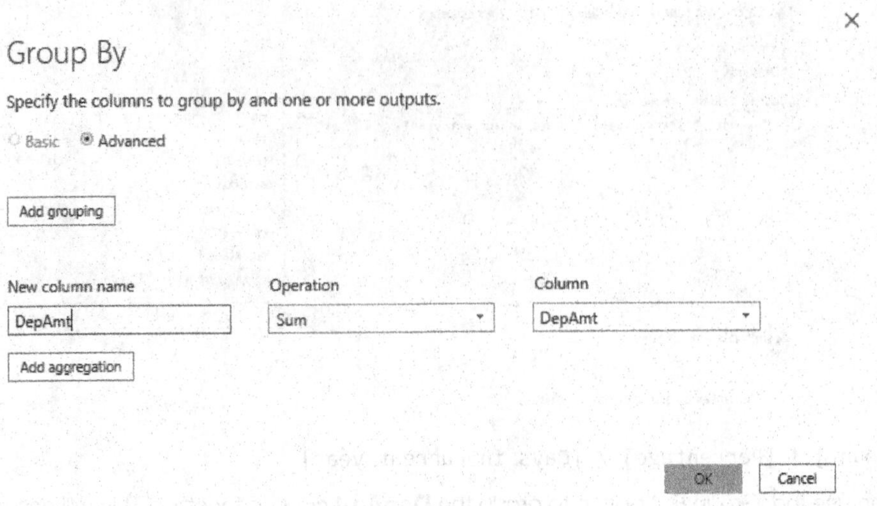

I shall rename this query to **FN_TaxDep**.

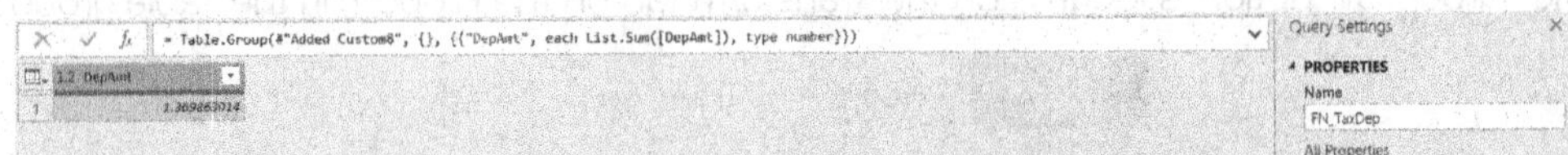

Now to turn this query into a function. To do this I will select **FN_TaxDep** and open the Advanced Editor:

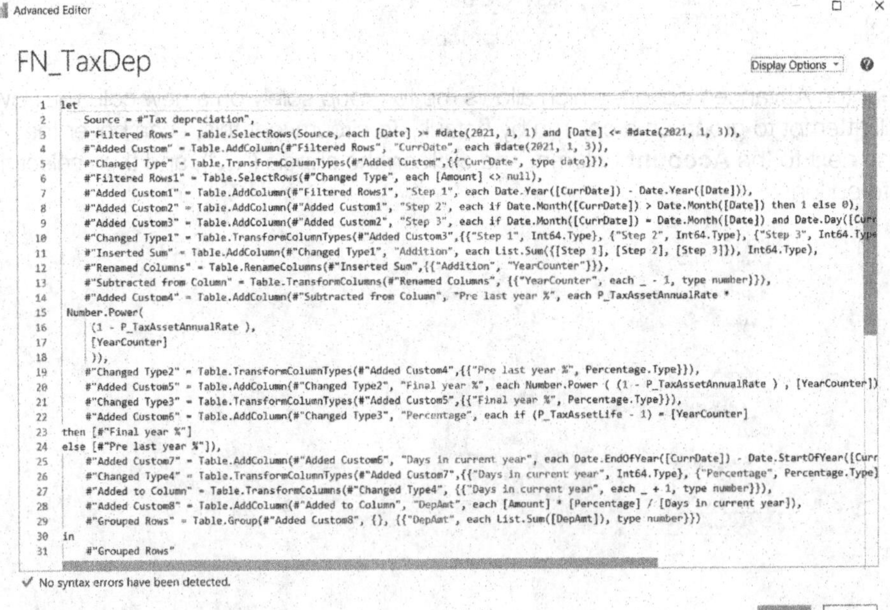


```
let
    Source = #"Tax depreciation",
    #"Filtered Rows" = Table.SelectRows(Source, each [Date] >= #date(2021, 1, 1) and [Date] <= #date(2021, 1, 3)),
    #"Added Custom" = Table.AddColumn(#"Filtered Rows", "CurrDate", each #date(2021, 1, 3)),
    #"Changed Type" = Table.TransformColumnTypes(#"Added Custom",{{"CurrDate", type date}}),
    #"Filtered Rows1" = Table.SelectRows(#"Changed Type", each [Amount] <> null),
    #"Added Custom1" = Table.AddColumn(#"Filtered Rows1", "Step 1", each Date.Year([CurrDate]) - Date.Year([Date])),
    #"Added Custom2" = Table.AddColumn(#"Added Custom1", "Step 2", each if Date.Month([CurrDate]) > Date.Month([Date]) then 1 else 0),
    #"Added Custom3" = Table.AddColumn(#"Added Custom2", "Step 3", each if Date.Month([CurrDate]) = Date.Month([Date]) and Date.Day([Curr
    #"Changed Type1" = Table.TransformColumnTypes(#"Added Custom3",{{"Step 1", Int64.Type}, {"Step 2", Int64.Type}, {"Step 3", Int64.Type
    #"Inserted Sum" = Table.AddColumn(#"Changed Type1", "Addition", each List.Sum({[Step 1], [Step 2], [Step 3]}), Int64.Type),
    #"Renamed Columns" = Table.RenameColumns(#"Inserted Sum",{{"Addition", "YearCounter"}}),
    #"Subtracted from Column" = Table.TransformColumns(#"Renamed Columns", {{"YearCounter", each _ - 1, type number}}),
    #"Added Custom4" = Table.AddColumn(#"Subtracted from Column", "Pre last year %", each P_TaxAssetAnnualRate *
 Number.Power(
    (1 - P_TaxAssetAnnualRate ),
    [YearCounter]
    )),
    #"Changed Type2" = Table.TransformColumnTypes(#"Added Custom4",{{"Pre last year %", Percentage.Type}}),
    #"Added Custom5" = Table.AddColumn(#"Changed Type2", "Final year %", each Number.Power ( (1 - P_TaxAssetAnnualRate ) , [YearCounter])
    #"Changed Type3" = Table.TransformColumnTypes(#"Added Custom5",{{"Final year %", Percentage.Type}}),
    #"Added Custom6" = Table.AddColumn(#"Changed Type3", "Percentage", each if (P_TaxAssetLife - 1) = [YearCounter]
then [#"Final year %"]
else [#"Pre last year %"]),
    #"Added Custom7" = Table.AddColumn(#"Added Custom6", "Days in current year", each Date.EndOfYear([CurrDate]) - Date.StartOfYear([Curr
    #"Changed Type4" = Table.TransformColumnTypes(#"Added Custom7",{{"Days in current year", Int64.Type}, {"Percentage", Percentage.Type}
    #"Added to Column" = Table.TransformColumns(#"Changed Type4", {{"Days in current year", each _ + 1, type number}}),
    #"Added Custom8" = Table.AddColumn(#"Added to Column", "DepAmt", each [Amount] * [Percentage] / [Days in current year]),
    #"Grouped Rows" = Table.Group(#"Added Custom8", {}, {{"DepAmt", each List.Sum([DepAmt]), type number}})
in
    #"Grouped Rows"
```

After I have stood and admired this code for a while, I then add the following code to the beginning of the code in the Advanced Editor:

```
let
 TaxDepCalc = (Tbl as table, LookBackDate as date, CurrDate as date) =>
```

and also add the following code at the end of the code in the Advanced Editor:

```
in
 TaxDepCalc
```

```
let
    TaxDepCalc = (Tbl as table, LookBackDate as date, CurrDate as date) =>

let
    Source = #"Tax depreciation",
    #"Filtered Rows" = Table.SelectRows(Source, each [Date] >= #date(2021, 1, 1) and [Date] <= #date(2021, 1, 3)),
    #"Added Custom" = Table.AddColumn(#"Filtered Rows", "CurrDate", each #date(2021, 1, 3)),
    #"Changed Type" = Table.TransformColumnTypes(#"Added Custom",{{"CurrDate", type date}}),
    #"Filtered Rows1" = Table.SelectRows(#"Changed Type", each [Amount] <> null),
    #"Added Custom1" = Table.AddColumn(#"Filtered Rows1", "Step 1", each Date.Year([CurrDate]) - Date.Year([Date])),
    #"Added Custom2" = Table.AddColumn(#"Added Custom1", "Step 2", each if Date.Month([CurrDate]) > Date.Month([Date]) then 1 else 0),
    #"Added Custom3" = Table.AddColumn(#"Added Custom2", "Step 3", each if Date.Month([CurrDate]) = Date.Month([Date]) and Date.Day([CurrDate]) >= Date.Day([Date]) then 1 else 0),
    #"Changed Type1" = Table.TransformColumnTypes(#"Added Custom3",{{"Step 1", Int64.Type}, {"Step 2", Int64.Type}, {"Step 3", Int64.Type}}),
    #"Inserted Sum" = Table.AddColumn(#"Changed Type1", "Addition", each List.Sum({[Step 1], [Step 2], [Step 3]}), Int64.Type),
    #"Renamed Columns" = Table.RenameColumns(#"Inserted Sum",{{"Addition", "YearCounter"}}),
    #"Subtracted from Column" = Table.TransformColumns(#"Renamed Columns", {{"YearCounter", each _ - 1, type number}}),
    #"Added Custom4" = Table.AddColumn(#"Subtracted from Column", "Pre last year %", each P_TaxAssetAnnualRate *
 Number.Power(
     (1 - P_TaxAssetAnnualRate ),
     [YearCounter]
     )),
    #"Changed Type2" = Table.TransformColumnTypes(#"Added Custom4",{{"Pre last year %", Percentage.Type}}),
    #"Added Custom5" = Table.AddColumn(#"Changed Type2", "Final year %", each Number.Power ( (1 - P_TaxAssetAnnualRate ) , [YearCounter])),
    #"Changed Type3" = Table.TransformColumnTypes(#"Added Custom5",{{"Final year %", Percentage.Type}}),
    #"Added Custom6" = Table.AddColumn(#"Changed Type3", "Percentage", each if (P_TaxAssetLife - 1) = [YearCounter]
then [#"Final year %"]
else [#"Pre last year %"]),
    #"Added Custom7" = Table.AddColumn(#"Added Custom6", "Days in current year", each Date.EndOfYear([CurrDate]) - Date.StartOfYear([CurrDate])),
    #"Changed Type4" = Table.TransformColumnTypes(#"Added Custom7",{{"Days in current year", Int64.Type}, {"Percentage", Percentage.Type}}),
    #"Added to Column" = Table.TransformColumns(#"Changed Type4", {{"Days in current year", each _ + 1, type number}}),
    #"Added Custom8" = Table.AddColumn(#"Added to Column", "DepAmt", each [Amount] * [Percentage] / [Days in current year]),
    #"Grouped Rows" = Table.Group(#"Added Custom8", {}, {{"DepAmt", each List.Sum([DepAmt]), type number}})
in
    #"Grouped Rows"
    in
    TaxDepCalc
```

I now feed in the variables in the function into the code.

```
let
    TaxDepCalc = (Tbl as table, LookBackDate as date, CurrDate as date) =>

let
    Source = #"Tax depreciation",
    #"Filtered Rows" = Table.SelectRows(Source, each [Date] >= #date(2021, 1, 1) and [Date] <= #date(2021, 1, 3)),
    #"Added Custom" = Table.AddColumn(#"Filtered Rows", "CurrDate", each #date(2021, 1, 3)),
    #"Changed Type" = Table.TransformColumnTypes(#"Added Custom",{{"CurrDate", type date}}),
```

- **#"Tax depreciation"** becomes **Tbl**
- **#date(2021, 1, 1)** becomes **LookBackDate**
- **#date(2021, 1, 3)** becomes **CurrDate**

The code will now look like this:

```
let
    TaxDepCalc = (Tbl as table, LookBackDate as date, CurrDate as date) =>

let
    Source = Tbl,
    #"Filtered Rows" = Table.SelectRows(Source, each [Date] >= LookBackDate and [Date] <= CurrDate,
    #"Added Custom" = Table.AddColumn(#"Filtered Rows", "CurrDate", each CurrDate,
    #"Changed Type" = Table.TransformColumnTypes(#"Added Custom",{{"CurrDate", type date}}),
```

Creating the tax depreciation table (continued)

I can now invoke the custom function in my **Tax depreciation** table. I navigate to the 'Add Column' tab on the Ribbon, and select the 'Invoke Custom Function' option located in the General group:

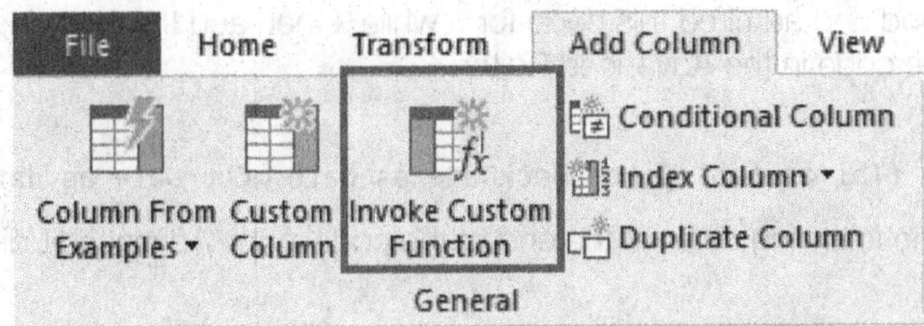

This will bring up the 'Invoke Custom Function' dialog, where I choose the following options from the dropdowns, and call the new column 'DepAmount':

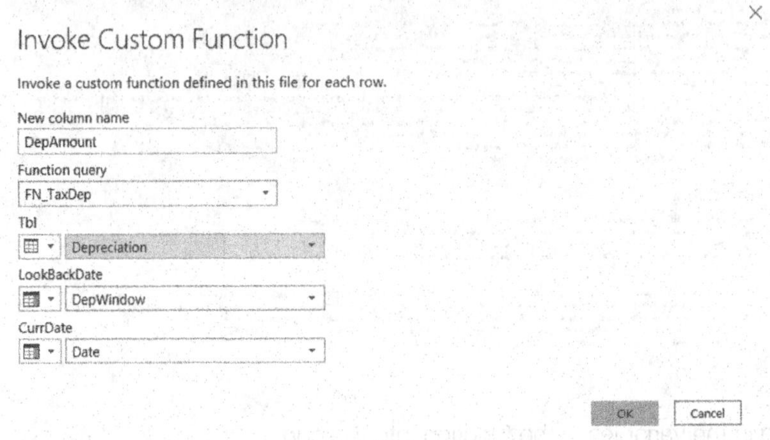

Note that the **Tbl** parameter is temporarily set to **Depreciation**. I will change the **Tbl** input to something else in the Formula Bar:

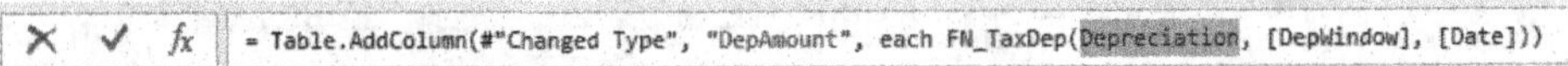

Looking at the Formula Bar, I select the **Depreciation** section and change it to **#"Changed Type"**. I then expand the table and change the resulting **DepAmt** column's data type to a decimal number.

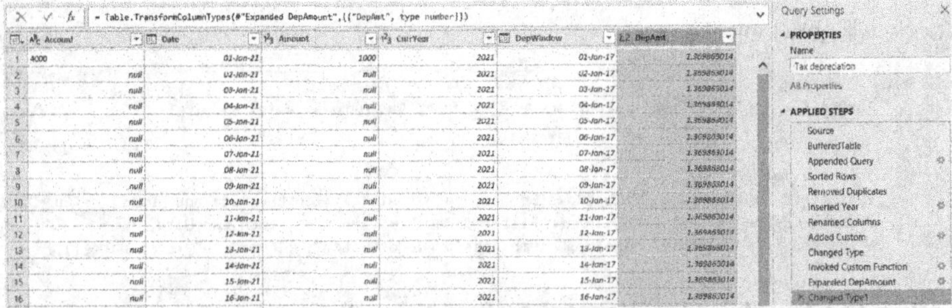

	Account	Date	Amount	CurrYear	DepWindow	DepAmt
1	4000	01-Jan-21	1000	2021	01-Jan-17	1.369863014
2	null	02-Jan-21	null	2021	02-Jan-17	1.369863014
3	null	03-Jan-21	null	2021	03-Jan-17	1.369863014
4	null	04-Jan-21	null	2021	04-Jan-17	1.369863014
5	null	05-Jan-21	null	2021	05-Jan-17	1.369863014
6	null	06-Jan-21	null	2021	06-Jan-17	1.369863014
7	null	07-Jan-21	null	2021	07-Jan-17	1.369863014
8	null	08-Jan-21	null	2021	08-Jan-17	1.369863014
9	null	09-Jan-21	null	2021	09-Jan-17	1.369863014
10	null	10-Jan-21	null	2021	10-Jan-17	1.369863014
11	null	11-Jan-21	null	2021	11-Jan-17	1.369863014
12	null	12-Jan-21	null	2021	12-Jan-17	1.369863014
13	null	13-Jan-21	null	2021	13-Jan-17	1.369863014
14	null	14-Jan-21	null	2021	14-Jan-17	1.369863014
15	null	15-Jan-21	null	2021	15-Jan-17	1.369863014
16	null	16-Jan-21	null	2021	16-Jan-17	1.369863014

As I have been practicing before, I should add the **Table.View** step at the end of this query to optimise it. This can be done by replacing the existing 'Changed Type1' step with the following code in the Advanced Editor:

```
#"Changed Type1" = Table.TransformColumnTypes(#"Expanded DepAmount",
{{"DepAmt", type number}}),
```

```
 OverrideZeroRowFilter = Table.View(
 null,
 [
 GetType = () =>
 type table[
 Account = Text.Type,
 Date = Date.Type,
 Amount = Int64.Type,
 CurrYear = Int64.Type,
 DepWindow = Date.Type,
 DepAmt = Number.Type
 ],
 GetRows = () =>
 #"Changed Type1",
 OnTake = (count as number) =>
 if count = 0 then
 #table(
 type table[
 Account = Text.Type,
 Date = Date.Type,
 Amount = Int64.Type,
 CurrYear = Int64.Type,
 DepWindow = Date.Type,
 DepAmt = Number.Type
 ],
 {}
 )
 else
 Table.FirstN(#"Changed Type1", count)]
 )
in
 OverrideZeroRowFilter
```

The final step is to 'Close & Apply'. Note that this involved query may take a noticeable amount of time to load to the model.

With my tax depreciation table now complete, I can move on to the tax measures that will feed into the tax control account.

Creating the tax measures (depreciation timing difference)

To begin, I create the relationship between the **Tax depreciation** table and the **Calendar** table.

Edit relationship

Select tables and columns that are related.

Tax depreciation

Account	Date	Amount	CurrYear	DepWindow	DepAmt
null	Sunday, 1 January 2023	null	2023	Tuesday, 1 January 2019	8.63013698630137
null	Monday, 2 January 2023	null	2023	Wednesday, 2 January 2019	8.63013698630137
null	Tuesday, 3 January 2023	null	2023	Thursday, 3 January 2019	8.63013698630137

Calendar

Date	Year	Month	Day	Month name	Qtr
Thursday, 1 July 2021	2021	7	1	Jul	Q3
Friday, 2 July 2021	2021	7	2	Jul	Q3
Saturday, 3 July 2021	2021	7	3	Jul	Q3

Cardinality: Many to one (*:1)

Cross filter direction: Single

☑ Make this relationship active

☐ Apply security filter in both directions

☐ Assume referential integrity

OK Cancel

Then, I construct the **Accounting depreciation** measure. Note the Home Table will be **Control account measures**:

```
Accounting depreciation =
-[Capex depreciation]
```


```
Accounting depreciation =
-[Capex depreciation]
```


This is followed by the **Tax depreciation** measure:

```
Tax depreciation =
-SUM('Tax depreciation'[DepAmt])
```


```
Tax depreciation =
-SUM('Tax depreciation'[DepAmt])
```


These two measures will be added together to calculate the **Depreciation timing difference** measure:

```
Depreciation timing difference =
[Accounting depreciation] + [Tax depreciation]
```


```
Depreciation timing difference =
[Accounting depreciation] + [Tax depreciation]
```


It might seem confusing, but clearly it's correct to add these two amounts together. This may be demonstrated when I plot these three measures in a matrix visualisation:

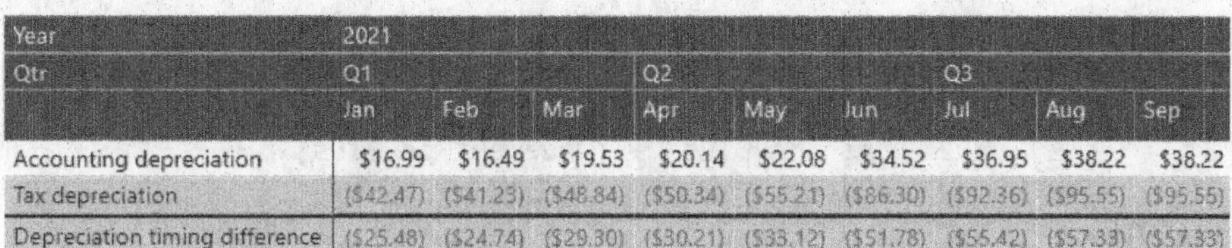

Year	2021								
Qtr	Q1			Q2			Q3		
	Jan	Feb	Mar	Apr	May	Jun	Jul	Aug	Sep
Accounting depreciation	$16.99	$16.49	$19.53	$20.14	$22.08	$34.52	$36.95	$38.22	$38.22
Tax depreciation	($42.47)	($41.23)	($48.84)	($50.34)	($55.21)	($86.30)	($92.36)	($95.55)	($95.55)
Depreciation timing difference	($25.48)	($24.74)	($29.30)	($30.21)	($33.12)	($51.78)	($55.42)	($57.33)	($57.33)

Now for the movements in the deferred tax losses control account:

The **Movement in DTLs** is calculated with the following **DAX** code:

```
Movement in DTLs =
-[Depreciation timing difference] * P_TaxRate
```

```
Movement in DTLs =
-[Depreciation timing difference] * P_TaxRate
```

The next measure I need to create is the cumulative measure for DTLs, **Movement in DTLs cum**. It uses the following **DAX** code:

```
Movement in DTLs cum =
    CALCULATE([Movement in DTLs],
        FILTER(
            ALL('Calendar'),
            'Calendar'[Date] <= MAX('Calendar'[Date])
        )
    )
```

```
Movement in DTLs cum =
 CALCULATE([Movement in DTLs],
 FILTER(
 ALL('Calendar'),
 'Calendar'[Date] <= MAX('Calendar'[Date])
 )
 )
```

I can now calculate the **Opening DTLs** with this **DAX** code:

```
Opening DTLs =
    IF(
        PREVIOUSDAY('Calendar'[Date]) = BLANK(),
        0,
        CALCULATE([Movement in DTLs cum],
        PREVIOUSDAY('Calendar'[Date])
        )
    )
```

```
Opening DTLs =
 IF(
 PREVIOUSDAY('Calendar'[Date]) = BLANK(),
 0,
 CALCULATE([Movement in DTLs cum],
 PREVIOUSDAY('Calendar'[Date])
 )
 )
```

This is followed by the **Closing DTLs** measure:

```
Closing DTLs =
[Opening DTLs] + [Movement in DTLs]
```



```
Closing DTLs =
[Opening DTLs] + [Movement in DTLs]
```


I can plot the three measures onto a matrix visualisation:

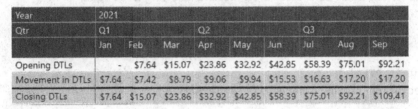

Year	2021								
Qtr	Q1			Q2			Q3		
	Jan	Feb	Mar	Apr	May	Jun	Jul	Aug	Sep
Opening DTLs	-	$7.64	$15.07	$23.86	$32.92	$42.85	$58.39	$75.01	$92.21
Movement in DTLs	$7.64	$7.42	$8.79	$9.06	$9.94	$15.53	$16.63	$17.20	$17.20
Closing DTLs	$7.64	$15.07	$23.86	$32.92	$42.85	$58.39	$75.01	$92.21	$109.41

I should then group the measures into its own display folder, I've called this one **09. Tax (depreciation timing difference)**.

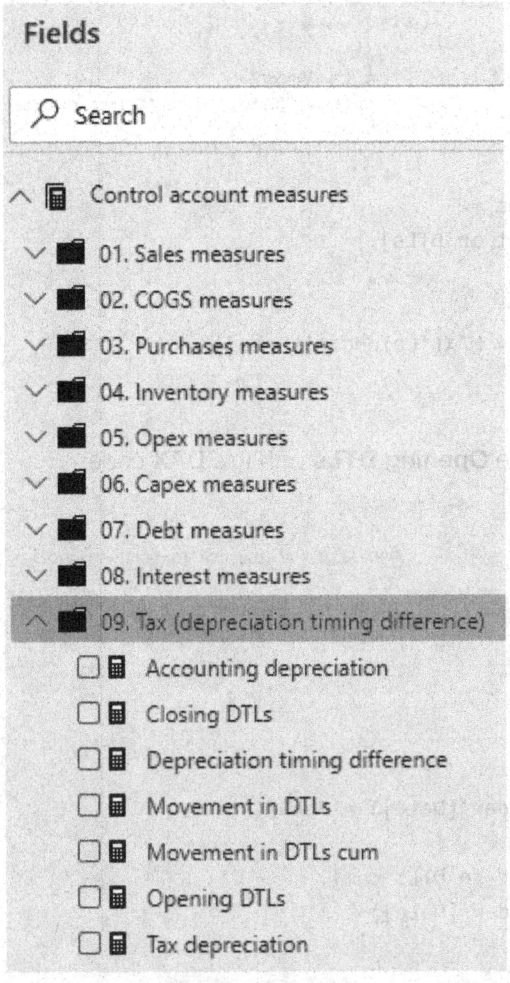

Creating the tax measures (tax losses memorandum)

I will detail the measures that relate to the tax losses memorandum. This control account will be comprised of four main measures:

1. Opening tax losses
2. Tax losses created during period
3. Tax losses used
4. Closing tax losses.

For the measures relating to this tax losses memorandum, I begin with the **Accounting taxable profit** measure:

```
Accounting taxable profit =
    [NPBT]
```

```
Accounting taxable profit =
 [NPBT]
```

I then calculate the **Taxable profit / (loss) before losses** measure with the following **DAX** code:

```
Taxable profit / (loss) before losses =
[Accounting taxable profit] + [Depreciation timing difference]
```

```
Taxable profit / (loss) before losses =
[Accounting taxable profit] + [Depreciation timing difference]
```

The next measure I will create is the **Tax losses created during period** measure. It will use the following **DAX** code:

```
Tax losses created during period =
MIN([Taxable profit / (loss) before losses] , 0)
```

```
Tax losses created during period =
MIN([Taxable profit / (loss) before losses] , 0)
```

As with all my control accounts so far, I need to create a cumulative measure for the **Tax losses created during period**. This is done with the following **DAX** code:

```
Tax losses created cum =
    CALCULATE([Tax losses created during period],
        FILTER(
            ALL('Calendar'),
            'Calendar'[Date] <= MAX('Calendar'[Date])
            )
        )
```

```
Tax losses created cum =
 CALCULATE([Tax losses created during period],
 FILTER(
```

```
ALL('Calendar'),
'Calendar'[Date] <= MAX('Calendar'[Date])
)
)
```

Upon closer inspection, this method of calculating the cumulative amounts does not seem to work in this scenario:

2022					2023				
Q3		Q4			Q1			Q2	
	Sep	Oct	Nov	Dec	Jan	Feb	Mar	Apr	May
9.97	$305.13	$329.48	$354.64	$378.99	$409.24	$435.84	$459.21	$484.37	$508.03
8.12	$931.92	$913.06	$941.11	$764.55	($267.53)	($239.49)	($262.76)	($251.97)	($257.98)
0.00	0.00	0.00	0.00	0.00	-267.53	-239.49	-262.76	-251.97	-257.98
0.00	0.00	0.00	0.00	0.00	0.00	0.00	0.00	0.00	0.00

This is because the **CALCULATE** function does not work well with Boolean logic. Boolean logic is logic that will test if the values are either true or false. Yes, I can use Boolean logic to filter a calculate function. However, Boolean logic does not work well when I use it in the **expression** of the **CALCULATE** function.

In this calculation tree, the Boolean logic arises in the **Tax losses created during period** measure:

```
Tax losses created during period =
MIN([Taxable profit / (loss) before losses] , 0)
```

This measure evaluates the **Taxable profit / (loss) before losses** at each filter context. This then determines if the value is lesser than zero, then return with true, if it is not, then false. However, the filter context may change, based upon how I filter my visualisations. Therefore, Power BI will not know how to properly evaluate this measure.

To calculate this properly, I have to specify which level of granularity I wish to evaluate the Boolean logic in. Do I want the measure to test if the value is positive or negative at the daily, weekly or monthly level? The answer is going to be daily, isn't it?

Further, I can create a table that only exists within the measure. From there, I can aggregate the value **[Taxable profit / (loss) before losses]** accordingly.

There are several functions that I can use to create a table that exists in a measure. The function I will use in this example is the **ADDCOLUMNS** function. The **ADDCOLUMNS** function uses the following syntax to operate:

ADDCOLUMNS(table, name, expression [, name, expression]...)

The square brackets delineate an optional input:

- the **table** parameter can be any **DAX** expression that returns with a table of data
- the **name** parameter is the name given to a column enclosed in double quotation marks
- the **expression** parameter is any **DAX** expression that returns with a scalar expression, this will be evaluated for each row of a table.

With this function, I can create a table that exists in a measure that will evaluate the **Taxable profit / (loss) before losses** at each row of my choosing.

```
Tax losses created during period =
VAR TaxPLTable =
ADDCOLUMNS(
    'Calendar',
    "TPLBL", MIN([Taxable profit / (loss) before losses], 0)
)

Return
SUMX(
    TaxPLTable,
    [TPLBL]
)
```


```
Tax losses created during period =
VAR TaxPLTable =
ADDCOLUMNS(
 'Calendar',
 "TPLBL", MIN([Taxable profit / (loss) before losses], 0)
)

Return
SUMX(
 TaxPLTable,
 [TPLBL]
)
```


In this measure I created a variable called **TaxPLTable**, short for 'Tax Profit / Loss Table'. In this table I used the **ADDCOLUMNS** function to create a table that exists only in the measure. The **TaxPLTable** table will be built off the **Calendar** table. Keep in mind that the **Calendar** table contains contiguous dates in my dataset, this will force the expression to be calculated each day.

I then use the **SUMX** function to evaluate the sum of the **Taxable profit / (loss) before losses** at each row in the table. This will then be filtered by the current filter context in the visualisation. The current filter context is currently set to a monthly level.

Year	2021									
Qtr	Q1			Q2			Q3			Q4
	Jan	Feb	Mar	Apr	May	Jun	Jul	Aug	Sep	Oct
Opening DTLs	-	$7.64	$15.07	$23.86	$32.92	$42.85	$58.39	$75.01	$92.21	$109.41
Taxable profit / (loss) before losses	$393.28	$1,706.11	$2,065.31	$1,894.45	$1,900.37	$1,626.19	$1,838.40	$1,764.14	$1,541.33	$1,590.16
Tax losses created during period	($137.63)	($11.58)	-	-	-	-	-	($10.17)	-	($10.06)
Tax losses created cum	($137.63)	($149.21)	($149.21)	($149.21)	($149.21)	($149.21)	($149.21)	($159.38)	($159.38)	($169.44)

Updating the **Tax losses created during period** measure allows the **Tax losses created cum** measure to calculate the proper cumulative amounts.

The next step here is to create the first version of the **Opening tax losses** measure. I have to create the **Opening tax losses** measure first because the **Tax losses used** measure is conditionally calculated based off the **Opening tax losses**.

The first version **Opening tax losses** measure is calculated with the following **DAX** code:

```
Opening tax losses =
    CALCULATE([Tax losses created cum],
        PREVIOUSDAY('Calendar'[Date])
    )
```

```
Opening tax losses =
 CALCULATE([Tax losses created cum],
 PREVIOUSDAY('Calendar'[Date])
 )
```

Now that I have the **Opening tax losses,** I can create the **Tax losses used** measure. This measure is a conditional measure that will first evaluate if the **Taxable profit / (loss) before losses** is positive. If it is positive, then it will calculate the lesser value between the **Opening tax losses** and the **Taxable profit / (loss) before losses**. Then check that the lesser value is greater than zero. Otherwise, it will return with zero [0].

It is written with the following **DAX** code:

```
Tax losses used =
    IF([Taxable profit / (loss) before losses] > 0,
        -MAX(
            MIN([Taxable profit / (loss) before losses], [Opening tax losses]),
            0
        ),
    0
    )
```

```
Tax losses used =
 IF([Taxable profit / (loss) before losses] > 0,
 -MAX(
 MIN([Taxable profit / (loss) before losses], [Opening tax losses]),
 0
 ),
 0
 )
```

This is followed by the **Tax losses used cum** measure:

```
Tax losses used cum =
    CALCULATE([Tax losses used],
        FILTER(
            ALL('Calendar'),
            'Calendar'[Date] <= MAX('Calendar'[Date])
            )
    )
```

```
Tax losses used cum =
 CALCULATE([Tax losses used],
 FILTER(
 ALL('Calendar'),
 'Calendar'[Date] <= MAX('Calendar'[Date])
 )
 )
```

I can now create the **Closing tax losses** measure:

```
Closing tax losses =
[Opening tax losses] + [Tax losses created during period] + [Tax losses used]
```

```
Closing tax losses =
[Opening tax losses] + [Tax losses created during period] + [Tax losses used]
```

At this point in time, the control account looks to be working fine:

Year	2021								
Qtr	Q1			Q2			Q3		
	Jan	Feb	Mar	Apr	May	Jun	Jul	Aug	Sep
Opening tax losses		($137.63)	($149.21)	($149.21)	($149.21)	($149.21)	($149.21)	($149.21)	($159.38)
Tax losses created during period	($137.63)	($11.58)	-	-	-	-	-	($10.17)	-
Tax losses used	-	-	-	-	-	-	-	-	-
Closing tax losses	($137.63)	($149.21)	($149.21)	($149.21)	($149.21)	($149.21)	($149.21)	($159.38)	($159.38)

However, I have to complete the loop where the Opening tax losses measure must evaluate the previous total of the Tax losses created during period and Tax losses used:

To complete the loop, I will have to revisit the **Opening tax losses** measure and add the following **DAX** code:

```
Opening tax losses =
    CALCULATE([Tax losses created cum] + [Tax losses used cum],
        PREVIOUSDAY('Calendar'[Date])
    )
```

```
Opening tax losses =
 CALCULATE([Tax losses created cum] + [Tax losses used cum],
 PREVIOUSDAY('Calendar'[Date])
 )
```

This is to ensure that the **Opening tax losses** measure will include the **Tax losses used** in its calculation. When I try to enter this change, an error message is displayed. The exact wording may vary according to your version of Power BI Desktop, but the result is the same.

Fields that need to be fixed

Something's wrong with one or more fields: (Control account measures) Opening tax losses: A circular dependency was detected: Measure: 'Control account measures'[Tax losses used cum], Measure: 'Control account measures'[Tax losses used], Measure: 'Control account measures'[Opening tax losses], Measure: 'Control account measures'[Tax losses used cum].

Close

Power BI is prompting that there is a circular dependency between the **Tax losses used** measure and the **Opening tax losses** measure. This is because I wanted the **Opening tax losses** measure to refer to the previous value of the **Tax losses used**. This is a form of recursion, which Power BI does not allow to be coded in **DAX** (at time of writing). There is a work around, which I will detail in the next chapter.

Before I move on, I should collect all the tax losses measures together into a folder.

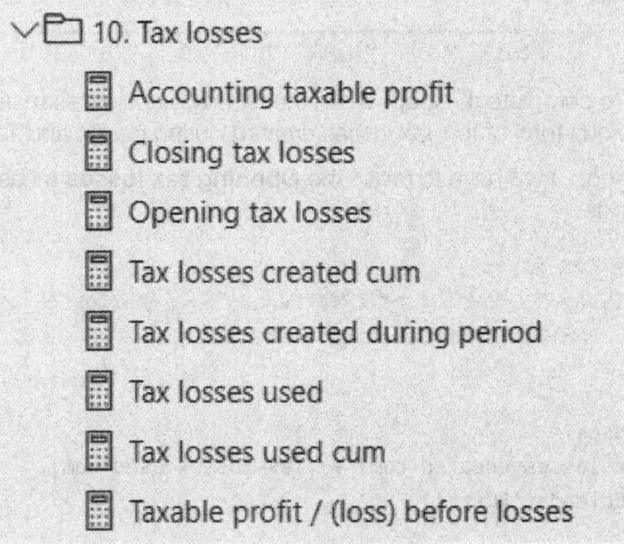

I need an excursion into a version of recursion aversion…

CHAPTER 21: Recursion Aversion

Upon discovering the problem from the last chapter, I had to explore several paths to a solution. This is not an insignificant issue as **DAX** is not Turing Complete, which means certain things are not possible to code in **DAX**. And this problem was *almost* one of those things!

As some of you may be aware, I have been fortunate enough to be awarded the Most Valuable Professional (MVP) status more than 10 times by Microsoft. This is not intended to be a boast; the point is, this means I am fortunate enough to discuss these sorts of issues with some of the greatest minds in Power BI. I would like to state this particular chapter has been a true collaborative effort between some great minds (although it was my idea in the end, he said modestly). Thank you in particular to Imke Feldmann, Tristan Malherbe, Marco Russo and Neil Hambly. We went down a lot of blind alleys, but we got there in the end!

For our particular problem, I found two paths that led to a feasible solution. I will cover both solutions below.

Before I get to the workaround ideas, I will create the **Taxable profit / (loss) before losses** cumulative measure (**TPLBL cum**):

```
TPLBL cum =
    CALCULATE([Taxable profit / (loss) before losses],
        FILTER(
            ALL('Calendar'),
            'Calendar'[Date] <= MAX('Calendar'[Date])
        )
    )
```

```
TPLBL cum =
 CALCULATE([Taxable profit / (loss) before losses],
 FILTER(
 ALL('Calendar'),
 'Calendar'[Date] <= MAX('Calendar'[Date])
 )
 )
```

Now, let's move on to the workaround alternatives.

Tax recursion workaround method A

The work around here involves backward solving the **Closing tax losses** measure from the **Total profit / (loss) before losses** measure. This is done in three steps:

1. Calculating the cumulative amount of **Total profit / (loss) before losses** (TPLBL)
2. Then calculate the historical maximum amount of the TPLBL
3. Subtract the historical maximum amount from the cumulative amount of TPLBL.

The following measure performs all three steps:

```
Closing tax losses (method A) =
VAR CurrentDate =
    MAX ( 'Calendar'[Date] )

VAR NetSum =
    CALCULATE ( [TPLBL cum], 'Calendar'[Date] <= CurrentDate )

VAR PreviousMax =
    MAXX (
        ADDCOLUMNS (
            DATESBETWEEN ( 'Calendar'[Date], BLANK (), CurrentDate - 1 ),
            "NetDayBefore",
                VAR CurrentIt =
                    CALCULATE ( MAX ( 'Calendar'[Date]) )
                Return
                    CALCULATE ( [TPLBL cum], DATESBETWEEN ( 'Calendar'[Date], BLANK (), CurrentIt ) )
        ),
        [NetDayBefore]
    )

VAR Result =
    MIN ( [TPLBL cum] - max( PreviousMax, 0 ), 0 )

Return
    -Result
```

```
Closing tax losses (method A) =
VAR CurrentDate =
 MAX ( ‘Calendar’[Date] )

VAR NetSum =
 CALCULATE ( [TPLBL cum], ‘Calendar’[Date] <= CurrentDate )

VAR PreviousMax =
 MAXX (
 ADDCOLUMNS (
 DATESBETWEEN ( ‘Calendar’[Date], BLANK (), CurrentDate - 1 ),
 "NetDayBefore",
 VAR CurrentIt =
 CALCULATE ( MAX ( ‘Calendar’[Date]) )
 Return
 CALCULATE ( [TPLBL cum], DATESBETWEEN ( ‘Calendar’[Date], BLANK (), CurrentIt ) )
 ),
 [NetDayBefore]
 )

VAR Result =
 MIN ( [TPLBL cum] - MAX( PreviousMax, 0 ), 0 )

Return
 -Result
```

This measure looks to calculate several variables first:

- the **CurrentDate** variable will evaluate to the maximum current date in the filter context
- the **NetSum** variable will evaluate to the cumulative taxable profit / losses before losses amount, up until the **CurrentDate**
- the **PreviousMax** variable attempts to determine the previous maximum amount of the taxable profit / losses before losses measure
- with the **PreviousMax** calculated, the **Result** variable calculates the **TPLBL** cumulative amount then subtracts the **PreviousMax** value
- Finally, I flip the sign of the **Result** by adding a minus sign in front of it after the **RETURN** function.

This measure will effectively return with the **Closing tax losses** in the control account:

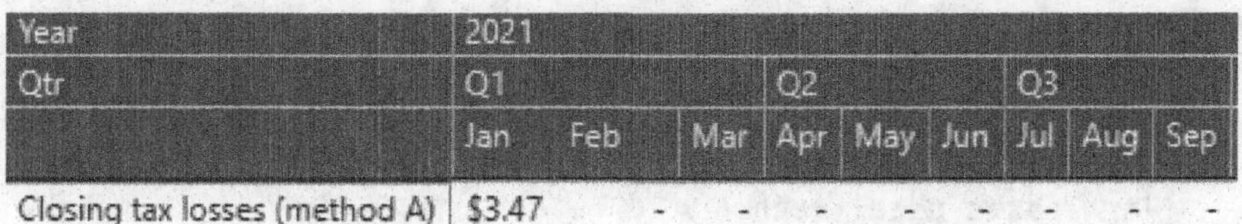

Year	2021								
Qtr	Q1			Q2			Q3		
	Jan	Feb	Mar	Apr	May	Jun	Jul	Aug	Sep
Closing tax losses (method A)	$3.47	-	-	-	-	-	-	-	-

With the **Closing tax losses** created, I can now create the **Opening tax losses**.

```
Opening tax losses (method A) =
CALCULATE(
    [Closing tax losses (method A)],
    PREVIOUSDAY(
        'Calendar'[Date]
    )
)
```

```
Opening tax losses (method A) =
CALCULATE(
 [Closing tax losses (method A)],
 PREVIOUSDAY(
 'Calendar'[Date]
 )
)
```

I can now back solve the two other measures in the control account: **Tax losses created during period**, and **Tax losses used** measures.

I will begin with the **Tax losses used** measure. It uses the following **DAX** code:

```
Tax losses used (method A) =
IF(
    [Taxable profit / (loss) before losses] > 0,
    -MAX(
        MIN(
            [Taxable profit / (loss) before losses],
            [Opening tax losses (method A)]),
            0
        ),
    0
)
```

```
Tax losses used (method A) =
IF(
 [Taxable profit / (loss) before losses] > 0,
 -MAX(
 MIN(
 [Taxable profit / (loss) before losses],
 [Opening tax losses (method A)]),
 0
 ),
 0
)
```

With all previous three measures created, I can derive the **Tax losses created during period** measure:

```
Tax losses created during period (method A) =
[Closing tax losses (method A)] - [Opening tax losses (liam) 2]
- [Tax losses used (method A)]
```

```
Tax losses created during period (method A) =
[Closing tax losses (method A)] - [Opening tax losses (method A)]
- [Tax losses used (method A)]
```

With all four measures created, the control account now correctly calculates the opening and closing tax losses:

Year	2021								
Qtr	Q1			Q2			Q3		
	Jan	Feb	Mar	Apr	May	Jun	Jul	Aug	Sep
Opening tax losses (method A)	-	$3.47	-	-	-	-	-	-	-
Tax losses created during period (method A)	$3.47	-	-	-	-	-	-	-	-
Tax losses used (method A)	-	($3.47)	-	-	-	-	-	-	-
Closing tax losses (method A)	$3.47	-	-	-	-	-	-	-	-

I collect the measures used into a folder.

11. Tax recursion workaround method A
- Closing tax losses (method A)
- Opening tax losses (method A)
- Tax losses created during period (method A)
- Tax losses used (method A)
- TPLBL cum

Tax recursion workaround method B

The other method I will cover is similar but uses a slightly different approach when calculating the closing balance measure.

Just like method A, this method will calculate the previous maximum of the TPLBL then subtract that amount from the current TPLBL. The difference in this approach is the method I use to calculate the previous maximum amount.

I begin with the **Closing tax losses** measure:

```
Closing tax losses (method B) =
VAR CurrentDate =
    MAX ( 'Calendar'[Date] )

VAR NetSum =
    CALCULATE ( [TPLBL cum], 'Calendar'[Date] <= CurrentDate )

VAR PreviousMax =
    MAXX (
        DATESBETWEEN ( 'Calendar'[Date], BLANK (), CurrentDate - 1 ),
        VAR CurrentIt =
            CALCULATE ( MAX ( 'Calendar'[Date] ) )
        Return
            CALCULATE (  [TPLBL cum], DATESBETWEEN ( 'Calendar'[Date], BLANK (), CurrentIt ) )
    )

VAR Result =
    MIN ( NetSum - MAX( PreviousMax, 0), 0 )

Return
    -Result
```

```
Closing tax losses (method B) =
VAR CurrentDate =
 MAX ('Calendar'[Date])

VAR NetSum =
 CALCULATE ([TPLBL cum], 'Calendar'[Date] <= CurrentDate)

VAR PreviousMax =
 MAXX (
 DATESBETWEEN ('Calendar'[Date], BLANK (), CurrentDate - 1),
 VAR CurrentIt =
 CALCULATE (MAX( 'Calendar'[Date]))
 Return
 CALCULATE ([TPLBL cum], DATESBETWEEN ('Calendar'[Date], BLANK (), CurrentIt
))
 )

VAR Result =
 MIN (NetSum - MAX(PreviousMax, 0), 0)

Return
 -Result
```

In method A, I used the **ADDCOLUMNS** function to create the table I want the **MAXX** function to evaluate in. Then, I wrapped the **DATESBETWEEN** function with the **ADDCOLUMNS** function to create the table I want to evaluate the maximum value of the **TPLBL** in. This method (B) improves on that logic and removes the **ADDCOLUMNS** step, reducing the calculation loop time.

The next step here is to calculate the **Opening tax losses**. This is done with the following **DAX** code:

```
Opening tax losses (method B) =
CALCULATE(
    [Closing tax losses (method B)],
    PREVIOUSDAY(
        'Calendar'[Date]
    )
)
```

```
Opening tax losses (method B) =
CALCULATE(
 [Closing tax losses (method B)],
 PREVIOUSDAY(
 ‘Calendar’[Date]
 )
)
```

Following a similar order to method A, I will then create the **Tax losses used** measure:

```
Tax losses used (method B) =
IF(
    [Taxable profit / (loss) before losses] > 0,
    -MAX(
        MIN(
            [Taxable profit / (loss) before losses],
            [Opening tax losses (method B)]),
            0
        ),
    0
)
```

```
Tax losses used (method B) =
IF(
 [Taxable profit / (loss) before losses] > 0,
 -MAX(
 MIN(
 [Taxable profit / (loss) before losses],
 [Opening tax losses (method B)]),
 0
 ),
 0
)
```

With the first three measures created I can backward solve for the **Tax losses created during period** measure:

```
Tax losses created during period (method B) =
[Closing tax losses (method B)] - [Opening tax losses (method B)] - [Tax losses used (method B)]
```

```
Tax losses created during period (method B) =
[Closing tax losses (method B)] - [Opening tax losses (method B)] - [Tax
losses used (method B)]
```

I can then apply the appropriate formatting to the measures and display them on a matrix visualisation:

Year	2021								
Qtr	Q1			Q2			Q3		
	Jan	Feb	Mar	Apr	May	Jun	Jul	Aug	Sep
Opening tax losses (method B)	-	$3.47	-	-	-	-	-	-	-
Tax losses created during period (method B)	$3.47	-	-	-	-	-	-	-	-
Tax losses used (method B)	-	($3.47)	-	-	-	-	-	-	-
Closing tax losses (method B)	$3.47	-	-	-	-	-	-	-	-

I collect the measures into a folder.

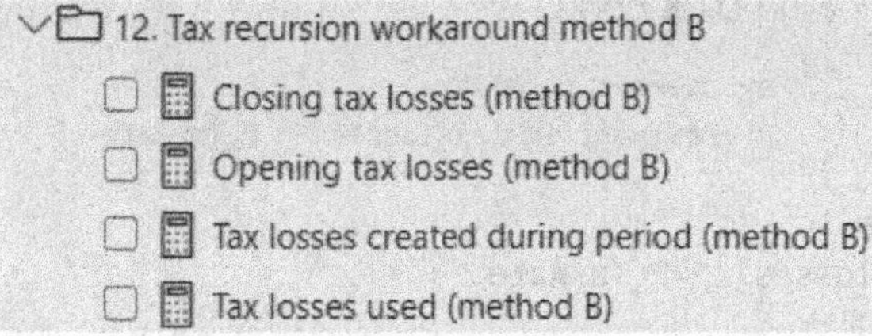

For the rest of the book, I will use method B, since it appears to be (in general) a more optimised solution when compared to method A. If your processing times have been adversely affected by having both methods, then the measures and matrix associated with method A can be safely removed from the model.

With that now complete, I can return to tax.

CHAPTER 22: Calculating Tax (Part 2)

In this section, I will revisit the rest of the calculations required for this model, beginning with the calculation of "Deferred Tax Assets" or DTAs.

Calculating the DTA control account

With the **Tax losses used** control account created I can now create the **Movement in tax losses** measure:

```
Movement in tax losses =
[Tax losses created during period (method B)] + [Tax losses used (method B)]
```

```
Movement in tax losses =
[Tax losses created during period (method B)] + [Tax losses used (method B)]
```

With the **Movement in tax losses** now constructed, I can now calculate the **Movement in DTAs** with the following **DAX** code:

```
Movement in DTAs =
[Movement in tax losses] * P_TaxRate
```

```
Movement in DTAs =
[Movement in tax losses] * P_TaxRate
```

As with other control accounts, I will have to create a cumulative measure for the **Movement in DTAs**:

```
Movement in DTAs cum =
CALCULATE([Movement in DTAs],
    FILTER(
        ALL('Calendar'),
        'Calendar'[Date] <= MAX('Calendar'[Date])
    )
)
```

```
Movement in DTAs cum =
CALCULATE([Movement in DTAs],
 FILTER(
 ALL('Calendar'),
 'Calendar'[Date] <= MAX('Calendar'[Date])
 )
)
```

I can then create the **Opening DTAs** measure with the following **DAX** code:

```
Opening DTAs =
    CALCULATE([Movement in DTAs cum],
        PREVIOUSDAY('Calendar'[Date])
    )
```

```
Opening DTAs =
 CALCULATE([Movement in DTAs cum],
 PREVIOUSDAY('Calendar'[Date])
 )
```

The next measure to follow is the **Closing DTAs** measure:

```
Closing DTAs =
[Opening DTAs] + [Movement in DTAs]
```


```
Closing DTAs =
[Opening DTAs] + [Movement in DTAs]
```


I can then plot the measure onto a matrix visualisation and apply the formatting consistent with the rest of the model:

Year	2021								
Qtr	Q1			Q2			Q3		
	Jan	Feb	Mar	Apr	May	Jun	Jul	Aug	Sep
Opening DTAs	-	$1.04	-	-	-	-	-	-	-
Movement in DTAs	$1.04	($1.04)	-	-	-	-	-	-	-
Closing DTAs	$1.04	-	-	-	-	-	-	-	-

Tax payable and paid

In this section, I will detail how to create the measures that will evaluate to the tax paid control account. I will reference / create no less than the following nine [9] measures:

1. Accounting taxable profit
2. Depreciation timing difference
3. Taxable profit / (loss) before losses
4. Tax losses used (method B)
5. Taxable profit / (loss) after losses
6. Tax payable for period
7. Tax opening payables
8. Tax paid
9. Tax closing payables.

The **Accounting taxable profit, Depreciation timing difference, Taxable profit / (loss) before losses** and **Tax losses used (method B)** measures have already been created. Building off them I will create the **Taxable profit / (loss) after losses** measure with the following **DAX** code:

```
Taxable profit / (loss) after losses =
[Taxable profit / (loss) before losses] + [Tax losses used (method B)]
```


```
Taxable profit / (loss) after losses =
[Taxable profit / (loss) before losses] + [Tax losses used (method B)]
```


The **Tax payable for period** measure will be calculated with the following **DAX** code:

```
Tax payable for period =
VAR CalcTable =
ADDCOLUMNS(
    'Calendar',
    "TPLAL", MAX( [Taxable profit / (loss) after losses] * P_TaxRate, 0)
)

Return
SUMX(
    CalcTable,
    [TPLAL]
)
```


```
Tax payable for period =
VAR CalcTable =
ADDCOLUMNS(
 'Calendar',
 "TPLAL", MAX( [Taxable profit / (loss) after losses] * P_TaxRate, 0)
)

Return
SUMX(
 CalcTable,
 [TPLAL]
)
```


I have adopted a variable that evaluates the **Taxable profit / (loss) after losses * P_TaxRate** in a table using the **ADDCOLUMNS** function. This is to evaluate the taxable profit or loss at a daily level, otherwise Power BI will evaluate this number based on the filter context in the visualisation. Evaluating this number based on the filter context of the visualisation can lead to miscalculations. This is because shifts at a daily level may not be reflected in the number when it is aggregated to a monthly level.

I can then plot the measures into a matrix visualisation:

Year	2021								
Qtr	Q1			Q2			Q3		
	Jan	Feb	Mar	Apr	May	Jun	Jul	Aug	Sep
Accounting taxable profit	$119.06	$681.90	$870.83	$790.79	$784.64	$649.01	$759.96	$717.58	$639.62
Depreciation timing difference	($25.48)	($24.74)	($29.30)	($30.21)	($33.12)	($51.78)	($55.42)	($57.33)	($57.33)
Taxable profit / (loss) before losses	$93.58	$657.16	$841.53	$760.59	$751.52	$597.22	$704.54	$660.25	$582.29
Tax losses used (method B)	-	($3.47)	-	-	-	-	-	-	-
Taxable profit / (loss) after losses	$93.58	$653.70	$841.53	$760.59	$751.52	$597.22	$704.54	$660.25	$582.29
Tax payable for period	$29.11	$196.11	$252.46	$228.18	$225.46	$179.17	$211.36	$198.07	$174.69

This takes me to the tax paid control account.

I have the **Tax payable for period** measure. The other line in the control account is the **Tax paid** measure. It is calculated with the following **DAX** code:

```
Tax paid =
CALCULATE(
    -[Tax payable for period],
    DATEADD(
        'Calendar'[Date],
        -P_DaysPayable,
        DAY
    )
)
```

```
Tax paid =
CALCULATE(
 -[Tax payable for period],
 DATEADD(
 'Calendar'[Date],
 -P_DaysPayable,
 DAY
 )
)
```

I will be using the **P_DaysPayable** parameter for this measure. However, this can be changed based on the tax rules of the region. The point here is I am trying to consider general concepts, not specific tax legislation!

Moving on, I can now create the cumulative measures for the **Tax payable for period** and **Tax paid** measures:

```
Tax payable for period cum =
    CALCULATE([Tax payable for period],
        FILTER(
            ALL('Calendar'),
            'Calendar'[Date] <= MAX('Calendar'[Date])
            )
        )
```

```
Tax payable for period cum =
 CALCULATE([Tax payable for period],
 FILTER(
 ALL('Calendar'),
 'Calendar'[Date] <= MAX('Calendar'[Date])
 )
 )
```

```
Tax paid cum =
    CALCULATE([Tax paid],
        FILTER(
            ALL('Calendar'),
            'Calendar'[Date] <= MAX('Calendar'[Date])
            )
        )
```

```
Tax paid cum =
 CALCULATE([Tax paid],
 FILTER(
 ALL('Calendar'),
 'Calendar'[Date] <= MAX('Calendar'[Date])
 )
 )
```

With both cumulative measures created, I can then create the **Tax opening payables** measure:

```
Tax opening payables =
    CALCULATE(
        [Tax payable for period cum] + [Tax paid cum],
        PREVIOUSDAY('Calendar'[Date])
    )
```

```
Tax opening payables =
 CALCULATE(
 [Tax payable for period cum] + [Tax paid cum],
 PREVIOUSDAY('Calendar'[Date])
 )
```

The final step in this control account is to create the **Tax closing payables** measure:

```
Tax closing payables =
[Tax opening payables] + [Tax payable for period] + [Tax paid]
```

```
Tax closing payables =
[Tax opening payables] + [Tax payable for period] + [Tax paid]
```

With all four measures of the control account created, I can now plot them into a matrix visualisation:

Year	2021								
Qtr	Q1			Q2			Q3		
	Jan	Feb	Mar	Apr	May	Jun	Jul	Aug	Sep
Tax opening payables		$29.11	$202.72	$328.87	$329.03	$291.87	$243.42	$279.47	$247.95
Tax payable for period	$29.11	$196.11	$252.46	$228.18	$225.46	$179.17	$211.36	$198.07	$174.69
Tax paid		($22.50)	($126.32)	($228.01)	($262.61)	($227.61)	($175.32)	($229.59)	($193.44)
Tax closing payables	$29.11	$202.72	$328.87	$329.03	$291.87	$243.42	$279.47	$247.95	$229.19

Tax control account

The final control account in this section is the Tax control account. This is comprised of the following line items:

1. Tax opening payables
2. Tax expense / (credit)
3. Tax paid

4. Movement in DTAs
5. Movement in DTLs
6. Tax closing payables.

The only measures that need to be created here are the: **Tax expense / (credit)**, **Tax opening payables**, and **Tax closing payables** measures, as the other three measures have already been created for previous control accounts.

Year	2021								
Qtr	Q1			Q2			Q3		
	Jan	Feb	Mar	Apr	May	Jun	Jul	Aug	Sep
Tax paid		($22.50)	($126.32)	($228.01)	($262.61)	($227.61)	($175.32)	($229.59)	($193.44)
Movement in DTAs	$1.04	($1.04)	-	-	-	-	-	-	-
Movement in DTLs	$7.64	$7.42	$8.79	$9.06	$9.94	$15.53	$16.63	$17.20	$17.20

The **Tax expense / (credit)** measure is calculated with the following **DAX** code:

```
Tax expense / (credit) =
[Accounting taxable profit] * P_TaxRate
```

```
Tax expense / (credit) =
[Accounting taxable profit] * P_TaxRate
```

I then create the cumulative measure, **Tax expense / (credit) cum** with the following **DAX** code:

```
Tax expense / (credit) cum =
    CALCULATE([Tax expense / (credit)],
        FILTER(
            ALL('Calendar'),
            'Calendar'[Date] <= MAX('Calendar'[Date])
        )
    )
```

```
Tax expense / (credit) cum =
CALCULATE([Tax expense / (credit)],
 FILTER(
 ALL(‘Calendar’),
 ‘Calendar’[Date] <= MAX(‘Calendar’[Date])
 )
)
```

With the cumulative measure calculated, I can now create the **Tax opening payables** measure. The difference here is I will name it **Tax opening payables CA**, where 'CA' is short for control account. This is because I have already created a **Tax opening payables** measure earlier, and Power BI Desktop does not allow for two measures to have the same name.

```
Tax opening payables CA =
    CALCULATE(
        [Tax expense / (credit) cum] + [Tax paid cum] + [Movement in DTAs cum]
        + [Movement in DTLs cum],
        PREVIOUSDAY('Calendar'[Date])
    )
```

```
Tax opening payables CA =
 CALCULATE(
 [Tax expense / (credit) cum] + [Tax paid cum] + [Movement in DTAs cum]
 + [Movement in DTLs cum],
 PREVIOUSDAY(‘Calendar’[Date])
 )
```

I shall also rename this measure when I plot it into the visualisation:

Year	2021								
Qtr	Q1			Q2			Q3		
	Jan	Feb	Mar	Apr	May	Jun	Jul	Aug	Sep
Tax opening payables	-	$44.40	$232.86	$376.58	$394.86	$377.58	$360.20	$429.49	$432.37
Tax expense / (credit)	$35.72	$204.57	$261.25	$237.24	$235.39	$194.70	$227.99	$215.27	$191.89
Tax paid		($22.50)	($126.32)	($228.01)	($262.61)	($227.61)	($175.32)	($229.59)	($193.44)
Movement in DTAs	$1.04	($1.04)	-	-	-	-	-	-	-
Movement in DTLs	$7.64	$7.42	$8.79	$9.06	$9.94	$15.53	$16.63	$17.20	$17.20

The last line of this control account is the **Tax closing payables** measure. I shall give this measure a similar name to the **Tax opening payables CA** measure for the same reason.

```
Tax closing payables CA =
[Tax opening payables CA] + [Tax expense / (credit)] + [Tax paid]
+ [Movement in DTAs] + [Movement in DTLs]
```

```
Tax closing payables CA =
[Tax opening payables CA] + [Tax expense / (credit)] + [Tax paid]
+ [Movement in DTAs] + [Movement in DTLs]
```

With the measures created, I can plot them into a visualisation:

Year	2021								
Qtr	Q1			Q2			Q3		
	Jan	Feb	Mar	Apr	May	Jun	Jul	Aug	Sep
Tax opening payables	-	$44.40	$232.86	$376.58	$394.86	$377.58	$360.20	$429.49	$432.37
Tax expense / (credit)	$35.72	$204.57	$261.25	$237.24	$235.39	$194.70	$227.99	$215.27	$191.89
Tax paid		($22.50)	($126.32)	($228.01)	($262.61)	($227.61)	($175.32)	($229.59)	($193.44)
Movement in DTAs	$1.04	($1.04)	-	-	-	-	-	-	-
Movement in DTLs	$7.64	$7.42	$8.79	$9.06	$9.94	$15.53	$16.63	$17.20	$17.20
Tax closing payables	$44.40	$232.86	$376.58	$394.86	$377.58	$360.20	$429.49	$432.37	$448.01

I add the remaining measures to folder **10. Tax losses** (do note this group contains the original measures used to demonstrate the *naive* problem):

- 10. Tax losses
  - Accounting taxable profit
  - Closing DTAs
  - Closing tax losses
  - Movement in DTAs
  - Movement in DTAs cum
  - Movement in tax losses
  - Opening DTAs
  - Opening tax losses
  - Tax closing payables
  - Tax closing payables CA
  - Tax expense / (credit)
  - Tax expense / (credit) cum
  - Tax losses created cum
  - Tax losses created during period
  - Tax losses used
  - Tax losses used cum
  - Tax opening payables
  - Tax opening payables CA
  - Tax paid
  - Tax paid cum
  - Tax payable for period
  - Tax payable for period cum
  - Taxable profit / (loss) after losses
  - Taxable profit / (loss) before losses

CHAPTER 23: Income Statement (Part 2)

Now that I have calculated the tax control account, I can revisit the Income Statement and calculate the final line. The net profit after tax or **NPAT. NPAT** is the **NPBT** less the **Tax expense**. In the model the **Tax expense** is currently calculated as a positive amount. Therefore, I shall first have to create a measure to flip the sign:

```
Tax expense = -[Tax expense / (credit)]
```


```
Tax expense = -[Tax expense / (credit)]
```


This measure should have **Financial account measures** as the Home Table, and be stored in the **Income statement** folder.

I can change **NPAT** measure, which I created as a placeholder, to use the following **DAX** code. Note that since **Tax expense** has been created as a negative of **Tax expense / (credit)**, I just need to add it:

```
NPAT =
[NPBT] + [Tax expense]
```


```
NPAT =
[NPBT] + [Tax expense]
```


With the final line calculated, I can clean up the matrix visualisation for the Income Statement. I have decided on the following layout:

Year	2021								
Qtr	Q1			Q2			Q3		
	Jan	Feb	Mar	Apr	May	Jun	Jul	Aug	Sep
Revenue	$599.40	$2,097.90	$2,447.55	$2,267.73	$2,297.70	$2,057.94	$2,267.73	$2,207.79	$1,918.08
COGS	($359.64)	($1,258.74)	($1,468.53)	($1,360.64)	($1,378.62)	($1,234.76)	($1,360.64)	($1,324.67)	($1,150.85)
Gross profit	$239.76	$839.16	$979.02	$907.09	$919.08	$823.18	$907.09	$883.12	$767.23
Operating expenditure	($93.84)	($130.56)	($77.52)	($85.68)	($102.00)	($130.56)	($102.00)	($120.36)	($83.64)
EBITDA	$145.92	$708.60	$901.50	$821.41	$817.08	$692.62	$805.09	$762.76	$683.59
Depreciation	($16.99)	($16.49)	($19.53)	($20.14)	($22.08)	($34.52)	($36.95)	($38.22)	($38.22)
EBIT	$128.93	$692.11	$881.97	$801.28	$795.00	$658.10	$768.15	$724.54	$645.37
Interest expense	($9.88)	($10.20)	($11.13)	($10.48)	($10.36)	($9.09)	($8.19)	($6.96)	($5.75)
NPBT	$119.06	$681.90	$870.83	$790.79	$784.64	$649.01	$759.96	$717.58	$639.62
Tax expense	($35.72)	($204.57)	($261.25)	($237.24)	($235.39)	($194.70)	($227.99)	($215.27)	($191.89)
NPAT	$83.34	$477.33	$609.58	$553.56	$549.25	$454.30	$531.97	$502.30	$447.73

CHAPTER 24: Calculating Equity and Dividends

With the Income Statement now completed, I now move on to what is missing in the Cash Flow Statement, the second smallest (conceptually) of our three financial statements:

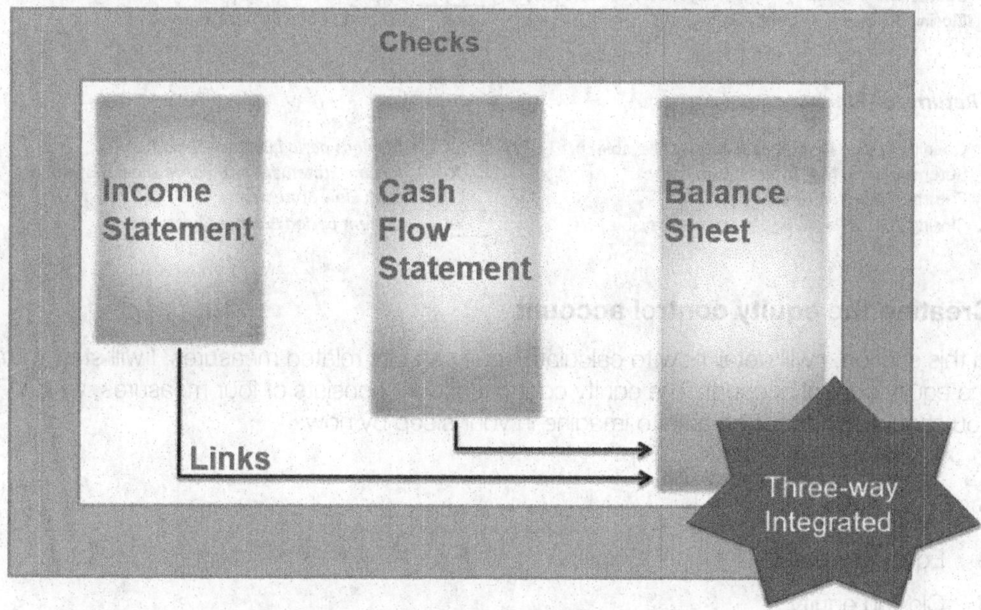

If I were developing the model in Excel, using the example from my first book, *An Introduction to Financial Modelling*, I would be able to prepare a Cash Flow Statement that looked something like this:

1. Cash Flow Statement

Direct Cash Flow Statement

Operating Cash Flow						
Cash Receipts	US$'000	334	440	485	526	554
Direct Cash Payments	US$'000	(90)	(131)	(145)	(157)	(166)
Indirect Cash Payments	US$'000	(60)	(65)	(68)	(70)	(71)
Cash Payments	US$'000	(150)	(196)	(212)	(226)	(237)
Interest Paid	US$'000	-	-	(1)	(3)	(2)
Tax Paid	US$'000	-	(48)	(33)	(46)	(58)
Net Operating Cash Flow	US$'000	**184**	**196**	**239**	**251**	**258**
Investing Cash Flows						
Interest Received	US$'000	-	0	1	1	3
Purchases of Non-Current Assets	US$'000	(150)	(180)	(120)	(90)	(100)
Net Investing Cash Flows	US$'000	**(150)**	**(180)**	**(119)**	**(89)**	**(97)**
Financing Cash Flows						
Debt Drawdowns	US$'000	20	20	-	-	-
Debt Repayments	US$'000	-	-	(15)	(25)	(10)
Ordinary Equity Issuances	US$'000					
Ordinary Equity Buybacks	US$'000					
Dividends Paid	US$'000					
Net Financing Cash Flows	US$'000	**20**	**20**	**(15)**	**(25)**	**(10)**
Net Increase / (Decrease) in Cash Held	US$'000	**54**	**36**	**104**	**137**	**151**

It is clear I have equity and dividends to construct. Similarly to debt, I have a return **OF** finance and a return **ON** finance. As a reminder:

Returns of Finance

Opening Balance (e.g. Debt / Equity) b/f	XX	*Previous period Balance Sheet item*
Additions (e.g. drawdowns / issuances / conversions)	X	*Typically in Cash Flow Statement*
Returns on finance rolled up (e.g. "interest capitalised")	X	*Usually a Balance Sheet movement*
Deductions (e.g. repayments / buybacks / conversions)	(X)	*Typically in Cash Flow Statement*
Closing Balance (e.g. Debt / Equity) c/f	**XX**	*Current period Balance Sheet item*

Returns on Finance

Opening Return Payable (e.g. Interest Payable) b/f	XX	*Previous period Balance Sheet item*
Return Accrued (e.g. Interest Expense)	X	*Income Statement or Balance Sheet movement*
Return Paid (e.g. Interest Paid)	(X)	*Cash Flow Statement*
Closing Return Payable (e.g. Interest Payable) c/f	**XX**	*Current period Balance Sheet item*

Creating the equity control account

In this section, I will detail how to calculate equity and its related measures. I will start with the equity control account. The equity control account consists of four measures, which you should just about be able to imagine in your sleep by now:

1. Opening equity
2. Equity issuances
3. Equity buybacks
4. Closing equity.

Before I create my measures, I must create a relationship between the **Equity** table and the **Calendar** table:

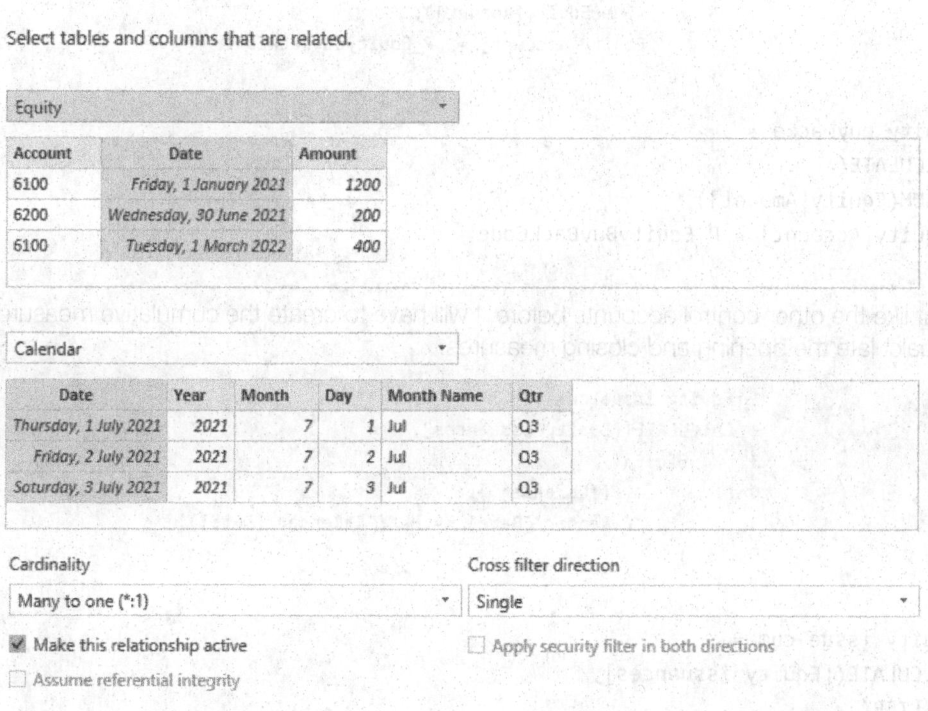

The first measure I will calculate is the **Equity issuances** measure. The Home Table for this measure will be **Control account measures**. I use the following **DAX** code:

```
Equity issuances =
CALCULATE(
    SUM(Equity[Amount]),
    Equity[Account] =  P_EquityIssueCode
)
```


```
Equity issuances =
CALCULATE(
 SUM(Equity[Amount]),
 Equity[Account] = P_EquityIssueCode
)
```


Whilst the **Account** field also occurs in the **Actuals** table, it makes sense from a performance perspective to take all fields in our **CALCULATE** function from the same table (not only is there the linkage to consider, but it would be reasonable to expect that the **Equity** table might be smaller than its **Actuals** counterpart).

This is followed by the **Equity buybacks** measure. The data is located in the **Equity** table, therefore, these two measures are simple sums of the **Amount** column:

```
Equity buybacks =
CALCULATE(
    -SUM(Equity[Amount]),
    Equity[Account] =  P_EquityBuyBackCode
)
```

```
Equity buybacks =
CALCULATE(
 -SUM(Equity[Amount]),
 Equity[Account] = P_EquityBuyBackCode
)
```

Just like the other control accounts before, I will have to create the cumulative measures to calculate the opening and closing measures.

```
Equity issue cum =
CALCULATE([Equity issuances],
    FILTER(
        ALL('Calendar'),
        'Calendar'[Date] <= MAX('Calendar'[Date])
    )
)
```

```
Equity issue cum =
CALCULATE([Equity issuances],
 FILTER(
 ALL(‘Calendar’),
 ‘Calendar’[Date] <= MAX(‘Calendar’[Date])
 )
)
```

```
Equity buybacks cum =
CALCULATE([Equity buybacks],
    FILTER(
        ALL('Calendar'),
        'Calendar'[Date] <= MAX('Calendar'[Date])
    )
)
```

```
Equity buybacks cum =
CALCULATE([Equity buybacks],
 FILTER(
 ALL(‘Calendar’),
 ‘Calendar’[Date] <= MAX(‘Calendar’[Date])
 )
)
```

I can now move on to the **Opening equity**:

```
Opening equity =
    IF(
        PREVIOUSDAY('Calendar'[Date]) = BLANK(),
        0,
        CALCULATE([Equity issue cum] + [Equity buybacks cum],
        PREVIOUSDAY('Calendar'[Date])
        )
    )
```

```
Opening equity =
 IF(
 PREVIOUSDAY('Calendar'[Date]) = BLANK(),
 0,
 CALCULATE([Equity issue cum] + [Equity buybacks cum],
 PREVIOUSDAY('Calendar'[Date])
 )
 )
```

I can then create the **Closing equity** measure, using the following **DAX** code:

```
Closing equity =
[Opening equity] + [Equity issuances] + [Equity buybacks]
```

```
Closing equity =
[Opening equity] + [Equity issuances] + [Equity buybacks]
```

I can then plot the four measures in a matrix visualisation and apply the usual appropriate formatting. The results in the visualisation may look like this:

Year	2021								
Qtr	Q1			Q2			Q3		
	Jan	Feb	Mar	Apr	May	Jun	Jul	Aug	Sep
Opening equity	$0.00	$1,200.00	$1,200.00	$1,200.00	$1,200.00	$1,200.00	$1,000.00	$1,000.00	$1,000.00
Equity issuances	$1,200.00								
Equity buybacks						($200.00)			
Closing equity	$1,200.00	$1,200.00	$1,200.00	$1,200.00	$1,200.00	$1,000.00	$1,000.00	$1,000.00	$1,000.00

I will then group the measures into their own display folder titled **13. Equity measures**:

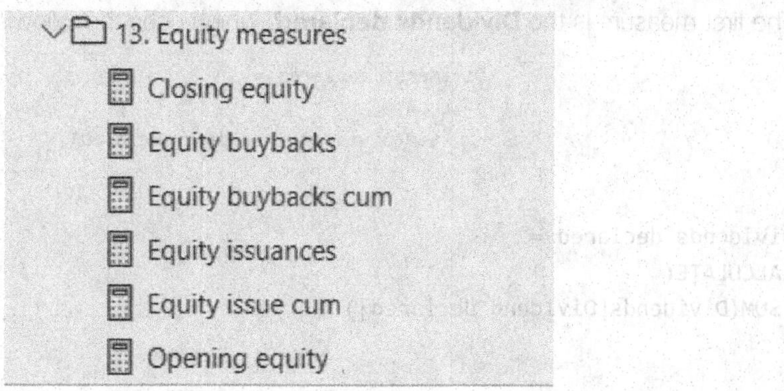

Before I create my next measures, there is another relationship to create, this time between the **Dividends** table and the **Calendar** table:

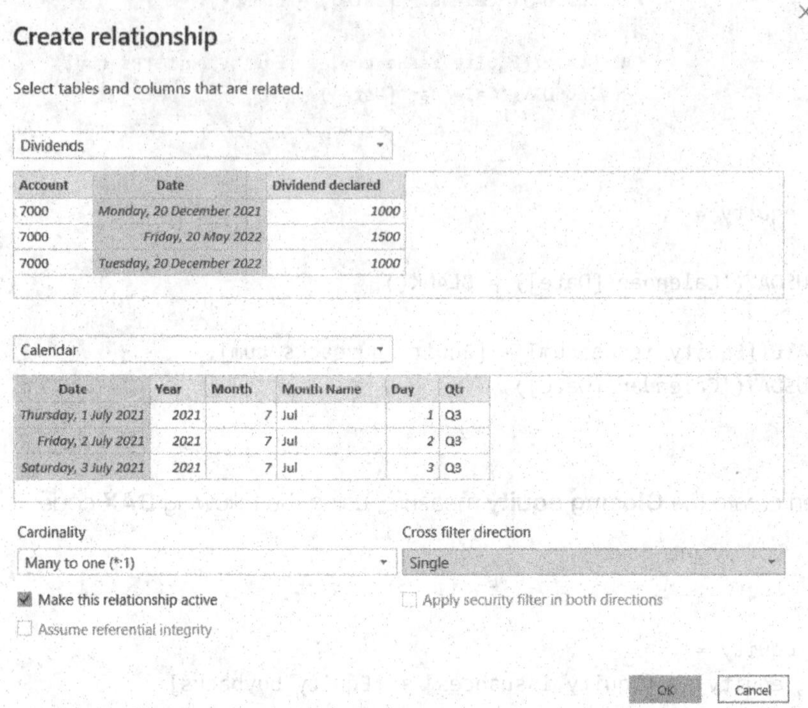

Creating the dividends control account

I am now able to create the related part of the equity section. Let's first review the measures needed to calculate the dividend control account:

1. Dividend opening payables
2. Dividends declared
3. Dividends paid
4. Dividend closing payables.

The first measure is the **Dividends declared**, which uses the following **DAX** code:

```
Dividends declared =
CALCULATE(
    SUM(Dividends[Dividend declared])
)
```

```
Dividends declared =
CALCULATE(
 SUM(Dividends[Dividend declared])
)
```

I will assume that dividends are paid 40 days after being declared. Therefore, I can use the **P_DaysPayable** parameter to calculate the **Dividends paid** measure.

```
Dividends paid =
    CALCULATE(-[Dividends declared],
        DATEADD('Calendar'[Date], -P_DaysPayable, DAY)
    )
```

```
Dividends paid =
 CALCULATE(-[Dividends declared],
 DATEADD(‘Calendar’[Date], -P_DaysPayable, DAY)
 )
```

With these two measures calculated, I can now move on to create the cumulative measures.

```
Dividends declared cum =
    CALCULATE([Dividends declared],
        FILTER(
            ALL('Calendar'),
            'Calendar'[Date] <= MAX('Calendar'[Date])
            )
        )
```

```
Dividends declared cum =
 CALCULATE([Dividends declared],
 FILTER(
 ALL(‘Calendar’),
 ‘Calendar’[Date] <= MAX(‘Calendar’[Date])
 )
 )
```

```
Dividends paid cum =
    CALCULATE([Dividends paid],
        FILTER(
            ALL('Calendar'),
            'Calendar'[Date] <= MAX('Calendar'[Date])
            )
        )
```

```
Dividends paid cum =
 CALCULATE([Dividends paid],
 FILTER(
 ALL(‘Calendar’),
 ‘Calendar’[Date] <= MAX(‘Calendar’[Date])
 )
 )
```

I can now use the two cumulative measures to calculate the **Dividend opening payables** measure:

```
Dividend opening payables =
    IF(
        PREVIOUSDAY('Calendar'[Date]) = BLANK(),
        0,
        CALCULATE([Dividends declared cum] + [Dividends paid cum],
        PREVIOUSDAY('Calendar'[Date])
        )
```

```
Dividend opening payables =
 IF(
 PREVIOUSDAY('Calendar'[Date]) = BLANK(),
 0,
 CALCULATE([Dividends declared cum] + [Dividends paid cum],
 PREVIOUSDAY('Calendar'[Date])
 )
 )
```

The **Dividend closing payables** measure is calculated with the following **DAX** code:

```
Dividend closing payables =
[Dividend opening payables] + [Dividends declared] + [Dividends paid]
```


```
Dividend closing payables =
[Dividend opening payables] + [Dividends declared] + [Dividends paid]
```


I can then plot the measure into a matrix visualisation and apply the standard formatting:

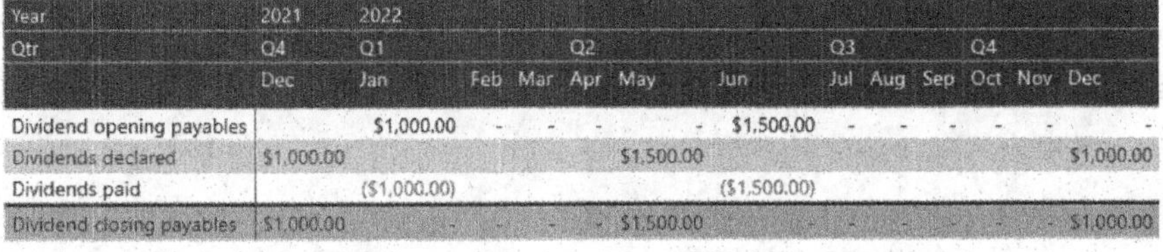

Year	2021	2022											
Qtr	Q4	Q1			Q2			Q3			Q4		
	Dec	Jan	Feb	Mar	Apr	May	Jun	Jul	Aug	Sep	Oct	Nov	Dec
Dividend opening payables		$1,000.00	-	-	-	-	$1,500.00	-	-	-	-	-	-
Dividends declared	$1,000.00					$1,500.00							$1,000.00
Dividends paid		($1,000.00)					($1,500.00)						
Dividend closing payables	$1,000.00	-	-	-	-	$1,500.00	-	-	-	-	-	-	$1,000.00

Déjà vu anyone?

I create a new folder for these measures called **14. Dividends measures:**

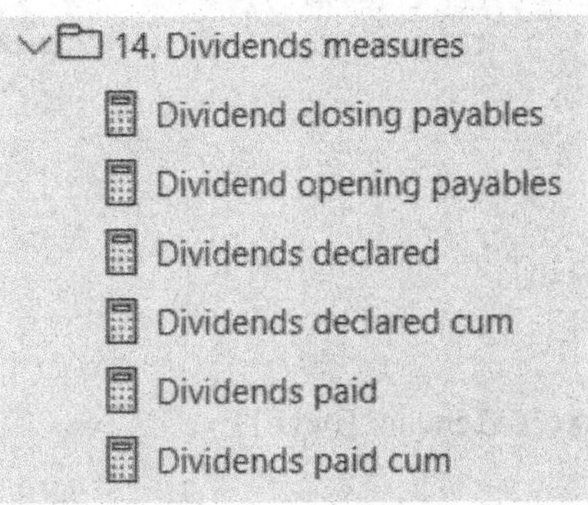

CHAPTER 25: Cash Flow Statement

With equity and dividends now constructed, I am now in a position to compile all of the measures required for the **Cash Flow Statement**. These measures are (deep breath!):

1. Operating cash flow
2. Cash receipts
3. Direct cash payments
4. Indirect cash payments
5. Cash payments
6. Interest paid (Interest cash paid)
7. Tax paid
8. Net operating cash flow
9. Investing cash flows
10. Purchases of non-current assets
11. Net investing cash flows
12. Financing cash flows
13. Debt drawdown
14. Debt repayment
15. Ordinary equity issuances
16. Ordinary equity buybacks
17. Dividends paid
18. Net financing cash flows
19. Net increase / (decrease) in cash held.

I shall break this section down further into four segments:

1. Operating cash flows
2. Investing cash flows
3. Financing cash flows
4. Increase / (decrease) in cash held.

Operating Cash Flows

There are several measures that will make up the Operating cash flow segment:

1. Operating cash flow
2. Cash receipts
3. Direct cash payments
4. Indirect cash payments (Opex cash payments)
5. Cash payments

6. Interest paid (Interest cash paid)
7. Tax paid
8. Net operating cash flow.

The first measure I am going to create is the **Operating cash flow** measure. This will have **Financial account measures** as the Home Table. One of the most complex measures in this book, it uses the following **DAX** code to evaluate:

```
Operating cash flow = ""
```

```
Operating cash flow = ""
```

This measure evaluates to a blank value because its purpose is just to serve as a title for a section within the measure. Plotting this measure into the visualisation will result in a blank row. I will demonstrate after I create the **Cash receipts** measure.

The next line item or measure in this case is the **Cash receipts** measure. The **Cash receipts** measure will use the following **DAX** code:

```
Cash receipts =
-[Sales cash receipts]
```

```
Cash receipts =
-[Sales cash receipts]
```

If I plot the **Cash receipts** and **Operating cash flow** measures into a visualisation, I get the following result:

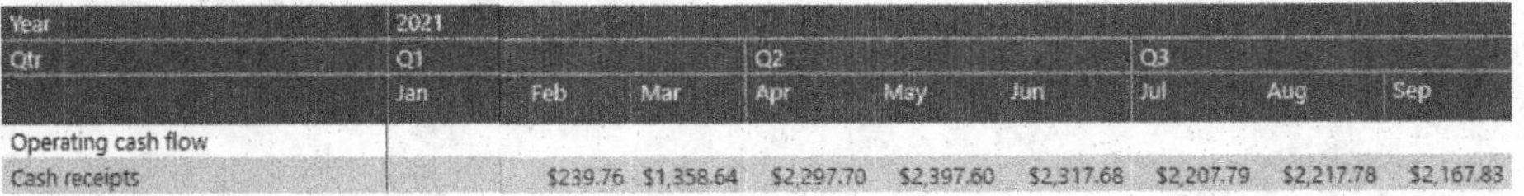

Year	2021								
Qtr	Q1			Q2			Q3		
	Jan	Feb	Mar	Apr	May	Jun	Jul	Aug	Sep
Operating cash flow									
Cash receipts		$239.76	$1,358.64	$2,297.70	$2,397.60	$2,317.68	$2,207.79	$2,217.78	$2,167.83

The result is **Operating cash flow** acting as a pseudo sub-heading, for the visualisation.

There is however a formatting issue here. Since the there is no data for **Cash receipts** in January 2021, the value is *null*, and there is no formatting which will show *null* as '-' in the same way that zero [0] is shown. This was acceptable for the control accounts, but this is a financial statement.

I can trap for *null* in the **Cash receipts** measure:

```
Cash receipts =
IF( [Sales cash receipts] = BLANK(), 0, -[Sales cash receipts])
```

```
Cash receipts =
If ([Sales cash receipts] = BLANK(), 0, -[Sales cash receipts])
```

This checks if **Sales cash receipts** is *null*, and if it is then **Cash receipts** is given a value of zero [0], otherwise **Cash receipts** is the negative of **Sales cash receipts**. This fixes my formatting issue:

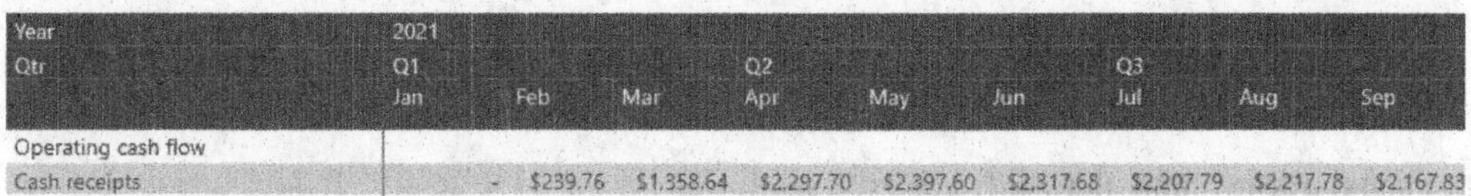

Year	2021								
Qtr	Q1			Q2			Q3		
	Jan	Feb	Mar	Apr	May	Jun	Jul	Aug	Sep
Operating cash flow									
Cash receipts	-	$239.76	$1,358.64	$2,297.70	$2,397.60	$2,317.68	$2,207.79	$2,217.78	$2,167.83

I could do this for every measure on the financial statements where I am getting a *null* value, but that would add to an already substantial text. Suffice to say, if you encounter any *null* values, this is how they can be dealt with. Let's move on; life's too short, but perhaps not as short as *null*! It's ironic it takes so long to write something that's shorter than nothing…

The next measure I shall create is the **Direct cash payments** measure. Direct cash payments are comprised of **COGS cash payments** and **Purchases cash payments ($)**. It uses the following **DAX** code:

```
Direct cash payments =
[COGS cash payments] + [Purchases cash payments ($)]
```


```
Direct cash payments =
[COGS cash payments] + [Purchases cash payments ($)]
```


The **Indirect cash payments** is another name for **Opex cash payments**, I can use this and rename the measure in the visual.

I can now create the **Cash payments** measure that will sum the **Direct cash payments** and **Opex cash payments** measures together:

```
Cash payments =
[Direct cash payments] + [Opex cash payments]
```


```
Cash payments =
[Direct cash payments] + [Opex cash payments]
```


The next two line items in the Cash Flow Statement are **Interest paid** and **Tax paid**. **Interest paid** is another name for the **Interest cash paid** measure, so I will use that measure and rename it in the visual. The **Tax paid** measure already exists.

I can plot the **Direct cash payments**, **Opex cash payments** (renamed to **Indirect cash payments**), **Cash payments** and **Interest cash paid** (renamed to **Interest paid**) measures into the visualisation. I have applied formatting and used the asterisk (*****) and blank (**""**) measures:

Year	2021								
Qtr	Q1			Q2			Q3		
	Jan	Feb	Mar	Apr	May	Jun	Jul	Aug	Sep
Operating cash flow									
Cash receipts	-	$239.76	$1,358.64	$2,297.70	$2,397.60	$2,317.68	$2,207.79	$2,217.78	$2,167.83
Direct cash payments		($231.78)	($1,001.04)	($1,828.63)	($1,978.46)	($1,772.64)	($1,894.78)	($2,249.57)	($2,177.75)
Indirect cash payments		($40.80)	($155.04)	($77.52)	($93.84)	($57.12)	($146.88)	($122.40)	($77.52)
Cash payments		($272.58)	($1,156.08)	($1,906.15)	($2,072.30)	($1,829.76)	($2,041.66)	($2,371.97)	($2,255.27)
Interest paid		($5.50)	($11.30)	($10.86)	($10.92)	($10.20)	($9.76)	($8.53)	($7.10)
Tax paid		($22.50)	($126.32)	($228.01)	($262.61)	($227.61)	($175.32)	($229.59)	($193.44)

Moving on, I now create the **Net operating cash flow** measure, to sum all the operating cash flows:

```
Net operating cash flow =
[Cash receipts] + [Cash payments] + [Interest cash paid] + [Tax paid]
```


```
Net operating cash flow =
[Cash receipts] + [Cash payments] + [Interest cash paid] + [Tax paid]
```


Year	2021								
Qtr	Q1			Q2			Q3		
	Jan	Feb	Mar	Apr	May	Jun	Jul	Aug	Sep
Operating cash flow									
Cash receipts	-	$239.76	$1,358.64	$2,297.70	$2,397.60	$2,317.68	$2,207.79	$2,217.78	$2,167.83
Direct cash payments		($231.78)	($1,001.04)	($1,828.63)	($1,978.46)	($1,772.64)	($1,894.78)	($2,249.57)	($2,177.75)
Indirect cash payments		($40.80)	($155.04)	($77.52)	($93.84)	($57.12)	($146.88)	($122.40)	($77.52)
Cash payments		($272.58)	($1,156.08)	($1,906.15)	($2,072.30)	($1,829.76)	($2,041.66)	($2,371.97)	($2,255.27)
Interest paid		($5.50)	($11.30)	($10.86)	($10.92)	($10.20)	($9.76)	($8.53)	($7.10)
Tax paid		($22.50)	($126.32)	($228.01)	($262.61)	($227.61)	($175.32)	($229.59)	($193.44)
Net operating cash flow	-	($60.83)	$64.95	$152.67	$51.76	$250.11	($18.95)	($392.31)	($287.98)

I know some of you may place **Interest paid** in financing, but I can't help it if you are wrong. Whilst that might be flippant, technically, **Interest paid** is an operating cost as it services debt on a mandatory basis of the debt raised to fund operations. Dividends are not included, as they represent a financial decision: you don't have to pay dividends if you don't want any friends, investors or a business. If it helps, think of operating cash flows as the cash proxy of the Income Statement. You would include **Interest expense** in the P&L – so you would include **Interest paid** in **Net operating cash flow**.

But hey, if you put it in Financing, it is what a lot of people do, and that's fine, as long as you are consistent.

Investing Cash Flows

The investing cash flows segment contains the following measures:

1. Investing cash flows
2. Purchases of non-current assets
3. Net investing cash flows.

Just like the operating cash flows segment, I shall create a header measure:

```
Investing cash flows = ""
```


```
Investing cash flows = ""
```


In this model, net investing cash flows consists of **Purchases of non-current assets**. This line item is calculated using the following **DAX** code:

```
Purchases of non-current assets = -[Capex]
```


```
Purchases of non-current assets = -[Capex]
```


Next up the **Net investing cash flows** measure. I know I could use the same measure twice and rename it once, but I include a new measure to avoid confusion:

```
Net investing cash flows =
[Purchases of non-current assets]
```

```
Net investing cash flows =
[Purchases of non-current assets]
```

I use the blank measure ("") after the **Net operating cash flow**. This is followed by the **Investing cash flows, Purchases of non-current assets** and **Net investing cash flows** measures.

Year	2021								
Qtr	Q1			Q2			Q3		
	Jan	Feb	Mar	Apr	May	Jun	Jul	Aug	Sep
Operating cash flow									
Cash receipts	-	$239.76	$1,358.64	$2,297.70	$2,397.60	$2,317.68	$2,207.79	$2,217.78	$2,167.83
Direct cash payments		($231.78)	($1,001.04)	($1,828.63)	($1,978.46)	($1,772.64)	($1,894.78)	($2,249.57)	($2,177.75)
Indirect cash payments		($40.80)	($155.04)	($77.52)	($93.84)	($57.12)	($146.88)	($122.40)	($77.52)
Cash payments		($272.58)	($1,156.08)	($1,906.15)	($2,072.30)	($1,829.76)	($2,041.66)	($2,371.97)	($2,255.27)
Interest paid		($5.50)	($11.30)	($10.86)	($10.92)	($10.20)	($9.76)	($8.53)	($7.10)
Tax paid		($22.50)	($126.32)	($228.01)	($262.61)	($227.61)	($175.32)	($229.59)	($193.44)
Net operating cash flow	-	[illegible]	$64.95	$152.67	$51.76	$250.11	[illegible]	[illegible]	[illegible]
Investing cash flows									
Purchases of non-current assets	($1,000.00)	($75.00)	($75.00)	($75.00)	($75.00)	($600.00)	($75.00)	($75.00)	($75.00)
Net investing cash flows	($1,000.00)	($75.00)	($75.00)	($75.00)	($75.00)	($600.00)	($75.00)	($75.00)	($75.00)

I may now proceed to the Financing cash flows segment.

Financing Cash Flows

The **Net financing cash flows** line is comprised of:

1. Financing cash flows
2. Debt drawdowns
3. Debt repayments
4. Ordinary equity issuances (Equity issuances)
5. Ordinary equity buybacks (Equity buybacks)
6. Dividends paid.

The only measure I need to create is the **Financing cash flows** measure:

```
Financing cash flows = ""
```

```
Financing cash flows = ""
```

The next two line items **Debt drawdown** and **Debt repayments** have already been created in the debt control account. For **Ordinary equity issuances,** I can rename **Equity issuances** in the visual. Similarly, for **Ordinary equity buybacks** I can rename **Equity buybacks**.

The next measure on the list is the **Dividends paid** measure, this measure has already been created in the dividends control account. Therefore, I can just plot these measures onto the visualisation:

Year	2021								
Qtr	Q1			Q2			Q3		
	Jan	Feb	Mar	Apr	May	Jun	Jul	Aug	Sep
Operating cash flow									
Cash receipts	-	$239.76	$1,358.64	$2,297.70	$2,397.60	$2,317.68	$2,207.79	$2,217.78	$2,167.83
Direct cash payments		($231.78)	($1,001.04)	($1,828.63)	($1,978.46)	($1,772.64)	($1,894.78)	($2,249.57)	($2,177.75)
Indirect cash payments		($40.80)	($155.04)	($77.52)	($93.84)	($57.12)	($146.88)	($122.40)	($77.52)
Cash payments		($272.58)	($1,156.08)	($1,906.15)	($2,072.30)	($1,829.76)	($2,041.66)	($2,371.97)	($2,255.27)
Interest paid		($5.50)	($11.30)	($10.86)	($10.92)	($10.20)	($9.76)	($8.53)	($7.10)
Tax paid		($22.50)	($126.32)	($228.01)	($262.61)	($227.61)	($175.32)	($229.59)	($193.44)
Net operating cash flow	-	($60.83)	$64.95	$152.67	$51.76	$250.11	($18.95)	($392.31)	($287.98)
Investing cash flows									
Purchases of non-current assets	($1,000.00)	($75.00)	($75.00)	($75.00)	($75.00)	($800.00)	($75.00)	($75.00)	($75.00)
Net investing cash flows	($1,000.00)	($75.00)	($75.00)	($75.00)	($75.00)	($800.00)	($75.00)	($75.00)	($75.00)
Financing cash flows									
Debt drawdown	$1,900.00								
Debt repayment		-	($50.00)	($50.00)	($100.00)	($200.00)	($200.00)	($200.00)	($150.00)
Ordinary equity issuances	$1,200.00								
Ordinary equity buybacks						($200.00)			
Dividends paid									

Note, I have followed the consistent structure as before. I have inserted blank ("") measures to create a small space before **Financing cash flows**.

I can now create the **Net financing cash flows** measure:

```
Net financing cash flows =
[Debt drawdown] + [Debt repayment] + [Equity issuances]
+ [Equity buybacks] + [Dividends paid]
```

```
Net financing cash flows =
[Debt drawdown] + [Debt repayment] + [Equity issuances]
+ [Equity buybacks] + [Dividends paid]
```

I shall insert a line, (asterisk measure (*)) before plotting the **Net financing cash flows** measure into the visualisation:

Year	2021								
Qtr	Q1			Q2			Q3		
	Jan	Feb	Mar	Apr	May	Jun	Jul	Aug	Sep
Operating cash flow									
Cash receipts	-	$239.76	$1,358.64	$2,297.70	$2,397.60	$2,317.68	$2,207.79	$2,217.78	$2,167.83
Direct cash payments		($231.78)	($1,001.04)	($1,828.63)	($1,978.46)	($1,772.64)	($1,894.78)	($2,249.57)	($2,177.75)
Indirect cash payments		($40.80)	($155.04)	($77.52)	($93.84)	($57.12)	($146.88)	($122.40)	($77.52)
Cash payments		($272.58)	($1,156.08)	($1,906.15)	($2,072.30)	($1,829.76)	($2,041.66)	($2,371.97)	($2,255.27)
Interest paid		($5.50)	($11.30)	($10.86)	($10.92)	($10.20)	($9.76)	($8.53)	($7.10)
Tax paid		($22.50)	($126.32)	($228.01)	($262.61)	($227.61)	($175.32)	($229.59)	($193.44)
Net operating cash flow	-	($60.83)	$64.95	$152.67	$51.76	$250.11	($18.95)	($392.31)	($287.98)
Investing cash flows									
Purchases of non-current assets	($1,000.00)	($75.00)	($75.00)	($75.00)	($75.00)	($800.00)	($75.00)	($75.00)	($75.00)
Net investing cash flows	($1,000.00)	($75.00)	($75.00)	($75.00)	($75.00)	($800.00)	($75.00)	($75.00)	($75.00)
Financing cash flows									
Debt drawdown	$1,900.00								
Debt repayment		-	($50.00)	($50.00)	($100.00)	($200.00)	($200.00)	($200.00)	($150.00)
Ordinary equity issuances	$1,200.00								
Ordinary equity buybacks						($200.00)			
Dividends paid									
Net financing cash flows	$3,100.00	-	($50.00)	($50.00)	($100.00)	($400.00)	($200.00)	($200.00)	($150.00)

Net increase / (decrease) in cash held measure

The final measure to create in the Cash Flow Statement, is the **Net increase / (decrease) in cash held** measure. It is calculated by adding the **Net operating cash flow, Net investing cash flows,** and the **Net financing cash flows** measures:

```
Net increase / (decrease) in cash held =
[Net operating cash flow] + [Net investing cash flows] + [Net financing cash flows]
```

```
Net increase / (decrease) in cash held =
[Net operating cash flow] + [Net investing cash flows] + [Net financing cash
flows]
```

I insert blank space measures ("") and an asterisk (*) measure before and after the **Net increase / (decrease) in cash held** measure to achieve this look. I also adjust the background colour where necessary. Note that in this final screenshot I have also trapped for any *null* values so that "–" appears where there is no data available:

Year	2021								
Qtr	Q1			Q2			Q3		
	Jan	Feb	Mar	Apr	May	Jun	Jul	Aug	Sep
Operating cash flow									
Cash receipts	-	$239.76	$1,358.64	$2,297.70	$2,397.60	$2,317.66	$2,207.79	$2,217.78	$2,167.83
Direct cash payments	-	($231.78)	($1,001.04)	($1,828.63)	($1,978.46)	($1,772.64)	($1,894.78)	($2,249.57)	($2,177.75)
Indirect cash payments	-	($40.80)	($155.04)	($77.52)	($93.84)	($57.12)	($146.88)	($122.40)	($77.52)
Cash payments	-	($272.58)	($1,156.08)	($1,906.15)	($2,072.30)	($1,829.76)	($2,041.66)	($2,371.97)	($2,255.27)
Interest paid	-	($5.50)	($11.30)	($10.86)	($10.92)	($10.20)	($9.76)	($8.53)	($7.10)
Tax paid	-	($22.50)	($126.32)	($228.01)	($262.61)	($227.61)	($175.32)	($229.59)	($193.44)
Net operating cash flow	-	[illegible]	$64.95	$152.67	$51.76	$250.11	[illegible]	[illegible]	[illegible]
Investing cash flows									
Purchases of non-current assets	($1,000.00)	($75.00)	($75.00)	($75.00)	($75.00)	($800.00)	($75.00)	($75.00)	($75.00)
Net investing cash flows	[illegible]	[illegible]	[illegible]	[illegible]	[illegible]	[illegible]	[illegible]	[illegible]	[illegible]
Financing cash flows									
Debt drawdown	$1,900.00	-	-	-	-	-	-	-	-
Debt repayment	-	-	($50.00)	($50.00)	($100.00)	($200.00)	($200.00)	($200.00)	($150.00)
Ordinary equity issuances	$1,200.00	-	-	-	-	-	-	-	-
Ordinary equity buybacks	-	-	-	-	-	($200.00)	-	-	-
Dividends paid	-	-	-	-	-	-	-	-	-
Net financing cash flows	$3,100.00	-	[illegible]	[illegible]	[illegible]	[illegible]	[illegible]	[illegible]	[illegible]
Net increase / (decrease) in cash held	$2,100.00	($135.83)	($60.05)	$27.67	($123.24)	($949.89)	($293.95)	($667.31)	($512.98)

Finally, I should move all the measures created for the Cash Flow Statement into a separate folder in **Financial account measures**.

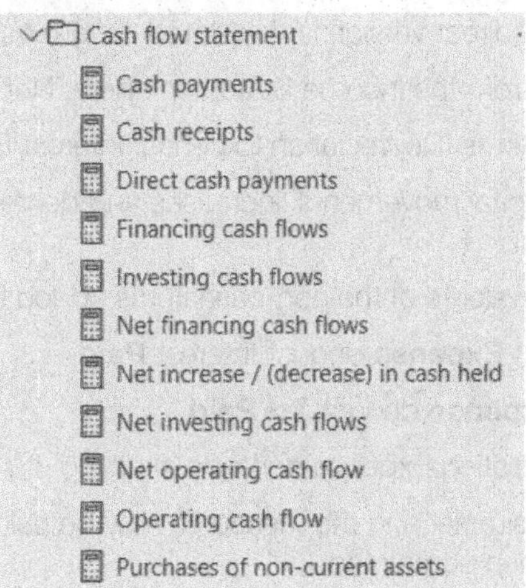

Here, I have only concentrated on creating just one version of the Cash Flow Statement. There are actually <u>two</u> forms the Cash Flow Statement may take: **direct** and **indirect**:

- **Direct:** This can reconcile Operating Cash Flows back to a large proportion of the bank statements. It is a summary of Cash Receipts, Cash Paid, Interest Paid and Tax Paid – this is what has been modelled here, and what supports my control account approach.
- **Indirect:** This starts with an element of the Income Statement and adds back non-cash items (deducting their cash equivalents) and adjusts for working capital movements.

The next section is optional: I will show how easy it is to compute the Indirect extract by simply summing the measures I have already created…

Indirect cash flow extract

A typical indirect Cash Flow Statement may compare to the direct version as follows:

1. Cash Flow Statement						
Direct Cash Flow Statement						
Operating cash flow						
Cash receipts	US$'000	1,303	2,829	4,536	6,435	8,578
Direct cash payments	US$'000	(1,834)	(4,319)	(2,456)	(4,059)	(7,296)
Indirect cash payments	US$'000	(60)	(65)	(68)	(70)	(71)
Cash payments	US$'000	(1,894)	(4,384)	(2,523)	(4,128)	(7,367)
Interest paid	US$'000	(20)	(9)	(12)	(13)	(14)
Tax paid	US$'000	(40)	-	-	(176)	(376)
Net Operating cash flow	US$'000	**(650)**	**(1,565)**	**2,001**	**2,117**	**822**
Indirect extract						
Operating cash flow						
NPAT	US$'000	17	10	484	803	694
Add back:						
Depreciation	US$'000	128	173	203	225	213
Interest Expense	US$'000	9	23	29	11	(4)
Tax Expense	US$'000	14	1	207	346	308
Movements in working capital:						
(inc) / dec in Current Assets	US$'000	(971)	(2,051)	1,189	667	(386)
inc / (dec) in Current Liabilities	US$'000	212	289	(100)	254	387
Deduct:						
Interest paid	US$'000	(20)	(9)	(12)	(13)	(14)
Tax paid	US$'000	(40)	-	-	(176)	(376)
Net Operating cash flow	US$'000	**(650)**	**(1,565)**	**2,001**	**2,117**	**822**

As explained above, the indirect version is calculated as follows:

- Start with a line item from the Income Statement (here, Net Profit After Tax)
- Add back non-cash items (Depreciation Expense, Interest Expense and Tax Expense)
- Adjust for working capital movements (increases and decreases in Current Assets and Current Liabilities)
- Deduct the cash equivalents of the non-cash items added back:
  - Instead of Interest **Expense** deduct Interest **Paid**
  - Instead of Tax **Expense** deduct Tax **Paid**
  - Instead of Depreciation Expense *don't do anything*. It's a double count.

All these calculations are simple, and the measures may be calculated readily once the Income Statement has been completed.

I start by taking a copy of the Cash Flow Statement visual and copying it to a new page which I call 'Indirect Cash Flow Extract'. I also take a copy of the **Gross margin** slicer. I remove everything under **Net operating cash flow** from the matrix and I am ready to begin.

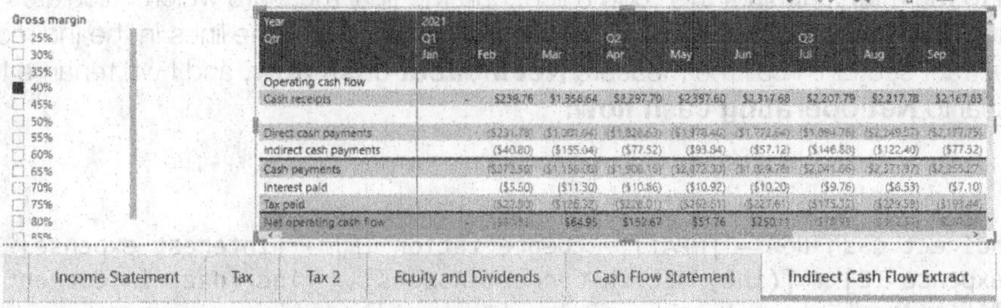

Gross margin
- ☐ 25%
- ☐ 30%
- ☐ 35%
- ■ 40%
- ☐ 45%
- ☐ 50%
- ☐ 55%
- ☐ 60%
- ☐ 65%
- ☐ 70%
- ☐ 75%
- ☐ 80%
- ☐ 85%

Year Qtr	2021 Q1 Jan	Feb	Mar	Q2 Apr	May	Jun	Q3 Jul	Aug	Sep
Operating cash flow									
Cash receipts	-	$238.76	$1,356.64	$2,297.70	$2,397.60	$2,317.68	$2,207.79	$2,217.78	$2,167.83
Direct cash payments		($231.78)	[illegible]	[illegible]	[illegible]	[illegible]	[illegible]	[illegible]	[illegible]
Indirect cash payments		($40.80)	($155.04)	($77.52)	($93.84)	($57.12)	($146.88)	($122.40)	($77.52)
Cash payments		[illegible]	[illegible]	[illegible]	[illegible]	[illegible]	[illegible]	[illegible]	[illegible]
Interest paid		($5.50)	($11.30)	($10.86)	($10.92)	($10.20)	($9.76)	($6.53)	($7.10)
Tax paid		[illegible]	[illegible]	[illegible]	[illegible]	[illegible]	[illegible]	[illegible]	[illegible]
Net operating cash flow	-	[illegible]	$64.95	$152.67	$51.76	$250.11	[illegible]	[illegible]	[illegible]

Income Statement | Tax | Tax 2 | Equity and Dividends | Cash Flow Statement | Indirect Cash Flow Extract

The first measure I need is the title **Indirect extract:**

```
Indirect extract = ""
```

Indirect extract = ""

I have already calculated **NPAT.** I need to subtract Capex depreciation, so I create a measure called **Depreciation IE** (IE for Indirect extract). I will rename this to **Depreciation** in the visualisation.

```
Depreciation IE = -[Capex depreciation]
```

Depreciation IE = -[Capex depreciation]

Interest expense has already been created. The next line requires me to subtract **Tax expense**, so I create a new measure to do this, which I will rename to **Tax expense** in the visualisation:

```
Tax expense IE = -[Tax expense]
```

Tax expense IE = -[Tax expense]

To make the calculations clearer, I insert a blank line before the next measure. The next measure calculates the movement in Accounts Receivable, which subtracts the movement in the sales control account.

```
(inc)/dec in Current Assets = -([Sales] + [Sales cash receipts])
```

(inc)/dec in Current Assets = -([Sales] + [Sales cash receipts])

The next related measure considers the movement in Accounts Payable. I sum the movements in the COGS, purchases and Opex control accounts, and then subtract the movement in the inventory control account. This is because of the relationship between COGS and inventory that we created earlier.

```
inc/(dec) in Current Liabilities = [COGS] + [COGS cash payments] + [Purchases ($)] + [Purchases cash payments ($)] + [Opex]
    + [Opex cash payments] - [Inventory purchases ($)] - [Inventory cost ($)]
```

inc/(dec) in Current Liabilities = [COGS] + [COGS cash payments] + [Purchases ($)] + [Purchases cash payments ($)] + [Opex] + [Opex cash payments] - [Inventory purchases ($)] - [Inventory cost ($)]

I insert another space. The next two lines are repeated from the upper part of the statement. **Interest cash paid** has already been renamed to **Interest paid** and will automatically use the visual name if I include the measure again. **Tax paid** is also added to the matrix again. I then add a line, and the final measure which calculates net operating cash flow using the indirect method by summing all the lines in the Indirect cash extract section. I call the measure **Net indirect cash flow**, and I will rename this in the visual to **Net operating cash flow:**

```
Net indirect cash flow = [NPAT] + [Depreciation IE] + [Interest expense] + [Tax expense IE] + [(inc)/dec in Current Assets]
  + [inc/(dec) in Current Liabilities] + [Interest cash paid] + [Tax paid]
```

```
Net indirect cash flow = [NPAT] + [Depreciation IE] + [Interest expense] +
[Tax expense IE] + [(inc)/dec in Current Assets] + [inc/(dec) in Current
Liabilities] + [Interest cash paid] + [Tax paid]
```

If you choose to produce a Cash Flow Statement with an Indirect cash extract, and apply all the formatting (including replacing *null* with zero [0]), it should look like this:

Gross margin
- ☐ 25%
- ☐ 30%
- ☐ 35%
- ■ 40%
- ☐ 45%
- ☐ 50%
- ☐ 55%
- ☐ 60%
- ☐ 65%
- ☐ 70%
- ☐ 75%
- ☐ 80%
- ☐ 85%

Year	2021								
Qtr	Q1			Q2			Q3		
	Jan	Feb	Mar	Apr	May	Jun	Jul	Aug	Sep
Operating cash flow									
Cash receipts	-	$239.76	$1,358.64	$2,297.70	$2,397.60	$2,317.68	$2,207.79	$2,217.78	$2,167.83
Direct cash payments	-	($231.78)	($1,001.04)	($1,828.63)	($1,978.46)	($1,772.64)	($1,894.78)	($2,249.57)	($2,177.75)
Indirect cash payments		($40.80)	($155.04)	($77.52)	($93.84)	($57.12)	($146.88)	($122.40)	($77.52)
Cash payments	-	($272.58)	($1,156.08)	($1,906.15)	($2,072.30)	($1,829.76)	($2,041.66)	($2,371.97)	($2,255.27)
Interest paid	-	($5.50)	($11.30)	($10.86)	($10.92)	($10.20)	($9.76)	($8.53)	($7.10)
Tax paid	-	($22.50)	($126.32)	($228.01)	($262.61)	($227.61)	($175.32)	($229.59)	($193.44)
Net operating cash flow	-	[illegible]	$64.95	$152.67	$51.76	$250.11	[illegible]	[illegible]	[illegible]
Indirect extract									
NPAT	$83.34	$477.33	$609.58	$553.56	$549.25	$454.30	$531.97	$502.30	$447.73
Depreciation	$16.99	$16.49	$19.53	$20.14	$22.08	$34.52	$36.95	$38.22	$38.22
Interest expense	$9.88	$10.20	$11.13	$10.48	$10.36	$9.09	$8.19	$6.96	$5.75
Tax expense	$35.72	$204.57	$261.25	$237.24	$235.39	$194.70	$227.99	$215.27	$191.89
(inc)/dec in Current Assets	($599.40)	($1,858.14)	($1,088.91)	$29.97	$99.90	$259.74	($59.94)	$9.99	$249.75
inc/(dec) in Current Liabilities	$453.48	$1,116.72	$389.97	($459.83)	($591.68)	($464.43)	($579.02)	($926.93)	($1,020.78)
Interest paid	-	($5.50)	($11.30)	($10.86)	($10.92)	($10.20)	($9.76)	($8.53)	($7.10)
Tax paid	-	($22.50)	($126.32)	($228.01)	($262.61)	($227.61)	($175.32)	($229.59)	($193.44)
Net operating cash flow	-	[illegible]	$64.95	$152.67	$51.76	$250.11	[illegible]	[illegible]	[illegible]

Finally, I collect the measures into a folder:

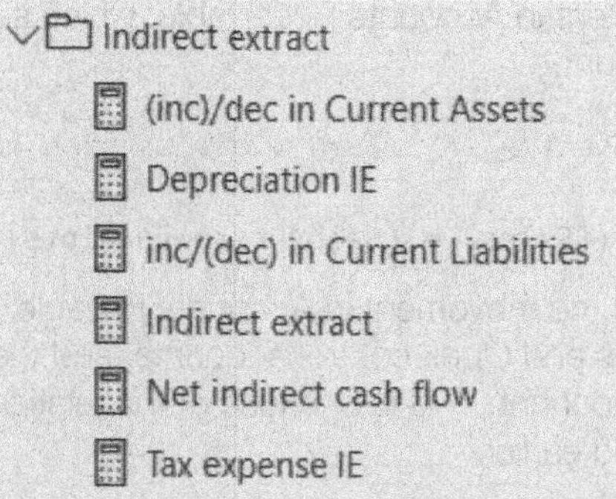

Whilst it is common practise to model an Income Statement and use that Income Statement to work back to the Cash Flow Statement, for this model I have made *transparent* assumptions instead using control accounts and that has necessitated using the direct method. Control accounts are a financial modeller's best friend(s).

CHAPTER 26: Balance Sheet

Last and completely least, the financial statement that draws fear in even the bravest financial modeller. I need to get the damned thing to balance. Don't forget, I assume here that I have a blank canvas for an opening Balance Sheet. If this seems like playing some sort of "Get Out of Jail Free" card, you're right. But there is a valid reason: every reader will have a different idea how to construct opening balance calculations and I didn't want this book to be 30 trillion pages long, even if that is what it feels like.

In this section, I will detail how to create the following measures:

1. Current assets
2. Cash
3. Accounts receivable
4. Inventory
5. Total current assets
6. Non-current assets
7. PP&E
8. Deferred tax assets
9. Total non-current assets
10. Total assets
11. Current liabilities
12. Accounts payable
13. Interest payable
14. Dividends payable
15. Tax payable
16. Total current liabilities
17. Non-current liabilities
18. Debt
19. Deferred tax liabilities
20. Total non-current liabilities
21. Total liabilities
22. Net assets
23. Equity
24. Ordinary equity
25. Opening retained profits
26. NPAT
27. Dividends declared
28. Retained profits

29. Total equity
30. Checks
31. Balance check.

I shall create the following segments of the Balance sheet separately:

1. Assets
2. Liabilities
3. Equity
4. Checks

Calculating Total Assets

I shall cover the following measures to calculate the **Total assets** measure:

1. Current assets
2. Cash
3. Accounts receivable (Sales closing receivables)
4. Inventory
5. Total current assets
6. Non-current assets
7. PP&E (Capex closing net book value)
8. Deferred tax assets (Closing DTAs)
9. Total non-current assets
10. Total assets.

The first measure I am going to create for this section is the **Current assets** measure. This is yet another one of the more complex notions in this book, only second to the **Operating cash flow** measure:

```
Current assets = ""
```


```
Current assets = ""
```


This measure will serve as a 'pseudo-title' for this section in the Balance sheet.

Year	2021		
Qtr	Q1		
	Jan	Feb	Mar
Current assets			

The next measure on the list is the **Cash** measure. It is calculated with the following **DAX** code:

```
Cash =
    CALCULATE( [Net increase / (decrease) in cash held],
        DATESBETWEEN('Calendar'[Date],
            FIRSTDATE(
                ALL('Calendar'[Date])),
                LASTDATE('Calendar'[Date])
        )
    )
```


```
Cash =
 CALCULATE( [Net increase / (decrease) in cash held],
 DATESBETWEEN('Calendar'[Date],
 FIRSTDATE(
 ALL('Calendar'[Date])),
 LASTDATE('Calendar'[Date])
 )
 )
```


Next in my list is **Accounts receivable.** I can rename the **Sales closing receivables** measure for this line.

Similarly for the **Inventory** line, I can rename **Inventory closing ($)**.

I can now summarise the current assets with the **Total current assets** measure:

```
Total current assets =
[Cash] + [Sales closing receivables] + [Inventory closing ($)]
```


```
Total current assets =
[Cash] + [Sales closing receivables] + [Inventory closing ($)]
```


I can plot the previous measures into the matrix visualisation, with additional blank ("") measures to create a gap between **Total current assets** and the next measure **Non-current assets**:

Year	2021								
Qtr	Q1			Q2			Q3		
	Jan	Feb	Mar	Apr	May	Jun	Jul	Aug	Sep
Current assets									
Cash	$2,100.00	$1,964.17	$1,904.12	$1,931.79	$1,808.55	$858.66	$564.71	($102.61)	($615.59)
Accounts receivable	$599.40	$2,457.54	$3,546.45	$3,516.48	$3,416.58	$3,156.84	$3,216.78	$3,206.79	$2,957.04
Inventory	$26.00	$150.00	$686.00	$1,132.00	$1,576.00	$2,264.00	$3,184.00	$4,062.00	$4,864.00
Total current assets	$2,725.40	$4,571.71	$6,136.57	$6,580.27	$6,801.13	$6,279.50	$6,965.49	$7,166.18	$7,205.45

The **Non-current assets** measure is created with the following **DAX** code:

```
Non-current assets = ""
```


```
Non-current assets = ""
```


Non-current assets are comprised of Plant Property and Equipment or **PP&E** and **Deferred tax assets**. For the **PP&E**, I can rename **Capex closing net book value,** and for **Deferred tax assets** I can rename the **Closing DTAs** measure.

To sum the total non-current assets as a line item, the **Total non-current assets** measure uses the following **DAX** code:

```
Total non-current assets =
[Capex closing net book value] + [Closing DTAs]
```

```
Total non-current assets =
[Capex closing net book value] + [Closing DTAs]
```

The next measure to be displayed is the **Total assets** line. It will be calculated with the following **DAX** code:

```
Total assets =
[Total current assets] + [Total non-current assets]
```

```
Total assets =
[Total current assets] + [Total non-current assets]
```

I can then plot the measures into the matrix visualisation. I have inserted blank measures ("") and an asterisk measure (*) between the **Total non-current assets** and **Total assets** measures.

Year	2021								
Qtr	Q1			Q2			Q3		
	Jan	Feb	Mar	Apr	May	Jun	Jul	Aug	Sep
Current assets									
Cash	$2,100.00	$1,964.17	$1,904.12	$1,931.79	$1,808.55	$858.66	$564.71	($102.61)	($615.59)
Accounts receivable	$599.40	$2,457.54	$3,546.45	$3,516.48	$3,416.58	$3,156.84	$3,216.78	$3,206.79	$2,957.04
Inventory	$26.00	$150.00	$686.00	$1,132.00	$1,576.00	$2,264.00	$3,184.00	$4,062.00	$4,864.00
Total current assets	$2,725.40	$4,571.71	$6,136.57	$6,580.27	$6,801.13	$6,279.50	$6,965.49	$7,166.18	$7,205.45
Non-current assets									
PP&E	$983.01	$1,041.52	$1,096.99	$1,151.85	$1,204.77	$1,970.25	$2,008.30	$2,045.08	$2,081.86
Deferred tax assets	$1.04	-	-	-	-	-	-	-	-
Total non-current assets	$984.05	$1,041.52	$1,096.99	$1,151.85	$1,204.77	$1,970.25	$2,008.30	$2,045.08	$2,081.86
Total assets	$3,709.45	$5,613.23	$7,233.56	$7,732.12	$8,005.90	$8,249.74	$8,973.79	$9,211.27	$9,287.32

Calculating Total Liabilities

To calculate the **Total liabilities** (which doesn't include me!), I shall create the following measures:

1. Current liabilities
2. Accounts payable
3. Interest payable (Interest closing payables)
4. Dividends payable (Dividend closing payables)
5. Tax payable (Tax closing payables CA)
6. Total current liabilities
7. Non-current liabilities
8. Debt (Debt closing payables)

9. Deferred tax liabilities
10. Total non-current liabilities
11. Total liabilities
12. Net assets.

Remember, to avoid redrawing the matrix, the measures can be created while I am on a blank page. The **Current liabilities** measure is calculated with the following **DAX** code:

```
Current liabilities = ""
```

```
Current liabilities = ""
```

In this model I calculate the **Total current liabilities** from the sum of: **Accounts payable, Interest payable, Dividends payable** and **Tax payable.**

The **Accounts payable** measure is calculated with the following **DAX** code:

```
Accounts payable =
[COGS closing payables] + [Opex closing payables] + [Purchases closing payables ($)]
```

```
Accounts payable =
[COGS closing payables] + [Opex closing payables] + [Purchases closing
payables ($)]
```

Some adjustments may be made:

- for the **Interest payable** line, I can rename the **Interest closing payables** measure
- for the **Dividends payable** line, I can rename the **Dividend closing payables** measure
- for the **Tax payable** line, I can rename the **Tax closing payables CA** measure.

I can then summarise the **Total current liabilities** with the following **DAX** code:

```
Total current liabilities =
[Accounts payable] + [Interest closing payables] + [Dividend closing payables] + [Tax closing payables CA]
```

```
Total current liabilities =
[Accounts payable] + [Interest closing payables] + [Dividend closing
payables] + [Tax closing payables CA]
```

I can plot the new measures onto the matrix visualisation with blank (**""**) measures between the **Total assets** and **Current liabilities** measures. This is to create a bit of a gap:

Year	2021								
Qtr	Q1			Q2			Q3		
	Jan	Feb	Mar	Apr	May	Jun	Jul	Aug	Sep
Current assets									
Cash	$2,100.00	$1,964.17	$1,904.12	$1,931.79	$1,808.55	$858.66	$564.71	($102.61)	($615.59)
Accounts receivable	$599.40	$2,457.54	$3,546.45	$3,516.48	$3,416.58	$3,156.84	$3,216.78	$3,206.79	$2,957.04
Inventory	$26.00	$150.00	$686.00	$1,132.00	$1,576.00	$2,264.00	$3,184.00	$4,062.00	$4,864.00
Total current assets	$2,725.40	$4,571.71	$6,136.57	$6,580.27	$6,801.13	$6,279.50	$6,965.49	$7,166.18	$7,205.45
Non-current assets									
PP&E	$983.01	$1,041.52	$1,096.99	$1,151.85	$1,204.77	$1,970.25	$2,008.30	$2,045.08	$2,081.86
Deferred tax assets	$1.04	-	-	-	-	-	-	-	-
Total non-current assets	$984.05	$1,041.52	$1,096.99	$1,151.85	$1,204.77	$1,970.25	$2,008.30	$2,045.08	$2,081.86
Total assets	$3,709.45	$5,613.23	$7,233.56	$7,732.12	$8,005.90	$8,249.74	$8,973.79	$9,211.27	$9,287.32
Current liabilities									
Accounts payable	$479.48	$1,720.20	$2,646.17	$2,632.33	$2,484.65	$2,708.21	$3,049.20	$3,000.26	$2,781.48
Interest payable	$9.88	$14.58	$14.41	$14.03	$13.46	$12.35	$10.78	$9.21	$7.86
Dividends payable	-								
Tax payable	$44.40	$232.86	$376.58	$394.86	$377.58	$360.20	$429.49	$432.37	$448.01
Total current liabilities	$533.76	$1,967.63	$3,037.16	$3,041.23	$2,875.69	$3,080.77	$3,489.47	$3,441.84	$3,237.36

Moving on to calculate the **Non-current liabilities**. I begin with the **Non-current liabilities** header measure; it is calculated with the following **DAX** code:

```
Non-current liabilities = ""
```

```
Non-current liabilities = ""
```

Non-current liabilities is comprised of **Debt** and **Deferred tax liabilities**. For the **Debt** line, I can rename the **Debt closing payables** measure.

The **Deferred tax liabilities** measure is calculated with the following **DAX** code:

```
Deferred tax liabilities = -[Closing DTLs]
```

```
Deferred tax liabilities = - [Closing DTLs]
```

I can then create the **Total non-current liabilities** measure with the following **DAX** code:

```
Total non-current liabilities =
[Debt closing payables] + [Deferred tax liabilities]
```

```
Total non-current liabilities =
[Debt closing payables] + [Deferred tax liabilities]
```

Next is to create the **Total liabilities** measure, which uses the following **DAX** code:

```
Total liabilities =
[Total current liabilities] + [Total non-current liabilities]
```

```
Total liabilities =
[Total current liabilities] + [Total non-current liabilities]
```

The **Net assets** measure can now be calculated with the following **DAX** code:

```
Net assets =
[Total assets] - [Total liabilities]
```

Net assets =
[Total assets] - [Total liabilities]

I have added the measures and some extra formatting by changing some of the backgrounds and adding a line before **Total current assets, Total non-current assets, Total current liabilities** and **Total non-current liabilities**. The Balance Sheet should now look like this with all the measures plotted on it so far:

Year	2021								
Qtr	Q1			Q2			Q3		
	Jan	Feb	Mar	Apr	May	Jun	Jul	Aug	Sep
Current assets									
Cash	$2,100.00	$1,964.17	$1,904.12	$1,931.79	$1,808.55	$858.66	$564.71	($102.61)	($615.59)
Accounts receivable	$599.40	$2,457.54	$3,546.45	$3,516.48	$3,416.58	$3,156.84	$3,216.78	$3,206.79	$2,957.04
Inventory	$26.00	$150.00	$686.00	$1,132.00	$1,576.00	$2,264.00	$3,184.00	$4,062.00	$4,864.00
Total current assets	$2,725.40	$4,571.71	$6,136.57	$6,580.27	$6,801.13	$6,279.50	$6,965.49	$7,166.18	$7,205.45
Non-current assets									
PP&E	$983.01	$1,041.52	$1,096.99	$1,151.85	$1,204.77	$1,970.25	$2,008.30	$2,045.08	$2,081.86
Deferred tax assets	$1.04	-	-	-	-	-	-	-	-
Total non-current assets	$984.05	$1,041.52	$1,096.99	$1,151.85	$1,204.77	$1,970.25	$2,008.30	$2,045.08	$2,081.86
Total assets	$3,709.45	$5,613.23	$7,233.56	$7,732.12	$8,005.90	$8,249.74	$8,973.79	$9,211.27	$9,287.32
Current liabilities									
Accounts payable	$479.48	$1,720.20	$2,646.17	$2,632.33	$2,484.65	$2,708.21	$3,049.20	$3,000.26	$2,781.48
Interest payable	$9.88	$14.58	$14.41	$14.03	$13.46	$12.35	$10.78	$9.21	$7.86
Dividends payable	-								
Tax payable	$44.40	$232.86	$376.58	$394.86	$377.58	$360.20	$429.49	$432.37	$448.01
Total current liabilities	$533.76	$1,967.63	$3,037.16	$3,041.23	$2,875.69	$3,080.77	$3,489.47	$3,441.84	$3,237.36
Non-current liabilities									
Debt	$1,900.00	$1,900.00	$1,850.00	$1,800.00	$1,700.00	$1,500.00	$1,300.00	$1,100.00	$950.00
Deferred tax liabilities	($7.64)	($15.07)	($23.86)	($32.92)	($42.85)	($58.39)	($75.01)	($92.21)	($109.41)
Total non-current liabilities	$1,892.36	$1,884.93	$1,826.14	$1,767.08	$1,657.15	$1,441.61	$1,224.99	$1,007.79	$840.59
Total liabilities	$2,426.11	$3,852.56	$4,863.30	$4,808.31	$4,532.84	$4,522.38	$4,714.45	$4,449.63	$4,077.94
Net assets	$1,283.34	$1,760.67	$2,370.26	$2,923.81	$3,473.06	$3,727.36	$4,259.33	$4,761.64	$5,209.37

Calculating Equity

This section is comprised of the following measures:

1. Equity
2. Ordinary equity (Closing equity)
3. Opening retained profits
4. NPAT
5. Dividends declared
6. Retained profits
7. Total equity.

The **Equity** measure is calculated from the following **DAX** code:

```
Equity = ""
```


Equity = ""

The **Ordinary equity** is next, I can rename the **Closing equity** measure.

The next line item is the **Opening retained profits** measure. However, this measure is part of a control account in the Balance sheet. Therefore, I first must create the cumulative **NPAT** and **Dividends declared** measures first.

The **NPAT** and **Dividends declared** measures have already been created in previous control accounts. Here I shall just create the cumulative variants. The **NPAT cum** measure is calculated with the following **DAX** code:

```
NPAT cum =
    CALCULATE(
        [NPAT],
        FILTER(
            ALL('Calendar'),
            'Calendar'[Date] <= MAX('Calendar'[Date])
            )
        )

```


```
NPAT cum =
 CALCULATE(
 [NPAT],
 FILTER(
 ALL('Calendar'),
 'Calendar'[Date] <= MAX('Calendar'[Date])
 )
 )
```


The **Dividends declared cum** measure should already have been created in the dividend control account. Therefore, I am just going to borrow it to calculate the **Opening retained profits** measure:

```
Opening retained profits =
    IF(
        PREVIOUSDAY(
            'Calendar'[Date]) = BLANK(),
            0,
        CALCULATE(
            [NPAT cum] - [Dividends declared cum],
        PREVIOUSDAY(
            'Calendar'[Date])
        )
    )
```

```
Opening retained profits =
 IF(
 PREVIOUSDAY(
 'Calendar'[Date]) = BLANK(),
 0,
 CALCULATE(
 [NPAT cum] - [Dividends declared cum],
 PREVIOUSDAY(
 'Calendar'[Date])
 )
 )
```

I can now calculate the **Retained profits**, it uses the following **DAX** code:

```
Retained profits =
[Opening retained profits] + [NPAT] - [Dividends declared]
```

```
Retained profits =
[Opening retained profits] + [NPAT] - [Dividends declared]
```

With that I can create the **Total equity** measure. It uses the following **DAX** code:

```
Total equity =
[Retained profits] + [Ordinary equity]
```

```
Total equity =
[Retained profits] + [Closing equity]
```

Year	2021								
Qtr	Q1			Q2			Q3		
	Jan	Feb	Mar	Apr	May	Jun	Jul	Aug	Sep
Current assets									
Cash	$2,100.00	$1,964.17	$1,904.12	$1,931.79	$1,808.55	$858.66	$564.71	($102.61)	($615.59)
Accounts receivable	$599.40	$2,457.54	$3,546.45	$3,516.48	$3,416.58	$3,156.84	$3,216.78	$3,206.79	$2,957.04
Inventory	$26.00	$150.00	$686.00	$1,132.00	$1,576.00	$2,264.00	$3,184.00	$4,062.00	$4,864.00
Total current assets	$2,725.40	$4,571.71	$6,136.57	$6,580.27	$6,801.13	$6,279.50	$6,965.49	$7,166.18	$7,205.45
Non-current assets									
PP&E	$983.01	$1,041.52	$1,096.99	$1,151.85	$1,204.77	$1,970.25	$2,008.30	$2,045.08	$2,081.86
Deferred tax assets	$1.04	-	-	-	-	-	-	-	-
Total non-current assets	$984.05	$1,041.52	$1,096.99	$1,151.85	$1,204.77	$1,970.25	$2,008.30	$2,045.08	$2,081.86
Total assets	$3,709.45	$5,613.23	$7,233.56	$7,732.12	$8,005.90	$8,249.74	$8,973.79	$9,211.27	$9,287.32
Current liabilities									
Accounts payable	$479.48	$1,720.20	$2,646.17	$2,632.33	$2,484.65	$2,708.21	$3,049.20	$3,000.26	$2,781.48
Interest payable	$9.88	$14.58	$14.41	$14.03	$13.46	$12.35	$10.78	$9.21	$7.86
Dividends payable	-								
Tax payable	$44.40	$232.86	$376.58	$394.86	$377.58	$360.20	$429.49	$432.37	$448.01
Total current liabilities	$533.76	$1,967.63	$3,037.16	$3,041.23	$2,875.69	$3,080.77	$3,489.47	$3,441.84	$3,237.36
Non-current liabilities									
Debt	$1,900.00	$1,900.00	$1,850.00	$1,800.00	$1,700.00	$1,500.00	$1,300.00	$1,100.00	$950.00
Deferred tax liabilities	($7.64)	($15.07)	($23.86)	($32.92)	($42.85)	($58.39)	($75.01)	($92.21)	($109.41)
Total non-current liabilities	$1,892.36	$1,884.93	$1,826.14	$1,767.08	$1,657.15	$1,441.61	$1,224.99	$1,007.79	$840.59
Total liabilities	$2,426.11	$3,852.56	$4,863.30	$4,808.31	$4,532.84	$4,522.38	$4,714.45	$4,449.63	$4,077.94
Net assets	$1,283.34	$1,760.67	$2,370.26	$2,923.81	$3,473.06	$3,727.36	$4,259.33	$4,761.64	$5,209.37
Equity									
Ordinary equity	$1,200.00	$1,200.00	$1,200.00	$1,200.00	$1,200.00	$1,000.00	$1,000.00	$1,000.00	$1,000.00
Opening retained profits	-	$83.34	$560.67	$1,170.26	$1,723.81	$2,273.06	$2,727.36	$3,259.33	$3,761.64
NPAT	$83.34	$477.33	$609.58	$553.56	$549.25	$454.30	$531.97	$502.30	$447.73
Dividends declared									
Retained profits	$83.34	$560.67	$1,170.26	$1,723.81	$2,273.06	$2,727.36	$3,259.33	$3,761.64	$4,209.37
Total equity	$1,283.34	$1,760.67	$2,370.26	$2,923.81	$3,473.06	$3,727.36	$4,259.33	$4,761.64	$5,209.37

Checks

This is followed by the **Checks** and the **Balance check** measures. The first one is our usual no-brainer:

```
Checks = ""
```


```
Checks = ""
```


I can create the **Balance check** measure (obviously, there would be many more in a "real life" model). I use the **ROUND** function to accommodate for any rounding errors in the calculation:

```
Balance check =
ROUND(
    [Total equity] - [Net assets],
    0
)
```


```
Balance check =
ROUND(
 [Total equity] - [Net assets],
 0
)
```


I format all the measures in the matrix and replace any null values with zero [0].

Year	2021								
Qtr	Q1			Q2			Q3		
	Jan	Feb	Mar	Apr	May	Jun	Jul	Aug	Sep
Current assets									
Cash	$2,100.00	$1,964.17	$1,904.12	$1,931.79	$1,808.55	$858.66	$564.71	($102.61)	($615.59)
Accounts receivable	$599.40	$2,457.54	$3,546.45	$3,516.48	$3,416.58	$3,156.84	$3,216.78	$3,206.79	$2,957.04
Inventory	$26.00	$150.00	$686.00	$1,132.00	$1,576.00	$2,264.00	$3,184.00	$4,062.00	$4,864.00
Total current assets	$2,725.40	$4,571.71	$6,136.57	$6,580.27	$6,801.13	$6,279.50	$6,965.49	$7,166.18	$7,205.45
Non-current assets									
PP&E	$983.01	$1,041.52	$1,096.99	$1,151.85	$1,204.77	$1,970.25	$2,008.30	$2,045.08	$2,081.86
Deferred tax assets	$1.04	-	-	-	-	-	-	-	-
Total non-current assets	$984.05	$1,041.52	$1,096.99	$1,151.85	$1,204.77	$1,970.25	$2,008.30	$2,045.08	$2,081.86
Total assets	$3,709.45	$5,613.23	$7,233.56	$7,732.12	$8,005.90	$8,249.74	$8,973.79	$9,211.27	$9,287.32
Current liabilities									
Accounts payable	$479.48	$1,720.20	$2,646.17	$2,632.33	$2,484.65	$2,708.21	$3,049.20	$3,000.26	$2,781.48
Interest payable	$9.88	$14.58	$14.41	$14.03	$13.46	$12.35	$10.78	$9.21	$7.86
Dividends payable	-	-	-	-	-	-	-	-	-
Tax payable	$44.40	$232.86	$376.58	$394.86	$377.58	$360.20	$429.49	$432.37	$448.01
Total current liabilities	$533.76	$1,967.63	$3,037.16	$3,041.23	$2,875.69	$3,080.77	$3,489.47	$3,441.84	$3,237.36
Non-current liabilities									
Debt	$1,900.00	$1,900.00	$1,850.00	$1,800.00	$1,700.00	$1,500.00	$1,300.00	$1,100.00	$950.00
Deferred tax liabilities	($7.64)	($15.07)	($23.86)	($32.92)	($42.85)	($58.39)	($75.01)	($92.21)	($109.41)
Total non-current liabilities	$1,892.36	$1,884.93	$1,826.14	$1,767.08	$1,657.15	$1,441.61	$1,224.99	$1,007.79	$840.59
Total liabilities	$2,426.11	$3,852.56	$4,863.30	$4,808.31	$4,532.84	$4,522.38	$4,714.45	$4,449.63	$4,077.94
Net assets	$1,283.34	$1,760.67	$2,370.26	$2,923.81	$3,473.06	$3,727.36	$4,259.33	$4,761.64	$5,209.37
Equity									
Ordinary equity	$1,200.00	$1,200.00	$1,200.00	$1,200.00	$1,200.00	$1,000.00	$1,000.00	$1,000.00	$1,000.00
Opening retained profits	-	$83.34	$560.67	$1,170.26	$1,723.81	$2,273.06	$2,727.36	$3,259.33	$3,761.64
NPAT	$83.34	$477.33	$609.58	$553.56	$549.25	$454.30	$531.97	$502.30	$447.73
Dividends declared BS	-	-	-	-	-	-	-	-	-
Retained profits	$83.34	$560.67	$1,170.26	$1,723.81	$2,273.06	$2,727.36	$3,259.33	$3,761.64	$4,209.37
Total equity	$1,283.34	$1,760.67	$2,370.26	$2,923.81	$3,473.06	$3,727.36	$4,259.33	$4,761.64	$5,209.37
Checks									
Balance check	-	-	-	-	-	-	-	-	-

There we have it, three-way integrated financial statements!

Before I get too excited, I should store any new measures away in their own folder.

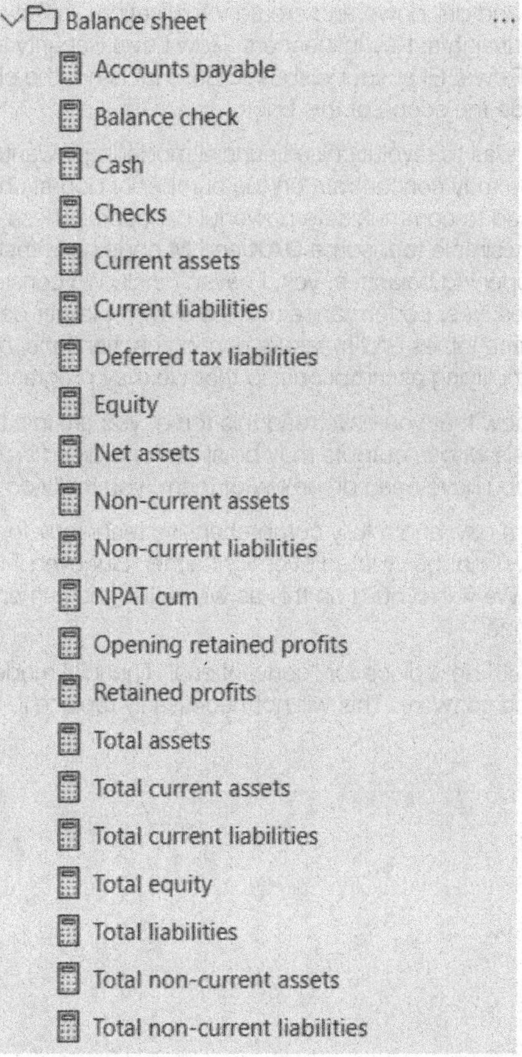

CHAPTER 27: And Finally...

That's it. Congratulations. You have completed your first financial model in Power BI. You may add slicers and drill down and create visualisations in Power BI to wow your audiences. You have Insights, Key Influencers, Row Level Security and many other powerful aspects of Power BI at your disposal. But that is not the objective of this exercise and is outside the scope of this book.

The aim of this book was to revolutionise financial modelling. I wanted to get the engine right. Now you may concentrate on the number of doors, chassis and colour. This exercise was used to communicate powerful concepts. These are *new* ideas, and they are relatively simple too, some **DAX** and **M** code notwithstanding. Yes, I haven't considered opening balances; yes, I haven't included consideration of different forecasting techniques; yes, performance may be slow for larger datasets; yes, I have had inconsistent source tables and measure naming conventions, *but this is all part of real life*. We make simplifying assumptions so that we may progress.

Think of it this way: now that you have read this tome, you are in a better position to create financial models whose outputs may be sliced and diced in ways you only dreamt of previously. And if you have been dreaming of them, you really do need to get out more.

Rome wasn't built in a day, and a fully comprehensive technique for developing financial models in Power BI will not be created overnight either. But even if I say so myself, it's a very exciting start. We will *all* build on this as we realise the immense potential for modelling in this manner.

Of course, there will still be a place for "conventional" financial modelling, in Excel or other similar spreadsheeting software. This will not necessarily replace it. But it will enhance it.

Happy modelling.

Index

Q

R

S

T

U

V

W

Y

Z